SOLDIER
LIFE
in the
Union and
Confederate
Armies

OTHER TITLES OF SIMILAR INTEREST FROM
RANDOM HOUSE VALUE PUBLISHING

2000 Questions and Answers About the Civil War

Diary from Dixie

The Civil War: Strange and Fascinating Facts

Civil War Battles

Civil War Generals

Soldier Life

in the Union and Confederate Armies

Edited, with an introduction and notes, by

PHILIP VAN DOREN STERN

from HARDTACK AND COFFEE *by*
John D. Billings *and* DETAILED MINUTIAE OF
SOLDIER LIFE IN THE ARMY OF
NORTHERN VIRGINIA *by* Carlton McCarthy

Original sketches by
Charles W. Reed and William L. Sheppard

Gramercy Books
New York

This 2001 edition is published by Gramercy™ Books, a division
of Random House Value Publishing, Inc., 280 Park Avenue,
New York, NY 10017.

Gramercy™ Books and design are registered trademarks of
Random House Value Publishing, Inc.

Random House
New York • Toronto • London • Sydney • Auckland
http://www.randomhouse.com/

Printed and bound in the United States of America

A catalog record for this title is available from the Library of
Congress.

Includes index.
ISBN 0-517-16395-0

9 8 7 6 5 4 3

Contents

Soldier Life in the Confederate Army

Introduction

*W*hen you walk through the stacks of a library that has a large collection of books dealing with the Civil War, you will pass thousands of volumes about the battles and leaders. You will find plenty of works on political history, foreign relations, the Navy, Army medical service, prisons, weapons, railroads, spies and secret service. If you look hard enough, you will discover some books on martial music, signalling, the military telegraph, and even aeronautics. But you will see very few books that tell how the common soldier lived and fought and died in that much-written-about war.

Notable among modern books on the subject are Bell Irvin Wiley's two volumes, The Life of Billy Yank, and its companion, The Life of Johnny Reb. Together they make an exhaustive treatise of nearly a thousand pages treating almost every aspect of the life of the common soldier in the Civil War. They are based largely on thousands of manuscript letters the author read while searching for material. Relatively few books are listed in his bibliographies. He calls John D. Billings' Hard Tack and Coffee (Boston, 1888) a "superb memoir" and says that it is "in essence a depiction of soldier life in the Army of the Potomac built around [Billings'] personal experience as an artilleryman" and that it is "rich in humor, franker than most reminiscences, and has the flavor of authenticity." He then says that Carlton McCarthy's Detailed Minutiae of Soldier Life in the Army of Northern Virginia (Richmond, 1882) "is the most interesting and the most informative of all memoirs written by privates."

Wiley was not the first to discover these two remarkable books. They have long been known to dealers and collectors and have been much sought after, especially in recent years when they soared in price as their availability diminished.

It is an odd coincidence that they were both written by artillerymen who may very well have met as foes in the relatively limited terrain covered by the two great armies. One wonders in what minor skirmish or major battle these authors-to-be may

vii

have fired lethal rounds at each other, never knowing that their destinies were someday to be linked together in one book. For here they both appear, each describing everyday life in the armies they knew so well.

Billings goes into greater detail and covers more topics. What he says applies in many instances to both armies, for they were very much alike, except that the Union Army was better provided with everything from new uniforms to good food and weapons. The miracle of the Confederacy was that it did so much with so little.

McCarthy's book is of more limited range, but it is also more intimate. Its discursive author departs from his main theme to tell the story of the Appomattox Campaign, but he describes it so well that one would not want to miss his lively narrative.

From both books there emerges a picture of the American fighting man as he was a hundred years ago. He was more naive then, more given to cheering and rallying around the flag than he is now. But the fresh-faced country boys and city clerks who fought the Civil War groused and beefed, played practical jokes, foraged for food and supplies, dreamed of going home, and waged desperate battle when they had to—very much as their descendants have done ever since the First World War.

The common soldier—genus Americanus especially—changes little. So do his customs and his special language. Words like "doughboy" go back to the Civil War, when the term was applied to Union infantrymen because the buttons they wore resembled balls of dough. The name stuck until the Second World War; then it was replaced by G. I. Joe. No one, apparently, remembered that long before G. I. meant Government Issue it was used in the Army to describe Galvanized Iron. And the word "beat," used here, seems oddly modern.

Similar words and incidents run from one war to another, echoing and re-echoing basic themes. Here is an account of a Civil War battle incident printed in 1884:

> A Confederate colonel ran ahead of his regiment at Malvern Hill [in 1862], and discovering that the men were not following him as closely as he wished, he uttered a fierce oath and exclaimed: "Come on! Do you want to live forever?"

Do these words sound familiar? They should, yet it seems unlikely that the Marine Corps sergeant who said the same thing at Belleau Wood in 1918 had any idea that he was repeating phrases already tried in battle.

As we read McCarthy and Billings, we note again and again how much alike everyday life was in the two armies. In the beginning men in both came to camp equipped with far too much unnecessary paraphernalia. They soon got rid of it, discarding it ruthlessly by the wayside when it encumbered them on the march. And troops in both armies looked forward to the comfort of winter quarters. When they built weather-tight homes from makeshift materials, their shelters were identical in plan and construction. They ate the same kind of food—although in differing quantity; sometimes wore the same clothing—often captured on the field; and used similar weapons—also often captured. They handled horses, mules, and wagons in exactly the same way. Except that one waxed fat while the other grew lean, almost everything about Billy Yank and Johnny Reb was similar, even, as the war eventually showed, their ability to fight.

And that was the great tragedy of the war—as it is of all civil wars. When a man meets his own kind on his own territory, the conflict is likely to be more than ordinarily bloody and terrible. Each knows the other's ways, the other's tricks, the other's limitations. The man seen through the smoke of battle is not an anonymous stranger but a former friend who has now become a personal enemy.

But the accounts of soldier life in the Civil War printed here have relatively little to do with the violence of actual conflict; they mirror the lighter side of army life. Seeing the men in the now almost legendary armies at ease and at play should give us a better idea of what they were really like.

PHILIP VAN DOREN STERN

Soldier Life

in the Union Army

from

HARDTACK AND COFFEE
by John D. Billings

1
Enlisting and Recruiting

The 16th of April [1861] was a memorable day in the history of the Old Bay State—a day made more uncomfortable by the rain and sleet which were falling with disagreeable constancy. Well do I remember the day. Possessing an average amount of the fire and enthusiasm of youth, I had asked my father's consent to go out with Company A of the old Fourth Regiment, which belonged to my native town. But he would not give ear to any such "nonsense," and having been brought up to obey his orders, although of military age (18), I did not enter the service in the first rally. This company did not go with full ranks. There were few that did. Several of my shopmates were in its membership. As those of us who remained gathered at the windows that stormy forenoon to see the company go by, the sight filled us with the most gloomy forebodings.

So the troops went forth from the towns in the shore counties of Massachusetts. Most of the companies in the regiments that were called reported for duty at Boston this very 16th—two companies from Marblehead being the first to arrive. One of these companies was commanded by Captain Knott V. Martin, who was engaged in slaughtering hogs when E. W. Hinks rode up and instructed him to report on Boston Common in the morning. Drawing the knife from the throat of a hog, the Captain uttered an exclamation which has passed into history, threw the knife with a light toss to the floor, went immediately and notified his Orderly Sergeant, and then returned to his butchering. In the morning he and his company were ready for business.

But their relatives who remained at home could not look calmly on the departure of these dear ones, who were going no one knew just where, and would return—perhaps never; so there were many touching scenes witnessed at the various railway stations as the men boarded the trains for Boston. When

13

these Marblehead companies arrived at that city the enthusiasm
was something unprecedented, and as a new detachment appeared in the streets it was cheered to the echo all along its line
of march. The early months of the war were stirring ones for
Boston; for not only did the most of the Massachusetts regiments march through her streets en route for the seat of war,
but also the troops from Maine and New Hampshire as well,
so that a regiment halted for rest on the Common, or marching
to the strain of martial music to some railway station, was at
times a daily occurrence.

It has always seemed to me that the "Three-months men"
have never received half the credit which the worth of their
services to the country deserved. The fact of their having been
called out for so short a time as compared with the troops that
came after them, and of their having seen little or no fighting
places them at a disadvantage. But to have so suddenly left
all, and gone to the defence of the Capital City, with no knowledge of what was in store for them, and impelled by no other
than the most patriotic of motives, seems to me fully as praise-
worthy as to have gone later under the pressure of urgent need
when the full stress of war was upon us, and when its realities
were better known, and the inducements to enlist greater in
some other respects. There is no doubt whatever but what the
prompt appearance of these short-term men not only saved
the Capital, but that it served also to show the Rebels that
the North at short call could send a large and comparatively
well-equipped force into the field, and was ready to back its
words by deeds. Furthermore, these soldiers gave the Government time to catch its breath, as it were, and looking the issue
squarely in the face to decide upon some settled plan of action.

On the 3d of May President Lincoln issued a call for United
States volunteers to serve three years, unless sooner discharged.

At once thousands of loyal men sprang to arms—so large a
number, in fact, that many regiments raised were refused until
later. The methods by which these regiments were raised were
various. In 1861 a common way was for some one who had
been in the regular army, or perhaps . . . prominent in the
militia, to take the initiative and circulate an enlistment paper
for signatures. His chances were pretty good for obtaining
a commission as its captain for his active interest, and men
who had been prominent in assisting him, if they were popular,
would secure the lieutenancies. On the return of the "Three-

months" troops many of the companies immediately re-enlisted in a body for three years, sometimes under their old officers. A large number of these short-term veterans, through influence at the various state capitals, secured commissions in new regiments that were organizing. In country towns too small to furnish a company, the men would post off to a neighboring town or city and there enlist.

In 1862 men who had seen a year's active service were selected to receive a part of the commissions issued to new organizations and should in justice have received all within the bestowal of governors. But the recruiting of troops soon resolved itself into individual enlistments or this program:—twenty, thirty, fifty or more men would go in a body to some recruiting station and signify their readiness to enlist in a certain regiment provided a certain specified member of their number should be commissioned captain. Sometimes they would compromise if the outlook was not promising and take a lieutenancy, but equally often it was necessary to accept their terms or count them out. In the rivalry for men to fill up regiments, the result often was officers who were diamonds in the rough, but liberally intermingled with veritable clod-hoppers whom a brief experience in active service soon sent to the rear.

This year the War Department was working on a more systematic basis, and when a call was made for additional troops each state was immediately assigned its quota, and with marked promptness each city and town was informed by the state authorities how many men it was to furnish under that call. The war fever was not at such a fervid heat in '62 as in the year before, and so recruiting offices were multiplied in cities and large towns. These offices were of two kinds, viz: those which were opened to secure recruits for regiments and batteries already in the field, and those which solicited enlistments in new organizations. Unquestionably, at this time the latter were more popular. The former office was presided over by a line officer directly from the front, attended by one or two subordinates, all of whom had smelled powder. The latter office might be in charge of an experienced soldier recently commissioned, or of a man ambitious for such preferment.

The flaming advertisements with which the newspapers of the day teemed, and the posters pasted on the bill-boards or the country fence, were the decoys which brought patronage to these fishers of men. Here is a sample:

More Massachusetts Volunteers Accepted ! ! !

Three Regiments to be Immediately Recruited!

GEN. WILSON'S REGIMENT,
To which CAPT. FOLLETT'S BATTERY
is attached;

COL. JONES' GALLANT SIXTH REGIMENT
WHICH WENT "THROUGH BALTIMORE";

THE N. E. GUARDS REGIMENT,
commanded by that excellent officer,
MAJOR J. T. STEVENSON

The undersigned has this day been authorized and directed to fill up the ranks of these regiments forthwith. A grand opportunity is afforded for patriotic persons to enlist in the service of their country under the command of as able officers as the country has yet furnished. Pay and rations will begin immediately on enlistment.

UNIFORMS ALSO PROVIDED!

Citizens of Massachusetts should feel pride in attaching themselves to regiments from their own state, in order to maintain the proud supremacy which the Old Bay State now enjoys in the contest for the Union and the Constitution. The people of many of the towns and cities of the Commonwealth have made ample provision for those joining the ranks of the army. If any person enlists in a Company or Regiment out of the Commonwealth, he cannot share in the bounty which has been thus liberally voted. Wherever any town or city has assumed the privilege of supporting the families of Volunteers, the Commonwealth reimburses such place to the amount of $12 per month for families of three persons.

Patriots desiring to serve the country will bear in mind that

THE GENERAL RECRUITING STATION

IS AT

No. 14 PITTS STREET, BOSTON!

WILLIAM F. BULLOCK,
General Recruiting Officer, Massachusetts Volunteers

[Boston Journal of Sept. 12, 1861]

Here is a call to a war meeting held out-of-doors:

TO ARMS! TO ARMS!!

GREAT WAR MEETING
IN ROXBURY.

Another meeting of the citizens of Roxbury, to re-enforce their brothers in the field, will be held in

ELIOT SQUARE, ROXBURY,

THIS EVENING AT EIGHT O'CLOCK
SPEECHES FROM

Paul Willard, Rev. J. O. Means, Judge Russell,
And other eloquent advocates

The Brigade Band will be on hand early. Come one, come all!
God and your Country Call ! !

Per Order

[*Boston Journal* of July 30, 1862]

Here are two which look quite businesslike:

GENERAL POPE'S ARMY.

*"Lynch Law for Guerillas and No Rebel
Property Guarded!"*

IS THE MOTTO OF THE

SECOND MASSACHUSETTS REGIMENT.

$578.50 for 21 months' service.
$252.00 State aid for families of four.
$830.50 and short service.
$125.00 cash in hand.

This Regiment, although second in number, is second to none in regard to discipline and efficiency, and is in the healthiest and most delightful country.

Office at Coolidge House, Bowdoin Square

CAPT. C. R. MUDGE
LIEUT. A. D. SAWYER

$100 BOUNTY!

CADET REGIMENT,
Company D,
NINE MONTH'S SERVICE

O. W. PEABODY . . . . Recruiting Officer

Headquarters, 113 Washington Street, Boston

[*Boston Journal*, Sept. 17, 1862]

War meetings similar to the one called in Roxbury were designed to stir lagging enthusiasm. Musicians and orators blew themselves red in the face with their windy efforts. Choirs improvised for the occasion, sang "Red, White, and Blue" and "Rallied 'Round the Flag" till too hoarse for further endeavor. The old veteran soldier of 1812 was trotted out and worked for all he was worth, and an occasional Mexican War veteran would air his nonchalance at grim-visaged war. At proper intervals the enlistment roll would be presented for signatures. There was generally one old fellow present who upon slight provocation would yell like a hyena and declare his readiness to shoulder his musket and go, if he wasn't so old, while his staid and half-fearful consort would pull violently at his coat-tails to repress his unseasonable effervescence ere it assumed more dangerous proportions. Then there was a patriotic maiden lady who kept a flag or a handkerchief waving with only the rarest and briefest of intervals, who "would go in a minute if she was a man." Besides these there was usually a man who would make one of fifty (or some other safe number) to enlist, when he well understood that such a number could not be obtained. And there was one more often found present who when challenged to sign would agree to, provided that A or B (men of wealth) would put down *their* names. I saw a man at a war meeting promise, with a bombastic flourishment, to enlist if a certain number (which I do not now remember) of the citizens would do the same. The number was obtained; but the small-sized patriot who was willing to sacrifice his *wife's* relations on the altar of his country crawled away amid the sneers of his townsmen.

Sometimes the patriotism of such a gathering would be

wrought up so intensely by waving banners, martial and vocal music, and burning eloquence, that a town's quota would be filled in less than an hour. It needed only the first man to step forward, put down his name, be patted on the back, placed upon the platform, and cheered to the echo as the hero of the hour, when a second, a third, a fourth would follow, and at last a perfect stampede set in to sign the enlistment roll, and a frenzy of enthusiasm would take possession of the meeting. The complete intoxication of such excitement, like intoxication from liquor, left some of its victims on the following day, especially if the fathers of families, with the sober second thought to wrestle with; but Pride, that tyrannical master, rarely let them turn back.

The next step was a medical examination to determine physical fitness for service. Each town had its physician for this work. The candidate for admission into the army must first divest himself of all clothing, and his soundness or unsoundness was then decided by causing him to jump, bend over, kick, receive sundry thumps in the chest and back, and such other laying-on of hands as was thought necessary. The teeth had also to be examined, and the eyesight tested, after which, if the candidate passed, he received a certificate to that effect.

His next move was toward a recruiting station. There he would enter, signify his errand, sign the roll of the company or regiment into which he was going, leave his description, including height, complexion, and occupation, and then accompany a guard to the examining surgeon, where he was again subjected to a critical examination as to soundness. Those men who, on deciding to "go to war," went directly to a recruiting office and enlisted, had but this simple examination to pass, the other being then unnecessary. It is interesting to note that in 1861 and '62 men were mainly examined to establish their fitness for service; in 1863 and '64 the tide had changed, and they were then only anxious to prove their unfitness.

After the citizen in question had become a soldier, he was usually sent at once to camp or the seat of war, but if he wanted a short furlough it was generally granted. If he had enlisted in a new regiment, he might remain weeks before being ordered to the front; if in an old regiment, he might find himself in a fight at short notice. Hundreds of the men who enlisted under the call issued by President Lincoln July 2, 1862, were killed or wounded before they had been in the field a week. . . .

The spirit of patriotism was at fever-heat, and animated both sexes of all ages. Such a display of the national colors had never been seen before. Flag-raisings were the order of the day in public and private grounds. The trinity of red, white, and blue colors was to be seen in all directions. Shopkeepers decked their windows and counters with them. Men wore them in neckties, or in a rosette pinned on the breast, or tied in the buttonhole. The women wore them conspicuously also. The bands played only patriotic airs, and "Yankee Doodle," "Red, White, and Blue," and the "Star-Spangled Banner" would have been worn threadbare if possible. Then other patriotic songs and marches were composed, many of which had only a short-lived existence; and the poetry of this period, some of it excellent, would fill a large volume.

2
How the Soldiers Were Sheltered

After enlistment, what? This deed done, the responsibility of the citizen for himself ceased in a measure, and Uncle Sam took him in charge. A word here to make clear to the uninformed the distinction between the militia and the volunteers. The militia are the soldiers of the state, and their duties lie wholly within its limits, unless called out by the President of the United States in an emergency. Such an emergency occurred when President Lincoln made his call for 75,000 militia. . . . The volunteers, on the other hand, enlist directly into the service of the United States, and it becomes the duty of the national Government to provide for them from the very date of their enlistment.

Before leaving the state, these volunteers were *mustered into service*. This often occurred soon after their enlistment, before they had been provided with the garb of Union soldiers.

The oath of muster, which they took with uplifted hand, ran as follows:

"I, A—— B——, do solemnly swear that I will bear true allegiance to the United States of America, and that I will serve them honestly and faithfully against all their enemies and opposers whatsoever, and observe and obey the orders of the President of the United States, and the orders of the officers appointed over me according to the rules and articles for the government of the armies of the United States."

The provision made for the shelter of these troops before they took the field was varied. Some of them were quartered at Forts Warren and Independence while making ready to depart. But the most of the Massachusetts volunteers were quartered at camps established in different parts of the state. Among the earliest of these were Camp Andrew in West Roxbury, and Camp Cameron in North Cambridge. Afterwards camps were laid out at Lynnfield, Pittsfield, Boxford, Readville, Worcester,

21

Lowell, Long Island, and a few other places. The "three-months militia" required no provision for their shelter as they were ordered away soon after reporting for duty. Faneuil Hall furnished quarters for a part of them one night. The first Massachusetts Regiment of Infantry quartered for a week in Faneuil Hall; but, this not being a suitable place for so large a body of men to remain, on the first day of June the regiment marched out to Cambridge, and took possession of an old ice-house on the borders of Fresh Pond, which had been procured by the state authorities and partially fitted up for barracks, and established their first camp. But this was not the first camp established in the state, for three years' troops had already been ordered into camp on Long Island and at Fort Warren.

Owing to the unhealthiness of the location selected for the First Regiment, their stay in it was brief, and a removal was soon had to North Cambridge, where . . . some new barracks had been built, and in honor of President Lincoln's Secretary of War had been named "Camp Cameron."

Sibley Tents

Barracks then, it will be observed, served to shelter some of the troops. To such as are not familiar with these structures, I will simply say that they were generally a long one-storied building not unlike a bowling alley in proportions, having the entrance at one end, a broad aisle running through the center, and a double row of bunks, one above the other, on either side. They were calculated to hold one company of a hundred men. . . . But while barracks were desirable quarters in the cooler weather of this latitude and sheltered many regiments during their stay in the state, a still larger number found shelter in tents prior to their departure for the field. These tents were of various patterns, but the principal varieties used were the *Sibley*, the A or *Wedge Tent*, and the *Hospital* or *Wall Tent*.

The Sibley tent was invented by Henry Sibley in 1857. He was a graduate of the United States military academy at West Point and accompanied Capt. John C. Fremont on one of his exploring expeditions. He evidently got his idea from the *Tepee* or *Tepar*, the Indian wigwam of poles covered with skins, having a fire in the center, which he saw on the plains. When the Rebellion broke out, Sibley cast in his fortune with the South. He afterwards attained the rank of brigadier-general, but performed no services so likely to hand down his name as the invention of this tent. It has recently been stated that Sibley was not the actual inventor, the credit being assigned to some private soldier in his command. On account of its resemblance to a huge bell, it has sometimes been called a *Bell Tent*. It is eighteen feet in diameter and twelve feet high, and is supported by a single pole which rests on an iron tripod. This pole is the exact radius of the circle covered by the tent. By means of the tripod the tent can be tightened or slackened at pleasure. At the top is a circular opening, perhaps a foot in diameter, which serves the double purpose of ventilation and of passing a stove pipe through in cool weather. This stove pipe connected with a cone-shaped stove suited to this shape of tent, which stood beneath the tripod. A small piece of canvas called a *cap*, to which were attached two long guys, covered the opening at the top in stormy weather. It was not an unusual sight in the service to see the top of one of these tents in a blaze caused by some one having drawn the cap too near an over-heated stove pipe. A chain depended from the fork of the tripod, with a hook on which a kettle could be hung; when the stove was wanting, the fire was built on the ground.

These tents are comfortably capacious for a dozen men. In cold or rainy weather, when every opening is closed, they are most unwholesome tenements, and to enter one of them of a rainy morning from the outer air and encounter the night's accumulation of nauseating exhalations from the bodies of twelve men (differing widely in their habits of personal cleanliness)

A, or Wedge Tents

was an experience which no old soldier has ever been known to recall with any great enthusiasm. Of course the air was of the vilest sort, and it is surprising to see how men endured it as they did. In the daytime these tents were ventilated by lifting them up at the bottom. Sibley tents went out of field service in 1862, partly because they were too expensive, but principally on account of being so cumbrous. They increased the amount of impedimenta too largely, for they required many wagons for their transportation, and so were afterwards used only in camps of instruction. . . . I remember having seen these tents raised on a stockade four feet high by some regiments during the war, and thus arranged they made very spacious and comfortable winter quarters. When thus raised they accommodated twenty men. The camp for convalescents near Alexandria, Va., comprised this variety of tent stockaded.

The A or Wedge tents were yet quite common. The origin of this tent is not known, so far as I can learn. It seems to be about as old as history itself. A German historian who wrote in 1751 represents the Amalekites as using them. Nothing simpler for a shelter could suggest itself to campers than some sort of awning stretched over a horizontal pole or bar. The setting-up of branches on an incline against a low horizontal branch of a tree to form a rude shelter may have been its earliest suggestion. But, whatever its orgin, it is *now* a canvas tent stretched over a horizontal bar, perhaps six feet long . . . supported on two upright posts of about the same length. It covers, when pitched, an area nearly seven feet square. The name of these tents is undoubtedly derived from the fact of the ends having the

Spooning Together

proportions of the Roman letter A, and because of their resem-
balance to a wedge. Four men was the number usually assigned
to one of them; but they were often occupied by five, and
sometimes six. When so occupied at night, it was rather necessary to comfort that all should turn over at the same time, for
six or even five men were a tight fit in the space enclosed, unless
"spooned" together. These tents when stockaded were quite
spacious and comfortable.

A word or two just here with regard to stockading. A stockade
proper is an enclosure made with posts set close together. In

Hospital or Wall Tent

stockading a tent the posts were split in halves, and the cleft
sides all turned inward so as to make a clean and comely inside
to the hut. But by far the most common way of logging up a
tent was to build the walls "cob-fashion," notching them together at the corners. This method took much less time and
material than the other. But whenever I use the word stockade
or stockading in any descriptions, I include either method. I
shall speak further of stockading by and by.

The A tents were in quite general use by the state and
also by the general Government the first two years of the war,
but, like the Sibley, they required too much wagon transportation to take along for use in the field, and so they also were
turned over to camps of instruction and to troops permanently
located in or near important military centers or stations.

The Hospital or Wall tent is distinguished from those already described by having four upright sides or walls. To this fact it probably owes the latter name, and it doubtless gets the former from being used for hospital purposes in the field. These tents, also, are not of modern origin. They were certainly used by Napoleon, and probably long before his day. On account of their walls they are much more comfortable and convenient to occupy than the two preceding, as one can stand erect or move about in them with tolerable freedom. They are made of different sizes. Those used as field hospitals were quite large, accommodating from six to twenty patients, according to circumstances. It was a common occurrence to see two or more of these joined, being connected by ripping the central seam in the two ends that came in contact. By looping back the flaps thus liberated, the tents were thrown together, and quite a commodious hospital was in that way opened with a central corridor running its entire length between a double row of cots. The smaller size of wall tent was in general use as the tent of commissioned officers, and so far as I recall, was used by no one else.

Officer's Wall Tent with Fly

While the Army of the Potomac was at Harrison's Landing under McClellan, he issued a General Order (Aug. 10, 1862) prescribing among other things wall tents for general field and staff officers, and a single shelter tent for each line officer; and the same order was reissued by his successors. But in some way many of these line officers managed to smuggle a wall tent into the wagon train, so that when a settled camp was entered upon they were provided with those luxurious shelters instead of the

shelter tent. Over the top an extra piece of canvas called a fly
was stretched as additional protection against sun and rain. . . .
The tents thus far described I have referred to as used largely
by the troops before they left the state. But there was another
tent, the most interesting of all, which was used exclusively in
the field, and that was Tente d'Abri—the Dog or Shelter Tent.

Just why it is called the shelter tent I cannot say, unless on
the principle stated by the Rev. George Ellis for calling the
pond on Boston Common a Frog Pond, viz: because there are
no frogs there. So there is little shelter in this variety of tent.
But about that later. I can imagine no other reason for calling
it a dog tent than this, that when one is pitched it would only
comfortably accommodate a dog, and a small one at that. This
tent was invented late in 1861 or early in 1862. I am told it was
made of light duck at first, then of rubber, and afterwards of
duck again, but I never saw one made of anything heavier than
cotton drilling. This was the tent of the rank and file. It did not
come into general use till after the Peninsular Campaign. Each
man was provided with a half-shelter, as a single piece was
called, which he was expected to carry on the march if he
wanted a tent to sleep under.

I will describe these more fully. One I recently measured is
five feet two inches long by four feet eight inches wide and is
provided with a single row of buttons and button holes on three
sides and a pair of holes for stake loops at each corner. A single
half-shelter, it can be seen, would make a very contracted and
uncomfortable abode for a man; but every soldier was expected
to join his resources for shelter with some other fellow. It was
only rarely that a soldier was met with who was so crooked a
stick that no one would chum with him, or that he cared for
no chum, although I have seen a few such cases in my experience. But the rule in the Army was similar to that in civil
life. Every man had his chum or friend with whom he associated
when off duty, and these tented together. By mutual agreement
one was the "old woman," the other the "old man" of the concern. A Marblehead man called his chum his "chicken," more
especially if the latter was a young soldier.

By means of the buttons and button holes two or more of
these half-shelters could be buttoned together, making a very
complete roofing. There were hundreds of men that came from
different sections of the same state, or from different states, who
joined their resources in this manner, and who, through this

accidental association, became the warmest of personal friends and continued so while they lived. It was not usual to pitch these tents every night when the army was on the march. The soldiers did not waste their time and strength much in that way. If the night was clear and pleasant, they lay down without roof-shelter of any kind; but if it was stormy or a storm was threaten-

The Dog or Shelter Tent

ing when the order came to go into camp for the night, the shelters were then quite generally pitched.

This operation was performed by the infantry in the following simple way: two muskets with bayonets fixed were stuck erect into the ground the width of a half-shelter apart. A guy rope which went with every half-shelter was stretched between the trigger-guards of the muskets, and over this as a ridge-pole the tent was pitched in a twinkling. Artillery men pitched theirs over a horizontal bar supported by two uprights. This framework was split out of fence rails, if fence rails were to be had conveniently; otherwise saplings were cut for the purpose. It often happened that men would throw away their shelters during the day, and take their chances with the weather, or of finding cover in some barn, or under the brow of some overhanging rock, rather than be burdened with them. In summer, when the Army was not in proximity to the enemy, or was lying off recuperating, as the Army of the Potomac did a few weeks after the Gettysburg Campaign, they would pitch their shelters

high enough to get a free circulation of air beneath, and to enable them to build bunks or cots a foot or two above the ground.
If the camp was not in the woods, it was common to build a
bower of branches over the tents, in order to ward off the
sun's heat.

When cold weather came on, the soldiers built the stockades
to which I have already referred. The walls of these structures
were raised from two to five feet, according to the taste or working inclination of the intended occupants. Oftentimes an ex-
cavation was made one or two feet deep. When such was the
case, the walls were not built so high. Such a hut was warmer
than one built entirely above ground. The size depended upon
the number of the proposed mess. If the hut was to be occupied by two, it was built nearly square, and covered by two
half-shelters. Such a stockade would and often did accommodate three men, the third using his half-shelter to stop up
one gable. When four men occupied a stockade, it was built
accordingly and covered by four half-shelters. In each case these
were stretched over a framework of light rafters raised on the
walls of the stockade. Sometimes the gables were built up to the
ridge poles with smaller logs, but just as often they were filled
by an extra half-shelter, a rubber blanket, or an old poncho. An
Army poncho, I may here say, is specified as made of un-
bleached muslin coated with vulcanized India rubber, sixty
inches wide and seventy-one inches long, having an opening
in the center lengthwise of the poncho, through which the
head passes, with a lap three inches wide and sixteen inches
long. This garment is derived from the woollen poncho worn
by the Spanish-Americans, but is of different proportions, these
being four feet by seven. The Army poncho was used in lieu
of the gum blanket.

The chinks between the logs were filled with mud, worked to
a viscous consistency, which adhered more or less tenaciously
according to the amount of clay in the mixture. It usually
needed renewing after a severe storm. The chimney was built
outside, after the Southern fashion. It stood sometimes at the
end and sometimes in the middle of one side of the stockade.
It started from a fireplace which was fashioned with more or
less skill, according to the taste or mechanical genius of the
workman, or the tools and materials used, or both. In my own
company there were two masons who had opportunities, whenever a winter camp was pitched, to practise their trade far more

than they were inclined to do. The fireplaces were built of brick, of stone, or of wood. If there was a deserted house in the neighborhood of the camp which boasted brick chimneys, they were sure to be brought low to serve the Union cause in the manner indicated, unless the house was used by some general officer as headquarters. When built of wood, the chimneys were lined with a very thick coating of mud. They were generally continued above the fireplace with split wood built cob-fashion, which was filled between and lined with the red clayey soil of Virginia; but stones were used when abundant.

Very frequently pork and beef barrels were secured to serve this purpose, being put one above another, and now and then a lively hurrah would run through the camp when one of these was discovered on fire. It is hardly necessary to remark that not all these chimneys were monuments of success. Too often the draught was down instead of up, and the inside of some stockades resembled smokehouses. Still, it was "all in the three years," as the boys used to say. It was all the same to the average soldier, who rarely saw fit to tear down and build anew more scientifically. The smoke of

A Poncho On

his camp fires in warm weather was an excellent preparative for the smoking fireplace of winter quarters.

Many of these huts were deemed incomplete until a sign appeared over the door. Here and there some one would make an attempt at having a door plate of wood suitably inscribed; but the more common sight was a sign over the entrance bearing such inscriptions, rudely cut or marked with charcoal, as: "Parker House," "Hole in the Wall," "Mose Pearson's," "Astor House," "Willard's Hotel," "Five Points," and other titles equally absurd, expressing in this ridiculous way the vagaries of the inmates.

The last kind of shelter I shall mention as used in the field, but not the least in importance, were the *Bomb-proofs* used by both Union and Rebel armies in the war. Probably there were more of these erected in the vicinity of Petersburg and Richmond than in all the rest of the South combined, if I except Vicksburg, as here the opposing armies established themselves —the one in defence, the other in siege of the two cities. These bomb-proofs were built just inside the fortifications. Their walls were made of logs heavily banked with earth and having a door or wider opening on the side away from the enemy. The roof was also made of heavy logs covered with several feet of earth.

The interior of these structures varied in size with the number that occupied them. Some were built on the surface of the ground to keep them drier and more comfortable; others were dug down after the manner of a cellar kitchen; but all of them were at best damp and unwholesome habitations—even where fireplaces were introduced, which they were in cool weather. For these reasons they were occupied only when the

A Common Bomb-Proof

enemy was engaged in sending over his iron compliments in the shape of mortar shells. For all other hostile missiles the breast-works were ample protection, and under their walls the men stretched their half-shelters and passed most of their time in the summer and fall of 1864, when their lot was cast in that part of the lines nearest the enemy in front of Petersburg.

A mortar is a short, stout cannon designed to throw shells *into* fortifications. This is accomplished by elevating the muzzle a great deal. But the higher the elevation the greater the strain upon the gun. For this reason it is that they are made so short and thick. They can be elevated so as to drop a shell just inside a fort, whereas a cannon ball would either strike it on the outside or pass over it far to the rear.

Mortars were used very little as compared with cannon. In the siege of Petersburg, I think, they were used more at night than in the daytime. This was due to the exceeding watchfulness of the pickets of both armies. At some periods in the siege each side was in nightly expectation of an attack from the other, and so the least provocation—an accidental shot, or a strange and unusual sound after dark—would draw the fire of the pickets, which would extend from the point of disturbance all along the line in both directions. Then the main lines, both infantry and artillery, thinking it might possibly be a night attack, would join in the fire, while the familiar Rebel yell, responded to by the Union cheer, would swell louder as the din and roar increased. But soon the yelling, the cheering, the artillery, the musketry would subside, and the mortar batteries with which each fort was supplied would continue the contest, and the sky would become brilliant with the fiery arches of these lofty-soaring and more dignified projectiles. As the mortar shells described their majestic curves across the heavens every other sound was hushed, and the two armies seemed to stand in mute and mutual admiration of these magnificent messengers of destruction and woe.

Sometimes a single shell could be seen climbing the sky from a Rebel mortar, but ere it had reached its destination as many as half a dozen from Union mortars would appear as if chasing each other through the air, anxious to be foremost in resenting such temerity on the part of the enemy. In this arm of the service, as in the artillery, the Union Army was greatly superior to the enemy.

These evening fusillades rarely did any damage. So harmless were they considered that President Lincoln and other officials frequently came down to the trenches to be a witness of them. But, harmless as they usually were to our side, they yet often enlisted our warm personal interest. The guns of my own company were several times a mark for their particular attentions by daylight. At such times we would watch the shells closely as they mounted the sky. If they veered to the right or left from a vertical in their ascent, we cared nothing for them as we then knew they would go one side of us. If they rose perpendicularly, and at the same time increased in size, our interest intensified. If they soon began to descend we lost interest, for that told us they would fall short; but if they continued climbing until much nearer the zenith, and we could hear the creaking whistle of the fuse as the shell slowly revolved through the air, *business of a very pressing nature suddenly called us into the bomb-proofs;* and it was not transacted until an explosion was heard, or a heavy jar told us that the bomb had expended its violence in the ground.

These mortar bombs could be seen very distinctly at times, but only when they were fired directly toward or from us. They can be seen immediately after they leave the gun if they come against the sky. Coming towards one they appear first as a black speck, increasing in size as stated. Besides mortar shells I have seen the shot and shell from twelve-pounders in transit, but never from rifled pieces, as their flight is much more rapid.

3
Life in Tents

Enter with me into a Sibley tent which is not stockaded. If it is cold weather, we shall find the cone-shaped stove, which I have already mentioned, setting in the center. These stoves were useless for cooking purposes, and the men were likely to burn their blankets on them in the night, so that many of the troops utilized them by building a small brick or stone oven below, in which they did their cooking, setting the stove on top as a part of the flue. The length of pipe furnished by the Government was not sufficient to reach the opening at the top, and the result was that unless the inmates bought more to piece it out, the upper part of such tents was as black and sooty as a chimney flue.

The dozen men occupying a Sibley tent slept with their feet toward the center. The choice place to occupy was that portion opposite the door, as one was not then in the way of passers in and out, although he was himself more or less of a nuisance to others when he came in. The tent was most crowded at meal times, for, owing to its shape, there can be no standing or sitting erect except about the center. But while there was more or less growling at accidents by some, there was much forbearance by others, and aside from the vexations arising from the constitutional blundering of the Jonahs and the Beats, whom I shall describe later, these little knots were quite family-like and sociable.

The manner in which the time was spent in these tents— and for that matter in all tents—varied with the disposition of the inmates. It was not always practicable for men of kindred tastes to band themselves under the same canvas, and so just as they differed in their avocations as citizens, they differed in their social life, and many kinds of pastimes went on simultaneously. Of course, all wrote letters more or less, but there were a few men who seemed to spend the most of their spare time

35

in this occupation. Especially was this so in the earlier part of a man's war experience. The side or end strip of a hardtack box, held on the knees, constituted the writing desk on which this operation was performed. It is well remembered that in the early months of the war silver money disappeared, as it commanded a premium, so . . . postage stamps were used instead.

Sibley Tent—Inside View

This was before scrip was issued by the Government to take the place of silver; and although the use of stamps as change was not authorized by the national Government, yet everybody took them, and the soldiers in particular just about to leave for the war carried large quantities away with them—not all in the best of condition. This could hardly be expected when they had been through so many hands. They were passed about in little envelopes, containing twenty-five and fifty cents in value.

Many an old soldier can recall his disgust on finding what a mess his stamps were in either from rain, perspiration, or compression, as he attempted after a hot march to get one for a letter. If he could split off one from a welded mass of perhaps a hundred or more, he counted himself fortunate. Of course they could be soaked out after a while, but he would need to dry them on a griddle afterwards, they were so sticky. It was later than this that the postmaster-general issued an order allowing soldiers to send letters without prepayment; but, if I recollect right, it was necessary to write on the outside "Soldier's Letter." I recall in this connection a verse that was to have appeared on a letter of this kind. It ran as follows:—

> *Soldier's letter, nary red,*
> *Hardtack and no soft bread,*
> *Postmaster, please put it through,*
> *I've nary cent, but six months due.*

There were a large number of fanciful envelopes got up during the war. I heard of a young man who had a collection of more than seven thousand such, all of different designs. I have several in my possession which I found among the numerous letters written home during war-time. One is bordered by thirty-four red stars—the number of states then in the Union —each star bearing the abbreviated name of a state. At the left end of the envelope hovers an eagle holding a shield and streamer, with this motto, "Love one another." Another one bears a representation of the earth in space, with "United States" marked on it in large letters, and the American eagle above it. Enclosing all is the inscription, "What God has joined, let no man put asunder." A third has a medallion portrait of Washington, under which is, "A SOUTHERN MAN WITH UNION PRINCIPLES." A fourth displays a man sitting among money-bags, on horseback, and driving at headlong speed. Underneath is the inscription, "FLOYD OFF FOR THE SOUTH. All that the Seceding States ask is to be let alone." Another has a Negro standing grinning, a hoe in his hand. He is represented as saying, "Massa can't have dis chile, dat's what's de matter"; and beneath is the title, "The latest contraband of war." Then there are many bearing the portraits of early Union generals. On others Jeff Davis is represented as hanged; while the national colors appear in a hundred or more ways on a number

—all of which, in a degree at least, expressed some phase of the sentiments popular at the North. The Christian Commission also furnished envelopes gratuitously to the armies, bearing their stamp and "Soldier's Letter" in one corner.

Besides letter writing the various games of cards were freely engaged in. Many men played for money. Cribbage and euchre were favorite games. Reading was a pastime quite generally indulged in, and there was no novel so dull, trashy, or sensational as not to find some one so bored with nothing to do that he would wade through it. I, certainly, never read so many such before or since. The mind was hungry for something, and took husks when it could get nothing better. A great deal of good might have been done by the Christian Commission or some other organization planned to furnish the soldiers with good literature, for in that way many might have acquired a taste for the works of the best authors who would not have been likely to acquire it except under just such a condition as they were then in, viz.: a want of some entertaining pastime. There would then have been much less gambling and sleeping away of daylight than there was.

Religious tracts were scattered among the soldiers by thousands, it is true, and probably did some good. A Massachusetts soldier was heard to say that when his regiment arrived in New York en route for the seat of war, the men were presented with "a plate of thin soup and a Testament." This remark to me was very suggestive. It reminded me of the vast amount of mistaken or misguided philanthropy that was expended upon the army by good Christian men and women, who, with the best of motives urging them forward no doubt, often labored under the delusion that the Army was composed entirely of men thoroughly bad, and governed their actions accordingly. That there were bad men in the Army is too well known to be denied if one cared to deny it; and, while I may forgive, I cannot forget a war governor who granted pardon to several criminals that were serving out sentences in prison, if they would enlist. But the morally bad soldiers were in the minority. The good men should have received some consideration, and the tolerably good even more. Men are only children of an older growth; they like to be appreciated at their worth at least, and the nature of many of the tracts was such that they defeated the object aimed at in their distribution.

Checkers was a popular game among the soldiers, backgammon less so, and it was only rarely that the statelier and less familiar game of chess was to be observed on the board. There were some soldiers who rarely joined in any games. In this class were to be found the illiterate members of a company. Of course they did not read or write, and they rarely played cards. They were usually satisfied to lie on their blankets and talk with one another or watch the playing. Yes, they did have one pastime—the proverbial soldier's pastime of smoking. A pipe was their omnipresent companion, and seemed to make up to them in sociability for whatsoever they lacked of entertainment in other directions.

Then there were a few men in every organization who engaged in no pastimes and joined in no social intercourse. These men were irreproachable as soldiers, it may have been, doing without grumbling everything that was expected of them in the line of military or fatigue duty, but they seemed shut up within an impenetrable shell, and would lie on their blankets silent while all others joined in the social round; or perhaps would get up and go out of the tent, as if its lively social atmosphere was uncongenial, and walk up and down the parade or company street alone. Should you address them, they would answer pleasantly but in monosyllables; and if the conversation was continued, it must be done in the same way. They could not be drawn out. They would cook by themselves, eat by themselves, camp by themselves on the march—in fact, keep by themselves at all times as much as possible. Guard duty was the one occupation which seemed most suited to their natures, for it provided them with the exclusiveness and comparative solitude that their peculiar mental condition craved. But these men were the exceptions. They were few in number, and the more noticeable on that account. They only served to emphasize the fact that the average soldier was a sociable being.

One branch of business which was carried on quite extensively was the making of pipes and rings as mementos of a camp or battlefield. The pipes were made from the root of the mountain laurel when it could be had, and often ornamented with the badges of the various corps either in relief or inlaid. The rings were made sometimes of dried horn or hoof, very often of bone, and some were fashioned out of large guttapercha buttons which were sent from home.

The evenings in camp were less occupied in game playing,

I should say, than the hours off duty in the daytime; partly, perhaps, because the tents were rather dimly lighted, and partly because of a surfeit of such recreations by daylight. But, whatever the cause, I think old soldiers will generally agree in the statement that the evenings were the time of sociability and reminiscence. It was then quite a visiting time among soldiers of the same organization. It was then that men from the same town or neighborhood got together and exchanged home gossip. Each one would produce recent letters giving interesting information about mutual friends or acquaintances, telling that such a girl or old schoolmate was married; that such a man had enlisted in such a regiment; that another was

Drafting

wounded and at home on furlough; that such another had been exempted from the forthcoming draft, because he had lost teeth; that yet another had suddenly gone to Canada on important business—which was a favorite refuge for all those who were afraid of being forced into the service.

And when the draft finally was ordered, such chucklings as these old schoolmates or fellow-townsmen would exchange as they again compared notes; first, to think that they themselves had voluntarily responded to their country's appeal, and, second, to hope that some of the croakers they left at home might be drafted and sent to the front at the point of the bayonet, interchanging sentiments of the following character: "There's A——, he was always urging others to go, and declaring he would himself make one of the next quota." "I want to see him out here with a Government suit on." "Yes, and there's B——, who has lots of money. If he's drafted, he'll send a substitute. The Government ought not to allow any able-bodied man, even if he has got money, to send a substitute." "Then there's C——, who declared he'd die on his doorstep rather than be forced into the service. I only hope that his courage will be put to the test." Such are fair samples of the remarks these fellow-soldiers would exchange. . . .

Then, there were many men not so fortunate as to have enlisted with acquaintances, or to be near them in the Army. These were wont to lie on their blankets and join in the general conversation, or exchange ante-war experiences and find much of interest in common; but, whatever the number or variety of the evening diversions, there is not the slightest doubt that home, its inmates, and surroundings were more thought of and talked of then than in all the rest of the twenty-four hours.

In some tents vocal or instrumental music was a feature of the evening. There was probably not a regiment in the service that did not boast at least one violinist, one banjoist, and a bone player in its ranks—not to mention other instruments generally found associated with these—and one or all of them could be heard in operation, either inside or in a company street, most any pleasant evening. However unskilful the artists, they were sure to be the center of an interested audience. The usual medley of comic songs and Negro melodies comprised the greater part of the entertainment, and, if the space admitted, a jig or clog dance was stepped out on a hardtack box or other crude platform. Sometimes a real Negro was brought in to enliven the occasion by patting and dancing "Juba," or singing his quaint music. There were always plenty of them in or near camp ready to fill any gap, for they asked nothing better than to be with "Massa Linkum's Sojers." But the men

played tricks of all descriptions on them, descending at times
to most shameful abuse until someone interfered. There were
a few of the soldiers who were not satisfied to play a reasonable
practical joke, but must bear down with all that the good-
natured Ethiopians could stand, and, having the fullest confidence in the friendship of the soldiers, these poor fellows stood
much more than human nature should be called to endure
without a murmur. Of course they were on the lookout a second time. There was one song which the boys of the old Third
Corps used to sing in the fall of 1863 to the tune of "When
Johnny Comes Marching Home," which is an amusing jingle
of historical facts. . . . It ran substantially as follows:

We are the boys of Potomac's ranks,
            Hurrah! Hurrah!
We are the boys of Potomac's ranks,
We ran with McDowell, retreated with Banks,
      And we'll all drink stone blind—
      Johnny, fill up the bowl.

We fought with McClellan, the Rebs, shakes and
            fever,
            Hurrah! Hurrah!
Then we fought with McClellan, the Rebs, shakes
            and fever,
But Mac joined the Navy on reaching James River,
      And we'll all drink, etc.

Then they gave us John Pope, our patience to tax,
            Hurrah! Hurrah!
Then they gave us John Pope our patience to tax,
Who said that out West he'd seen naught but
            Gray backs.*

He said his headquarters were in the saddle,
            Hurrah! Hurrah!
He said his headquarters were in the saddle,
But Stonewall Jackson made him skedaddle.

*An allusion to a statement in the address made by Pope, on taking
command of the Army of Virginia, "I have come to you from the
West where we have always seen the backs of our enemies."

Then Mac was recalled, but after Antietam,
Hurrah! Hurrah!
Then Mac was recalled, but after Antietam
Abe gave him a rest, he was too slow to beat 'em.

Oh, Burnside then he tried his luck,
Hurrah! Hurrah!
Oh, Burnside then he tried his luck,
But in the mud so fast got stuck.

Then Hooker was taken to fill the bill,
Hurrah! Hurrah!
Then Hooker was taken to fill the bill,
But he got a black eye at Chancellorsville.

Next came General Meade, a slow old plug,
Hurrah! Hurrah!
Next came General Meade, a slow old plug,
For he let them away at Gettysburg.

I think there were other verses, and some of the above may have got distorted with the lapse of time. But they are essentially correct.

Here is the revised prayer of the soldier while on the celebrated "Mud March" of Burnside:*

Now I lay me down to sleep
In mud that's many fathoms deep;
If I'm not here when you awake,
Just hunt me up with an oyster rake.

It was rather interesting to walk through a company street of an evening and listen to a few words of the conversation in progress in the tents—all lighted up, unless some one was saving or had consumed his allowance of candle. It would read much like a chapter from the telephone—noted down by a listener from one end of the line only. Then to peer into the

*After losing the Battle of Fredericksburg on December 13, 1862, Burnside started out again on January 20, 1863. A two-day rainstorm made the roads so impassable that the ill-fated attempt was called "the Mud March."

tents as one went along, just time enough to see what was going on, and excite the curiosity of the inmates as to the identity of the intruder, was a feature of such a walk.

While the description I have been giving applies in some particulars to life in Sibley tents, yet so far as much of it is concerned, it describes equally well the life of the private soldier in any tent. But *the* tent of the Army was the shelter or dog tent, and the life of the private soldier in log huts under these tents requires treatment by itself in many respects. I shall therefore leave it for consideration in another chapter.

4
Life in Log Huts

The camp of a regiment or battery was supposed to be laid out in regular order as definitely prescribed by Army Regulations. Those, I may state in a general way, provided that each company of a regiment should pitch its tents in two files, facing on a street which was at right angles with the color line of the regiment. This color line was the assigned place for regimental formation. Then, without going into details, I will add that the company officers' tents were pitched in rear of their respective companies, and the field officers in rear of these. Cavalry had something of the same plan, but with one row of tents to a company, while the artillery had three files of tents, one to each section.

All of this is preliminary to saying that while there was in Army Regulations this prescribed plan for laying out camps, yet the soldiers were more distinguished for their breach than their observance of this plan. Army Regulations were adopted for the guidance of the regular standing Army; but this same regular Army was now only a very small fraction of the Union forces, the largest portion by far—"the biggest half," to use a Hibernianism—were volunteers who could not or would not all be bound by Army Regulations. In the establishing of camps therefore, there was much of the go-as-you-please order of procedure. It is true that regiments commanded by strict disciplinarians were likely to and did keep pretty close to regulations. Many others approximated this standard, but still there then remained a large residuum who suited themselves, or did not attempt to suit anybody unless compelled to by superior authority; so that in entering some camps one might find everything betokening the supervision of a critical military spirit, while others were such a hurly-burly lack of plan that a mere plow-jogger might have been, and perhaps was, the controlling genius of the camp. When troops located in the woods, as they

45

always did for their winter cantonments, this lack of system in the arrangement was likely to be deviated from on account of trees. . . .

Come with me into one of the log huts. I have already spoken of its walls, its roof, its chimney, its fireplace. The door we are to enter may be cut in the same end with the fireplace. Such was often the case, as there was just about unoccupied space enough for that purpose. But where four or more soldiers located together it was oftener put in the center of one side. In that case the fireplace was in the opposite side as a rule. In entering a door at the end one would usually observe two bunks across the opposite end, one near the ground (or floor, when there was such a luxury, which was rarely), and the other well up towards the top of the walls. I say, usually. It depended upon circumstances. When only two men occupied the hut there was one bunk. Sometimes when four occupied it there was but one, and that one running lengthwise. There are other exceptions which I need not mention; but the average hut contained two bunks.

The construction of these bunks was varied in character. Some were built of boards from hardtack boxes; some of barrelstaves laid crosswise on two poles; some men improvised a springbed of slender saplings, and padded them with a cushion of hay, oak, or pine leaves; others obtained coarse grain sacks from an artillery or cavalry camp, or from some wagon train, and by making a hammock-like arrangement of them thus devised to make repose a little sweeter. At the head of each bunk were the knapsacks or bundles which contained what each soldier boasted of personal effects. These were likely to be underclothes, socks, thread, needles, buttons, letters, stationery, photographs, etc. The number of such articles was fewer among infantry than among artillery, who, on the march, had their effects carried for them on the gun carriages and caissons. But in winter quarters both accumulated a large assortment of conveniences from home, sent on in the boxes which so gladdened the soldier's heart. The haversacks, canteens, and the equipments usually hung on pegs inserted in the logs. The muskets had no regular abiding place. Some stood them in a corner, some hung them on pegs by the slings.

Domestic conveniences were not entirely wanting in the best ordered of these rude establishments. A hardtack box nailed end upwards against the logs with its cover on leather hinges serving as a door, and having suitable shelves inserted, made a very passable dish closet; another such box put upside down on legs did duty as a table—small, but large enough for the family and useful. Over the fireplace one or more shelves were sometimes put to catch the *bric à brac* of the hut; and three- or four-legged stools were manufactured for the inmates. But such a hut as this one I have been describing was rather *high-toned*. There were many huts without any of these conveniences.

A soldier's table furnishings were his tin dipper, tin plate, knife, fork, and spoon. When he had finished his meal, he did not in many cases stand on ceremony, and his dishes were tossed under the bunk to await the next meal. Or, if he condescended to do a little dish cleaning, it was not of an esthetic kind. Sometimes he was satisfied to scrape his plate out with his knife and let it go at that. Another time he would take a wisp of straw or a handful of leaves from his bunk and wipe it out. When soft bread was abundant, a piece of that made a convenient and serviceable dishcloth and towel. Now and then a man would pour a little of his hot coffee into his plate to cleanse it. While here and there one with neither pride, nor shame, nor squeamishness would take his plate out just as he last used it, to get his ration, offering no other remark to the comment of the cook than that he guessed the plate was a fit receptacle for the ration. As to the knife and fork, when they got too black to be tolerated—and they had to be of a very sable hue, it should be said—there was no cleansing process so inexpensive, simple, available, and efficient as running them vigorously into the earth a few times.

For lighting these huts the Government furnished candles in limited quantities: at first long ones, which had to be cut for distribution; but later they provided short ones. I have said that they were furnished in limited quantities. I will modify that statement. Sometimes they were abundant, sometimes the contrary; but no one could account for a scarcity. It was customary to charge quartermasters with peculation in such cases, and it is true that many of them were rascals; but I think they were sometimes saddled with burdens that did not belong to them. Some men used more light than others. Indeed, some men were constitutionally out of everything. They seemed to have conscientious scruples against keeping rations of any description in stock for the limit of time for which they were drawn.

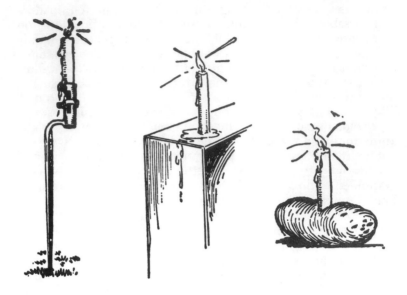

Army Candlesticks

As to candlesticks, the Government provided the troops with these by the thousands. They were of steel and very durable, but were supplied only to the infantry, who had simply to unfix bayonets, stick the points of the same in the ground, and their candlesticks were ready for service. As a fact, the bayonet shank was *the* candlestick of the rank and file who used that implement. It was always available, and just filled the bill in other respects. Potatoes were too valuable to come into very general use for this purpose. Quite often the candle was set up on a box in its own drippings.

Whenever candles failed, *slush lamps* were brought into use. These I have seen made by filling a sardine box with cookhouse grease, and inserting a piece of rag in one corner for a wick. The whole was then suspended from the ridge pole of the hut by a wire. This wire came to camp around bales of hay brought to the horses and mules.

The bunks were the most popular institutions in the huts. Soldiering is at times a lazy life, and bunks were then liberally patronized; for, as is well known, ottomans, lounges, and easy chairs are not a part of a soldier's outfit. For that reason the bunks served as a substitute for all these luxuries in the line of furniture.

I will describe in greater detail how they were used. All soldiers were provided with a woollen and a rubber blanket. When they retired, after tattoo roll call, they did not strip to the skin and put on night dresses as they would at home. They were satisfied ordinarily with taking off coat and boots, and perhaps the vest. Some, however, stripped to their flannels, and donning a smoking cap would turn in and pass a very comfortable night. There were a few in each regiment who never took off anything night or day unless compelled to; and these turned in at night in full uniform with all the covering they could muster. I shall speak of this class in another connection.

There was a special advantage in two men bunking together in winter quarters, for then each got the benefit of the other's blankets—no mean advantage either in much of the weather. It was a common plan with the soldiers to make an undersheet of the rubber blanket, the lining side up, just as when they camped out on the ground, for it excluded the cold air from below in the one case as it kept out dampness in the other. Moreover, it prevented the escape of animal heat.

I think I have said that the half-shelters were not impervious to a hard rain. But I was about to say that whenever such a storm came on it was often necessary for the occupants of the upper bunk to cover that part of the tent above them with their rubber blankets or ponchos; or, if they did not wish to venture out to adjust such a protection, they would pitch them on the inside. When they did not care to bestir themselves enough to do either, they would compromise by spreading a rubber blanket over themselves and let the water run off on to the tent floor.

At intervals, whose length was governed somewhat by the movements of the Army, an inspector of Government property put in an appearance to examine into the condition of the belongings of the Government in the possession of an organization, and when in his opinion any property was unfit for further service it was declared condemned and marked with his official brand, I C, meaning, *Inspected Condemned*. This I C became a byword among the men, who made an amusing application of it on many occasions.

In the daytime the men lay in their bunks and slept, or

read a great deal, or sat on them and wrote their letters. Unless otherwise forbidden, callers felt at liberty to perch on them; but there was such a wide difference in the habits of cleanliness of the soldiers that some proprietors of huts had, as they thought, sufficient reasons why no one else should occupy their berths but themselves, and if the three-legged stools or boxes did not furnish seating capacity enought for company and the regular boarders too, the r. b. would take to the bunks with a dispatch which betokened a deeper interest than that required of simple etiquette. This remark naturally leads me to say something of the insect life which seemed to have enlisted with the soldiers for "three years or during the war," and which required and received a large share of attention in quarters, much more, in fact, than during active campaigning. I refer now to the *Pediculus Vestimenti*, as the scientific men call him, but whose picture when it is well taken, and somewhat magnified, bears this familiar outline. Old soldiers will recognize the picture if the name is an odd one to them. This was the historic "grayback" which went in and out before Union and Confederate soldiers without ceasing. Like death, it was no respecter of persons. It preyed alike on the just and the unjust. It inserted its bill as confidingly into the body of the major-general as of the lowest private. I once heard the orderly of a company officer relate that he had picked fifty-two graybacks from the shirt of his chief at one sitting. Aristocrat or plebeian it mattered not. Every soldier seemed foreordained to encounter this

*Pediculus
Vestimenti*

pest at close quarters. Eternal vigilance was not the price of liberty. That failed the most scrupulously careful veteran in active campaigning. True, the neatest escaped the longest, but sooner or later the time came when it was simply impossible for even them not to let the left hand know what the right hand was doing.

The secretiveness which a man suddenly developed when he found himself inhabited for the first time was very entertaining. He would cuddle all knowledge of it as closely as the old Forty-Niners did the hiding place of their bag of gold dust. Perhaps he would find only one of the vermin. This he would secretly murder, keeping all knowledge of it from his tent mates, while he nourished the hope that it was the Robinson Crusoe of its race cast away on a strange shore with none of its kind at hand to cheer its loneliness. Alas, vain delusion! In ninety-nine cases out of a hundred this solitary *pediculus* would prove to be the advance guard of generations yet to come, which had been stealthily engaged in sowing its seed; and in a space of time all too brief, after the first discovery the same soldier would appoint himself an investigating committee of one to sit with closed doors and hie away to the desired seclusion. There he would seat himself taking his garments across his knees in turn, conscientiously doing his (k)nitting work, inspecting every fiber with the scrutiny of a dealer in broadcloths.

The feeling of intense disgust aroused by the first contact with these creepers soon gave way to hardened indifference, as a soldier realized the utter impossibility of keeping free from them, and the privacy with which he carried on his first "skirmishing," as this "search for happiness" came to be called, was soon abandoned, and the warfare carried on more openly. In fact, it was the mark of a cleanly soldier to be seen engaged at it, for there was no disguising the fact that everybody needed to do it.

In cool weather "skirmishing" was carried on in quarters, but in warmer weather the men preferred to go outside of camp for this purpose; and the woods usually found near camps were full of them sprinkled about singly or in social parties of two or three slaying their victims by the thousands. Now and then a man could be seen just from the quartermaster with an entire new suit on his arm, bent on starting afresh. He would hang the suit on a bush, strip off every piece of the old, and set fire to the same, and then don the new suit of blue. So far well; but he was a lucky man if he did not share his new clothes with other hungry *pediculi* inside of a week.

"Skirmishing," however, furnished only slight relief from the oppressive attentions of the grayback, and furthermore took much time. Hot water was the sovereign remedy, for it penetrated every mesh and seam, and cooked the millions yet unborn, which Job himself could not have exterminated by the thumbnail process unaided. So tenacious of life were these creatures that some veterans affirm they have seen them still creeping on garments taken out of *boiling water*, and that only by putting salt in the water were they sure of accomplishing their destruction.

I think there was but one opinion among the soldiers in regard to the graybacks; viz., that the country was being ruined
by overproduction. What the Colorado beetle is to the potato
crop they were to the soldiers of both armies. . . . From all this
it can readily be seen why no good soldier wanted his bunk to
be regarded as common property.

I may add in passing that no other variety of insect life
caused any material annoyance to the soldier. Now and then
a wood tick would insert his head, on the sly, into some part
of the human integument; but these were not common.

I have already related much that the soldier did to pass away
time. I will add to that which I have already given two branches
of domestic industry that occupied a considerable time in log
huts with a few, and less—very much less indeed—with others.
I refer to washing and mending. Some of the men were just
as particular about changing their underclothing at least once
a week as they would be at home; while others would do so
only under the severest pressure. It is disgusting to remember.
. . . how little care hundreds of the men bestowed on bodily
cleanliness. The story, quite familiar to old soldiers, about the
man who was so negligent in this respect that when he finally
took a bath he found a number of shirts and socks which he
supposed he had lost, arose from the fact of there being a few
men in every organization who were most unaccountably regardless of all rules of health, and of whom such a statement
would seem to those that knew the parties only slightly ex-
aggerated.

How was this washing done? Well, if the troops were camping near a brook, that simplified the matter somewhat; but
even then the clothes must be boiled, and for this purpose there
was but one resource—the mess kettles. . . . In regard to using
our mess kettles to boil clothes in, it might be asked "Why
not?" Were they not used to boil our meat and potatoes in, to
make our bean, pea, and meat soups in, to boil our tea and
coffee in, to make our apple and peach sauce in? Why not use
them as washboilers? While it might at first interfere somewhat
with your appetite to have your food cooked in the washboiler,
you would soon get used to it; and so this complex use of the
mess kettles soon ceased to affect the appetite, or to shock the
sense of propriety of the average soldier as to the eternal fitness
of things, for he was often compelled by circumstances to endure much greater improprieties. It would indeed have been

a most admirable arrangement in many respects could each man have been provided with an excellent Magee Range with copper-boiler annex, and set tubs near by; but the line had to be drawn somewhere, and so everything in the line of *impedimenta* was done away with, unless it was absolutely essential to the service. For this reason we could not take along a well-equipped laundry, but must make some articles do double or triple service.

It may be asked what kind of a figure the men cut as washerwomen. Well, some of them were awkward and imperfect enough at it; but necessity is a capital teacher, and in this as in many other directions men did perforce what they would not have attempted at home. It was not necessary, however, for every man to do his own washing, for in most companies there was at least one man who, for a reasonable recompense, was ready to do such work, and he usually found all he could attend to in the time he had off duty. There was no ironing to be done, for "boiler shirts," as white-bosomed shirts were

A Housewife

called, were almost an unknown garment in the army except in hospitals. Flannels were the order of the day. If a man had the courage to face the ridicule of his comrades by wearing a white‧ collar, it was of the paper variety, and white cuffs were unknown in camp.

In the department of mending garments each man did his own work, or left it undone, just as he thought best; but no one hired it done. Every man had a "housewife" or its equivalent, containing the necessary needles, yarn, thimble, etc., furnished him by some mother, sister, sweetheart, or Soldier's

Aid Society, and from this came his materials to mend or darn with.

Now, the average soldier was not so susceptible to the charms and allurements of sock darning as he should have been; for this reason he always put off the direful day until both heels looked boldly and with hardened visage out the back door, while his ten toes ranged themselves en échelon in front of their quarters. By such delay or neglect good ventilation and the opportunity of drawing on the socks from either end were secured. The task of once more restricting the toes to quarters was not an easy one, and the processes of arriving at this end were not many in number. Perhaps the speediest and most unique, if not the most artistic, was that of tying a string around the hole. This was a scheme for cutting the Gordian knot of darning, which a few modern Alexanders put into execution. But I never heard any of them commend its comforts after the job was done.

Then, there were other men who, having arranged a checkerboard of stitches over the holes, as they had seen their mothers do, had not the time or patience to fill in the squares, and the inevitable consequence was that both heels and toes would look through the bars only a few hours before breaking jail again. But there were a few of the boys who were kept furnished with homemade socks, knit, perhaps by their good old grandmas, who seemed to inherit the patience of the grandams themselves; for, whenever there was mending or darning to be done, they would sit by the hour and do the work as neatly and conscientiously as any one could desire. I am not wide of the facts when I say that the heels of the socks darned by these men remained firm when the rest of the fabric was well spent.

There was little attempt made to repair the socks drawn from the Government supplies, for they were generally of the shoddiest description and not worth it. In symmetry, they were like an elbow of stove pipe; nor did the likeness end here, for while the stove pipe is open at both ends, so were the socks within forty-eight hours after putting them on.

Cooking was also an industry which occupied more or less of the time of individuals; but when the Army was in settled camp company cooks usually took charge of the rations. Sometimes, where companies preferred it, the rations were served out to them in the raw state; but there was no invariable rule in this matter. I think the soldiers as a whole preferred to receive their coffee and sugar raw, for rough experience in campaigning soon made each man an expert in the preparaticn of this beverage. Moreover, he could make a more palatable cup for himself than the cooks made for him; for too often their handiwork betrayed some of the other uses of the mess kettles to which I have made reference. Then again some men liked their coffee strong, others weak; some liked it sweet, others wished little or no sweetening; and this latter class could and did save their sugar for other purposes. I shall give other particulars about this when I take up the subject of Army Rations.

It occurs to me to mention in this connection a circumstance which may seem somewhat strange to many, and that is that some parts of the army burned hundreds of cords of green pinewood while lying in winter quarters. It was very often their only resource for heat and warmth. People at the North would as soon think of attempting to burn water as green pine. But the explanation of the paradox is this—the pine of southern latitudes has more pitch in it than that of northern latitudes. Then, the heartwood of all pines is comparatively dry. It seemed especially so South. The heartwood was used to kindle with, and the pitchy sapwood placed on top, and by the time the heartwood had burned, the sappy portion had also seasoned enough to blaze and make a good fire. These pines had the advantage over the hard woods of being more easily worked up—an advantage the average soldier appreciated.

Nearly every organization had its barber in established camp. True, many men never used the razor in the service, but allowed a shrubby, straggling growth of haii and beard to grow, as if to conceal them from the enemy in time of battle. Many more carried their own kit of tools and shaved themselves, frequently shedding innocent blood in the service of their country while undergoing the operation. But there was yet a large number left who, whether from lack of skill in the use or care of the razor, or from want of inclination, preferred to patronize the camp barber. This personage plied his vocation inside the tent in cold or stormy weather, but at other times took his post in rear of the tent, where he had improvised a chair for the comfort(?) of his victims. This chair was a product of home manufacture. Its framework was four stakes driven into the ground, two long ones for the back legs, and two shorter ones for the front. On this foundation a superstructure was raised which made a passable barber's chair. But not all the professors who

presided at these chairs were finished tonsors, and the back of
a soldier's head whose hair had been "shingled" by one of them
was likely to show each course of the shingles with painful
distinctness. The razors, too, were of the most barbarous sort.

One other occupation of a few men in every camp, which
I must not overlook, was that of studying the tactics. Some
were doing it, perhaps, under the instructions of superior officers; some because of an ambition to deserve promotion. Some
were looking to passing a competitive examination with a view

The Camp Barber

of obtaining a furlough; and so these men from various motives were "booking" themselves. But the great mass of the rank and file had too much to do with the practice of war to take much interest in working out its theory, and freely gave themselves up when off duty to every available variety of physical or mental recreation, doing their uttermost to pass away the time rapidly; and even those troops having nearly three years to serve would exclaim with a cheerfulness more feigned than real as each day dragged to its close, "It's only two years and a but."

5

Jonahs and Beats

In a former chapter I made the statement that Sibley tents furnished quarters capacious enough for twelve men. That statement is to be taken with some qualifications. If those men were all lying down asleep there did not seem much of a crowd. But if one man of the twelve happened to be on guard at night and was on what we used to know as the Third Relief guard, which in my company was posted at 12 midnight and came off post at 2 A.M., when all were soundly sleeping, and . . . if this man chanced to quarter in that part of the tent opposite the entrance, and if, in seeking his blanket and board in the darkness, it was his luck to step on the stockinged foot of a recumbent form having a large voice, a large temper, but a small though forcible selection of English defiled, straightway that selection was hurled at the head of the offending even though well-meaning guard. And if, under the excitement of his mishap, the luckless guard makes a spring thinking to clear all other intervening slumberers and score a home run, but alights instead amidships of the comrade who sleeps next him, expelling from him a groan that by all known comparisons should have been his last, the poor guard has only involved himself the more inextricably in trouble; for as soon as his latest victim recovers consciousness sufficiently to know that it was not a twelve-pound cannon ball that has doubled him up and that stretcher bearers are not needed to take him to the rear, he strikes up in the same strain and pitch and force as that of the first victim, and together they make the midnight air vocal with choice invective against their representative of the Third Relief. By this time the rest of the tent's crew have been waked up, cross enough, too, at being thus rudely disturbed, and they all come in heavily on the chorus. As the wordy assault continues the inmates of adjoining tents who have also been aroused take a hand in it, and "Shut up!"
58

"Sergeant of the Guard!" "Go lie down!" "Shoot him on the spot!" "Put him in the guardhouse!" are a few of the many impromptu orders issued within and without the tent in question.

At last the tempest in a teapot expends itself, and by the time the sergeant of the guard has arrived to seek out the cause of the tumult and enforce the instructions of the officer of the day by putting the offenders against the rules and discipline of camp under arrest for talking and disturbance after Taps, all are quiet, for no one would make a complaint against the culprits. Their temporary excitement has cooled, and the discreet sergeant is even in doubt as to which tent contains the offenders.

Now accidents will happen to the most careful and the best of men, but the soldier whom I have been describing could be found in every squad in camp—that is, a man of his kind. Such men were called "Jonahs" on account of their ill luck. Perhaps this particular Jonah after getting his tin plate level full of hot pea soup was sure, on entering the tent, to spill a part of it down somebody's back. The higher he could hold it the better it seemed to please him as he made his way to his accustomed place in the tent, and in bringing it down into a latitude where he proposed to eat it he usually managed to dispose of much of the remainder, either on his own or somebody else's blankets. When pea soup failed him for a diversion, he was a dead shot on kicking over his neighbor's pot of coffee, which the owner had put down for a moment while he adjusted his lap table to receive his supper. The profuseness of the Jonah's apologies—and they always were profuse and undoubtedly sincere—was utterly inadequate as a balm for the wounds he made. Anybody else in the tent might have kicked the coffee to the remotest bounds of camp with malice aforethought, and it would not have produced a tithe of the aggravation which it did to have this constitutional blunderer do it by accident. It may be that he wished to borrow your ink. Of course you could not refuse him. It may have been made by you with some ink powders sent from home—perhaps the last you had and which you should want yourself that very day. It mattered not. He took it with complacency and fair promises, put it on a box by his side and tipped the box over five minutes afterward by the watch.

Cooking was the forte of this Jonah. He could be found

most any time of day—or night, if he was a guardsman—
around the camp fire with his little mess of something in his
tomato can or tin dipper, which he would throw an air of
mystery around every now and then by drawing a small package from the depths of his pocket or haversack and scattering
some of its contents into the brew. But there was a time
in the history of his culinary pursuits when he rose to a su-
preme height as a blunderer. It was when he appeared at the
camp fire which, by the way, he never kindled himself, ready
to occupy the choice places with his dishes; and after the
two rails, between which fires were usually built, had been
well burdened by the coffee pots of his comrades it presented
an opportunity which his evil genius was likely to take advantage of, for then he was suddenly seized with a thought of
something else that he had forgotten to borrow. Turning in
his haste to go to the tent for this purpose he was sure to
stumble over the end of one or both of the rails, when the
downfall of the coffee pots and the quenching of the fire
followed as a matter of course. At just this point in his career
it would be to the credit of his associates to drop the curtain
on the picture; but the sequel must be told. The average
soldier was not an especially devout man, and while in times
of imminent danger he had serious thoughts, yet at other times
his many trials, his privations, and the rigors of a necessary
discipline all conduced to make him a highly explosive crea-
ture on demand. Moreover, coffee and sugar were stable
articles with the soldier, and the least waste of them was not
to be tolerated under ordinary circumstances; but to have a
whole line of coffee pots with their precious contents upset
by the Jonah of the tent in his recklessness was the last ounce
of pressure removed from the safety valve of his tent mates,
wrath; and such a discharge of hard names and oaths, "long,
loud, and deep," as many of these sufferers would deliver
themselves of, if it could have been utilized against the enemy,
might have demolished a regiment. And the others who did
not give vent to their passions by blows or the use of strong
language seemed to sympathize very keenly with those who
did. Two chaplains apiece to some of the men would have been
none too many to hold them in check.

I remember one man who seemed always to have hard luck
in spite of himself. He was a good soldier and meant well
but would blunder badly now and then. His last act in the

service was to plunge an axe through his boot while he was
cutting wood. Unfortunately for him as it happened his foot
was in it at the time. On pulling it out of the boot and looking
it over he found that several of his toes had "got left"; so
he took up his boot, turned it upside down, and shook out
a shower of toes as complacently as if that was what he enlisted for. This casualty closed his career in active service.

There were divers other directions in which the Jonah distinguished himself; but I must leave him for the present to
direct attention to the other class of men of whom I wish
to say something. These were the *beats* of the service—a name
given them by their comrades-in-arms. There were all grades
of beats. The original idea of beat was that of a lazy man or
a shirk who would by hook or by crook get rid of all military
or fatigue duty that he could; but the term grew to have a
broader significance.

One of the milder forms of beat was the man who sat over
the fire in the tent piling on wood all the time, and roasting
out the rest of the tent's crew, who seemed to have no rights
that this fireman felt bound to respect. He was always cold.
He wore overcoat, dress coat, blouse, and flannels in the full
Government allowance all at once, but never complained of
being too warm. He never took off any of these garments
night or day unless compelled to on inspection. He was most
at home on fatigue duty, for he seemed fatigued from the start
and moved like real estate. A sprinkling of this class seemed
necessary to the success of the Union arms, for they were
certainly to be found in every organization.

Another and more positive type of beat were the men who
never had any water in their canteens. Even when the Army
was in settled camp, water was not always to be had without
going some distance for it; but these men were never known
to go after any. They always managed to hang their canteen
on someone else who was bound for the spring. If, when
the Army was on the move, a rush was made during a temporary halt for a spring or stream some distance away, these
men never rushed. They were satisfied to lie down and drink
a supply which they took their chances of begging from some
recruit who did not know their propensities. If it happened
to any man to be so straitened in his cooking operations as
to be under the necessity of borrowing from one of these, he

was sure of being called upon to requite the favor fully as
many times as his temper would endure it.

Then, as to rations, their hardtack never held out, and they
were ever on the alert to borrow. It mattered not how great
the scarcity, real or anticipated, they could not provide for a
contingency, and their neighbors in the same squad were mean
and avaricious—so the beats said—if they would not give of
their husbanded resources to these profligate, improvident
comrades. But this class did not stop at borrowing hardtack.
They were not all of them particular, and when hardtack could
not be spared they would get along with coffee or sugar or
salt pork; or, if they could borrow a *dollar* "just for a day or
two," they would then repay it surely, because several letters
from their friends at home, each one containing money, were
already overdue. People in civil life think they know all about
the imperfections of the United States postal service, and tell
of their letters and papers [being] lost, miscarried, or in some
way delayed, with much pedantry; but they have yet to learn
the A B C of its imperfections, and no one that I know of is so
competent to teach them as certain of the Union soldiers. I
could have produced men in 1862–5, who lost more letters in
one year, three out of every four of which contained considerable sums of money, than any postmaster-general yet appointed
is willing to admit have been lost since the establishment of
a mail service. This, remember, the loss of one man; and when
it is multiplied by the number of men just like him, a special
reason is obvious why the Government should be liberal in
its dealings with the old soldier.

In this connection I am reminded‧ of another interesting
feature of army experience, which is of some historical value.
It was this: whenever the troops were paid off, a very large
majority of them wished to send the most of their pay home
to their families or their friends for safe keeping. Of course
there was some risk attending the sending of it in the mails.
To obviate this risk an "allotment" plan was adopted by
means of which when the troops were visited by the paymaster, on signing a roll prepared for that purpose, so much
of their pay as they wished was allotted or assigned by the
soldiers to whomsoever they designated at the North. To illustrate: John Smith had four months' pay due him at the
rate of $13 a month. He decided to allot $10 per month of
this to his wife at Plymouth, Mass.; so the paymaster pays

him $12, and the remaining $40 is paid to his wife by check in Plymouth, without any further action on the part of John.

This plan was a great convenience to both the soldiers and their families. In this division of his income the calculation of the soldier was to save out enough for himself to pay all incidental expenses of camp life, such as washing, tobacco, newspapers, pies and biscuits, bought of "Aunty," and cheese and cakes of the sutler. But in spite of his nice calculations the rule was that the larger part of the money allotted home was returned, by request of the sender, in small amounts of a dollar or the fraction of a dollar. I have previously stated that at that time silver had gone out of use, it being only to be had by paying the premium on it, just as on gold, and so to take its place the Government issued what was generally known as scrip, being paper currency of the denominations of fifty, twenty-five, ten, five, and, later, fifteen and three-cent pieces. . . . They were a great convenience to the soldiers and their friends. But to resume:

If the statements made by these beats as to the amount of money they had sent for and were expecting were to be believed, they must not only have sent for their full allotment but have drawn liberally on their home credit or the charity of their friends besides. In truth, however, the genuine beat never intended to return borrowed money. It is currently believed by outsiders that the soldiers who stood shoulder to shoulder battling for the Union, sharing the same exposures, the same shelter, the same mess would ever afterwards be likely to stand steadfastly by one another. The organization of the Grand Army of the Republic seems to strengthen such an opinion, yet human nature remains pretty much the same in all situations. If a man was a shirk or a thief or a beat or a coward or a worthless scoundrel generally in the Army, it was because he had been educated to it before he enlisted. The leopard cannot change his spots nor the Ethiopian his skin. It will therefore create no great surprise when I remark that a large amount of money borrowed by one soldier of another has never been repaid; and such is the lack of honesty and manliness on the part of these men that they can meet the old comrades of whom in those trying war days they borrowed one, two, five, or ten dollars, and in some cases more, without so much as a blush or betraying in any manner the slightest recognition of their long standing obligation. Some are so worthless and brazen-faced even as to ask the same victims for more. . . .

One favorite dodge of the beat was to have the corporal arouse him twice or three times before he would finally get out of his bunk, and then he would prepare to go out at a snail's pace. Once on his beat, his next dodge was to maneuver so as to have the corporal of his relief do the most of his duty for him, for hardly would he have been posted before the corporal must be summoned, the beat having been seized with a desire to go to the company sink. That is good for half an hour out of the corporal at least. At last the dodger reappears moving at a slow pace, and wearing the appearance of a man suffering for his discharge from service. He retails his woes to the corporal as he resumes his equipments in a most doleful strain. But the corporal is in no mood to listen after his long wait and hastily directs his steps towards the guard tent.

He is not allowed to remain there long, however, ere a summons reaches him from the same post, to which he responds with excusable ill-humor and mutterings at the duplicity of the guardsman in question. This time the patient has happened to think of some medicine at his tent which will be of benefit to him. Of course the corporal is anxious enough to have him healed, and so he again assumes the duties of the post for the shirk, who does not reappear until his last hour of duty is well on its second quarter, feigning in excuse that he could not find his own panacea and so was obliged to go elsewhere. Thus in one way and another, by using the kind offices of his messmates together with those of the corporal, he would manage to get out of at least two-thirds of his guard duty.

After the battle of Fredericksburg a soldier belonging to a gallant regiment in Burnside's corps, whose courage had evidently been put to a sore test in the above engagement, resorted to the rheumatic dodge to secure his discharge. He responded daily to sick call, pitifully warped out of shape, was prescribed for, but all to no avail. One leg was drawn up so that, apparently, he could not use it, and groans indicative of excruciating agony escaped him at studied intervals and on suitable occasions. So his case went on for six weeks, till at last the surgeon recommended his discharge. It was approved at regimental, brigade, and division headquarters, and had reached corps headquarters when the corps was ordered to

Kentucky. At Covington the party having the supposed invalid in charge gained access in some manner to a barrel of whiskey. Not being a temperance man, the dodger was thrown off his guard by this spiritual bonanza, and, taking his turn at the straw, for which entry had been made into the barrel, he was soon as sprightly on both legs as ever. In this condition his colonel found him. Of course his discharge was recalled from

Water for the Cook-house

corps headquarters, and the way of this transgressor was made hard for months afterwards.

There was another field in which the beat played an interesting part. I use *played* with a double significance, for he never *worked* if he could avoid it. It was when a detail of men was made to do some line of *fatigue duty*, by which is meant all the labors of the service distinct from strict military duty, such as the "policing" or clearing up of camp, procuring wood and water for the company, digging and fitting up of sinks (the water closets of the army), and, in addition to these duties, in cavalry and artillery, procuring grain and forage for the horses. It was a sad fate to befall a good duty soldier to get on to a detail to procure wood where every second or

third man was a shirk or beat, for while they must needs bear
the appearance of doing something, they were really in the
way of those who could work and were willing to. Many of
these shirkers would waste a great deal of time and breath
maligning the Government or their officers for requiring them
to do such work, indignantly declaring that "they enlisted to
fight and not to chop wood or dig sinks." But it was noticeable
that when the fight came on, if any of these heroes got into
it, they then appeared just as willing to bind themselves by
contract to cut all the wood in Virginia, if they could only
be let go just that once. These were the men who were "invincible in peace and invisible in war," as the late Senator
Hill of Georgia once said. I may add here that, coming as the
soldiers did from all avocations and stations in life, these details
for fatigue often brought together men few of whom had any
practical knowledge of the work in hand; so that aside from
the shirks, who *could* work but *would* not, there were others
who *would* but *could* not, at least intelligently. Still, the Army
was a great educator in many ways to men who cared to learn,
and some of the most ignorant became by force of circumstances quite expert in time in channels hitherto untraversed
by them.

But there was one detail upon which our shirks, beats, and
men unskilled in manual labor, such as the handling of the
spade and pickaxe, appeared in all the glory of their artful
dodging and ignorance. If a man did not take hold of the
work lively, whether because he preferred to shirk it or because
he did not understand it, the worse for him. The detail in
question was one made to administer the last rites to a batch
of deceased horses. It happened to the artillery and cavalry
to lose a large number of these animals in winter, which,
owing to the freezing of the ground, could not be buried
until the disappearance of the frost in spring; but by that
time, through the action of rain and sun and the frequent
depredations of dogs, buzzards, and crows, the remains were
not always in the most inviting condition for the administra-
tions of the sexton. Then, again, during the summer season,
when the Army made a halt for rest and recruiting, another
sacrifice of glanders-infected and generally used-up horses was
made to the god of war. But as they were not always promptly
committed to mother earth, either from a desire to show a
decent respect for the memory of the deceased or for some

other reason best known to the red tape of military rule, the odors that were wafted from them on the breezes were wont to become far more "spicy" than agreeable, so that a speedy interment was generally ordered by the military Board of Health.

As soon as the nature of the business for which such a detail was ordered became generally known, the fun began, for a lively protest was wont to go up from the men against being selected to participate in the impending equine obsequies. Perhaps the first objection heard from a victim who has drawn a prize in the business is that "he was on guard the day before, and is not yet physically competent for such a detail." The sergeant is charged with unfairness and with having pets that he gives all the soft jobs to, etc. But the warrior of the triple chevron is inexorable, and his muttering, much injured subordinate finally reports to the corporal in charge of the detail in front of the camp, betraying in his every word and movement a heartfelt desire for his term of service or this cruel war to be over.

Another one whom his sergeant has booked for the enterprise has got wind of what is to be done, so that when found he is tucked up in his bunk. He stoutly insists that he is an invalid and is only waiting for the next sounding of Sick Call to respond to it. But his attack is so sudden, and his language and lungs so strong for a sick man that he finds it difficult to establish his claim. He calls on his tent mates to swear that he is telling the truth but finds them strangely devout and totally ignorant of his ailments, for they are chuckling internally at their own good fortune in not being selected, which, if he proves his case, one of them may be; so, unless his plea is a pitiful and deserving one, they keep mum.

A third victim does not claim to have been selected out of turn, but nevertheless alleges that "the deal is unfair, because he was on the last detail but one made for this horse-burying business, and he does not think that he ought to be the chief mourner for his detachment, for a paltry thirteen dollars a month. Besides, there may be others who would like to go on this detail." But as he is unable to name or find the man or men having this highly refined ambition he finally goes off grumbling and joins the squad.

A fourth victim is the constitutionally high-tempered and profane man. He finds no fault with the justice of the sergeant

in assigning to him a participation in the ceremonies of the
hour; but he had got comfortably seated to write a letter when
the summons came, and pausing only long enough to inquire
the nature of the detail, he pitches his half-written letter and
materials in one direction, his lap board in another, gets up,
kicks over the box or stool on which he was sitting, pulls on
his cap with a vehement jerk, and then opens his battery.
He directs none of his unmilitary English at the sergeant—
that would hardly do; but he lays his furious lash upon the
poor innocent back of the Government, though just what
branch of it is responsible he does not pause between his oaths
long enough to state. He pursues it with the most terrible of
curses uphill, and then with like violent language follows it
down. He blank blanks the whole blank blank war and hopes
that the South may win. He wishes that all the blank horses
were in blank and adds by way of self-reproach that it serves
anyone who is such a blank blank fool as to enlist *right* to have
this blank, filthy, disgusting work to do. And he leaves the
stockade shutting the door behind him "with a wooden damn,"
as Holmes says and goes off to report, making the air blue
with his cursing. Let me say for this man, before leaving him,
that he is not so hardened and bad at heart as he makes himself appear, and in the shock of battle he will be found standing manfully at his post minus his temper and profanity.

There is one more man whom I will describe here, representing another class than either mentioned, whose unlucky
star has fated *him* to take a part in these obsequies, but he
is not a shirk nor a beat. He is the *paper-collar* young man,
just from the recruiting station, with enamelled long-legged
boots and custom-made clothes, who yet looks with some measure of disdain on Government clothing, and yet eats in a
most gingerly way of the stern, unpoetical Government rations.
He is an only son, and was a dry-goods clerk in the city at
home, where no reasonable want went ungratified; and now
when he is summoned forth to join the burial party, he responds at once. True, his heart and stomach both revolt at the
work ahead, but he wants to be—not an angel—but a veteran
among veterans, and his pride prevents his entering any remonstrance in the presence of the older soldiers. As he clutches
the spade pointed out to him with one hand, he shoves the
other vacantly to the bottom of his breeches pocket, his mouth
drawn down codfish-like at the corners. He attempts to appear

indifferent as he approaches the detail, and as they congratulate him on his good fortune a sickly smile plays over his countenance; but it is Mark Tapley feigning a jollity which he does not feel and which soon subsides into a pale melancholy. His fellow-victims feel their ill luck made more endurable by seeing him also drafted for the loathsome task; but their glow of satisfaction is only superficial and speedily wanes as the officer of the day who is to superintend the job appears and orders them forward.

And now the fitness of the selection becomes apparent as the squad moves off, for a more genuine body of mourners, to the eye, could not have been chosen. Their faces with . . . a hardened or indifferent exception wear the most solemn of expressions, and their step is as slow as if they were following a muffled drum beating the requiem of a deceased comrade.

Having arrived at the place of sepulture, the first business is to dig a grave close to each body, so that it may be easily rolled in. But if there has been no fun before, it commences when the rolling in begins. The Hardened Exception, who has occupied much of his time while digging in sketching distasteful pictures for the Profane Man to swear at, now makes a change of base and calls upon the Paper-Collar Young Man to "take hold and help roll in," which the young man reluctantly and gingerly does; but when the noxious gases begin to make their presence manifest, and the Hardened Wretch hands him an axe to break the legs that would otherwise protrude from the grave, it is the last straw to an already overburdened sentimental soul; his emotions overpower him, and turning his back on the deceased he utters something which sounds like "hurrah! without the h," as Mark Twain puts it, repeating it with increasing emphasis. But he is not to express his enthusiasm on this question alone a great while. There are more sympathizers in the party than he had anticipated, and not recruits either; and in less time than I have taken to relate it more than half the detail, gallantly led off by the officer of the day, are standing about, leaning over at various angles like the tombstones in an old cemetery, disposing of their hardtack and coffee, and looking as if ready to throw up even the contract. The profane man is among them, and just as often as he can catch his breath long enough he blank blanks the Government and then dives again. The rest of the detail stand not far away holding on to their sides and roaring with laughter. But I must drop the curtain on this picture. It has been said that one touch of nature makes the whole world kin. Be that as it may, certain it is that the officer, the good duty soldier, the recruit, and the beat, after an occasion of this kind, had a common bond of sympathy, which went far towards levelling military distinctions between them.

6
Army Rations

Fall in for your rations, Company A!" My theme is Army Rations. And while what I have to say on this subject may be applicable to all of the armies of the Union in large measure, yet, as they did not fare just alike, I will say once for all that my descriptions of army life pertain, when not otherwise specified, especially to that life as it was lived in the Army of the Potomac.

In beginning, I wish to say that a false impression has obtained more or less currency both with regard to the quantity and quality of the food furnished the soldiers. I have been asked a great many times whether I always got enough to eat in the Army, and have surprised inquirers by answering in the affirmative. Now, some old soldier may say who sees my reply, "Well, you were lucky. I didn't." But I should at once ask him to tell me for how long a time his regiment was ever without food of some kind. Of course, I am not now referring to our prisoners of war who starved by the thousands. And I should be very much surprised if he should say more than twenty-four or thirty hours at the outside. I would grant that he himself might have been so situated as to be deprived of food a longer time, possibly when he was on an exposed picket post, or serving as rear guard to the Army, or doing something which separated him temporarily from his company; but his case would be the exception and not the rule. Sometimes, when active operations were in progress, the Army was compelled to wait a few hours for its trains to come up, but no general hardship to the men ever ensued on this account. Such a contingency was usually known some time in advance, and the men would husband their last issue of rations, or, perhaps, if the country admitted, would make additions to their bill of fare in the shape of poultry or pork—usually it was the latter, for Southerners do not pen up their swine as

71

do the Northerners, but let them go wandering about, getting their living much of the time as best they can. This led some one to say jocosely, with no disrespect intended to the people however, "that every other person one meets on a Southern street is a hog." They certainly were quite abundant, and are today, in some form, the chief meat food of that section. But on the point of scarcity of rations I believe my statement will be generally agreed to by old soldiers.

Now, as to the quality the case is not quite so clear, but still the picture has been often overdrawn. There were, it is true, large quantities of stale beef or salt horse—as the men were wont to call it—served out, and also rusty, unwholesome pork; and I presume the word "hardtack" suggests to the uninitiated a piece of petrified bread honeycombed with bugs and maggots, so much has this article of army diet been reviled by soldier and civilian. Indeed, it is a rare occurrence for a soldier to make any sort of allusion to it without some reference to its hardness, the date of its manufacture, or its propensity for travel. But in spite of these unwholesome rations, whose existence no one calls in question, of which I have seen—I must not say eaten—large quantities, I think the Government did well under the circumstances to furnish the soldiers with so good a quality of food as they averaged to receive. Unwholesome rations were not the rule, they were the exception, and it was not the fault of the Government that these were furnished, but very often the intent of the rascally, thieving contractors who supplied them, for which they received the price of good rations; or, perhaps, of the inspectors who were in league with the contractors, and who therefore did not always do their duty. No language can be too strong to express the contempt every patriotic man, woman, and child must feel for such small-souled creatures, many of whom ended up rolling in the riches acquired in this way and other ways equally disreputable and dishonorable.

I will now give a complete list of the rations served out to the rank and file, as I remember them. They were salt pork, fresh beef, salt beef, rarely ham or bacon, hard bread, soft bread, potatoes, an occasional onion, flour, beans, split pease, rice, dried apples, dried peaches, desiccated vegetables, coffee, tea, sugar, molasses, vinegar, candles, soap, pepper, and salt. It is scarcely necessary to state that these were not all served out at one time. There was but one kind of meat served at once, and this, to use a Hibernianism, was usually pork. When it was hard bread, it wasn't *soft* bread or flour, and when it was pease or beans it wasn't rice.

Here is just what a single ration comprised, that is, what a soldier was entitled to have in one day. He should have had twelve ounces of pork or bacon, or one pound four ounces of salt or fresh beef; one pound six ounces of soft bread or flour, or one pound of hard bread, or one pound four ounces of corn meal. With every hundred such rations there should have been distributed one peck of beans or pease; ten pounds of rice 'or hominy; ten pounds of green coffee, or eight pounds of roasted and ground, or one pound eight ounces of tea; fifteen pounds of sugar; one pound four ounces of candles; four pounds of soap; two quarts of salt; four quarts of vinegar; four ounces of pepper; a half bushel of potatoes when practicable, and one quart of molasses. Desiccated potatoes or desiccated compressed vegetables might be substituted for the beans, pease, rice, hominy, or fresh potatoes. Vegetables, the dried fruits, pickles, and pickled cabbage were occasionally issued to prevent scurvy, but in small quantities.

But the ration thus indicated was a camp ration. Here is the *marching* ration: one pound of hard bread; three-fourths of a pound of salt pork, or one and one-fourth pounds of fresh meat; sugar, coffee, and salt. The beans, rice, soap, candles, etc., were not issued to the soldier when on the march, as he could not carry them; but singularly enough, as it seems to me, unless the troops went into camp before the end of the month, where a regular depot of supplies might be established from which the other parts of the rations could be issued, they were *forfeited* and *reverted to the Government*—an injustice to the rank and file, who through no fault of their own were thus cut off from a part of their allowance at the time when they were giving most liberally of their strength and perhaps of their very heart's blood. It was possible for company commanders and *for no one else* to receive the equivalent of these missing parts of the ration *in cash* from the brigade commissary, with the expectation that when thus received it would be distributed among the rank and file to whom it belonged. Many officers did not care to trouble themselves with it, but many others did and—forgot to pay it out afterwards. I have yet to learn of the first company whose members ever received any revenue from such a source, although the name of Company Fund is a familiar one to every veteran.

The commissioned officers fared better in camp than the enlisted men. Instead of drawing rations after the manner of the latter, they had a certain cash allowance, according to rank, with which to purchase supplies from the Brigade Commissary, an official whose province was to keep stores on sale for their convenience. The monthly allowance of officers in infantry, including servants, was as follows: Colonel, six rations worth $56, and two servants; Lieutenant-Colonel, five rations worth $45, and two servants; Major, four rations worth $36, and two servants; Captain, four rations worth $36, and one servant; First and Second Lieutenants, jointly, the same as Captains. In addition to the above, the field officers had an allowance of horses and forage proportioned to their rank.

I will speak of the rations more in detail, beginning with the hard bread, or, to use the name by which it was known in the Army of the Potomac, Hardtack. What was hardtack? It was a plain flour-and-water biscuit. Two which I have in my possession as mementos measure three and one-eighth by two and seven-eighths inches and are nearly half an inch thick. Although these biscuits were furnished to organizations by weight, they were dealt out to the men by number, nine constituting a ration in some regiments, and ten in others; but there were usually enough for those who wanted more, as some men would not draw them. While hardtack was nutritious, yet a hungry man could eat his ten in a short time and still be hungry. When they were poor and fit objects for the soldiers' wrath, it was due to one of three conditions: First, they may have been so hard that they could not be bitten; it then required a very strong blow of the fist to break them. The cause of this hardness it would be difficult for one not an expert to determine. This variety certainly well deserved their name. They could not be soaked soft, but after a time took on the elasticity of gutta percha.

The second condition was when they were moldy or wet, as sometimes happened, and should not have been given to the soldiers. I think this condition was often due to their having been boxed up too soon after baking. It certainly was frequently due to exposure to the weather. It was no uncommon sight to see thousands of boxes of hard bread piled up at some railway station or other place used as a base of supplies, where they were only imperfectly sheltered from the weather, and too often not sheltered at all. The failure of inspectors to do their full duty was one reason that so many of this sort reached the rank and file of the service.

The third condition was when from storage they had become infested with maggots and weevils. These weevils were, in my experience, more abundant than the maggots. They were a little, slim, brown bug an eighth of an inch in length, and were great *bores* on a small scale, having the ability to completely riddle the hardtack. I believe they never interfered with the hardest variety.

When the bread was moldy or moist, it was thrown away and made good at the next drawing, so that the men were not the losers; but in the case of its being infested with the weevils, they had to stand it as a rule; for the biscuits had to be pretty thoroughly alive and well covered with the webs which these creatures left to insure condemnation. An exception occurs to me. Two cargoes of hard bread came to City Point, and on being examined by an inspector were found to be infested with weevils. This fact was brought to Grant's attention, who would not allow it landed, greatly to the discomfiture of the contractor, who had been attempting to bulldoze the inspector to pass it.

The quartermasters did not always take as active an interest in righting such matters as they should have done; and when the men growled at them, of course they were virtuously indignant and prompt to shift the responsibility to the next higher power, and so it passed on until the real culprit could not be found.

But hardtack was not so bad an article of food, even when traversed by insects, as may be supposed. Eaten in the dark, no one could tell the difference between it and hardtack that was untenanted. It was no uncommon occurrence for a man to find the surface of his pot of coffee swimming with weevils, after breaking up hardtack in it, which had come out of the fragments only to drown; but they were easily skimmed off, and left no distinctive flavor behind. If a soldier cared to do

so, he could expel the weevils by heating the bread at the fire.
The maggots did not budge in that way. The most of the
hard bread was made in Baltimore, and put up in boxes of
sixty pounds gross, fifty pounds net; and it is said that some
of the storehouses in which it was kept would swarm with
weevils in an incredibly short time after the first box was
infested with them, so rapidly did these pests multiply.

Having gone so far, I know the reader will be interested
to learn of the styles in which this particular article was
served up by the soldiers. I say *styles* because I think there
must have been at least a score of ways adopted to make
this simple *flour tile* more edible. Of course, many of them
were eaten just as they were received—hardtack *plain;*
then I have already spoken of their being crumbed in coffee,
giving the "hardtack and coffee." Probably more were eaten
in this way than in any other, for they thus frequently furnished the soldier his breakfast and supper. But there were
other and more appetizing ways of preparing them. Many
of the soldiers, partly through a slight taste for the business
but more from force of circumstances, became in their way
and opinion experts in the art of cooking the greatest variety
of dishes with the smallest amount of capital.

Some of these crumbed them in soups for want of other
thickening. For this purpose they served very well. Some
crumbed them in cold water, then fried the crumbs in the
juice and fat of meat. A dish akin to this one, which was
said to "make the hair curl," and certainly was indigestible
enough to satisfy the cravings of the most ambitious dys-
peptic, was prepared by soaking hardtack in cold water, then
frying them brown in pork fat, salting to taste. Another
name for this dish was "skillygalee." Some liked them
toasted, either to crumb in coffee, or, if a sutler was at
hand whom they could patronize, to butter. The toasting
generally took place from the end of a split stick, and if
perchance they dropped out of it into the camp fire, and
were not recovered quickly enough to prevent them from
getting pretty well charred, still they were not thrown away
on that account, being then thought to be good for weak
bowels.

Then they worked into milk toast made of condensed
milk at seventy-five cents a can; but only a recruit with a
big bounty, or an old vet the child of wealthy parents, or a

re-enlisted man did much in that way. A few who succeeded
by hook or by crook in saving up a portion of their sugar
ration spread it upon hardtack. The hodge-podge of lobscouse also contained this edible among its divers other
ingredients; and so in various ways the ingenuity of the
men was taxed to make this plainest and commonest yet
most serviceable of army food to do duty in every conceiv-
able combination. There is an old song, entitled "Hard
Times," which some one in the army parodied. I do not
remember the verses, but the men used to sing the following
chorus:

> 'Tis the song of the soldier, weary, hungry, and faint,
> Hardtack, hardtack, come again no more;
> Many days have I chewed you and uttered no complaint,
> O Greenbacks, come again once more!

It is possible at least that this song, sung by the soldiers
of the Army of the Potomac, was an outgrowth of the following circumstance and song. I am quite sure, however,
that the verses were different.

For some weeks before the battle of Wilson's Creek, Mo.,
where the lamented Lyon fell, the First Iowa Regiment had
been supplied with a very poor quality of hard bread (they
were not then (1861) called hardtack). During this period
of hardship to the regiment, so the story goes, one of its
members was inspired to produce the following touching
lamentation:

> Let us close our game of poker,
> Take our tin cups in our hand,
> While we gather round the cook's tent door,
> Where dry mummies of hard crackers
> Are given to each man;
> O hard crackers, come again no more!

> CHORUS: 'Tis the song and sigh of the hungry,
> Hard crackers, hard crackers, come again no
> more!
> Many days have you lingered upon our
> stomachs sore,
> O hard crackers, come again no more!

There's a hungry, thirsty soldier
Who wears his life away,
With torn clothes, whose better days are o'er;
He is sighing now for whiskey,
And, with throat as dry as hay,
Sings, "Hard crackers, come again no more!"—CHORUS.

'Tis the song that is uttered
In camp by night and day,
'Tis the wail that is mingled with each snore,
'Tis the sighing of the soul
For spring chickens far away,
"O hard crackers, come again no more!"—CHORUS.

When General Lyon heard the men singing these stanzas
in their tents, he was said to have been moved by them to
the extent of ordering the cook to serve up corn-meal mush
for a change, when the song received the following altera-
tion:

But to groans and to murmurs
There has come a sudden hush,
Our frail forms are fainting at the door;
We are starving now on horse feed
That the cooks call mush,
O hard crackers, come again once more!

CHORUS: It is the dying wail of the starving,
          Hard crackers, hard crackers, come again once
            more;
          You were old and very wormy, but we pass
            your failings o'er.
          O hard crackers, come again once more!

The name hardtack seems not to have been in general use
among the men in the Western armies.

But I now pass to consider the other bread ration—the
loaf or soft bread. Early in the war the ration of flour was
served out to the men uncooked; but as the eighteen ounces
allowed by the Government more than met the needs of the
troops, who at that time obtained much of their living from
outside sources (to be spoken of hereafter), it was allowed,

as they innocently supposed, to be sold for the benefit of the
Company Fund, already referred to. Some organizations
drew, on requisition, ovens, semi-cylindrical in form, which
were properly set in stone, and in these regimental cooks or
bakers baked bread for the regiment. But all of this was
in the tentative period of the war. As rapidly as the needs

An Army Oven

of the troops pressed home to the Government, they were
met with such despatch and efficiency as circumstances
would permit. For a time, in 1861, the vaults under the
broad terrace on the western front of the Capitol were converted into bakeries, where sixteen thousand loaves of bread
were baked daily. The chimneys from the ovens pierced the
terrace where now the freestone pavement joins the grassy
slope, and for months smoke poured out of these in dense
black volumes. The greater part of the loaves supplied to
the Army of the Potomac up to the summer of 1864 were
baked in Washington, Alexandria, and at Fort Monroe,
Virginia. The ovens at the latter place had a capacity of
thirty thousand loaves a day. But even with all these
sources worked to their uttermost, brigade commissaries
were obliged to set up ovens near their respective depots,
to eke out enough bread to fill orders. These were erected
on the sheltered side of a hill or woods, then enclosed in a
stockade, and the whole covered with old canvas.

When the army reached the vicinity of Petersburg, the
supply of fresh loaves became a matter of greater difficulty

and delay, which Grant immediately obviated by ordering ovens built at City Point. A large number of citizen bakers were employed to run them night and day, and as a result *one hundred and twenty-three thousand fresh loaves* were furnished the Army daily from this single source; and so closely did the delivery of these follow upon the manipulations of the bakers that the soldiers quite frequently received them while yet warm from the oven. Soft bread was always a very welcome change from hard bread; yet, on the other hand, I think the soldiers tired sooner of the former than of the latter. Men who had followed the sea preferred the hard bread. Jeffersonville, in Southern Indiana, was the headquarters from which bread was largely supplied to the Western armies.

I began my description of the rations with the bread as being the most important one to the soldier. Some old veterans may be disposed to question the judgment which gives it this rank, and claim that coffee, of which I shall speak next, should take first place in importance; in reply to which I will simply say that he is wrong, because coffee, being a stimulant, serves only a temporary purpose, while the bread has nearly or quite all the elements of nutrition necessary to build up the wasted tissues of the body, thus conferring a permanent benefit. Whatever words of condemnation or criticism may have been bestowed on other Government rations, there was but one opinion of the coffee which was served out, and that was of unqualified approval.

The rations may have been small, the commissary or quartermaster may have given us a short allowance, but what we got was good. And what a perfect Godsend it seemed to us at times! How often, after being completely jaded by a night march—and this is an experience common to thousands—have I had a wash, if there was water to he had, made and drunk my pint or so of coffee, and felt as fresh and invigorated as if just arisen from a night's sound sleep! At such times it could seem to have had no substitute.

It would have interested a civilian to observe the manner in which this ration was served out when the army was in active service. It was usually brought to camp in an oatsack, a regimental quartermaster receiving and apportioning his among the ten companies, and the quartermaster-sergeant of a battery apportioning his to the four or six detachments.

Then the orderly-sergeant of a company or the sergeant of a detachment must devote himself to dividing it. One method of accomplishing· this purpose was to spread a rubber blanket on the ground—more than one if the company was large—and upon it were put as many piles of the coffee as there were men to receive rations; and the care taken to make the piles of the same size to the eye to keep the men from growling, would remind one of a country physician making his powders, taking a little from one pile and adding to another. The sugar which always accompanied the coffee was spooned out at the same time on another blanket. When both were ready they were given out, each man taking a pile, or in some companies, to prevent any charge of unfairness or injustice, the sergeant would turn his back on the rations and take out his roll of the com-

Apportioning Coffee and Sugar

pany. Then, by request, some one else would point to a pile and ask, "Who shall have this?" and the sergeant, without turning, would call a name from his list of the company or detachment, and the person thus called would appropriate the pile specified. This process would be continued until the last pile was disposed of. There were other plans for distributing the rations, but I describe this one because of its being quite common.

The manner in which each man disposed of his coffee and sugar ration after receiving it is worth noting. Every soldier of a month's experience in campaigning was provided with some sort of bag into which he spooned his coffee; but the kind of bag he used indicated pretty accurately . . . the length of time he had been in the service. For example, a raw recruit just arrived would take it up in a paper and stow it away in that well-known receptacle for all eatables, the soldier's haversack, only to find it a part of a general mixture of hardtack, salt pork, pepper, salt, knife, fork, spoon, sugar and coffee by the time the next halt was made. A recruit of longer standing, who had been through this experience and had begun to feel his wisdom-teeth coming, would take his up in a bag made of a scrap of rubber blanket or a poncho; but after a few days carrying the rubber would peel off or the paint of the poncho would rub off from contact with greasy pork or boiled meat ration which was its traveling companion, and make a black, dirty mess, besides leaving the coffee bag unfit for further use. Now and then some young soldier, a little starchier than his fellows, would bring out an oil-silk bag lined with cloth, which his mother had made and sent him; but even oil-silk couldn't stand everything, certainly not the peculiar inside furnishings of the average soldier's haversack, so it too was not long in yielding. But your plain, straightforward old veteran, who had shed all his poetry and romance, if he had ever possessed any, who had roughed it up and down "Old Virginny," man and boy, for many months, and who had tried all plans under all circumstances took out an oblong plain cloth bag, which looked as immaculate as the every-day shirt of a coal heaver, and into it scooped without ceremony both his sugar and coffee, and stirred them thoroughly together.

There was method in this plan. He had learned from a hard experience that his sugar was a better investment thus disposed of than in any other way; for on several occasions he had eaten it with his hardtack a little at a time, had got it wet and melted in a rain, or, what happened fully as often, had sweetened his coffee to his taste when the sugar was kept separate, and in consequence had several messes of coffee to drink without sweetening, which was not to his taste. There was now and then a man who could keep the two separate, sometimes in different ends of the same bag, and serve them up proportionately. The reader already knows that milk was a luxury in the army.

It was a new experience for all soldiers to drink coffee without milk. But they soon learned to make a virtue of a necessity, and I doubt whether one man in ten, before the war closed, would have used the lactic fluid in his coffee from choice. Condensed milk of two brands, the *Lewis* and *Borden*, was to be had at the sutler's when sutlers were handy, and occasionally milk was brought in from the udders of stray cows, the men milking them into their canteens, but this was early in the war. Later, war-swept Virginia afforded very few of these brutes, for they were regarded by the armies as more valuable for beef than for milking purposes, and only those survived that were kept apart from lines of march. In many instances they were the chief reliance of Southern families, whose able-bodied men were in the Rebel army, serving both as a source of nourishment and as beasts of burden.

When the army was in settled camp, company cooks generally prepared the rations. These cooks were men selected from the company, who had a taste or an ambition for the business. If there were none such, turns were taken at it; but this did not often happen, as the office excused men from all other duty.

When company cooks prepared the food, the soldiers, at the bugle signal, formed single file at the cook-house door, in winter, or the cook's open fire, in summer, where, with a long-handled dipper he filled each man's tin with coffee from the mess kettles and dispensed to him such other food as was to be given out at that meal.

For various reasons, some of which I have previously hinted at, the coffee made by these cooks was of a very inferior quality and unpleasant to taste at times. It was not to be compared in excellence with what the men made for themselves. I think that when the soldiers were first thrown upon their own resources to prepare their food, they almost invariably cooked their coffee in the tin dipper with which all were provided, holding from a pint to a quart, perhaps. But it was an unfortunate dish for the purpose, forever tipping over and spilling the coffee into the fire, either because the coals burned away beneath, or because the Jonah upset it. Then if the fire was new and blazing, it sometimes needed a hand that could stand heat like a steam safe to get it when it was wanted, with the chance in favor of more than half of the coffee boiling out before it was rescued, all of which was conducive to ill-temper, so that such utensils would soon disappear, and a recruit would afterwards be seen with his pint or quart preserve can, its improvised wire bail held on the end of a stick, boiling his coffee at the camp fire, happy in the security of his ration from Jonahs and other casualties. His can soon became as black as the blackest, inside and out. This was the typical coffee boiler of the private soldier and had the advantage of being easily replaced when lost, as canned goods were in very general use by commissioned officers and hospitals. Besides this, each man was generally supplied with a small tin cup as a drinking cup for his coffee and water.

The coffee ration was most heartily appreciated by the soldier. When tired and foot-sore, he would drop out of the marching column, build his little camp fire, cook his mess of coffee, take a nap behind the nearest shelter, and, when he woke, hurry on to overtake his company. Such men were sometimes called stragglers; but it could, obviously, have no offensive meaning when applied to them. Tea was served so rarely that it does not merit any particular description. In the latter part of the war, it was rarely seen outside of hospitals.

One of the most interesting scenes presented in army life took place at night when the army was on the point of bivouacking. As soon as this fact became known along the column, each man would seize a rail from the nearest fence and with this additional·arm on the shoulder would enter the proposed camping ground. In no more time than it takes to tell the story, the little camp fires, rapidly increasing to hundreds in number, would shoot up along the hills and plains, and as if by magic acres of territory would be luminous with them. Soon they would be surrounded by the soldiers, who made it an almost invariable rule to cook their coffee first, after which a large number, tired out with the toils of the day, would make their supper of hardtack and coffee and roll up in their blankets for the night. If a march was ordered at midnight, unless a surprise was intended, it must be preceded by a pot of coffee; if a halt was ordered in mid-forenoon or afternoon, the same dish was inevitable, with hardtack accompaniment usually. It was coffee at meals and between meals; and men going on guard or coming off guard drank it at all hours of the night. . . .

At a certain period in the war, speculators bought up all the coffee there was in the market with a view of compelling the Government to pay them a very high price for the Army supply;

but on learning of their action the agents of the United States in England were ordered to purchase several ship loads then anchored in the English Channel. The purchase was effected, and the coffee "corner" tumbled in ruins.

At one time, when the Government had advertised for bids to furnish the armies with a certain amount of coffee, one Sawyer, a member of a prominent New York importing firm, met the Government official having the matter in charge— I think it was General Joseph H. Eaton—on the street, and anxiously asked him if it was too late to enter another bid, saying that he had been figuring the matter over carefully, and found that he could make a bid so much a pound lower than his first proposal. General Eaton replied that while the bids had all been opened, yet they had not been made public, and the successful bidder had not been notified, so that no injustice could accrue to any one on that account; he would therefore assume the responsibility of taking his new bid. Having done so, the General informed Sawyer that he was the lowest bidder, and that the Government would take not only the amount asked for but all his firm had at its disposal at the same rate. But when General Eaton informed him that his first bid was also lower than any other offered, Sawyer's rage at Eaton and disgust at his own undue ambition to bid a second time can be imagined. The result was the saving of many thousands of dollars to the Government.

I have stated that by Army Regulations the soldiers were entitled to either three-quarters of a pound of pork or bacon or one and one-fourth pounds of fresh or salt beef. I have also stated, in substance, that when the Army was settled down for a probable long stop company cooks did the cooking. But there was no uniformity about it, each company commander regulating the matter for his own command. It is safe to remark, however, that in the early history of each regiment the rations were cooked for its members by persons especially selected for the duty, unless the regiment was sent at once into active service, in which case each man was immediately confronted with the problem of preparing his own food. In making this statement I ignore the experience which troops had before leaving their native state, for in the different state rendezvous I think the practice was general for cooks to prepare the rations; but their culinary skill—or lack of it—was little appreciated by men within easy reach of home, friends, and cooky shops, who displayed as yet no undue anxiety to anticipate the unromantic living provided for Uncle Sam's patriot defenders.

Having injected so much, by way of further explanation I come now to speak of the manner in which the fresh-meat ration was cooked. If it fell into the hands of the company cooks, it was fated to be boiled twenty-four times out of twenty-five. There are rare occasions on record when these cooks attempted to broil steak enough for a whole company, and they would have succeeded tolerably if this particular tid-bit could be found all the way through a steer, from the tip of his nose to the end of his tail, but as it is only local and limited the amount of nice or even tolerable steak that fell to the lot of one company in its allowance was not very large. For this reason among others the cooks did not always receive the credit which they deserved for their efforts to change the diet or extend the variety on the bill of fare. Then, on occasions equally rare, when the beef ration drawn was of such a nature as to admit of it, roast beef was prepared in ovens such as I have already described, and served "rare," "middling," or "well done." More frequently, yet not very often, a soup was made for a change, but it was usually boiled meat; and when this accumulated, the men sometimes fried it in pork fat for a change.

When the meat ration was served out raw to the men to prepare after their own taste, although the variety of its cooking may not perhaps have been much greater, yet it gave more general satisfaction. The growls most commonly heard were that the cooks kept the largest or choicest portions for themselves, or else that they sent them to the company officers, who were not entitled to them. Sometimes there was foundation for these complaints.

In drawing his ration of meat from the commissary the quartermaster had to be governed by his last selection. If it was a hindquarter then, he must take a forequarter the next time, so that it will at once be seen, by those who know anything about beef, that it would not always cut up and distribute with the same acceptance. One man would get a good solid piece, the next a flabby one. When a ration of the latter description fell into the hands of a passionate man, such as I have described in another connection, he would instantly hurl it across the camp and break out with such remarks as "something not being fit for hogs," "always his blank luck," etc. There was likely to

be a little something gained by this dramatic exhibition, for
the distributor would give the actor a good piece for several
times afterwards to restrain his temper.

The kind of piece drawn naturally determined its disposition in the soldier's cuisine. If it was a stringy, flabby piece,
straightway it was doomed to a dish of lobscouse, made with
such other materials as were at hand. If onions were not in
the larder, and they seldom were, the little garlic found growing wild in some places furnished a very acceptable substitute.
If the meat was pretty solid, even though it had done duty
when in active service well down on the shank or shin, it was
quite likely to be served as beefsteak, and prepared for the
palate in one of two ways: either fried in pork fat, if pork was
to be had, otherwise tallow fat, or impaled on a ramrod or
forked stick; it was then salted and peppered and broiled in the
flames; or it may have been thrown on the coals. This broiling
was, I think, the favorite style with the oldest campaigners. It
certainly was more healthful and palatable cooked in this wise
and was the most convenient in active service, for any of the
men could prepare it thus at short notice.

The meat generally came to us quivering from the butcher's
knife and was often eaten in less than two hours after slaughtering. To fry it necessitated the taking along of a frying pan with
which not many of the men cared to burden themselves.
These fry pans—Marbleheadmen called them Creepers—were
yet comparatively light, being made of thin wrought iron. They
were of different sizes and were kept on sale by sutlers. It was a
common sight on the march to see them borne aloft on a musket to which they were lashed, or tucked beneath the straps of
a knapsack. But there was another fry pan which distanced
these both in respect of lightness and space. The soldier called
in his own ingenuity to aid him here as in so many other directions, and consequently the men could be seen by scores
frying the food in their tin plate, held in the jaws of a split
stick, or fully as often an old canteen was unsoldered and its
concave sides mustered into active duty as fry pans. The fresh-
meat ration was thoroughly appreciated by the men, even
though they rarely if ever got the full allowance stipulated in
Army Regulations, for it was a relief from the salt pork, salt
beef, or boiled fresh meat ration of settled camp. I remember
one occasion in the Mine Run Campaign during the last days
of November, 1863, when the Army was put on short beef ra-

tions, that the men cut and scraped off the little rain-bleached shreds of meat that remained on the head of a steer which lay near our line of battle at Robertson's Tavern. The animal had been slaughtered the day before, and what was left of its skeleton had been soaking in the rain, but not one ounce of muscular tissue could have been gleaned from the bones when our men left it.

The liver, heart, and tongue were perquisites of the butcher. For the liver, the usual price asked was a dollar, and for the heart or tongue fifty cents.

The "salt horse" or salt beef, of fragrant memory, was rarely furnished to the Army except when in settled camp, as it would obviously have been a poor dish to serve on the march when water was often so scarce. But even in camp the men quite generally rejected it. Without doubt, it was the vilest ration distributed to the soldiers.

It was thoroughly penetrated with saltpeter, was often yellow-green with rust from having lain out of brine, and, when boiled was four times out of five if not nine times out of ten a stench in the nostrils, which no delicate palate cared to encounter at shorter range. It sometimes happened that the men would extract a good deal of amusement out of this ration when an extremely unsavory lot was served out, by arranging a funeral, making the appointments as complete as possible, with bearers, a bier improvised of boards or a hardtack box, on which was the beef accompanied by scraps of old harness to indicate the original of the remains, and then, attended by solemn music and a mournful procession, it would be carried to the company sink and dumped, after a solemn mummery of words had been spoken, and a volley fired over its unhallowed grave.

So salt was this ration that it was impossible to freshen it too much, and it was not an unusual occurrence for troops encamped by a running brook to tie a piece of this beef to the end of a cord, and throw it into the brook at night to remain freshening until the following morning as a necessary preparative to cooking.

Salt pork was the principal meat ration—the mainstay as it were. Company cooks boiled it. There was little else they could do with it, but it was an extremely useful ration to the men when served out raw. They almost never boiled it, but, as I have already shown, much of it was used for frying purposes. On the march it was broiled and eaten with hard bread, while much of it was eaten raw, sandwiched between hardtack. Of course it was used with stewed as well as baked beans and was an ingredient of soups and lobscouse. Many of us have since learned to call it an indigestible ration, but we ignored the existence of such a thing as a stomach in the Army and then regarded pork as an indispensable one. Much of it was musty and rancid, like the salt horse, and much more was flabby, stringy, "sow-belly," as the men called it. . . . The Government had a pork-packing factory of its own in Chicago from which tons of this ration were furnished.

Once in a while a ration of ham or bacon was dealt out to the soldiers, but of such quality that I do not retain very grateful remembrances of it. It was usually black, rusty, strong, and decidedly unpopular. Once only do I recall a lot of smoked shoulders as being supplied to my company, which were very good. They were never duplicated. For that reason, I presume, they stand out prominently in memory.

The bean ration was an important factor in the sustenance of the Army, and no edible, I think, was so thoroughly appreciated. Company cooks stewed them with pork, and when the pork was good and the stew or soup was well done and not burned—a rare combination of circumstances—they were quite palatable in this way. Sometimes ovens were built of stones on top of the ground, and the beans were baked in these in mess pans or kettles. But I think the most popular method was to bake them in the ground. This was the almost invariable course pursued by the soldiers when the beans were distributed for them to cook. It was done in the following way: A hole was dug large enough to set a mess pan or kettle in and have ample space around it besides. Mess kettles are cylinders made of heavy sheet iron. They are from thirteen to fifteen inches high,

Mess Kettles and a Mess Pan

and vary in diameter from seven inches to a foot. A mess pan
stands about six inches high, and is a foot in diameter at the
top. I think one will hold nearly six quarts. To resume—in the
bottom of the hole dug a flat stone was put, if it could be obtained, then a fire was built in the hole and kept burning
some hours, the beans being prepared for baking meanwhile.
When all was ready, the coals were shovelled out, the kettle
of beans and pork set in, with a board over the top, while
the coals were shovelled back around the kettle; some poles
or boards were then laid across the hole, a piece of sacking
or other material spread over the poles to exclude dirt, and
a mound of earth piled above all; the net result of which, when
the hole was opened the next morning, was the most enjoyable
dish that fell to the lot of the common soldier. Baked beans
at the homestead seemed at a discount in comparison. As it
was hardly practicable to bake a single ration of beans in this
way, a tent's crew either saved their allowance until enough
accumulated for a good baking, or a half-dozen men would
form a joint-stock company and cook in a mess kettle; and
when the treasure was unearthed in early morning not a stock-
holder would be absent from the roll call, but all were promptly
on hand with plate or coffee dipper to receive their dividends.

Here is a post-bellum jingle sung to the music of "The Sweet
By and By," in which some old veteran conveys the affection
he still feels for this edible of precious memory:

THE ARMY BEAN

There's a spot that the soldiers all love,
    The mess tent's the place that we mean,
And the dish we best like to see. there
    Is the old-fashioned, white Army Bean.

CHORUS.—'Tis the bean that we mean,
    And we'll eat as we ne'er ate before;
The Army Bean, nice and clean,
    We'll stick to our beans evermore.

Now the bean, in its primitive state,
    Is a plant we have all often met;
And when cooked in the old Army style
    It has charms we can never forget.—CHORUS

The German is fond of sauerkraut,
The potato is loved by the Mick,
But the soldiers have long since found out
That through life to our beans we should
*   stick.*
                                    —CHORUS.

Boiled potatoes were furnished us occasionally in settled camp. On the march we varied the program by frying them. Onions, in my own company at least, were a great rarity, but highly appreciated when they did appear, even in homœopathic quantities. They were pretty sure to appear on the army table, fried.

Split peas were also drawn by the quartermaster now and then, and stewed with pork by the cooks for supper, making pea soup, or "Peas on a Trencher"; but if my memory serves me right, they were a dish in no great favor, even when they were not burned in cooking, which was usually their fate.

The dried-apple ration was supplied by the Government, "to swell the ranks of the Army," as some one wittily said. There seemed but one practicable way in which this could be prepared, and that was to stew it; thus cooked it made a sauce for hardtack. Sometimes dried peaches were furnished instead, but of such a poor quality that the apples, with the fifty per cent of skins and hulls which they contained, were considered far preferable.

At remote intervals the cooks gave for supper a dish of boiled rice (burned, of course), a sergeant spooning out a scanty allowance of molasses to bear it company.

Occasionally, a ration of what was known as desiccated vegetables was dealt out. This consisted of a small piece per man, an ounce in weight and two or three inches cube of a sheet or block of vegetables, which had been prepared and apparently *kiln-dried* as sanitary fodder for the soldiers. In composition it looked not unlike the large cheeses of beefscraps that are seen in the markets. When put in soak for a time, so perfectly had it been dried and so firmly pressed that it swelled to an amazing extent, attaining to several times its dried proportions. In this pulpy state a favorable opportunity was afforded to analyze its composition. It seemed to show, and I think really *did* show, layers of cabbage leaves and turnip tops stratified with layers of sliced carrots, turnips, parsnips, a bare suggestion of onions—they were too valuable to waste in this compound—and some other among known vegetable quantities, with a large residuum of insoluble and insolvable material which appeared to play the part of warp to the fabric, but which defied the powers of the analyst to give it a name. An inspector found in one lot which he examined powdered glass thickly sprinkled through it, apparently the work of a Confederate emissary; but if not it showed how little care was exercised in preparing this diet for the soldier. In brief, this coarse vegetable compound could with much more propriety have been put before Southern swine than Northern soldiers. "Desecrated vegetables" was the more appropriate name which the men quite generally applied to this preparation of husks.

I believe it was the Thirty-Second Massachusetts Infantry which once had a special ration of three hundred boxes of strawberries dealt out to it. But if there was another organization in the Army anywhere which had such a delicious experience, I have yet to hear of it.

I presume that no discussion of Army rations would be considered complete that did not at least make mention of the whiskey ration so called. This was not a ration, properly speaking. The Government supplied it to the army only on rare occasions, and then by order of the medical department. I think it was never served out to my company more than three or four times, and then during a cold rainstorm or after unusually hard service. Captain N. D. Preston of the Tenth New York Cavalry, in describing Sheridan's raid to Richmond in the spring of 1864, speaks of being instructed by his brigade commander to make a light issue of whiskey to the men of the brigade, and adds, "the first and only regular issue of whiskey I ever made or know of being made to an enlisted man." But although he belonged to the arm of the service called "the eyes and ears of the army" and was no doubt a gallant soldier, he is not well posted; for men who belonged to other organizations in the Army of the Potomac assure me that it was served out to them much more frequently than I have related as coming under my observation. I think there can be no doubt on this point.

The size of the whiskey allowance was declared, by those whose experience had made them competent judges, as trifling and insignificant, sometimes not more than a tablespoonful; but the quantity differed greatly in different organizations. The opinion was very prevalent, and undoubtedly correct, that the liquor was quite liberally sampled by the various headquarters, or the agents through whom it was transmitted to the rank and file. While there was considerable whiskey drunk by the men "unofficially," that is, which was obtained otherwise than on the order of the medical department, yet, man for man, the private soldiers were as abstemious as the officers. The officers who did not drink more or less were too scarce in the service. They had only to send to the commissary to obtain as much as they pleased, whenever they pleased, by paying for it; but the private soldier could only obtain it of this official on an order signed by a commissioned officer—usually the captain of his company. In fact, there was nothing but his sense of honor, his self-respect, or his fear of exposure and punishment, to restrain a captain, a colonel, or a general, of whatever command, from being intoxicated at a moment when he should have been in the full possession of his senses leading his command on to battle; and I regret to relate that these motives, strong as they are to impel to right and restrain from wrong-doing, were no barrier to many an officer whose appetite in a crisis thus imperilled the cause and disgraced himself. Doesn't it seem strange that the enforcement of the rules of war was so lax as to allow the lives of a hundred, a thousand, or perhaps fifty or a hundred thousand sober men to be jeopard ized, as they so often were, by holding them rigidly obedient to the orders of a man whose head at a critical moment might be crazed with commissary whiskey? Hundreds if not thousands of lives were sacrificed by such leadership. I may state here that drunkenness was equally as common with the Rebels as with the Federals.

The devices resorted to by those members of the rank and file who hungered and thirsted for commissary to obtain it, are numerous and entertaining enough to occupy a chapter; but these I must leave for some one of broader experience and observation. I could name two or three men in my own company whose experience qualified them to fill the bill completely. They were always on the scent for something to drink. Such men were to be found in all organizations.

It has always struck me that the Government should have increased the size of the marching ration. If the soldier on the march had received one and one-half pounds of hard bread and one and one-half pounds of fresh beef daily with his sugar, coffee, and salt, it would have been no more than marching men require to keep up the requisite strength and resist disease.

By such an increase the men would have been compensated for the parts of rations not issued to them, or the increase might have been an equivalent for these parts, and the temptation to dishonesty or neglect on the part of company commanders thus removed. But, more than this, the men would not then have eaten up many days' rations in advance. It mattered not that the troops, at a certain date, were provided with three, four, or any number of days' rations; if these rations were exhausted before the limit for which they were distributed was even half reached, more must be immediately issued. As a consequence, in every summer campaign *the troops had drawn ten or fifteen days' marching rations ahead of time,* proving season after season the inadequacy of this ration. This deficiency of active service had to be made up by shortening the rations issued in camp when the men could live on a contracted diet without detriment to the service. But *they* knew nothing of this shortage at the time—I mean now the rank and file—else what a universal growl would have rolled through the camps of each army corps while the commissary was "catching up."

7
Offences and Punishments

No popular history of the war has yet treated in detail of the various indiscretions of which soldiers were guilty, nor of the punishments which followed breaches of discipline. Perhaps such a record is wanting because there are many men yet alive who cannot think with equanimity of punishments to which they were at some period of their service subjected. Indeed, within a few months I have seen veterans who, if not breathing out threatenings and slaughter like Saul of Tarsus, are still unreconciled to some of their old commanders, and are brooding over their old-time grievances, real or imaginary, or both, when they ought to be engaged in more entertaining and profitable business. I shall not, because I cannot, name all the offences of soldiering to which punishments were affixed, as no two commanding officers had just the same violations of military discipline to deal with, but I shall endeavor in this chapter to include all those which appeal to a common experience.

The most common offences were drunkenness, absence from camp without leave, insubordination, disrespect to superior officers, absence from roll call without leave, turbulence after taps, sitting while on guard, gambling, and leaving the beat without relief. To explain these offences a little more in detail—no soldier was supposed to leave camp without a pass or permit from the commander of the regiment or battery to which he belonged. A great many did leave for a few hours at a time, however, and took their chances of being missed and reported for it. In some companies, when it was thought that several were absent without a permit, a roll call was ordered simply to catch the culprits. Disrespect to a superior officer was shown in many ways. Some of the more common ways were to "talk back" in strong unmilitary language and to refuse to salute him or recognize him on duty, which military etiquette requires to

95

A Loaded Knapsack

be done. The other offences named explain themselves. The methods of punishment were as diverse as the dispositions of the officers who sat in judgment on the cases of the offenders. In the early history of a regiment there was a guard house or guard tent where the daily guard were wont to assemble and which was their rendezvous when off post during their twenty-four hours of duty. But when the ranks of the regiment had become very much depleted, and the men pretty well seasoned in military duty, the guard tent was likely to be dispensed with. In this guard tent offenders were put for different periods of time. Such confinement was a common punishment for drunkenness. This may not be thought a very severe penalty; still, the men did not enjoy it as it imposed quite a restriction on their freedom to be thus pent up and cut off from their associates.

Absence from camp or roll call without leave was punished in various ways. There was no special penalty for it. I think every organization had what was known as a Black List, on which the names of all offenders against the ordinary rules of camp were kept for frequent reference, and when there was any particularly disagreeable task about camp to be done the blacklist furnished a quota for the work. The galling part of membership in the ranks of the blacklist was that all of the work done as one of its victims was a gratuity, as the member must stand his regular turn in his squad for whatever other fatigue duty was required.

Among the tasks that were thought quite interesting and profitable pastimes for the blacklisted to engage in, were policing the camp and digging and fitting up new company sinks or filling abandoned ones. A favorite treat meted out to the unfortunates in the artillery and cavalry was the burying of dead horses or cleaning up around the picket rope where the animals were tied. In brief, the men who kept off the blacklist in a company were spared many a hard and disagreeable job by the existence of a long list of offenders against camp discipline.

This placing of men on the blacklist was not as a rule resorted to by officers who cherished petty spites or personal malice, but by it they designed rather to enforce a salutary discipline. Such officers had no desire to torture the erring but aimed to combine a reasonable form of punishment with utility to the camp and to the better behaved soldiers, and in this they were successful.

But there was a class of officers who felt that every violation of camp rules should be visited with the infliction of bodily pain in some form. As a consequence, the sentences imposed by these military judges all looked towards that end. Some would *buck and gag* their victims; some would *stand them on a barrel* for a half-day or a day at a time; a favorite punishment with some was to knock out both heads of a barrel, then make the victim stand on the ends of the staves; some would compel them to wear an inverted barrel for several hours, by having a hole cut in the bottom, through which the head passed, making a kind of wooden overcoat; some culprits were compelled to stand a long time with their arms, extending horizontally at the side, lashed to a heavy stick of wood that ran across their backs; others were lashed to a tall wooden horse which stood perhaps eight or nine feet high; some underwent the knapsack drill, that is, they walked a beat with a guardsman two hours on and two or four hours off, wearing a knapsack filled with bricks or stones.

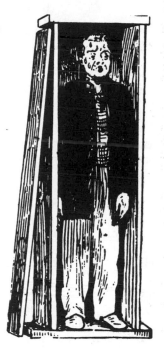

Here is an incident related by a veteran who served in the Gulf Department: One day a captain in General Phelps' Brigade put a man on knapsack drill; in other words, he filled his knapsack with bricks and made him march with it up and down the company street. The General had the habit of going through the camps of his brigade quite fre-

In the Sweatbox

quently and that day he happened around just in time to see the performance but returned to his quarters apparently without noticing it. Soon, however, he sent his Orderly to the Captain with a request to come to his tent. The Captain was soon on his way, dressed in his best uniform, probably expect-

On a Wooden Horse

ing, at least, a commendation for his efficiency, or perhaps a promotion. On reaching the General's tent, he was admitted, when, after the usual salute, the following dialogue took place:

General P. "Good-morning, Captain."

Captain. "Good-morning, General."

General P. "I sent for you, Captain, to inquire of you what knapsacks were made for."

Captain. "Knapsacks!—why, I suppose they were made for soldiers to carry their spare clothing in."

General P. "Well, Captain, I passed your camp a short time ago and saw one of your men carrying bricks in his knapsack up and down the company street. Now, go back to your company, send that man to his quarters and don't let me know of your ordering any such punishment again while you are in my brigade."

One regiment I know of had a platform erected, between twenty-five and thirty feet high, on which the offender was isolated from the camp and left to broil in the sun or soak in the rain while a guard paced his beat below to keep away any who might like to communicate with him. Some were tied up by the thumbs with arms extended full length and compelled to stand in that position for hours; some were put into what was known as the sweat-box. This was a box eighteen inches square, and of the full height of a man, into which the culprit was placed to stand until released. Some had their full offence written out on a board with chalk, and with this board strapped to their backs were marched up and down through camp the entire day, without rest or refreshment.

In the artillery, the favorite punishment was to lash the guilty party to the spare wheel—the extra wheel carried on the rear of every caisson in a battery. In the cavalry, men were some-times punished by being compelled to carry their packed saddle a prescribed time—no small or insignificant burden to men un-used to a knapsack. Sometimes the guilty parties were required

Isolated on a Platform

On the Chines

to carry a heavy stick of wood on the shoulder. I knew one such man, who, because of this punishment, took a solemn oath that he would never do another day's duty in his company; and he never did. From that day forward he reported at sick call, but the surgeon could find no traces of disease about him and so returned him for duty. Still the man persistently refused to do duty, claiming that he was not able, and continued to report at sick call. By refusing to eat anything, he reduced himself to such a condition that he really appeared diseased and at last was discharged, went home, and boasted of his achievement.

Sometimes double guard duty was ordered for a man on account of an omission or act of his while on guard. This punishment gave him four hours on and two off his post or beat instead of the reverse. His offence may have been failing or refusing to salute his superior officer. It may have been that he was not properly equipped. It may have been for being found off his beat, or for leaving it without having been properly relieved; or he may have failed in his duty when the "Grand Rounds" appeared.

When non-commisioned officers sinned, which they did sometimes, they were punished by being reduced to the ranks.

In some organizations gambling was not allowed, in others it was carried on by both officers and privates. In one command, at least, culprits were punished by having one-half of the head shaved—a most humiliating and effective punishment.

Then "back talk," as it was commonly called, which, interpreted, means answering a superior officer insolently, was a
prolific cause of punishments. It did not matter in some organizations who the officer was, from colonel or captain to the last
corporal, to hear was to obey, and under such discipline the
men became the merest puppets. In theory, such a regiment
was the perfect military machine, where every man was in
complete subordination to one master mind. But the value of
such a machine, after all, depended largely upon the kind of a
man the ruling spirit was, and whether he associated his in-
flexibility of steel with the justice of Aristides. If he did that,
then was it indeed a model organization; but such bodies were
rare, for the conditions were wanting to make them abundant.
The master mind was too often tyrannical and abusive, either

Posted

by nature, or from having
been suddenly clothed with a
little brief authority over men.
And often when nature, if left
to herself, would have made
him a good commander, an
excessive use of "commissary"
interfered to prevent, and the
subordinates of such a leader,
many of them appointed by
his influence, would naturally
partake of his characteristics;
so that such regiments, instead of standing solidly on all
occasions, were weakened as a
fighting body by a lack of
confidence in and personal respect for their leaders, and by
a hatred begotten of unjust
treatment. Hundreds of officers were put in commission
through influence at court,
wealth or personal influence
deciding appointments that
should have been made solely
on the basis of merit. At the
beginning of the war it was
inevitable that the officers

should have been inexperienced and uninstructed in the details of warfare, but later this condition changed, and the service would have been strengthened and materially improved by promoting men who had done honorable service and shown good conduct in action to commissions in new regiments. It

Strapped to a Stick

is true that such was the intent and partial practice in some states, but the governors, more or less from necessity, took the advice of some one who was a warm personal friend of the applicant, so that shoulder straps, instead of being always conferred for gallant conduct in the front rank, were sometimes a mark of distinguished prowess in the mule train or the cook-house, which seemed to maintain readier and more influential communication with the appointing power at the rear than did the men who stood nearest to the enemy.

To bow in meek submission to the uneducated authority of the civilian, or to the soldier whose record was such as not to command the respect of his fellows, was the lot of thousands of intelligent and brave soldiers, the superiors in all respects save that of military rank alone of these selfsame officers; and to be commanded not to answer back, when they felt that they must utter a protest against injustice, was a humiliation that the average volunteer did not fully realize when he put his name to the roll—a humiliation which grew bitterer with every new in-dignity. Punishments or rebukes administered by social inferiors were galling even when deserved.

It seems ludicrous to me when I recall the threats I used to hear made against officers for some of their misdeeds. Many a wearer of shoulder straps was to be shot by his own men in the first engagement. But, somehow or other, when the engagement came along there seemed to be Rebels enough to shoot without throwing away ammunition on Union men; and about that time

On a Spare Wheel

too the men, who in more peaceful retreats were so anxious to shoot their own officers, could not always be found, when wanted, to shoot more legitimate game. After the war, when private soldiers were so scarce and officers so exceedingly abun-dant, the question might very naturally arise how the abun-dance came about if the officers were so often between two fires; but what I have said will furnish a solution to the mystery.

Then, there were hundreds of officers that were to be settled
with when they reached home, and were on an equality with
the private soldier so far as military rank was concerned. But
while there were, as I have previously intimated, a few who took
their resentments out of the service with them, they were only
few in number, and it is doubtful whether any of them ever
executed their threatened deeds of violence. Poor underpaid
non-commissioned officers, who occupied the perplexing and
uncomfortable position of go-betweens, were frequently invited
by privates to strip off their chevrons and be handsomely
whipped for some act annoying to said privates; but I never
heard of any n. c. o. sacrificing his chevrons to any such ambition—and not necessarily for fear of a thrashing.

There were regiments each of which, when off duty, seemed
to contain at least two or three hundred colonels and captains,
so much social freedom obtained between officers and rank and
file, yet at the proper time there was just one commander of
such a regiment to whom the men looked ready to do his bidding, even to follow him into the jaws of death. These officers
were not always devout men; at an earlier period in their lives
some of them may have learned to be profane; some drank commissary whiskey occasionally, it may be; but in all their dealings
with subordinates, while they made rigid exactions of them as
soldiers, they never forgot that they were men, and hence, endeavoring to be just in the settlement of camp troubles, protecting their command in the full enjoyment of all its rights among
similar organizations, never saying "go!" but "come!" in the
hour of danger, they welded their regiment into a military
engine as solid and reliable as the old Grecian Phalanx. Punishments in such regiments were rare, for manliness and self-respect
were never crushed out by tyrants in miniature. The character
of the officers had so much to do with determining the nature
and amount of the punishments in the Army that I consider
what I have thrown in here as germane to this chapter.

It should be said, in justice to both officers and privates, that
the first two years of the war, when the exactions of the service
were new, saw three times the number of punishments administered in the two subsequent years; but, aside from the getting
accustomed to the restraints of the service, campaigning was
more continuous in the later years, and this kept both mind
and body occupied. It is inactivity which makes the growler's
paradise. Then, in the last years of the war the rigors of military

discipline, the sharing of common dangers and hardships, and promotions from the ranks, had narrowed the gap between officers and privates so that the chords of mutual sympathy were stronger than before, and trivial offences were slightly rebuked or passed unnoticed.

At the beginning of the war many generals were very fearful lest some of the acts of the common soldier should give offence to the Southern people. This encouraged the latter to report every chicken lost, every bee hive borrowed, every rail burnt, to headquarters, and subordinates were required to in-

Bucked and Gagged

stitute the most thorough search for evidence that should lead to the detection and punishment of the culprits, besides requiring them to make full restitution of the value of the property taken. Our Government and its leading officers, military and civil, seemed at that time to stand hat in hand apologizing to the South for invading its sacred territory, and almost appearing to want only a proper pretext to retire honorably from the conflict. But by the time that the Peninsular Campaign was brought to a close this kid-glove handling of the enemy had come to an end, and the wandering shote, the hen roosts, the

Virginia fence, and the straw stack came to be regarded in a sense as perquisites of the Union army. Punishments . . . were much rarer, and the difficulty of finding the culprits increased, as the officers were becoming judiciously nearsighted.

Drumming out of camp was a punishment administered for cowardice. Whenever a man's courage gave out in the face of the enemy, at the earliest opportunity after the battle he was stripped of his equipments and uniform, marched through the camp with a guard on either side and four soldiers following behind him at "charge bayonets," while a fife and drum corps brought up the rear, droning out the "Rogue's March." He was sure of being hooted and jeered at throughout the whole camp. There were no restraints put upon the language of his recent associates, and their vocabularies were worked up to their full capacity in reviling him. After he had been thoroughly shown off to the entire command, he was marched outside the lines and set free. This whole performance may seem at first thought a very light punishment for so grave an offence, and an easy escape from the service for such men. But it was considered a most disgraceful punishment. No man liked to be called a coward, much less to be turned out of the Army in that disreputable way, and the facts recorded on his regimental roll next to the honorable record of his fellows. He was liable to the death penalty if found in camp afterwards. Many more men deserved this punishment than ever received it. There were very few soldiers put out of the service by this method.

Somtimes an officer was assaulted by a private soldier or threatened by him. For all such offences soldiers were tried by court martial, and sentenced to the guard house or to hard labor at the Rip Raps or the Dry Tortugas with loss of pay; or to wear a ball and chain attached to their ankles for a stated period. These offences were often committed under the influence of liquor, but freqently through temper or exasperation at continued and unreasonable exactions, as the victim believed.

The penalty for sleeping at one's post when it was a post of danger, was death; but whether this penalty was ever enforced in our army I am unable to state. There is a very touching story of a young soldier who was pardoned by President Lincoln for this offence, through the pitiful intercession of the young man's mother. Whether it was a chapter from real life, I am in doubt. I certainly never heard of a sentinel being visited with this extreme penalty for this offence.

The penalty attaching to desertion is death by shooting, and this was no uncommon sight in the army; but it did not seem to stay the tide of desertion in the least. I have seen it stated that there was no time in the history of the Army of the Potomac, after its organization by McClellan, when it reported less than one-fourth its full membership as absent without leave. The general reader will perhaps be interested in the description of the first execution of a deserter I ever witnessed. It took place about the middle of October, 1863. I was then a member of Sickles' Third Corps, and my company was attached for the time being to General Birney's First Division, then covering Fairfax Station on the extreme left of the army. The guilty party was a member of a Pennsylvania regiment. He had deserted more than once, and was also charged with giving information to the enemy whereby a wagon train had been captured. The whole division was ordered out to witness the execution. The troops were drawn up around three sides of a rectangle in two double ranks, the outer facing inward and the inner facing outward. Between these ranks, throughout their entire extent, the criminal was obliged to march, which he did with lowered head. The order of the solemn procession was as shown in the diagram, the arrows indicating its direction.

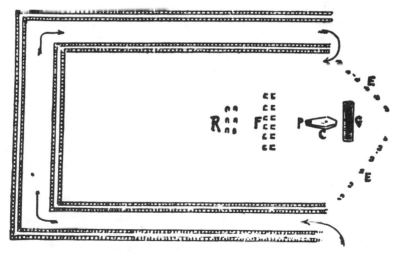

P, prisoner; C, coffin; G, Grave; F, firing party;
R, reserve firing party; E, twelve guards.

First came the provost-marshal—the sheriff of the army,—mounted; next, the band playing (what to me from its associations has now come to be the saddest of all tunes) Pleyel's Hymn, even sadder than the Dead March in "Saul," which I heard less frequently; then followed twelve armed men, who were deployed diagonally across the open end of the space after the procession had completed its round to guard against any attempt the prisoner might make to escape; fourth in order came four men bearing the coffin, followed by the prisoner attended by a chaplain and a single guard on either side; next, a shooting detachment of twelve men. Eleven of these had muskets loaded with ball, while the twelfth had a blank cartridge in his musket; but as the muskets had been loaded beforehand by an officer and mixed up afterwards, no one knew who had possession of the musket with the blank cartridge, so that each man, if he wanted it, had the benefit of a faint hope that his was the musket loaded without ball. After these marched an additional shooting force of six, to act in case the twelve should fail in the execution of their duty

When the slow and solemn round had been completed, the prisoner was seated on an end of his coffin which had been placed in the center of the open end of the rectangle near his grave. The chaplain then made a prayer and addressed a few words to the condemned man, which were not audible to any one else, and followed them by another brief prayer. The provost-marshal next advanced, bound the prisoner's eyes with a handkerchief, and read the general order for the execution. He then gave the signal for the shooting party to execute their orders. They did so, and a soul passed into eternity. Throwing his arms convulsively into the air, he fell back upon his coffin but made no further movement, and a surgeon who stood near, upon examination, found life to be extinct. The division was then marched past the corpse, off the field, and the sad scene was ended.

I afterwards saw a deserter from the First Division of the Second Corps meet his end in the same way down before Petersburg in the summer of 1864. These were the only exhibitions of this sort that I ever witnessed, although there were others that took place not far from my camp. The artillery was brigaded by itself in 1864 and 1865, and artillerymen were not then compelled to attend executions which took place in the infantry.

Here is a story of another deserter and spy who was shot in or near Indianapolis in 1863. He had enlisted in the Seventy-First Indiana Infantry. Not long afterwards he deserted and went over to the enemy but soon reappeared in the Union lines as a Rebel spy. While in this capacity he was captured and taken to the headquarters of General Henry B. Carrington, who was then in command of this military district. He indignantly protested his innocence of the charge, but a thorough search for evidence of his treachery was begun. His coat was first taken and cut into narrow strips and carefully scrutinized to assure that it contained nothing suspicious. One by one, the rest of his

Death of a Deserter

garments were examined and thrown aside until at last he stood naked before his captors with no evidence of his guilt having been discovered. He was then requested to don a suit of clothes that was brought in. This he did and then triumphantly demanded his release. But the General told him to keep cool, as the search was not yet completed; that full justice should be done him whether guilty or innocent. Taking up the trousers again, the General noticed that one of the spring bottoms was a little stiffer than the other, and on further investigation with his scissors found a pass from the Rebel General Kirby Smith carefully sewed in under the buckram.

At this discovery the culprit dropped on his knees and begged for his life. He was tried by court martial and sentenced to be hanged—hanging is the penalty for treason, shooting being considered too honorable a death for traitors. But General Carrington, wishing the influence of the execution to be exerted as a check against desertion, which was very common, decided that he should be shot. It is customary to detail the shooting squad from the company to which the deserter belongs. But so enraged were the members of this man's company at his offence that they sent a unanimous request that the entire company might act as firing party. This request was refused, however, and a detail of fifteen men made for that purpose. But whereas it is usual for the sergeant in charge of such a detail to load the muskets himself, putting blank cartridges into one, two, or three of the muskets, on this occasion the men were allowed to load for themselves, and when the surgeon examined the lifeless body he found *fifteen bullets* in it, showing that each one of the fifteen men had felt it to be his duty to shoot his former comrade, and that he had conscientiously acted up to that duty.

Shocking and solemn as such scenes were, I do not believe that the shooting of a deserter had any great deterring influence on the rank and file; for the opportunities to get away safely were most abundant. Indeed, any man who was base enough to desert his flag could almost choose his time for doing it. The wife of a man in my own company brought him a suit of citizen's clothing to desert in, which he availed himself of later; but even citizen's clothes were not always necessary to ensure safety for deserters. When a man's honor failed to hold him in the ranks, his exit from military life in the South was easy enough.

I have been asked if all deserters captured were shot. No; far from it. There were times in the war when the death penalty for this offence was entirely ignored, and then it would be revived again with the hope of diminishing the rapid rate at which desertions took place. Desertion was the most prevalent in 1864, when the town and city governments hired so many foreigners, who enlisted solely to get the large bounties paid and then deserted, many of them before getting to the field or immediately afterwards. They had no interest in the cause and could not be expected to have. These men were called bounty jumpers, and having deserted went to some other state and enlisted again to secure another bounty. In this manner many of them obtained hundreds of dollars without being detected; but many more were apprehended and suffered for it. I knew of three such being shot at one time, each having taken three bounties before they were finally captured. The greater part of these bounty jumpers came from Canada. A large number of reliable troops were necessary to take these men from the recruiting rendezvous to the various regiments which they were to join.

The mass of recaptured deserters were put to hard labor on Government works. Other were confined in some penitentiary to work out their unexpired term of service. I believe the penitentiary at Albany was used for this purpose, as was also the Old Capitol Prison in Washington. Many more were sent to the Rip Raps near Fort Monroe. On the 11th of March, 1865, President Lincoln issued a proclamation offering full pardon to all deserters who should return to their respective commands within sixty days, that is, before May 10, 1865, with the understanding that they should serve out the full time of their respective organizations and make up all time lost as well. A large number whose consciences had given them no peace since their lapse availed themselves of this proclamation to make amends as far as possible and leave the service with a good name. This act was characteristic of the Emancipator's matchless magnanimity and forgiving spirit but scarcely deserved by the parties having most at stake.

I have already intimated that death by hanging was a punishment meted out to certain offences against military law. One of these offences was desertion to the enemy, that is, going from our army over to the enemy and enlisting in his ranks to fight on that side. In the autumn of 1864—near Fort Welch, I think it was—I saw three military criminals hanged at the same moment from the same gallows for this crime against the Government. They were members of the Sixth Corps. There was less ceremony about this execution than that of the deserter whose end I more fully described. The condemned men were all foreigners and rode to the gallows in an ambulance attended by a chaplain. The ambulance was well guarded in front, in rear, and on the flanks. The gallows also was strongly guarded. If I recollect aright, the troops were not ordered out to witness the spectacle. Nevertheless, thousands of them from adjoining camps lined the route and standing around the gallows saw the prisoners meet their fate. No loyal heart gave them any sympathy.

In April, 1864, I saw a man hanged for a different offence, on the plains of Stevensburg. He belonged to the second division of my own corps. Most of the corps, which was then twenty-seven thousand strong, must have witnessed the scene from near or afar. In hanging the culprit the provost marshal made a dreadful botch of the job, for the rope was too long and when the drop fell the man's feet touched the ground. This obliged the provost-marshal to seize the rope and by main strength to hold him clear of the ground till death ensued. It is quite probable that strangulation instead of a broken neck ended his life. His body was so light and emaciated that it is doubtful if, even under more favorable circumstances, his fall could have broken his neck.

The report of the Adjutant-General made in 1870 shows that there were one hundred and twenty-one men executed during the war—a very insignificant fraction of those who, by military law, were liable to the death penalty.

8

A Day in Camp

The private soldiers in every arm of the service had many experiences in common in camp life, so that it will not be profitable to describe each in detail, but where the routine differs I shall adhere to the branch with which I am the most familiar, the light artillery.

Beginning the army day, the first bugle-call blown was one known in artillery tactics as the *Assembly of Buglers*, to sound which the corporal or sergeant of the guard would call up the bugler.

ASSEMBLY OF BUGLERS (artillery)

ASSEMBLY OF BUGLERS (infantry)

It was sounded in summer about five o'clock and in winter at six. It was the signal to the men to get out of their blankets and prepare for the morning roll call, known as *Réveillé*. At this signal the hum of life could be heard within the tents. "Put the bugler in the guard house!" "Turn out!" "All up!" and other similar expressions, mingled with yawns, groans, and exclamations of deep disgust, formed a part of the response to

113

this always unwelcome summons. But as only the short space of fifteen minutes was to intervene before the next call, the *Assembly*, would be blown, the men had to bestir themselves. Most of them woud arise at once, do the little dressing that was required, and perform or omit their toilet, according to the inclination or habit or time of the individual.

A common mode of washing was for one man to pour water from a canteen into the hands of his messmate, and thus take turns; but this method was practised most on the march. In settled camp, some men had a short log scooped out for a washbasin. Some were not so particular about being washed every day, and in the morning would put the time required for the toilet into another "turn over" and nap. As such men always slept with their full uniform on, they were equivalent to a kind of Minute Men, ready to take the field for roll call, or any other call, at a minute's notice.

ASSEMBLY *(artillery)*

ASSEMBLY *(infantry)*

As soon as the Assembly sounded, the sight presented was quite an interesting one. The men could be seen emerging from their tents or huts, their toilet in various stages of completion. Here was a man with one boot on and the other in his hand; here, one with his clothes buttoned in skips and blouse in hand, which he was putting on as he went to the line; here was one with a blouse on; there, one with his jacket or overcoat (unless uniformity of dress on line was required—it was not always at the morning roll calls, and in some companies never, only on inspections). Here and there was a man just about half awake, having a fist at each eye and looking as disconsolate and forsaken as men usually do when they get from the bed before the public at short notice.

Then, this roll call was always a powerful cathartic on a large number, who must go at once to the sinks and let the Rebel army wait, if it wanted to fight, until their return. The exodus in that direction at the sounding of the assembly was really quite a feature. All enlisted men in a company, except the guard and sick, must be present at this roll call, unless excused for good reasons. But as the shirks always took pride in dodging it, their notice of intention to be absent from it for any reason was looked at askance by the sergeants of detachments. The studied agony that these men would work not only into their features but their voice and even their gait would have been ludicrous in the extreme if frequent repetitions had not ren-

RÉVEILLÉ

dered it disgusting; and the humorous aspect of these dodgers was not a little enhanced by the appearance which they usually had of having been dressed much as is a statue about to be dedicated, which, at the signal, by the pulling of a single cord is stripped of all its drapery and displayed in its full glory.

Other touches which old soldiers not artillerymen would readily recognize as familiar might be added to the scene presented in camp when the bugle or the drum called the men into line for the first time in the day. When at last the line was formed, it was dressed by the orderly—later called, I believe, first sergeant—and while at "Parade Rest" the bugles blew.

There were words improvised to many of these calls, which I wish I would accurately remember: Those adapted to Réveillé, in some regiments, ran as follows:

I can't get 'em up, I can't get 'em up,
I can't get 'em up, I tell you.
I can't get 'em up, I can't get 'em up,
I can't get 'em up at all.

The corporal's worse than the private,
The sergeant's worse than the corporal,

The lieutenant's worse than the sergeant,
But the captain's worst of all.

I can't get 'em up, I can't get 'em up,
I can't get 'em up this morning;
I can't get 'em up, I can't get 'em up,
I can't get 'em up today.

These are more appropriate when applied to the infantry, where the call was blown before the men came into line.

When the bugle ceased to sound, the orderly-sergeant of a battery said, "Pay attention to roll call"; and the roll was called by the six line or duty sergeants, each of whom had charge of twenty-five men, more or less. These sergeants then made their report of "all present or accounted for" (or whatever the report was) to the orderly-sergeant, who in turn reported to the officer of the day in charge. If there were no special orders to be issued for fatigue duty or no checks or rebukes or instructions to be given "for the good of the order" the line was dismissed. Any men who were absent without leave were quite likely to be put on the Black List. . . .

Shortly after Réveillé, the buglers sounded forth the shrill notes of the

STABLE CALL

Here are the words sung to this call:

Go to the stable, as quick as you're able,
And groom off your horses, and give them some corn;
For if you don't do it the captain will know it,
And then you will rue it, as sure as you're born.

This call summoned all the drivers in the company to assemble at the grain pile with their pair of canvas nose bags, where the stable sergeant, so called (his rank was that of a private though he sometimes put on the airs of a brigadier-general), furnished each with the usual ration of grain, either oats or corn.

With this forage and a curry comb and brush, they at once proceeded to the picket rope, where, under the inspection of the six sergeants, supervised also by the officer of the day and orderly, the horses were thoroughly groomed. At a given signal, the grooming ceased, and the nose bags were strapped on. Sometimes the feed was given while the grooming was in progress.

The only amusing phase of this duty that I now recall, occurred when some luckless cannoneer, who would insist that he did not know the difference between a curry comb and a curry of mutton, was detailed to minister to the sanitary needs of some poor, unsavory, glanders-infected, or greasy-heeled, or sore-backed, or hoof-rotten brute that could not be entirely neglected until he was condemned by Governmental authority. Now the cannoneers of a battery, who constituted what was known as the Gun Detachment, were an aristocracy. It is worthy of notice that when artillery companies received their first outfit of horses, there were always at least three men who wished to be drivers to one who cared to serve as a cannoneer, the prevailing idea among the uninitiated being that a driver's position was a safer place in battle than that of a cannoneer. They were much disappointed...when they came to the reality. But the cannoneers, taking the recognized post of danger from choice, a post whose duties when well executed were the most showy on parade as well as the most effective in action, upon whose coolness and courage depended the safety not only of their own company but often that of regiments, were nursed by these facts into the belief that they rightfully outranked

the rest of the rank and file. The posturings and facial con-
tortions of a cannoneer who cherished these opinions, when
called upon to perform such a task as I have specified, can
readily be imagined; if they cannot, I will only say that they
would have excited the risibilities of the most sympathetic
heart. The four-footed patients alluded to were usually assigned
to the charge of "Spare Men," that is, men who were neither
drivers nor members of the gun detachments, who by use had
come to fill the situation meekly and gracefully. There was one
service that a cannoneer would occasionally condescend to do a
driver. When the army was on the march, a driver would sometimes get weary of riding and ask a cannoneer to spell him while
he stretched his legs; and just to oblige him the cannoneer
would get into the saddle and ride two or three miles, but
beyond that he kept to his own sphere.

Following close upon the completion of stable duties came
Breakfast Call, when the men prepared and ate their breakfast
or received their dipper of coffee and other rations from the
company cook house. I can add nothing in this connection to
what I have already related in the chapter on rations.

BREAKFAST CALL (in artillery)

BREAKFAST CALL (in infantry)

At eight o'clock the bugler blew

SICK CALL *(in artillery)*

SICK CALL *(in infantry)*

Here are the words improvised to this call:

> Dr. Jones says, Dr. Jones says:
> Come and get your quin, quin, quin, quinine,
> Come and get your quinine,
>   Q-u-i-n-i-n-e ! ! !

In response to this call some who were whole and needed not a physician, as well as those who were sick, reported at the surgeon's tent for prescriptions. Much used to be said by the soldiers in regard to the competency or incompetency of Army surgeons. It was well understood in war time that, even though an examination of fitness was required of surgeons to secure an appointment in the Army—at least in some states—many charlatans by some means received commissions. Such an examination had as much value as those the medicine men made of recruits in '64 and '65, for . . . a number of men too old or diseased came to the front in those years—no, they did not all get as far as the front—to stock all the hospitals in the country. A part of this showing must be charged to incompetent physicians, and a part to the strait the Government was in for recruits. The

appointment of incompetent surgeons, on the other hand, is
to be condoned in a Government sorely pressed for medical assistance and all too indifferent in its strait to the qualifications
of candidates.

Nothing in this line of remark is to be construed as reflecting
on the great mass of Army surgeons who were most assiduous
workers and whose record makes a most creditable chapter in
the history of the Rebellion. There are incompetents in every
class.

Every soldier who tried to do his duty and only responded to
sick call when in the direst need should have received the most
skilful treatment to be had; but a strict regard for the facts
compels the statement that a large number of those who waited
upon the doctor deserved no better treatment than the most
ignorant of these men of medicine were likely to administer.
Yes, there were a few individuals to be found, I believe, in
every company in the service, who to escape guard or fatigue
duty would feign illness, and if possible delude the surgeon into
believing them proper subjects for his tenderest care. Too often
they succeeded and threw upon their own intimate associates
the labors of camp, which they themselves were able to perform and degraded their bodies by swallowing drugs for the ailments to which they laid claim. One of my most vivid
memories of camp life is of these "beats on the Government"
emerging from their tents at sick call in the traditional Army
overcoat with one hand tucked into the breast, the collar up,
cap drawn down, one trousers-leg hung up on the strap of a
Government boot, and a pace slow and measured, appearing to
bear as many of the woes and ills of mankind as Landseer has
depicted in his "Scapegoat."

Sometimes the surgeons were shrewd enough to read the
frauds among the patients, in which case they often gave
them an unpalatable but harmless dose and reported them
back for duty, or perhaps reported them back for duty without
prescription, at the same time sending an advisory note to the
captain of the company to be on the lookout for them. It was,
of course, a great disappointment to these would-be shirkers to
fail in their plans, but some of the more persistent would stick
to their program and by refusing food and taking but little
exercise would in a short time make invalids of themselves
in reality. There were undoubtedly many men in the service
who secured admission to the hospitals and finally their dis-

charge by this method; and some of these men by such a course of action planted the seeds of real diseases, to which they later succumbed.

I must hasten to say that this is not a burlesque on *all* the soldiers who answered to sick call. God forbid! The genuine cases went with a different air from the shams. I can see some of my old comrades now, God bless them! sterling fellows, soldiers to the core, stalwart men when they entered the Army, but, overtaken by disease, they would report to sick call, day after day, hoping for a favorable change; yet in spite of medicine and the nursing of their messmates, pining away until at last they disappeared—went to the hospitals and there died. Oh, if such men could only have been sent to their homes before it was too late, where the surroundings were more congenial and comfortable, the nursing tender, and more skilful, because administered by warmer hearts and the more loving hands of mother, wife, or sister, thousands of these noble souls could have been saved to the Government and to their families. But it was not to be, and so they wasted away, manfully battling for life against odds, dying with the names of dear ones on their lips, dear ones whose presence at the death bed was in so many cases impossible, but dying as honorable deaths as if they had gone down

With their back to the field and their feet to the foe.

The proverbial prescription of the average Army surgeon was quinine, whether for stomach or bowels, headache or toothache, for a cough or for lameness, rheumatism, or fever and ague. Quinine was always and everywhere prescribed with a confidence and freedom which left all other medicines far in the rear. Making all due allowances for exaggerations, that drug was unquestionably the popular dose with the doctors.

After Sick Call came *Water Call,* or

WATERING CALL

at which the drivers in artillery and the full rank and file of the cavalry repaired to the picket rope, and taking their horses set out to water them. This was a very simple and expeditious matter when the Army was encamped near a river as it frequently was; but when it was not, the horses were ridden from one-half a mile to two miles before a stream or pond was found adequate to the purpose. It was no small matter to provide the animals of the Army of the Potomac with water, as can be judged from the following figures: After Antietam McClellan had 38,800 horses and mules. When the Army crossed the Rapidan into the Wilderness in 1864, there were 56,499 horses and mules in it. Either of these is a large number to provide with water. But of course they were not all watered at the same pond or stream, since the Army stretched across many miles of territory. In the summer of 1864, the problem of water-getting before Petersburg was quite a serious one for man and beast. No rain had fallen for several weeks, and the animals belonging to that part of the Army which was at quite a remove from the James and Appomattox Rivers had to be ridden nearly two miles ... for water, and then got only a warm, muddy, and stagnant fluid that had accumulated in some hollow. The soldiers were sorely pressed to get enough to supply their own needs. They would scoop out small holes in old water courses, and patiently await a dipperful of a warm, milky-colored fluid to ooze from the clay, drop by drop. Hundreds wandered through the woods and valleys with their empty canteens, barely finding water enough to quench thirst. Even places usually dank and marshy became dry and baked under the continuous drought. But such a state of affairs was not to be endured a great while by live, energetic Union soldiers; and as the heavens continued to withhold the much needed supply of water, shovels and pickaxes were forthwith diverted from the warlike occupation of intrenching to the more peaceful pursuit of well digging, it soon being ascertained that an abundance of excellent water was to be had ten or twelve feet below the surface of the ground. These wells were most of them dug broadest at the top and with shelving sides to prevent them from caving, stoning a well being obviously out of the question. Old-fashioned well-curbs and sweeps were then erected over them, and man and beast were provided with excellent water in camp.

Fatigue call was the next in regular order.

FATIGUE CALL

FATIGUE CALL (infantry)

The artillery were almost never detailed for fatigue duty outside of their own company. The only exception now occurring to me was when an artillery brigade headquarters was established near by, and an occasional detail was made and sent there for temporary service, but that was all. Our camp fatigue duty consisted in policing or cleaning camp, building stables (or perhaps I should more accurately designate them if I called them shelters) for the horses and mules, burying horses, getting wood and water, and washing gun carriages and caissons for inspections.

This building of horse shelters was at times no mean or trivial enterprise and sometimes employed a great many men a great many days. When the Army was on the march, with no danger impending, the horses were unharnessed and tied to the picket rope. This was a rope about two hundred feet long and two inches in diameter, which, when the battery was drawn up in park, was hitched to the outer hind wheel of a caisson on one flank of the battery and then carried through the hind wheels and over the ammunition chests of the intervening caissons and made fast to a hind wheel of the caisson on the other flank. In camp, a different plan was adopted. If it was in the open, a line of posts was set at intervals to keep the rope from sagging and to them it was secured. The earth for ten feet on either side was then thrown up so as to drain off readily. Sometimes the picket was established in the edge of woods, in which case the rope ran from tree to tree. In summer camp a shelter of boughs was constructed over the picket. In winter, a wall of pine boughs was set up around to fend off bleak winds. Now and then one was roofed with a thatch of confiscated straw, and I remember seeing one nearly covered with long clapboard-like shingles rifted out of pine logs.

The character and stability of all such structures depended largely upon the skill displayed by regimental and company commanders in devising means to keep men employed, and on the tenure of a company's stay in a place. But I fail to recall a single instance where the men called a meeting and gave public expression to their gratitude and appreciation in a vote of thanks for the kind thoughtfulness displayed by said commanders. In fact, not this alone but all varieties of fatigue were accompanied in their doing with no end of growling.

It was aggravating after several days of exhausting labor, of cutting and carting and digging and paving—for some of the "high-toned" commanders had the picket paved with cobblestones—to have boot-and-saddle call blown, summoning the company away, never to return to that camp but to go elsewhere and repeat their building operations. It was the cheapest kind of balm to a company's feelings, where so much of love's—or rather unwilling—labor had been lost, to see another company appear just as the first was leaving and literally enter into the labors of the former, taking quiet and full possession of everything left behind. Yet such was one of the inevitable concomitants of war, and so used did the men become to such upsettings of their calculations that twenty-four hours sufficed as a rule to wipe out all yearnings for what so recently had been.

I will add a few words in this connection in regard to the mortality of horses. Those who have not looked into the matter have the idea that actual combat was the chief source of the destruction of horseflesh. But, as a matter of fact, that source is probably not to be credited with one-tenth of the full losses of the Army in this respect. It is to be remembered that the exigencies of the service required much of the brutes in the line of hard pulling, exposure, and hunger, which conspired to use them up very rapidly; but the various diseases to which horses are subject largely swelled the death list. Every few weeks a veterinary surgeon would look over the sick list of animals and prescribe for such as seemed worth saving or within the reach of treatment, while others would be condemned, led off, and shot. . . .

The procuring of wood was often a task involving no little labor for all arms of the military service. At Brandy Station, Virginia, before the Army left there on the 3d of May, 1864, some commands were obliged to go four or five miles for it. The inexperienced can have little idea of how rapidly a forest containing many acres of heavy growth would disappear before an army of seventy-five or a hundred thousand men camped in and about it. The scarcity of wood was generally made apparent by this fact, that when an army first went into camp, trees were cut two or three feet above the ground, but as the scarcity increased these stumps would get chipped down often below the ground.

After fatigue call the next business, as indicated by the drum or army bugle, was to respond to

DRILL CALL *(artillery)*

DRILL CALL *(infantry)*

I will anticipate a little by saying that the last drill of any kind in which my own company engaged took place among the hills of Stevensburg but a day or two before the Army started into the Wilderness in '64. From that time until the close of the war batteries were kept in constant motion or placed in the intrenchments on siege duty, thus putting battery drill out of the question; such at least was the fact with light batteries attached to the various Army corps. The Artillery Reserve belonging to the Army of the Potomac may have been an exception to this. I have no information in regard to it.

The artillery, like the infantry, had its squad drill but as the marchings and facings were of only trifling importance there was an insignificant amount of time spent on them. The drivers were usually exempted from drill of this kind, the cannoneers of the gun detachments doing enough of it to enable them while drilling the standing-gun drill—a drill without horses—to get from line into their respective stations about the gun and limber and vice versa. But long after this drill became obsolete and almost forgotten, the men seemed never to be at a loss to find their proper posts whenever there was need of it.

So far as I know, artillerymen never piqued themselves on their skill in marchings by platoons, keeping correct alignment meanwhile, whether to the front, the rear, obliquely, or in wheelings. Indeed, I remember this part of their schooling as rather irksome to them, regarding it as they did, whether rightfully or wrongfully, as ornamental and not essential. It undoubtedly *did* contribute to a more correct military bearing and soldierly carriage of the body, and in a general way improved military discipline: but these advantages did not always appear to the average member of the rank and file, and, when they did, were not always appreciated at their worth.

The drill of light-artillerymen in the school of the piece occupied a considerable time in the early history of each company. Before field movements could be undertaken, and carried out either with much variety or success, it was indispensable for the cannoneers and drivers to be fully acquainted with their respective duties; and not only was each man drilled in the duties of his own post but in those of every other man as well.* The cannoneers must know how to be drivers, and the

*This was done so the gun could remain in action even when some of its crew were shot down. [Ed.]

drivers must have some knowledge of the duties of cannoneers. This qualified a man to fill not only any other place than his own when a vacancy occurred, but another place *with* his own if need came. This education included a knowledge of the ordinary routine of loading and firing, the ability to estimate distances with tolerable accuracy, cut fuses, take any part in the dismounting of the piece and carriage, the transfer of limber chests, the mounting of a spare wheel or insertion of a spare pole, the slinging of the gun under the limber in case a piece-wheel should be disabled; even all the parts of the harness must be known by cannoneer as well as driver, so that by the time a man had graduated from this school he was possessed of quite a liberal military education.

Doing this sort of business over and over again, day after day, got to be quite tedious, but it all helped to pass away the three years. One part of this instruction was quite interesting, particularly if the exercise was a match against time, or if there was competition between detachments or sections; this was the dismounting and remounting the piece and carriage. In this operation each man must know his precise place and fit into it as accurately as if he were a part of a machine. This was absolutely necessary in order to secure facility and despatch. In just the measure that he realized and lived up to this duty, did his gun detachment succeed in reducing the time of the exercise. One gun's crew in my company worked with such speed, strength, unanimity, and precision, that they reduced the time for performing this maneuver, including loading and firing, to forty-nine seconds. Other batteries may have done even better. The guns we then used were the steel Rodmans weighing something over eight hundred pounds, and four of us could toss them about pretty much at will. I say four of us, because just four were concerned in the lifting of the gun. We could not have handled the brass Napoleons with equal readiness, for they are somewhat heavier.

After cannoneers and drivers came to be tolerably familiar with the school of the piece, field maneuvers with the battery began. The signal which announced this bit of entertainment for man and beast is known to Army Regulations as *Boots and Saddles*, a call whose tones at a later period sent the blood of artillerymen and cavalrymen coursing more rapidly through the veins when it denoted that danger was nigh and seeking encounter.

BOOTS AND SADDLES

Battery drill was an enterprise requiring ample territory. When the vicinity of the camp would not furnish it, the battery was driven to some place that would. If cannoneers as a class were more devout than the other members of a light-artillery company, it must have been because they were stimulated early in their military career to pray—to pray that the limits of the drill ground should be so contracted that the battery could not be cantered up and down a plain more than half a mile in extent, with cannoneers dismounted and strung along in the rear at intervals varying with their running capacity or the humor of the commanding officer; or, if mounted, clutching at the handles or edge of the limber-chest, momently expecting to be hurled headlong as the carriages plunged into an old sink or tent ditch or the gutter of an old company street, or struck against a stump or stone with such force as to shake the ammunition in the chests out of its packing, making it liable to explode from the next concussion—at least so feared the more timid of the cannoneers, when their fears of being thrown off were quieted so that they could think of anything else. On such occasions they appreciated the re-enforced trousers peculiar to artillerymen, and wished Government had been even more liberal in that direction. But this mental state of timidity soon wore off, and the men came to feel more at home while mounted on these noisiest and hardest-riding of vehicles; or else sulked in the rear with less indifference to consequences.

Notwithstanding the monotony that came of necessity to be inseparable from them, battery drills were often exhilarating occasions. It was in the nature of things for them to be so, as when the artillery in action moved at all it must needs move promptly. A full six-gun battery going across a plain at a trot is an animated spectacle. To see it quietly halted, then, at the command, "Fire to the rear. Caissons pass your pieces-trot-march. In Battery," break into moving masses, is a still more animated and apparently confused scene, for horses and men seem to fly in all directions. But the apparent confusion is only brief, for in a moment the guns are seen unlimbered in line, the cannoneers at their posts, and the piece-limbers and caissons aligned at their respective distances in the rear.

There was an excitement about this turmoil and despatch which I think did not obtain in any other branch of the service. The rattle and roar was more like that which is heard in a cotton factory or machine shop than anything else with which I can compare it. The drill of a light battery possessed much interest to outsiders, when well done. It was not unusual, when the drill ground was in proximity to an infantry camp, for the men to look on by hundreds. To see six cannons, with their accompanying six caissons, sped by seventy-two horses across the plain at a lively pace, the cannoneers either mounted or in hot pursuit, suddenly halt at the bugle signal, and in a moment after appear "In Battery" belching forth mimic thunder in blank cartridge at a rapid rate, and in the next minute limbered up and away again to another part of the field, was a sight full of interest and spirit to the unaccustomed beholder; and if, as sometimes happened, there was a company of cavalry out on drill, to engage in a sham fight with the battery, a thrilling and exciting scene ensued which later actual combats never superseded in memory; for while the cavalry swept down on the guns at a gallop, with sabers flashing in the air, the cannoneers with guns loaded with blank cartridges stand rigid as death awaiting the onset, until they are within a few rods of the battery. Then the lanyards are pulled, and the smoke, belched suddenly forth, completely envelops both parties to the bloodless fray.

As the drilling of a battery was done for the most part by sounding the commands upon a bugle, it became necessary for cannoneers and drivers to learn the calls; and this they did after a short experience. Even the horses became perfectly familiar with some of these calls, and would proceed to execute them without the intervention of a driver. Cavalry horses, too, exhibited great sagacity in interpreting bugle signals.

Sometimes the lieutenants who were chiefs of sections were sent out with their commands for special drill. A section comprised two guns with their caissons. There was little enthusiasm in this piecemeal kind of practice, especially after familiarity and experience in the drill of the full battery; but it performed a part in making the men self-possessed and expert in their special arm of the service. Beyond that, it gave men and horses exercise and appetite for Government food, which without the exercise would have been wanting, to a degree at least, and occupied time that would otherwise have been devoted to the soldier's pastime of grumbling.

At twelve o'clock the *Dinner Call* was sounded.

DINNER CALL

DINNER CALL (*Infantry*)

Again, I can add nothing of interest here beyond what I have already presented on rations.

There was nothing in the regular line of duty in light artillery for afternoons which could be called routine, although there was more or less standing-gun drill for cannoneers early in the service. In the infantry, battalion drill often occupied the time.

The next regular call for a battery was *Water Call*, sounded of four o'clock, or perhaps a little later. On the return of the horses *Stable Call* was again blown, and the duties of the morning repeated.

At about 5.45 P. M., *Attention* was blown, soon to be followed by the *Assembly*, when the men fell in again for *Retreat* roll call.

The music for this was arranged in three parts, and when there were three bugles to blow it the effect was quite pleasing. The name *Retreat* was probably given this call because it came when there was a general retiring from the duties of the day. This roll call corresponded with the *Dress Parade* of the infantry.

RETREAT

Uniformity of dress was a necessity at this time with the latter, and quite generally too in the artillery; but the commanders of batteries differed widely in taste and military discipline. A company of soldiers was what its captain made it. Some were particular, others were not, but all should have been in this matter of dress for at least one roll call in the day. At this parade all general orders were read, with charges, specifications, and findings of courts martial, etc., so that the name of E. D. Townsend, Assistant Adjutant-General, became a household word. At this time, too, lectures on the shortcomings of the company were in order. The lecturer employed by the Government to do this was usually the officer of the day, though now and then the captain would spell him. A lecturer of this kind had two great advantages over a lecturer in civil life; first, he was always sure of an audience, and, second, he could hold their attention to the very close. None of them left while the lecture was in progress. Now and then an orderly-sergeant would try his hand in the lecture field, but unless he was protected by the presence of a pair of shoulder straps he was quite likely to be coughed or groaned down, or in some other way discouraged from repeating the effort.

The shortcomings alluded to were of a varied character. I think I mentioned some of them in the chapter on punishments. Sometimes the text was the general delinquency of the men in getting into line; sometimes it was a rebuke for being lax in phases of discipline; the men were not sufficiently respectful to superior officers, did not pay the requisite attention to *saluting*, had too much *back talk*, were *too boisterous in camp*, *too untidy in line*. These and twenty other allied topics all having a bearing on the characteristics essential in the makeup of a good soldier were preached upon with greater or less unction and frequency as circumstances seemed to require, or the standard in a given company demanded.

After the dismission of the line, guard mounting took place; but in the artillery this was a very simple matter. The guard at once formed on the parade line were assigned to their reliefs and dismissed till wanted. Sometimes the guard mounting took place in the morning as did that of the infantry. The neatest and most soldierly appearing guardsman was selected as captain's orderly. But guard mounting in light artillery was not always this simple. Camp Barry near Washington was used as a school of instruction for light batteries for a period of at least three years. During the greater part of this time there were ten or a dozen batteries there on an average. Under one of its commandants, at least, a brigade guard mounting was held at eight A. M., and here members of my company responded to the bugle-call known as the Assembly of Guard for the first and last time.

ASSEMBLY OF GUARD

The infantry bugle call for the same purpose was more familiar as it was heard daily for months. It ran as follows:

This call was immediately followed by other music, either a brass band or a fife-and-drum corps, to which the details from the various companies marched out to the colorline, where the usual formalities ensued. . . . The guard necessary in a single company of artillery was so small that the call with the bugle was rarely if ever sounded, at least in volunteer companies. A detail of cannoneers stood guard over the guns night and day, and over the cook house and quartermaster's stores at night, and sometimes there was one posted in front of company headquarters. A detail of drivers also went on duty at night at the picket rope, to assure that the horses were kept tied and not stolen by marauding cavalrymen.

In the safe rear, where, as the men used to say, the officers were wont to sit up late at night burning out Government candles while they devised ways and means to keep the men exercised as well as exorcised, a guard tent was pitched in front of the camp, in which the guard were compelled to stay when off post, much to their disgust sometimes; but when the company or regiment was in line along the glorious front, that unpopular lodging house was abandoned, and each guardsman slept in his own quarters, on his own Army feather bed, whither the corporal of the guard must come for his victim in the silent hours when that victim was wanted to go on post.

With the infantry, guard mounting took place in the morning at eight o'clock. The guard was divided into three equal portions, called reliefs, first, second, and third, each relief being on post two hours and off four, thus serving eight hours out of the twenty-four. With all the irksomeness of the detail, the guardsman enjoyed a temporary triumph as such, for on that day at least he could snap his fingers at roll calls and all calls for fatigue duty—in short was an independent gentleman within certain limits.

I have stated it to have been the duty of the corporal of the guard to seek out the members of the various reliefs in their quarters when the time came for them to go on post. There was more or less of lively incident attending these explorations —not, however, with the sanction of the corporal, to whom the liveliness was anything but amusing. Your corporal of the guard was up to the average of ordinary officers in intelligence, and as he was just started on the ladder of promotions, fully intended to do his whole duty at least; and so he was wont to prepare himself for his nightly rounds by obtaining such a knowledge of the local geography of the camp as would enable him to arouse and assemble his guard with the least inconvenience to himself and the least commotion to the camp. But the best laid plans of corporals of the guard would frequently "gang agley," even though they used every precaution, and so it was the rule rather than the exception for him to get into the wrong tent, and after waking up all the inmates and getting the profane to swearing and all to abusing him for his stupid intrusion, to retreat in as good order as possible and try again. The next time perhaps he would get into the right one, and after scrutinizing his list of the guard once more, call out the name of *Smith*, for example. No answer. There was a kind of deafness generated in the service, which was almost epidemic among guardsmen, especially night guard; at least, such seemed to be the case, for the man that was wanted to go out and take his post was invariably the last one in the tent to be awakened by the summons of the corporal; and long before that waking moment came, the corporal had as aids on his staff all these self-same inmates who had been victims to the assumed deafness of the man sought, and whose voices now furnished no mean chorus to the corporal's refrain.

Sometimes, when the knight of the double chevron was a man of retiring and quiet demeanor, he would save his lungs and make an effort to find his man by stepping inside the tent, and flashing the light of his Army candle from the open side of his tin lantern upon the features of each of the slumberers until he came to his victim, when he would shake him by the shoulder and arouse him. The only drawback to this method occurred when the reflections of the corporal woke up the wrong man, who, if he happened to be one of those explosive creatures whom I have before mentioned, was not always complimentary to the intruder in his use of language.

Once in a while in making his midnight rounds, when calling the name of one of his guard through the door of the stockade, the corporal would be politely directed by some one from within (perhaps the very man he wanted) to "Next tent below"; and many a time this officer succeeded in getting such an innocent and unsuspecting household completely by the ears before being convinced of the joke which had been played on him, when he would return to the first tent in no enviable humor; for meanwhile the men to be relieved were chafing and sputtering away at the non-appearance of the corporal and the relief. I think there was no one minor circumstance which vexed soldiers more than tardy relief from their posts, for every minute that they waited after the expiration of their allotted time seemed to them at least ten; so that the reception which the corporal and relief received when they *did* arrive was likely to be far from fraternal.

Speaking of the corporal of the guard reminds me of a snatch of a song which used to be sung in camp to the tune of "When Johnny Comes Marching Home." Here is the fragment:

> *My Johnny he now a Corporal is!*
> *Hurrah! Hurrah!*
> *My Johnny he now a Corporal is,*
> *You bet he knows his regular biz,*
> *And we'll all feel gay, etc.*

At 8.30 P. M., the bugle again sounded "Attention," followed by "Assembly" about five minutes afterwards, and the tumbling out of the company from their evening sociables to form in line for the final roll call of the day, known as *Tattoo*.

Tattoo was blown in artillery with the company at "Parade Rest" as at Réveillé. The roll call and reports followed just as before, and the company was then dismissed. Well do I recall, the melodious tones of this bit of army music coming to our ears so consecutively from various spots as to make continuous vibrations for nearly fifteen minutes, softened and sweetened by varying distances, as more than a thousand bugles gave tongue to the still and clear evening air, telling us that in the time specified a hundred thousand men had come out of their rude temporary homes—possibly the last ones they would ever

occupy—to respond to their names and give token that though
Nature's pall had now overshadowed the earth, they were yet
at their posts awaiting further orders for their country's service.

TATTOO

But this was Tattoo in the artillery. A somewhat more in-
spiriting call was that of the infantry, which gave the bugler
quite full scope as a soloist. Here it is:

Ere the last tone had died away, we could hear, when camped near enough to the infantry for the purpose, a very comical medley of names and responses coming from the several company streets of the various regiments within earshot. It was "Jones!" "Brown!" "Smith!" "Joe Smith!" "Green!" "Gray!" "O'Neil!" "O'Reilly!" "O'Brien!" and so on through the nationalities, only that the names were intermingled. Then the responses were replete with character. I believe it to be among the abilities of a man of close observation to write out quite at length prominent characteristics of an entire company, by noting carefully the manner in which the men answer "Here!" at roll call. Every degree of pitch in the gamut was represented. Every degree of force had its exponent. Some answered in a low voice, only to tease the sergeant, and roar out a second answer when called again. There were upward slides and downward slides, guttural tones and nasal tones. Occasionally, someone would answer for a messmate who was absent without leave and take his chances of being detected in the act. Darkness gave cover to much good-natured knavery.

After this roll call was over, the men had half an hour in which to make their beds, put on their nightcaps, and adjust themselves for sleep, as at nine o'clock Taps was sounded, which in the artillery ran as follows:

TAPS

In the infantry, the bugle call for Taps was identical with the Tattoo call in artillery. At its conclusion a drummer beat a few single, isolated taps, which closed the Army day. At this signal all lights must be put out, all talking and other noises cease, and every man except the guard be inside his quarters. In a previous chapter I think I stated that the Black List caught the men who violated this regulation. Some officers enforced it with greater rigidity than others, but all must have a quiet camp. Yet here as elsewhere rank interposed to shield culprits from violations of military regulations, and while the private soldier was punished for burning his candle or talking to his messmate after the bugle signal, general, field, staff, or line officers could and did get together and carouse and make the night turbulent with their revelry into the small hours, with no one to molest or call them to an account for it, although making tenfold the disturbance ever caused by the high private after hours.

Taps ended the Army day for all branches of the service, and, unless an alarm broke in upon the stillness of the night, the soldiers were left to their slumbers; or, what was oftener the case, to meditations on home; the length of time in months and days they must serve before returning thither; their prospects of surviving the vicissitudes of war; of the boys who once answered roll call with them, now camped over across the Dark River; or of plans for business, or social relations to be entered upon if they should survive the war. All these and a hundred other topics which furnished abundant field for air-castle-building would chase one another through the mind of the soldier-dreamer, till his brain would grow weary, his eyes heavy, and balmy sleep would softly steal him away from a world of trouble into the realm of sweet repose and pleasant dreams.

9

Raw Recruits

The reader will pardon me, I trust, for injecting a little bit of personal history to illustrate what thousands of young men were doing at the time and had been doing for months, as it leads up directly to the theme about to be considered.

After I had obtained the reluctant consent of my father to enlist—my mother never gave hers—the next step necessary was to make selection of the organization with which to identify my fortunes. I well remember the to me eventful August evening when that decision to enlist was arrived at. The Union army, then under McClellan, had been driven from before Richmond in the disastrous Peninsular Campaign, and now the Rebel army under General Lee was marching on Washington. President Lincoln had issued a call for three hundred thousand three-years' volunteers. One evening, shortly after this call was made, I met three of my former school mates and neighbors in the chief village of the town I then called home, and after a brief discussion of the outlook, one of the quartette challenged, or "stumped," the others to enlist. The challenge was promptly accepted all around, and hands were shaken to bind the agreement. I will add in passing that three of the four stood by that agreement; the fourth was induced by increased wages to remain with his employer, although he entered the service later in the war and bears a shell scar on his face to attest his honorable service.

After the decision had been reached . . . I returned to my home and either that night or the next morning informed my father of the resolution I had taken. Instead of interposing an emphatic objection as he had done the previous year, he said, "Well, you know I do not want you to go, but it is very evident that a great many more must go, and if you have fully determined upon it I shall not object."

Having already determined upon the arm of the service

139

VOLUNTEER ENLISTMENT

STATE OF  TOWN OF

I,   born in

in the State of   aged   years,
and by occupation a   Do HEREBY ACKNOWLEDGE to have
volunteered this   day of   18 ,
to serve as a **Soldier** in the 𝔄rmy of the 𝔘nited 𝔖tates of 𝔄merica, for
the period of *THREE YEARS*, unless sooner discharged by proper
authority: Do also agree to accept such bounty, pay, rations, and
clothing, as are, or may be, established by law for volunteers. And
I,   do solemnly swear, that I will bear
true faith and allegiance to the **United States of America,**
and that I will serve them honestly and faithfully against all their
enemies or opposers whomsoever; and that I will observe and
obey the orders of the President of the United States, and the
orders of the officers appointed over me, according to the Rules
and Articles of War.

Sworn and subscribed to, at
     this   day of   18 , }
BEFORE

     I CERTIFY, ON HONOR, That I have carefully examined the above
named Volunteer, agreeably to the General Regulations of the Army, and
that in my opinion he is free from all bodily defects and mental infirmity,
which would, in any way, disqualify him from performing the duties of a
soldier.

EXAMINING SURGEON

     I CERTIFY, ON HONOR, That I have minutely inspected the Vol-
unteer,   previously to his enlistment, and that he was
entirely sober when enlisted; that, to the best of my judgment and
belief, he is of lawful age; and that, in accepting him as duly qualified to
perform the duties of an able-bodied soldier, I have strictly observed the
Regulations which govern the recruiting service. This soldier has
eyes,   *hair,*   *complexion, is*   *feet*   *inches high.*

Regiment of   *Volunteers.*
RECRUITING OFFICER

DECLARATION OF RECRUIT.

I   desiring
to VOLUNTEER as a Soldier in the Army of the United
States, for the term of THREE YEARS, DO Declare, That
I am   years and   months of age; That I have
never been discharged from the United States service on account of disability or by sentence of a court-martial, or by
order before the expiration of a term of enlistment; and I
know of no impediment to my serving honestly and faithfully
as a soldier for three years.

GIVEN at
The   day of

Witness:

No. —   Volunteered at —   By —   18 —   Regiment of · —   enlistment; last served in Company ( ) —   Reg't of —   Discharged —   18 ·

CONSENT IN CASE OF MINOR.

I,   DO CERTIFY, That I am the father
of   that he said   is
years of age; and I do hereby freely give my CONSENT to his
volunteering as a SOLDIER IN THE ARMY OF THE UNITED
STATES for the period of THREE YEARS.

GIVEN at   the   day of   186

Witness:

which I should enter, accompanied by three other acquaintances of the same opinion, two of them the school fellows mentioned, I started for Cambridge with a view of seeing Captain Porter, who was then at home recruiting for the First Massachusetts Battery, which he commanded, and enlisting with him, as there were at least two men in his company who were fellow-townsmen. But we were much disappointed when the Captain informed us that his company was now recruited to the number required. However, we directed our steps back to Boston without delay, and there, in the second story of the Old State House, enlisted in a new organization then rapidly filling.

A copy of a certificate which I was to present on enlisting tells its own story. (See pages 140-141.)

How often in later years did the disappointment I experienced at not obtaining membership in the company I at first decided upon recur to me, and how grateful I always felt for the fate which thus controlled my enlistment. For the lot of a recruit in an old company was at best not an enviable one, and sometimes was made very disagreeable for him. He stood in much the same relation to the veterans of his company that the Freshman in college does to the Sophomores, or did when hazing was the rule and not the exception. It is to be remembered that he was utterly devoid of experience in everything which goes to make up the soldier, the details of camping, cooking, drilling, marching, fighting, etc., which put him at a disadvantage on all occasions. For this reason he easily became the butt of a large number of his company—not all, for there were some men who were ever ready to extend sympathy and furnish information to him when they saw it was needed, and did what they could to raise him to the same general plane occupied by the old members. But many of the veterans seemed to forget how they themselves obtained their army education little by little, and so ofttimes bore down on recruits severely.

In the later years of the war, when large bounties were being paid by town, city, and state governments to encourage enlistments, these recruits were often addressed as "bounty jumpers" by the evil disposed among the old members. But that term was a misnomer, unless these men proved later that they were deserving of it, for a bounty jumper was a man—I hate to call him one—who enlisted only to get the bounty and deserted at the earliest opportunity.

Recruits, as a class, stood the abuse which was heaped upon them with much greater serenity of temper than they should have done, and indeed so anxious were they to win favor with the veterans and to earn the right to be called and pass for old soldiers that they generally bore indignities without turning upon their assailants. The term "recruit" in the mouth of a veteran was a very reproachful one, but after one good brush with the enemy it was dropped if the new men behaved well under fire. In fact, those who abused the recruits most were themselves, as a rule, the most unreliable in action and the greatest shirks when on camp duty.

A Wood Detail

When a detail made up of recruits and veterans was sent with the wagons for wood, the recruits would be patted on the back by their wily associates and cajoled into doing most of the chopping, and then challenged to lift the heaviest end of the logs into the wagons, which they seldom refused to do. In the artillery, it usually fell to their lot to care for the spare and used-up horses, not from any intention of imposing upon them but because cannoneers and drivers had their regular tasks to perform, and all recruits entering the artillery began as spare men, and worked up from the position of private to that of the highest private—a cannoneer.

They always came to camp "flush" with money and received every encouragement from the bummers of the company to spend it freely; if they did not do this they were in a degree ostracised and their lot made much harder. When their boxes of goodies arrived from home, the lion's share went to the old hands. If the recruit did not give it to them, the meanest of them would steal it when he was away on detail.

All sorts of games were played on recruits by men who liked nothing so well as a practical joke. I recall the case of a young man in my own company who had just arrived, and, having been to the quartermaster for his outfit of clothing and equipments, was asked by one of the practical jokers why he did not get his umbrella.

"Do they furnish an umbrella?" he asked.

"Why, certainly," said his persecutor, unblushingly. "It's just like that fraud of a quartermaster to cheat a recruit out of a part of his outfit to sell for *his* own benefit. Go back and demand your umbrella of him and a good one too!"

And the poor beguiled recruit returned to the quartermaster in high dudgeon at the imagined attempt to swindle him, only to find that he had been victimized by one of the practical jokers of the camp.

There were at least two kinds of recruits to be found in every squad that arrived in camp. One of these classes was made up of modest, straightforward men who accepted their new situation with its deprivations gracefully and brought no sugar plums to camp with which to ease their entrance into stern life on Government fare and the hardships of Government service. They wore the Government clothing as it was furnished them, from the unshapely, uncomely forage cap to the shoddy, inelastic sock. It mattered naught to them that the limited stock of the quartermaster furnished nothing that fitted them. They accepted what he tendered cheerfully, believing it to be all right, and seemed as happy and as much at ease in a wilderness of overcoat and breeches as others did who had been artistically renovated by the company tailor. But they were none the less ludicrous and unsoldierly sights to look upon in such rigs and after a while would see themselves as others saw them and "spruce up" somewhat.

These men drew their Army rations to the full, not slighting the "salt horse," which I have intimated was rarely taken by old soldiers. They found no fault when detailed for fatigue duty, were always ready to learn, and in every way seemed anxious only to do the proper thing to be done, hoping by such a course to win a speedy and easy ascent to the plane of importance occupied by the veterans; and this course undoubtedly did much to give them caste in the eyes of the latter.

Unlike these men in many particulars was the other class of recruits. This latter class was not modest or retiring in demeanor. Its members came to camp in a uniform calculated to provoke impertinent remarks from the old vets. Their caps were from the store of a professional hatter, and the numbers and emblem on the crown were of silver and gilt instead of homely brass. Their clothing was generally custom-made. The pantaloons in particular were not only made to fit well, but were of the finest material obtainable, much unlike the Government shoddy which covered the old veteran, and through whose meshes peas of ordinary caliber would almost rattle.

Then, their boots! Such masterpieces of elegance and extravagance! Of the cavalry pattern, reaching above the knee, almost doing away with the necessity for pantaloons, sometimes of plain grained leather, sometimes of enamelled, elaborately stitched and stamped, but always seeming to mark their occupant as a man of note and distinction among his comrades. They seemed a sort of fortification about their owner, protecting him from too close contact with his vulgar surroundings. Alas! it never required more than one day's hard march in these dashing appendages to humble their possessor so much that he would evacuate in as good order as possible when camp was reached, if not compelled to before.

Their underwear was such as the common herd did not use in service. Their shirts were "boiled," that is, white ones, or, if woollen, were of some loud checkered pattern, only less conspicuous than the flag which they had sworn to defend. In brief, their general makeup would have stamped them as military dudes, had such a class of creatures been then extant. Of course, it was their privilege to wear whatever did not conflict with Army Regulations, but I am giving the impressions they made on the minds of the old soldiers.

As for Government rations, they scoffed at them so long as there was a dollar of bounty left and a sutler within reach of camp to spend it with. But when the treasury was exhausted they were disconsolate indeed and wished that the wicked war was over with all their hearts. On fatigue duty they were useless at first, and the old soldiers made their lot an unhappy one; but by dint of bulldozing and an abundance of hard service, most of them got their fine sentimental notions pretty well knocked out before they had been many weeks in camp. The sergeants into whose hands they were put for instruction did not spare them, keeping them hard at work until the recall from drill.

It was fun in the artillery to see one of these dainty men on his first arrival put in charge of a pair of spare horses—spare enough, too, usually. It was expected of him that he would groom, feed, and water them. As it often happened that such a man had had no experience in the care of horses, he would naturally approach the subject with a good deal of awe. When the *Watering Call* blew, and the bridles and horses were pointed out to him by the sergeant, the fun began. Taking the bridle, he would look first at it, then at the horse, as if in doubt which end of him to put it on. In going to water, the drivers always bridled the horse which they rode and led the other by the halter. But our unfledged soldier seemed innocent of all proper information. For the first day or two he would *lead* his charges; then, as his courage grew with acquaintance, he would finally mount the near one and with his legs crooked up like a V, cling for dear life until he got his lesson learned in this direction. But all the time that he was getting initiated he was a ridiculous object to observers.

The drilling of raw recruits of both the classes mentioned was no small part of the trials that fell to the lot of billeted officers, for they got hold of some of the crookedest sticks to make straight military men of that the country—or, rather, *countries*—produced. Not the least among the obstacles in the way of making good soldiers of them was the fact that the recruits of 1864-5, in particular, included many who could neither speak nor understand a word of English. In referring to the disastrous battle of Reams Station, the late General Hancock told me that the Twentieth Massachusetts Regiment had received an accession of about two hundred German recruits only two or three days before the battle, not one of whom could understand the orders of their commanding officers. It can be easily imagined how much time and patience would be required to mould such subjects as those into intelligent, reliable soldiery.

But outside of this class there were scores of men that spoke

English who would "hay-foot" every time when they should "straw-foot."* They were incorrigibles in almost every military respect. Whenever they were out with a squad—usually the awkward squad—for drill, they made business lively enough for the sergeant in charge. When they stood in the rear rank

Drilling the Awkward Squad

their loftiest ambition seemed to be to walk up the backs of their file leaders, and then they would insist that it was the file leaders who were out of step. Members of the much abused front rank often had occasion to wish that the regulation thirteen inches from breast to back might be extended to as many feet; but ·when the march was backward in line, these front rank men would get square with their persecutors in the rear.

To see such men attempt to change step while marching was no mean show. I can think of nothing more apt to compare it with than the game of Hop Scotch, in which the player hops

*Since some of the illiterate soldiers did not know what right or left meant, the drill sergeants would have them tie wads of straw and hay on their feet and give orders by calling out "hay-foot" or "straw-foot." [Ed.]

first on one foot, then on both; or to the blue jay, which in uttering one of its notes jumps up and down on the limb; and if such a squad under full headway were surprised with a sudden command to halt they went all to pieces. It was no easy task to align them, for each man had a line of his own, and they would crane their heads out to see the buttons on the breast of the second man, to such an extent that the sergeant might have exclaimed, with the Irish sergeant under like circumstances, "O be-gorra, what a bint row! Come out here, lads, and take a look at yoursels!"

The awkward squad excelled equally in the infantry manual-of-arms. Indeed, they displayed more real individuality here, I think, than in the marchings, probably because it was the more noticeable. At a "shoulder," their muskets pointed at all angles, from forty-five degrees to a vertical. In the attempt to change to a "carry," part of them would drop their muskets. At an "order," no two of the butts reached the ground together, and if a man could not always drop his musket on his own toe he was a pretty correct shot with it on the toe of his neighbor. But, with all their awkwardness and slowness at becoming acquainted with a soldier's duties, the recruits of the earlier years in time of need behaved manfully. They made a poor exhibition on dress parade, but could generally be counted on when more serious work was in hand. Sometimes, when they made an unusually poor display on drill or parade, they were punished—unjustly it may have been, for what they could not help—by being subjected to the knapsack drill, of which I have already spoken.

It was a prudential circumstance that the war came to an end when it did, for the quality of the material that was sent to the army in 1864 and 1865 was for the most part of no credit or value to any arm of the service. The period of enlistments from promptings of patriotism had gone by, and the man who entered the Army solely from mercenary motives was of little or no assistance to that Army when it was in need of valiant men, so that the chief burden and responsibility of the closing wrestle for the mastery necessarily fell largely on the shoulders of the men who bared their breasts for the first time in 1861, '62, and '63.

I have thus far spoken of a recruit in the usual sense of a man enlisted to fill a vacancy in an organization already in the field. But this seems the proper connection in which to say

something of the experiences of men who enlisted with original regiments, and went out with the same in '61 and '62. In
many respects their education was obtained under as great
adversity as fell to the lot of recruits. In some respects, I think
their lot was harder. They knew absolutely nothing of war.
They were stirred by patriotic impulse to enlist and crush out
treason and hurl back at once in the teeth of the enemy the
charge of cowardice and accept their challenge to the arbitra-
ment of war. These patriots planned just two moves for the
execution of this desire: first, to enlist—to join some company
or regiment; second, to have that regiment transferred at once
to the immediate front of the Rebels, where they could fight
it out and settle the troubles without delay. Their intense
fervor *to do something right away* to humble the haughty
enemy, made them utterly unmindful that they must first go
to school and learn the art of war from its very beginnings,
and right at that point their sorrows began.

I think the greatest cross they bore consisted in being compelled to settle down in home camp, as some regiments did for
months, waiting to be sent off. Here they were in sight of
home in many cases, yet outside of its comforts to a large extent; soldiers, yet out of danger; bidding their friends a tender
adieu today, because they are to leave them—perhaps forever—
tomorrow. But the morrow comes, and finds them still in
camp. Yes, there were soldiers who bade their friends a long
good-bye in the morning, and started for camp expecting that
very noon or afternoon to leave for the tented field, but who
at night returned again to spend a few hours more at the
homestead, as the departure of the regiment had been unex-
pectedly deferred.

The soldiers underwent a great deal of wear and tear from
false alarms of this kind, owing to various reasons. Sometimes
the regiment failed to depart because it was not full; sometimes it was awaiting its field officers; sometimes complete
equipments were not to be had; sometimes it was delayed to
join an expedition not yet ready; thus in one way or other, the
men and their friends were kept long on the tiptoe of expectation. Whenever a rumor became prevalent that the regiment
was surely going to leave on a certain day near at hand, straightway there was an exodus from camp for home, some obtaining
a furlough, but more going without one, to take another touching leave all around for the dozenth time perhaps. Many of

those who lived too far away to be sure of returning in time, remained in camp and telegraphed friends to meet them at some large center as they passed through on the specified day, which of course the friends faithfully tried to do and succeeded if the regiment set forth as rumored.

I said that many soldiers went home *without* furloughs. There was a camp guard hemming in every rendezvous for troops, with which I was familiar; but no sentinel could see a man cross his beat *if he did not look at him*, and this few of them did. Indeed, many of the sentinels themselves as soon as they were posted and the relieving squad were out of sight, stuck their inverted muskets into the ground and decamped, either for their two hours or for the day, and took their chances of being brought to answer for it. The fact is the men of '61 and '62 *wanted to go to war*, and whether they left the camp with or without leave, they were sure to return to it. This fact was quite generally understood by their superiors.

This home camp life seems interesting to look back upon. Hundreds of men did not spend one day in six in camp. They came often enough to have it known that they had not deserted and then flitted again, but other hundreds conscientiously remained. The company streets on every pleasant day were radiant with the costumes of "fair women and brave men"—to be. On such a day a young man sauntering along the parade, or winding in and out of the various company streets, the willing prisoner of one or more interesting young women—his sisters, perhaps, or somebody else's—walked, the envy of the men who had no such friends to enliven their camp life, or whose friends were too far away to visit them. If these latter men secured an introduction to such a party, it tempered their loneliness somewhat. And if such a party entered a tent and joined in' the social round, it made a merry gathering while they tarried. But there were other promenaders whose passing aroused no emotions of envy. The husband and father attended by the loving wife and mother whose brow had already begun to wear that sober aspect arising from a forecasting of the future, seeing possibly in the contingencies of war, herself a widow, her children fatherless—dependent on her own unaided hands for all of this world's comforts, which must be provided for the helplessness of childhood and youth. The husband, too, leading his boy or girl by the hand as he walks is not unmindful of the risks he has assumed or the comforts he must sacrifice. But his hand is on the plow, and he will not turn back.

Another interesting party often to be seen in the company street comprised a father, mother, and son, perhaps an only boy, who had volunteered for the war. Their reluctance at the step he had taken was manifested by turns in their looks, words, and acts. But while he remained in the state, they must be with him as much as possible. See that carpet bag which the mother opens as they take a seat on the straw in the son's tent! Notice the solicitude which she betrays as she takes out one comfort or convenience after another—the socks for cold weather, the woollens to ward off fever and ague, the medicine to antidote foul water, the little roll of bandages which—may he never have occasion for; the dozen other comforts that he ought to be provided with, including some goodies which he had better take along if the regiment should chance to go in a day or two. And so she loads him up—God bless her!—utterly unmindful that the Government has already provided him with more than he can carry very far with his unaided strength.

Then the camps were full of pedlars of "Yankee notions," which soldiers were supposed to stand in need of. I shall refer to some of these in another connection.

The lesson of submission to higher military authority was a hard one for free, honest American citizens to learn, and while learning it they chafed tremendously. It was difficult for them to realize the difference between men *with* shoulder straps and *without* them; in fact, they *would not* realize it for a long time. When the straps crowned the shoulders of social inferiors, submission to such authority was at times degrading indeed. I have already touched upon this subject. But the most judicious code of military discipline, even if administered by an accomplished officer of estimable character, would have met with vigorous opposition for a time from these impetuous and hitherto untrammelled American citizens. Fortunately for them, perhaps, but unfortunately for the service, the line officers were men of their own selection, their neighbors and friends, who had met them as equals on all occasions. But now, if such an officer attempted to enforce the authority conferred by his rank in the interest of better drill or discipline, he was at once charged by his late equals with "showing off his authority," "putting on airs," "feeling above his fellows"; and letters written home advertised him as a "miniature tyrant," etc., which made his position a very uncomfortable one to hold for a time. But this condition of affairs wore away soon after troops left the state, when the necessity for rigid discipline became apparent to every man. And when the private soldier saw that his captain was held responsible by the colonel for uncleanly quarters or arms, or unsoldierly and ill disciplined men, the colonel in turn being held to accountability by his next superior, the growls grew less frequent or were aimed at the Government rather than the captain, and the growlers began to settle down and accept the inevitable, taking lessons in something new every day.

It will be readily seen, I think, that the men composing the earliest regiments and batteries had also their trials to endure, and they were many; for not only they but their superiors were learning by rough experience the art of war. They were, in a sense, "achieving greatness," while the recruits had "greatness thrust upon them," often at short notice. Furthermore, recruits from the latter part of 1862 forward went out with a knowledge of much which they must undergo in the line of hardship and privation, which the first rallies had to learn by actual experience. And while it may be said that it took more courage for men to go with the stern facts of actual war confronting them than when its realities were unknown to them, yet it is also true that many of these later enlistments were made under the advantage of pecuniary and other inducements, without which many would not have been made. For patriotism unstimulated by hope of reward saw high-water mark in 1861, and rapidly receded in succeeding years, so that whereas men enlisted in 1861 and early in '62 because they wanted to go, and without hope of reward, later in '62 towns and individuals began to offer bounties to stimulate lagging enlistments, varying in amount from $10 to $300; and increased in '63 and '64 until, by the addition of state bounties, a recruit enlisting for a year received in the fall of '64 from $700 to $1000 in some instances. It was this large bounty which led old veterans to haze recruits in many ways. Of course, there was no justification for their doing it, only as the recruits in some instances provoked it.

There was a song composed during the war, entitled the "Raw Recruit," sung to the tune of "Abraham's Daughter," which I am wholly unable to recall, but a snatch of the first verse, or its parody, ran about as follows:

> *I'm a raw recruit, with a bran'-new suit,*
> *Nine hundred dollars bounty,*
> *And I've come down from Darbytown*
> *To fight for Oxford County.*

The name of the town and county were varied to suit the circumstances.

In 1863 a draft was ordered to fill the ranks of the Army, as volunteers did not come forward rapidly enough to meet the exigencies of the service. Men of means, if drafted, hired a substitute, as allowed by law, to go in their stead, when patriotism failed to set them in motion. Many of these substitutes did good service, while others became deserters immediately after enlisting. Conscription was never more unpopular than when enforced upon American citizens at this time.

Here is a suggestive extract from a rhyme of that period, entitled

THE SUBSTITUTE

> *A friend stepped up to me one day;*
> *These are the words that he did say:*
> *"A thousand dollars to you I'll owe,*
> *If in my place to war you'll go."*
> *"A thousand dollars? Done!" says I;*
> *" 'Twill help to keep my family."*
> *I soon was clothed in a soldier's suit,*
> *And off to war as a substitute.*
>
> *To a conscript camp first I was sent*
> *And to the barracks my steps I bent.*
> *I saw many there who wore blue suits,*
> *And learned they were all substitutes.*
> *Then orders came for us to go,*
> *Way down where blood like rivers flow.*
> *When the soldiers saw me, they yelled,*
> *"Recruit!*
> *Why did you come as a substitute?"*

10
Special Rations –
Boxes from Home – Sutlers

If there was a red-letter day to be found anywhere in the army life of a soldier, it occurred when he was the recipient of a box sent to him by the dear ones and friends he left to enter the service. Whenever it became clear, or even tolerably clear, that the Army was likely to pause in one place for at least two or three weeks, straightway the average soldier mailed a letter home to mother, father, wife, sister, or brother, setting forth in careful detail what he should like to have sent in a box at the earliest possible moment, and stating with great precision the address that must be put on the cover in order to have it reach its destination safely. Here is a specimen address:

Sergeant JOHN J. SMITH,
Company A., 19th Mass. Regiment,
SECOND BRIGADE, SECOND DIVISION, SECOND CORPS,
ARMY OF THE POTOMAC,
STEVENSBURG, VA.
Care Capt. James Brown

As a matter of fact much of this address was unnecessary, and the box would have arrived just as soon and safely if the address had only included the name, company, and regiment with Washington, D. C. added, for everything was forwarded from that city to Army headquarters, and thence distributed through the Army. But the average soldier wanted to make a sure thing of it and so told the whole story.

The boxes sent were usually of good size, often either a shoe case or a common soap box, and were rarely if ever less than a peck in capacity. As to the contents, I find on the back

154

of an old envelope a partial list of such articles ordered at some period in the service. I give them as they stand, to wit: "Round-headed nails" (for the heels of boots), "hatchet" (to cut kindlings, tent poles, etc.), "pudding, turkey, pickles, onions, pepper, paper, envelopes, stockings, potatoes, chocolate, condensed milk, sugar, broma, butter, sauce, preservative" (for the boots). The *quantity* of the articles to be sent was left to the discretion of thoughtful and affectionate parents.

In addition to the above, such a list was likely to contain an order for woollen shirts, towels, a pair of boots made to order, some needles, thread, buttons, and yarn, in the line of dry goods, and a boiled ham, tea, cheese, cake, preserve, etc., for edibles. As would naturally be expected, articles for the repair and solace of the inner man received most consideration in making out such a list.

How often the wise calculations of the soldier were rudely dash to earth by the Army being ordered to move before the time when the box should arrive! And how his mouth watered as he read over the invoice, which had already reached him by mail, describing with great minuteness of detail all the delicacies he had ordered, and many more that kind and loving hearts and thoughtful minds had put in. For the neighborhood generally was interested when it became known that a box was making up to send to a soldier, and each one must contribute some token of kindly remembrance, for the enjoyment of the far-away boy in blue. But the thought that some of these good things might spoil before the Army would again come to a stand-still came upon the veteran now and then with crushing force. Still, he must needs endure and take the situation as coolly as possible.

It was a little annoying to have every box opened and inspected at brigade or regimental headquarters to assure that no intoxicating liquors were smuggled into camp in that way, especially if one was not addicted to their use. There was many a growl uttered by men who had lost their little pint or quart bottle of some choice stimulating beverage, which had been confiscated from a box as "contraband of war," although the sender had marked it with an innocent name in the hope of passing it through unsuspected and uninspected. Yet the inspectors were often baffled. A favorite ruse was to have the bottle introduced into a well roasted turkey, a place that no one would for a moment suspect of containing such unique stuffing. In such a case the bottle was introduced into the bird empty, and filled after the cooking was completed, the utmost care being taken to cover up all marks of its presence. Some would conceal it in a tin can of small cakes; others inserted it in a loaf of cake, through a hole cut in the bottom. One member of my company had some whiskey sent for his enjoyment, sealed up in a tin can; but when the box was nailed up a nail was driven into the can, so that the owner found only an empty can and a generally diffused odor of "departed spirits" pervading the entire contents of food and raiment which the box contained.

It was really vexing to have one's knick-knacks and dainties overhauled by strangers under any circumstances, and all the more so when the box contained no proscribed commodity. Besides, the boxes were so nicely packed that it was next to impossible for the inspector to return all the contents, having once removed them; and he often made more or less of a jumble in attempting to do so. I think I must have had as many boxes sent as the average among the soldiers, and simple justice to those who had the handling of them requires me to state that I never missed a single article from them, and barring the breakage of two or three bottles, which may or may not have been the fault of the opener, the contents were always undamaged. Sometimes the boxes were sent directly from brigade headquarters to the headquarters of each company without inspection, and there only those were opened whose owners were known to imbibe freely on occasion.

The boxes came, when they came at all, by wagon loads— mule teams of the company going after them. I have already intimated that none were sent to the army when it was on the move or when a campaign was imminent; and as these moves were generally foreshadowed with tolerable accuracy, the men were likely to send their orders home at about the same time, and so they would receive their boxes together. In this way it happened that they came to camp by wagon loads, and a happier, lighter-hearted body of men than those who were gathered around the wagons could not have been found in the service. I mean now those who were the fortunate recipients of a box, for there was always a second party on hand who did not expect a box, but who were on the spot to offer congratulations to the lucky ones; perhaps these would receive an invitation to quarters to see the box unpacked.

This may seem a very tantalizing invitation for them to accept; but, nevertheless, next to being the owner of the prize, it was most entertaining to observe what some one else was to enjoy.

I think the art of box packing must have culminated during the war. It was simply wonderful, delightfully so, to see how each little corner and crevice was utilized. Not stuffed with paper by those who understood their business, thus wasting space, but filled with a potato, an apple, an onion, a pinch of dried apples, a handful of peanuts, or some other edible substance. These and other articles filled the crannies between carefully wrapped glass jars or bottles of toothsome preserves, or boxes of butter, or cans of condensed milk or well-roasted chickens, and the turkey that each box was wont to contain. If there was a new pair of boots among the contents, the feet were filled with little notions of convenience. Then, there was likely to be amid all the other merchandise already specified, a roll of bandages and lint, for the much-feared but unhoped-for contingency of battle. It added greatly to the pleasures of the investigator to come now and then upon a nicely wrapped package, labelled "From Mary," "From Cousin John," and perhaps a dozen other relatives, neighbors, school mates or shop mates, most of which contributions were delicious surprises, and many of them accompanied by notes of personal regard and good wishes.

There were some men in every company who had no one at home to remember them in this tender and appreciative manner, and as they sat or stood by the hero of a box and saw one article after another taken out and unwrapped, each speaking so eloquently of the loving care and thoughtful remembrance of kindred or friends, they were moved by mingled feelings of pleasure and sadness: pleasure at their comrade's good fortune and downright enjoyment of his treasure, and sadness at their own lonely condition with no one to remember them in this pleasant manner, and often their eyes would fill with tears by the contrast of their own situation with the pleasant scene before them. But these men were generally remembered by a liberal donation whenever a box came to camp.

Still, there were selfish men in every company, and if they were selfish by nature, the war, I think, had a tendency to make them more so. Such men would keep their precious box and its precious contents away from sight, smell, and taste of all outsiders. It was a little world to them, and all their own. "Send for a box yourself if you want one," appeared in their every look, and often found expression in words. As a boy I have seen a school mate munching an apple with two or three of his less favored acquaintances wistfully watching and begging for the core. But the men of whom I speak never had any core to their apples; they absorbed everything sent them.

I knew one man who came uncomfortably near belonging to to this class of soldiers. The first box he ever received contained, among other delicacies, about a peck of raw onions. Before these onions had been reached in this man's consumption of the contents of his box a move was ordered. What was to be done? It was one of the trying moments of his life. Nineteen out of every twenty men, if not ninety-nine out of every hundred, would at this eleventh hour have set them outside of the tent and said, "Here they are, boys. Take hold and help yourselves!" But not he. He was the hundredth man, the exception. So, packing them up with some old clothes, he at once expressed them back to his home. But as I have intimated, such men were few in number, and while war made this class more selfish, yet its community of hardship and danger and suffering developed sympathy and large-hearted generosity among the rank and file generally, and they shared freely with their less fortunate but worthy comrades.

Nothing, to my mind, better illustrates the fraternity developed in the army than the following poem, composed by Private Miles O'Reilly:

WE'VE DRANK FROM THE SAME CANTEEN

There are bonds of all sorts in this world of ours,
Fetters of friendship and ties of flowers,
    And true lover's knots, I ween.
The girl and the boy are bound by a kiss,
But there's never a bond, old friend, like this—
    We have drank from the same canteen.

It was sometimes water, and sometimes milk,
And sometimes apple jack fine as silk.
    But, whatever the tipple has been,
We shared it together, in bane or bliss,
And I warm to you friend, when I think of this
    We have drank from the same canteen.

The rich and the great sit down to dine,
And they quaff to each other in sparkling wine,
    From glasses of crystal and green.
But I guess in their golden potations they miss
The warmth or regard to be found in this—
    We have drank from the same canteen.

We have shared our blankets and tents together,
And have marched and fought in all kinds of weather.
    And hungry and full we have been;
Had days of battle and days of rest;
But this memory I cling to, and love the best—
    We have drank from the same canteen.

For when wounded I lay on the outer slope,
With my blood flowing fast, and but little to hope
    Upon which my faint spirit could lean,
Oh, then I remember you crawled to my side,
And, bleeding so fast it seemed both must have died,
    We drank from the same canteen.

But I will now leave this—to me deeply interesting theme
—and introduce

THE ARMY SUTLER

This personage played a very important part as quarter-master extraordinary to the soldiers. He was not an enlisted man, only a civilian. By Army Regulations sutlers could be appointed "at the rate of one for every regiment, corps, or separate detachment, by the commanding officer of such regiment, corps, or detachment," subject to the approval of higher authority. These persons made a business of sutling, or supplying food and a various collection of other articles to the troops. Each regiment was supplied with one of these traders, who pitched his hospital tent near camp and displayed his wares in a manner most enticing to the needs of the soldier. The sutler was of necessity both a dry-goods dealer and a grocer, and kept besides such other articles as were likely to be called for in the service. He made his chief reliance, however, a stock of goods that answered the demands of the stomach. He had a line of canned goods which he sold mostly for use in officers' messes. The canning of meats, fruits, and vegetables was then in its infancy, and the prices, which in time of peace were high, by the demands of war were so inflated that the highest of high privates could not aspire to sample them unless he was the child of wealthy parents who kept him supplied with a stock of scrip or greenbacks. It can readily be seen that his thirteen dollars a month (or even sixteen dollars, to which the pay was advanced June 20, 1864, through the efforts of Henry Wilson, who strove hard to make it twenty-one dollars) would not hold out a great while to patronize an army sutler, and hundreds of the soldiers when the paymaster came round had the pleasure of signing away the entire amount due them, whether two three, or four months' pay, to settle claims of the sutler upon them. Here are a few of his prices as I remember them:

Butter (warranted to be rancid), one dollar a pound; cheese, fifty cents a pound; condensed milk, seventy-five cents a can; navy tobacco, of the blackest sort, one dollar and a quarter a plug.* Other than the milk I do not remember any of the prices of canned goods. The investment that seemed to pay the largest dividend to the purchaser was the *molasses cakes* or *cookies* which the sutlers vended at the rate of six for a quarter. They made a pleasant and not too rich or expensive dessert when hardtack got to be a burden. Then one could buy sugar or molasses or flour of them, though at a higher price than the commissary charged for the same articles.

The commissary was an officer in charge of Government rations. From him quartermasters obtained their supplies for the rank and file on a written requisition given by the commander of a regiment or battery. He also sold supplies for officers' messes at cost price, and also to members of the rank and file if they presented an order signed by a commissioned officer.

Towards the end of the war sutlers kept self-rising flour, which they sold in packages of a few pounds. This the men bought quite generally to make into fritters or pancakes. It would have pleased the celebrated four-thousand-dollar cook at the Parker House, in Boston, could he have seen the men cook these fritters. The mixing was a simple matter, as water

*It must be remembered that the prices of these commodities on the civilian market were much less than they are today. [Ed.]

was the only addition which the flour required, but the fun was in the turning. A little experience enabled a man to turn them without the aid of a knife by first giving the fry pan a little toss upward and forward. This threw the cake out and over to be caught again the uncooked side down—all in a half-second. But the miscalculations and mishaps experienced in performing this piece of culinary detail were numerous and amusing, many a cake being dropped into the fire or taken by a sudden puff of wind just as it got edgewise in the air and whisked into the dirt.

Then, the sutler's pies! Who can forget them? "Moist and indigestible below, tough and indestructible above, with untold horrors within." The most mysterious products that he kept, I have yet to see the soldier who can furnish a correct analysis of what they were made from. Fortunately for the dealer, it mattered very little as to that, for the soldiers were used to mystery in all its forms, and the pies went down by hundreds; price, twenty-five cents each. Not very high, it is true, compared with other edibles, but they were small and thin, though for the matter of thickness several times the amount of such stuffing could have added but little to the cost.

I have said that these army merchants were dry-goods dealers. The only articles which would come under this head that I now remember of seeing were Army Regulation hats, cavalry boots, flannels, socks, and suspenders. They were not allowed to keep liquors, and any one of them found guilty of this act straightway lost his permit to suttle for the troops, if nothing worse happened him.

I am of the opinion that the sutlers did not always receive the consideration they deserved. Owing to the high prices which they asked the soldiers for their goods, the belief found ready currency that they were little better than extortioners; and I think that the name "sutler" today calls up in the minds of many a reader a man who would not enlist and shoulder his musket, but who was better satisfied to take his pack of goods and get his living out of the soldiers who were doing his fighting for him. But there is something to be said on the other side. In the first place, he filled a need recognized long before the Rebellion by Army Regulations. Such a personage was considered a convenience if not a necessity at military posts and in campaigns, and certain privileges were accorded him.

In the second place, no soldier was compelled to patronize him, and yet I question whether there was a man in the service any great length of time within easy reach of one of these traders, who did not patronize him more or less. In the third place, when one carefully considers the expense of transporting his goods to the Army, the wastage of the same from exposure to the weather, the cost of frequent removals, and the risk he carried of losing his stock of goods in case of a disaster to the Army, added to the constant increase in the cost of the necessaries of life, of which the soldiers were not cognizant, I do not believe that sutlers as a class can be justly accused of overcharging. I have seen one of these merchants after the war, who seemed seized with the fullest appreciation of the worth of his own services to the country, and with an innocent earnestness most refreshing, applied for membership in the Grand Army of the Republic, into which only men who have an honorable discharge from the Government are admitted.

There undoubtedly were Shylocks among them, and they often had a hard time of it; and this leads me to speak of another risk that sutlers had to assume—the risk of being raided—or "cleaned out," to quote the language of the expressive army slang. This meant the secret organization of a party of men in a regiment to fall upon a sutler in the darkness of night, throw down his tent, help themselves liberally to whatever they wanted, and then get back speedily and quietly to quarters. It did not do to carry stolen goods to the tents, for the next day was likely to see a detachment of men accompanied by the sutler searching the quarters for the missing property. Sometimes this raiding was done in a spirit of mischief by unprincipled men, sometimes to get satisfaction for what they considered his exorbitant charges. Sometimes the officers of a regiment sympathized in such a movement, if they thought the sutler's exactions deserved a rebuke. When this was the case, it was no easy task to find the criminals, for the officers were very blind and stupid, or, if the culprits were detected, they were quietly reminded that if they were foolish enough to get caught they must suffer the penalty. But sutlers, like other people, profited by the teachings of experience, and if they had faults, soon mended them, so that late in the war they rarely found it necessary to beg deliverance from their friends.

The following incident came under my own knowledge in

the winter of '64, while the Artillery Brigade of the Third Corps lay encamped in the edge of a pine woods near Brandy Station, Virginia. Just in rear of the Tenth Battery camp, near company headquarters, the brigade sutler had erected his tent, and every wagon load of his supplies passed through this camp under the eyes of anyone who cared to take note. A load of this description was thus inspected on a particular occasion, and while the wagon was standing in front of the tent waiting to be unloaded, and without special guarding—an always thirsty veteran stole up to it, seized upon a case of whiskey, said to have been destined for a battery commander, and was off in a jiffy. Less than three minutes elapsed before the case was missed. At once the captain of the company was notified, who immediately gave his instructions to the officer of the day. The bugler blew the *Assembly*, summoning every man into line; and every man had to be there or be otherwise strictly accounted for by his sergeant. What it all meant no one apparently knew. Meanwhile, two lieutenants and the orderly were carrying on a thorough search of the men's quarters. When it was completed, the orderly returned to the line, and the company was dismissed in a curious frame of mind as to the cause of all the stir. This soon leaked out, as did also the fact that no trace of the missing property had been discovered. All was again quiet along the Potomac, except when the culprit and his coterie waxed a little noisy over imbibitions of *ardent* mysteriously obtained, and not until after the close of the war was the mystery made clear.

It seems that as soon as he had seized his prize he passed swiftly down through the camp to the picket rope where the horses were tied, and there, *in a pile of manure thrown up behind them*, quickly concealed the case and at the bugle signal was prompt to fall into line. Under cover of darkness the same night, the plunder was taken from the manure heap and carried to a hill in front of the camp, where it was buried in a manner which would not disclose it to the casual traveler, and yet leave it easily accessible to its unlawful possessor, and here he resorted periodically for a fresh supply until it was exhausted.

I have quoted a few of the prices charged by sutlers. Here are a few of the prices paid by people in Richmond, during the latter part of the war, in Confederate money:

Potatoes $80 a bushel; a chicken $50; shad $50 per pair;

beef $15 a pound; bacon $20 a pound; butter $20 a pound; flour $1500 a barrel; meal $140 a bushel; beans $65 a bushel; cow-peas $80 a bushel; hard wood $50 a cord; green pine $80 a cord; and a dollar in gold was worth $100 in Confederate money.

11
Foraging

There was one other source from which soldiers—at least, some soldiers—replenished their larder or added to its variety. The means employed to accomplish this end was known as *Foraging*, which is generally understood to mean a seeking after food, whether for man or beast, and appropriating to one's own use whatsoever is found in this line, wheresoever it is found in an enemy's country. It took the Army some time to adopt this mode of increasing its stores. This arose from the fact that early in the war many of the prominent Government and military officers thought that a display of force with consideration shown the enemy's property would win the South back to her allegiance to the Union; but that if they devastated property and appropriated personal effects, it would only embitter the enemy, unite them more solidly, and greatly prolong the war; so that for many months after war began, Northern troops were prohibited from seizing fence rails, poultry, swine, straw, or any similar merchandise in which they might under some circumstances feel a personal interest; and whenever straw stacks and fences were appropriated by order of commanding officers, certificates to that effect were given the owners, who might expect at some time to be reimbursed. But the Rebellion waxed apace and outgrew all possibility of certificating everybody whose property was entered upon or absorbed, and furthermore it came to be known that many who had received certificates were in collusion with the enemy, so that the issuance of these receipts gradually grew beautifully less.

Then there was another obstacle in the way of a general adoption of foraging as an added means of support. It was the presence in the Army of a large number of men who had learned the ten commandments, and could not, with their early training and education, look upon this taking to themselves

165

the possessions of others without license as any different from
stealing. These soldiers would neither forage nor share in the
fruits of foraging. It can be readily imagined then that when
one of this class commanded a regiment the diversion of foraging was not likely to be very general with his men. But as the
war wore on, and it became more evident that such tender
regard for Rebel property only strengthened the enemy and
weakened the cause of the Union, conscientious scruples
stepped to the rear, and the soldier who had them at the end
of the war was a curiosity indeed.

There are some phases of this question of foraging which
at this late day may be calmly considered, and the right and
wrong of it carefully weighed. In the first place, international
law declares that in a hostile section an army may save its
rations and live off the country. To the large majority of the
soldiers this would be sufficient warrant for them to appropriate
from the enemy whatever they had a present liking for in
the line of provisions. If all laws were based on absolute justice,
the one quoted would settle the question finally and leave
nothing as an objection to foraging. But while the majority
make the laws, the consciences and convictions of the minority
are not changed thereby. Each man's conscience must be a
final law unto himself. It is well for it to be so. I only enlarge
upon this for a moment to show that on all moral questions
every intelligent man must in a measure make his own law,
having conscience as a guide.

The view which the average soldier took was, as already
intimated, in harmony with the international law quoted.
This view was, in substance, that the people of the South
were in a state of rebellion against the Government, notwithstanding that they had been duly warned to desist from war
and return to their allegiance; that they had therefore forfeited
all claim to whatever property the soldier chose to appropriate;
that this was one of the risks they assumed when they raised
the banner of secession; that for this, and perhaps other reasons, they should be treated just as a foreign nation waging
war against the United States, all of which may seem plausible
at first view, and indeed it may be said just here that if the
soldiers had always despoiled the enemy to supply their own
pressing personal needs, or if they had always taken or destroyed only those things which could be of service to the
enemy in the prosecution of the war, the arguments against

foraging would be considerably weakened; but the authority to forage carried with it also the exercise of the office of judge and jury, from whom there was no appeal. If the owner of a lot of corn or poultry was to protest against losing it, on the ground that he was a Unionist, unless the proof was at hand, he would lose his case—that is, his corn and chickens. However sincere he may have been, it was not possible for him to establish his Union sentiments at short notice. Indeed, so many who really were "secesh" claimed to be good Union men, it came latterly to be assumed that the victim was playing a false rôle on all such occasions, and so the soldiers went straight for the plunder, heeding no remonstrances. Without doubt, hundreds of Union men throughout the South suffered losses in this way, which if their loyalty could have been clearly shown they would have been spared.

A good deal of the foraging, while unauthorized and forbidden by commanding officers, was often connived at by them, and they were frequently sharers in the spoils; but I was about to say that it was not always of the most judicious kind. No one better than the old soldiers knows how destitute many, if not most, of the houses along the line of march were of provisions, clothing, and domestic animals after the first few months of the war. I will amend that statement. There was one class who knew better than the soldiers,— the tenants of those houses knew that destitution better—sometimes feigned, it may be, but as a rule it was the ugly and distressing reality. I am dealing now with the Army of the Potomac, which traveled the same roads year after year, either before or behind the Rebel Army of Northern Virginia. In or near the routes of these bodies little was attempted by the people in the way of crop raising, for their products were sure to feed one or the other of the two armies as they tramped up and down the state, so that destitution in some of the wayside cabins and farm houses was often quite marked. No one with a heart less hard than flint could deprive such families of their last cow, shote, or ear of corn. Yet there were many unauthorized foragers who would not hesitate a moment to seize and carry off the last visible mouthful of food. So it has seemed to me that the cup of Rebellion was made unnecessarily bitter from the fact that such appeals too often fell on deaf ears. Granting it to be true that the Rebels had forfeited all right to whatever property their antagonists saw fit to appropriate, yet in the absence of those Rebels their families ought not to suffer want and distress; the innocent should not suffer for the guilty, and when nothing was known against them they should not have been deprived of their last morsel. But there were exceptions. There were some families who gave information to the Rebel army or detachments of it, by which fragments of ours were killed or captured, and when this was known the members of that family were likely sooner or later to suffer for it, as would naturally be expected.

Some of these families were so destitute that they were at times driven to appeal to the nearest Army headquarters for rations to relieve their sufferings. To do this it was often necessary for them to walk many miles. Horses they had not. They could not keep them, for if the Union cavalry did not "borrow," the Rebel cavalry would impress them; so that they were not only without a beast of burden for farm work, but had none to use as a means of transportation. Now and then a sore-backed, emaciated, and generally used-up horse or mule, which had been abandoned and left in the track of the Army to die, was taken charge of when the coast was clear, and nursed back into vitality enough to stand on at least three of his legs, when, by means of bits of tattered rope, twisted corn husks, and odds and ends of leather which had seen better days, the sorry-looking brute, still bearing the brand U. S. or C. S. on his rump, partly concealed perhaps by his rusty outfit, was tackled into a nondescript vehicle, possibly the skeleton remains of what had been, in years gone by, the elegant and stylish family carriage, but fully as often into a two-wheeled cart, which now answered all the purposes of the family in its altered circumstances. One would hardly expect to find in such a brute a Goldsmith Maid or a Jay Eye See in locomotion, and so as a matter of fact such a beast was urged on from behind by lusty thwacks from a cudgel, propelling the family at a headlong walk—headlong, because he was likely to go headlong at any moment, from lack of strength, over the rough Virginia roads.

When such a brute got to be pretty lively once more, unless he was concealed, he would soon fall into service again in one of the armies, and possibly another gasping skeleton left in his place; but later in the war all animals abandoned by the Union Army were shot if any life remained in them, so that even this resource was to that extent cut off from the inhabitants, and the family cow, while she was spared, was fitted out for such service.

But the soldiers did not always content themselves with taking eatables and forage. Destruction of the most wanton and inexcusable character was sometimes indulged in. It is charged upon them when the Army entered Fredericksburg in 1862, that they took especial delight in bayonetting mirrors, smashing piano keys with musket butts, pitching crockery out of windows, and destroying other such inoffensive material, which could be of no possible service to either party. If they had been imbibing commissary whiskey, they were all the more unreasonable and outrageous in their destruction. Whenever a man was detected in the enactment of such disgraceful and unsoldierly conduct, he was put under arrest, and sentenced by court martial. But this class of men was an insignificantly small fraction of an army, although seeming very numerous to their victims.

A regularly authorized body of foragers in charge of a commissioned officer never gave way to excesses like those I have mentioned. Their task was usually well defined. It was to go out with wagons in quest of the contents of smoke houses or barns or corn barns; and if a flock of fowls or a few swine chanced to be a part of the livestock of the farms visited, the worse for the livestock and Secessia, and the better for the Union Army. The usual plunder secured by regular foraging parties was hams, bacon sides, flour, sweet potatoes, corn meal, corn on the cob, and sometimes corn shooks as they were called, that is, corn leaves stripped from the stalks, dried and bundled, for winter fodder. The neat cattle in the South get the most of their living in the winter by browsing, there being but little hay cured.

In traversing fresh territory, the army came upon extensive quantities of corn in corn ricks. At Wilcox's Landing on the James River, where we crossed in June, 1864, the Rebel Wilcox, who had a splendid farm on the left bank of the river, had hundreds of bushels of corn, I should judge, which the forage trains took aboard before they crossed over; and on the south side of the James, east from Petersburg, where Northern troops had never before penetrated, many such stores of corn were appropriated to feed the thousands of loyal quadrupeds belonging to Uncle Sam.

In this section, too, and in the territory stretching from the

Wilderness to Cold Harbor, immense quantities of tobacco were found in the various stages of curing. The drying-houses were full of it. These houses were rude structures, having watertight roofs, but with walls built of small logs placed two or three inches apart to admit a free circulation of air. On poles running across the interior hung the stalks of tobacco, root upwards. Then, in other buildings were hogsheads pressed full of the weed in another stage of the curing. It is well known that Petersburg was the center of a very extensive tobacco trade, and in that city were large tobacco factories. But the war put a summary end to this business for the time, by closing Northern markets and blockading Southern ports, so that this article of foreign and domestic commerce accumulated in the hands of the producers to the very great extent found by the Army when it appeared in that vicinity. Every soldier who had a liking for tobacco helped himself as freely as he pleased, with no one caring to stay his hand. But I believe that the experts in smoking and chewing preferred the black navy plug of the sutler, at a dollar and a quarter, to this unprepared but purer article to be had by the taking.

While the Army lay at Warrenton Sulphur Springs, after Gettysburg in '63, a detail of men was made from my company daily to take scythes from the Battery Wagon, and with a six-mule team go off and mow a load of grass wherever they could find it within our lines to eke out the Government forage. The same program was enacted by other batteries in the corps.

As Sherman's Bummers achieved a notoriety as foragers *par excellence*, some facts regarding them will be of interest in this connection. Paragraphs 4 and 6 of Sherman's *Special Field Orders* 120, dated Nov. 9, 1864, just before starting for Savannah, read as follows:

"4. The Army will forage liberally on the country during the march. To this end each brigade commander will organize a good and sufficient foraging party under the command of one or more discreet officers, who will gather, near the route traveled, corn or forage of any kind, meat of any kind, vegetables, corn meal or whatever is needed by the command, aiming at all times to keep in the wagons at least ten days' provisions for his command, and three days' forage. Soldiers must not enter the dwellings of the inhabitants or commit any trespass; but during a halt or camp they may be permitted to gather turnips, potatoes, and other vegetables, and to drive in stock in sight of their camp. To regular foraging parties must be intrusted the gathering of provisions and forage at any distance from the road traveled."

"6. As for horses, mules, wagons, etc., belonging to the inhabitants, the cavalry and artillery may appropriate freely and without limit; discriminating, however, between the rich, who are usually hostile, and the poor and industrious, usually neutral or friendly. Foraging parties may also take mules or horses to replace the jaded animals of their trains or to serve as pack mules for the regiments or brigades. In all foraging of whatever kind the parties engaged will refrain from abusive or threatening language, and may where the officer in command thinks proper give written certificates of the facts, but no receipts; and they will endeavor to leave with each family a reasonable portion for their maintenance."

As Sherman was among the commanders who believed most heartily in having those who provoked the conflict suffer the full measure of their crime, the above instructions seem certainly very mild and humane. On page 182, Vol. II., of his Memoirs, and also on pages 207-8, in a letter to Grant describing the march, he presents a summary of the working of the plan. His brigade foraging parties, usually comprising about fifty men, would set out before daylight, knowing the line of march for the day, and proceeding on foot five or six miles from the column, visit every farm and plantation in range. Their plunder consisted of bacon, meal, turkeys, ducks, chickens, and whatever else was eatable for man or beast. These they would load into the farm wagon or family carriage and rejoin the column, turning over their burden to the brigade commissary. "Often," says Sherman, "would I pass these foraging parties at the roadside, waiting for their wagons to come up and was amused at their strange collections—mules, horses, even cattle packed with old saddles, and loaded with hams, bacon, bags of corn meal, and poultry of every description. . . . No doubt, many acts of pillage, robbery, and violence were committed by these foragers, usually called 'bummers'; for I have since heard of jewelry taken from women, and the plunder of articles that never reached the commissary; but these acts were exceptional and incidental." Sherman further states that his army started with about five thousand head of cattle and arrived at the sea with about ten thousand, and that the State of Georgia must have lost by his operations fifteen thousand first-rate mules. As to horses, he says that every one of the foraging party of fifty who set out daily on foot invariably returned mounted, accompanying the various wagon loads of provisions and forage seized, and as there were forty brigades, an appproximation to the number of horses taken can be made.

But this traveling picnic of the Western armies was unique. There is nothing like it elsewhere in the history of the war. Certainly the Army of the Potomac could not present anything to compare with it. As a matter of fact, there was no other movement in the war whose nature justified such a season of riotous living as this one. But it illustrates in a *wholesale* way the kind of business other armies did on a *retail* scale.

There was no arm of the service that presented such favorable oppertunities for foraging as did the cavalry, and none, I may add, which took so great an advantage of its opportunity. In the first place, being the eyes and the ears of the army, and usually going in advance, cavalrymen skimmed the cream off the country when a general movement was making. Then when it was settled down in camp they were the outposts and never let anything in the line of poultry, bee hives, milk houses, and apple jack (not to enumerate other delicacies which outlying farmhouses afforded) escape the most rigid inspection. Again, they were frequently engaged in raids through the country, from the nature of which they were compelled to live in large measure off Southern products, seized as they went along; but infantry and artillery must needs confine *their* quests for special rations to the homesteads near the line of march. The cavalry not only could and did search these when they led the advance but also made requisitions on all houses in sight of the thoroughfares traveled, even when they were two or three miles away, so that in all probability they ate a smaller quantity of Government rations, man for man, than did any other branch of the land service; but they did not therefore always fare sumptuously, for now and then the cavalry too were in a strait for rations.

Next to the cavalry, the infantry stood the best chance of good living on foraged edibles, as their picket duty took them away some distance from the main lines and often into the neighborhood of farmhouses, from which they would buy or take such additions to their rations as the premises afforded. Then, they went out in reconnoitring parties, or perhaps to do

fatigue duty such as the building of bridges, or the corduroying of roads, which also opened opportunities for them to
enlist a few turkeys or chickens in the Union cause.

Perhaps the most unfortunate natives were those who
chanced to live in a house by the roadside in the direct line
of march of the Army, for from the time the head of the
column struck such a house until the last straggler left it, there
was a continuous stream of officers and men thronging into
and about the premises, all ambitious to buy or beg or take
whatsoever in the line of eatables and drinkables was to be had
by either of these methods. The net result of this was to leave
such families in a starving condition and finally begging rations from the Army. Those families by whose premises both
armies marched were in the depths of distress, for Confederate
soldiers let little in the way of provisions escape their maws on
their line of march, even in Virginia; so that it was not unusual
for such families to meet the Union advance with tearful cyes
and relate the losses which they had sustained and the beggary
to which they had been reduced by the seizure of their last cow
and last ounce of corn meal. Sometimes, no doubt, they de-
ceived to ward off impending search and seizure from a new
quarter, but as a rule the premises showed their statements
to be true.

Sometimes the inhabitants were shrewd and watchful
enough to scent danger and secrete the articles most precious
to them till the danger was past; but not infrequently they
were a little tardy in adopting such a measure and were overhauled just before they had reached cover and despoiled of the
whole or a part of their treasure. The corn fields of these roadside residents were the saddest of spectacles after the army had
passed along in the early fall, for no native-born Southron had
a finer appreciation of the excellent qualities of "roasting ears"
than the average Yankee soldier, who left no stalk unstripped
of its burden. Even the stalks themselves were used to regale
the appetites of the horses and mules.

Volumes might be filled with incidents of foraging. I will
relate one or two that came under my own personal observation.

The people of Maryland undoubtedly enjoyed greater ex-
emption from foragers, as a whole, than did those of Virginia,
for a larger number of the former than of the latter were supposed to be loyal and were therefore protected. I say supposed,

for personally I am of the opinion that the Virginians were fully as loyal as the Marylanders. But a large number of the soldiers when fresh and new in the service saw an enemy in every bush and recognized no white man south of Mason and Dixon's line as other than a "secesh." Very often they were right, but the point I wish to make is that they indulged in foraging to a greater extent probably than troops which had been longer in service. Before my own company had seen any hard service it was located at Poolesville, thirty-eight miles from Washington, where it formed part of an independent brigade which was included in the defences of Washington under the command of General Heintzelman. While we lay there drilling, growling, and feeding on Government rations, a sergeant of the guard imperilled his chevrons by leading off a midnight foraging party, after having first communicated the general countersign to the entire party. On this particular occasion a flock of sheep was the subject of the expedition. These sheep had been looked upon with longing eyes many times by the men as they rode their horses to water by their pasture, which was perhaps half a mile or more from camp.

As soon as the foragers came upon them in the darkness, the sheep cantered away, and their adversaries, who could only see them when near them, followed in full pursuit. As the chase up and down the enclosure (which was not a very large one) waxed warm, one of the party more noted for his zeal than his discretion drew a revolver and emptied nearly every barrel among the flock, doing no bodily injury to the sheep, however, but he *did* succeed in calling down upon his head the imprecations of the sergeant for his lack of good sense, and with reason, for in a few minutes the fire of the outer pickets was drawn. This being heard and reported in camp, the long-roll was sounded, calling into line the two regiments of infantry that lay near us and causing every preparation to be made to resist the supposed attack. The foragers, meanwhile, skulked back to camp by the shortest route, bringing with them two sheep that had been run down by some of the fleeter of the party But no one save an interested few, inside or outside of the company, ever knew, until the story was told at a reunion of the company in '79 or '80, the cause of all the tumult in camp that dark winter's night.

On another occasion a party of five or six men stole out of camp at midnight in quest of poultry. They knew of a farmhouse where poultry was kept, but to ascertain its exact where-abouts at night was no easy task. On looking around the premises they found that there was no isolated outbuilding, whereupon they at once decided that the ell to the main house must be the place which contained the "biddies"; but to enter that might rouse the farmer and his family, which they did not care to do. However, a council of war decided to take the risk and storm the place. Investigation showed the door to be padlocked, but a piece of iron which lay conveniently on a win-dowsill served to pull out the staple, and the door was open. Meanwhile, guards had been posted at the corners of the house, with drawn revolvers (which they would not have dared to fire), and the captures began. One man entered the ell, and lighting a match discovered that he had called at the right house and that the feathered family were at home. Among them he caught a glimpse of two turkeys, and these, with four fowls taken one at a time by the neck to control their noise, were passed to another man standing at the door with a penknife, who, having performed a successful surgical operation on each, gave them to a third party to put in a bag.

Back of our camp stood the house of a secessionist (at least, Black Mary, his colored servant, said he was one) and in his kitchen and cookstove for the sum of twenty-five cents in scrip, having previously dressed and stuffed them, Mary cooked the turkeys most royally, and one commissioned officer of our company, at least, sat down to one of the feasts, bliss-fully ignorant, of course, as to the source from which the special ration was drawn.

Bee hives were among the most popular products of foraging, The soldiers tramped many a mile by night in quest of these depositories of sweets. I recall an incident occurring in the Tenth Vermont Regiment—once brigaded with my company —when some of the foragers who had been out on a tramp brought a hive of bees into camp, after the men had wrapped themselves in their blankets, and by way of a joke set it down stealthily on the stomach of the captain of one of the com-panies, making business quite lively in that neighborhood shortly afterwards.

Foragers took other risks than that of punishment for ab-sence from camp or the column without leave. They were not infrequently murdered on these expeditions. On the 7th of December, 1864, Warren's Fifth Corps was started southward from Petersburg to destroy the Weldon Railroad still further. On their return they found some of their men, who had straggled and foraged, lying by the roadside murdered, their bodies stark naked and shockingly mutilated. One of Sherman's men afterwards told how in the Carolinas one of his comrades was found hanged on a tree, bearing this inscription: "Death to all foragers." A large number of men were made prisoners while away from their commands after the usual fruits of foraging—just how many no one will ever know; and many of those not killed on the spot by their captors ended their lives in the prison pens.

During the expedition of the Fifth Corps alluded to, while the column had halted at some point in its march, a few uneasy spirits wishing for something eatable to turn up had made off down a hill ahead of the column, had crossed a stream, and reached the vicinity of a house on the high ground the other side. Here a keen-scented cavalryman from the party had started up two turkeys, which as the pursuit grew close flew up on to the top of the smokehouse, whence, followed by their relentless pursuer, they went still higher to the ridgepole of the main house adjoining. Still up and forward pressed the trooper, his "soul in arms and eager for the fray," and as the turkeys with fluttering wings edged away, the hungry veteran, now astride the ridgepole, hopped along after, when *ping!* a bullet whistled by uncomfortably near him.

"What in thunder are you about!" blurted the cavalryman, suspecting his comrades of attempting to shoot his quarry in the moment of victory.

Receiving no satisfactory response from his innocent companions, who had stood interested spectators of his exploit, yet unconscious of what he was exclaiming at, he once more addressed himself to the pursuit when, chuck! a bullet struck a shingle by his leg and threw the splinters in his face. There was no mistaking the mark or the marksman this time, and our trooper suddenly lost all relish for turkey, and standing not on the order of his going, came sliding and tumbling down off the roof, striking the ground with too much emphasis and a great deal of feeling, where joined by his comrades, who by this time had taken in the situation, he beat a hasty retreat, followed by the jeers of the Johnnies, and rejoined the column.

A veteran of the Seventh New Hampshire tells of one Charley Swain who was not only an excellent duty soldier but a champion forager. While this regiment lay at St. Augustine, Fla., in 1863, Swain started out on one of his quests for game, and although it had grown rather scarce, at last found two small pigs penned up in the suburbs of the town. His resolve was immediately made to take them into camp. Securing a barrel, he laid it down, open at one end, in a corner of the pen and without commotion soon had both grunters inside the barrel and the barrel standing on end. By hard tugging he lifted it clear of the pen, and taking it on his back started rapidly for camp. But his passengers were not long reconciled to such quick and close transit, for he had not proceeded far before grunts developed into squeals, squeals into internal dissensions, to which the bottom of the barrel at last succumbed, and a brace of pigs were coursing at liberty. Here was a poser for the spoilsman. If he caught them again, how should he carry them? While he was attempting to solve this problem the cavalry patrol hove in sight, and Swain made for camp, where crestfallen and chagrined, he related how he had left to the greedy maws of the provost guard the quarry which he had hoped to share with his mess that night.

In considering this question of foraging, it has not been my purpose to put the soldiers of the Union Armies in an unfair or unfavorable position as compared with their opponents. It has been claimed that Southerners on Northern soil were more vindictive and wanton than Northerners on Southern soil; and the reason on which this statement is based is that the South hated the Yankees, but the North hated only slavery. Nor is it my intention to charge atrocities upon the best men of either army. They were committed by the few. And I do not wish to be understood as declaring foraging a black and atrocious act, for as I have shown, it had a legal warrant. I only claim that when the order once goes forth it leads to excesses, which it is difficult to control, and such excesses are likely to seriously affect the unoffending, defenceless women and children with woes out of all proportion with their simple part in bringing on the strife. But so it always has been, and so it probably always will be, till wars and rumors of wars shall cease.

12

Corps and Corps Badges

W hat was an army corps? The name is one adopted into the English language from the French and retains essentially its original meaning. It has been customary since the time of Napoleon I to organize armies of more than fifty or sixty thousand men into what the French call *corps d'armée* or, as we say, army corps. . . .

Bull Run, while comparatively disastrous as a battlefield, was a grand success to the North in other respects. It sobered, for a time at least, the hasty reckless spirits who believed that the South would not fight. . . .

General George B. McClellan took command of the forces in and around Washington on July 27, 1861, a command which then numbered about 50,000 infantry, 1,000 cavalry and 650 artillerymen, with nine field batteries, such as they were, of thirty guns. In organizing the Army of the Potomac McClellan first arranged the infantry in brigades of four regiments each. Then, as fast as new regiments arrived—and at that time, under a recent call of the President for 500,000 three-years' volunteers, they were coming in very rapidly—they were formed into temporary brigades and placed in camp in the suburbs of the city to await their full equipment, which many of them lacked, to become more efficient in the tactics of "Scott" or "Hardee," [training manuals] and in general to acquire such discipline as would be valuable in the service before them as soldiers of the Union. As rapidly as these conditions were fairly complied with, regiments were permanently assigned to brigades across the Potomac.

After this formation of brigades had made considerable headway, and the troops were becoming better disciplined and tolerably skilled in brigade movements, McClellan began the organization of Divisions, each comprising three brigades. Before the middle of October, 1861, eleven of these divisions had

178

been organized, each including, besides the brigades of infantry specified, from one to four light batteries, and from a company to two regiments of cavalry which had been specially assigned to it.

The next step in the direction of organization was the formation of Army Corps; but in this matter McClellan moved slowly, not deeming it best to form them until his division commanders had, by experience in the field, shown which of them, if any, had the ability to handle so large a body of troops as a corps. This certainly seemed good judgment. The Confederate authorities appear to have been governed by this principle, for they did not adopt the system of army corps until after the battle of Antietam, in September, 1862. But months had elapsed since Bull Run; 1862 had dawned. "All quiet along the Potomac" had come to be used as a byword and reproach. That powerful moving force, Public Sentiment, was . . . making itself felt. . . . President Lincoln, goaded to desperation by its persistence and insistence, issued a War Order [dated] March 8, 1862, *requiring* McClellan to organize his command into five Army Corps. So far, well enough; but the order went further and specified who the corps commanders should be, thus depriving him of doing that for which he had waited, and giving him officers in those positions not, in his opinion, the best in all respects that could have been selected.

But my story is not of the commanders, nor of McClellan, but of the corps, and what I have said will show how they were composed. Let us review for a moment: first, the *regiments*, each of which, when full, contained 1,046 men; *four* of these composed a *brigade; three brigades* were taken to form a *division,* and *three divisions* constituted a *corps.* This system was not always rigidly adhered to. Sometimes a corps had a *fourth* division, but such a case would be a deviation, and not the regular plan. So, too, a division might have an extra brigade. For example, a brigade might be detached from one part of the service and sent to join an army in another part. Such a brigade would not be allowed to remain independent in that case, but would be at once assigned to some division, usually a division whose brigades were small in numbers.

I have said that McClellan made up his brigades of four regiments. I think the usual number of regiments for a brigade is three. That gives a system of three throughout. But in this matter also, after the first organization, the plan was modified.

As a brigade became depleted by sickness, capture, and the bullet, new regiments were added, until, as the work of addition and depletion went on, I have known a brigade to have within it the skeletons of ten regiments, and even then its strength [was] not half that of the original body. My camp was located at one time near a regiment which had only *thirty-eight men present for duty*.

There were twenty-five army corps in the service at different times, exclusive of cavalry, engineer, and signal corps, and Hancock's veteran corps. The same causes which operated to reduce brigades and divisions naturally decimated corps, so that some of them consolidated; as, for example, the First and Third Corps were merged in the Second, Fifth, and Sixth, in the spring of 1864. At about the same time the Eleventh and Twelfth were united to form the Twentieth. But enough of corps for the present. What I have stated will make more intelligible what I shall say about corps badges.

What are corps badges? The answer to this question is somewhat lengthy, but I think it will be considered interesting. The idea of corps badges undoubtedly had its origin with General Philip Kearny, but just *how* or exactly *when* is somewhat legendary and uncertain. Not having become a member of Kearny's old corps until about a year after the idea was promulgated, I have no tradition of my own in regard to it, but I have heard men who served under him tell widely differing stories of the origin of the "Kearny Patch," yet all agreeing as to the author of the idea, and also in its application being made first to officers. General E. D. Townsend, former Adjutant-General of the United States Army, in his *Anecdotes of the Civil War*, has adopted an explanation which, I have no doubt, is substantially correct. He says:

"One day, when his brigade was on the march, General Philip Kearny, who was a strict disciplinarian, saw some officers standing under a tree by the roadside; supposing them to be stragglers from his command, he administered to them a rebuke, emphasized by a few expletives. The officers listened in silence, respectfully standing in the 'position of a soldier' until he had finished, when one of them, raising his hand to his cap, quietly suggested that the general had possibly made a mistake as they none of them belonged to his command. With his usual courtesy, Kearny exclaimed, 'Pardon me; I will take steps to know how to recognize my own men hereafter.' Immediately on reaching camp, he issued orders that all officers and men of his brigade should wear conspicuously on the front of their caps a round piece of red cloth to designate them. This became generally known as the 'Kearny Patch.' "

I think General Townsend is incorrect in saying that Kearny issued orders immediately on reaching camp for all "officers and men" to wear the patch; first, because the testimony of officers of the old Third Corps implies that the order was first directed to officers only, and this would be in harmony with the explanation which I have quoted; and, second, after the death of Kearny and while his old division was lying at Fort Lyon, Va., Sept. 4, 1862, General D. B. Birney, then in command of it, issued a general order announcing his death, which closed with the following paragraph:

"As a token of respect for his memory, all the officers of this division will wear crepe on the left arm for thirty days, and the colors and drums of regiments and batteries will be placed in mourning for sixty days. To still further show our regard, and to distinguish his ·officers as he wished, each officer will continue to wear on his cap a piece of scarlet cloth, or have the top or crown-piece of the cap made of scarlet cloth."

The italics in the above extract are my own; but we may fairly infer from it:

First, that up to this date the patch had been required for officers alone, as no mention is made of the rank and file in this order.

Second, that General Kearny did not specify the lozenge as the shape of the badge to be worn, as some claim; for, had such been the case, so punctilious a man as General Birney would not have referred in general orders to a lozenge as "a piece of scarlet cloth," nor have given the option of having the crown-piece of the cap made of scarlet cloth if the lamented Kearny's instructions had originally been to wear a lozenge. This being so, General Townsend's quoted description of the badge as "a round piece of red cloth" is probably erroneous.

As there were no red goods at hand when Kearny initiated this move, he is said to have given up his own red blanket to be cut into these patches.

Soon after these emblems came into vogue among the officers there is strong traditional testimony to show that the men of the rank and file, without general orders, of their own accord cut pieces of red from their overcoat linings, or obtained them from other sources to make patches for themselves; and as to the shape, there are weighty reasons for believing that any piece of red fabric of whatsoever shape was considered to answer the purpose. These red patches took immensely with the boys. Kearny was a rough soldier in speech, but a perfect daredevil in action, and his men idolized him. Hence they were only too proud to wear a mark which should distinguish them as members of his gallant division. It was said to have greatly reduced the straggling in this body, and also to have secured for wounded or dead that fell into the Rebels' hands a more favorable and considerate attention.

There was a special reason, I think, why Kearny should select a red patch for his men, although I have never seen it referred to. On the 24th of March, 1862, General McClellan issued a general order prescribing the kinds of flags that should designate corps, division, and brigade headquarters. In this he directed that the First Division flag should be a red one, six feet by five; the Second Division blue, and the Third Division a red and blue one—both of the same dimensions as the first. As Kearny commanded the First Division, he would naturally select the same color of patch as his flag. Hence the red patch.

The contagion to wear a distinguishing badge extended widely from this simple beginning. It was the most natural thing that could happen for other divisions to be jealous of any innovation which, by comparison, should throw them into the background, for by that time the esprit de corps, the pride of organization, had begun to make itself felt. Realizing this fact, and regarding it as a manifestation that might be turned to good account, Major-General Joseph Hooker promulgated a scheme of army corps badges on the 21st of March, 1863, which was the first systematic plan submitted in this direction in the armies. Hooker took command of the Army of the Potomac Jan. 26, 1863. General Daniel Butterfield was made his chief-of-staff, and he, it is said, had much to do with designing and perfecting the first scheme of badges for the Army, which appears in the following circular:

Headquarters Army of the Potomac
Circular   March 21, 1863

For the purpose of ready recognition of corps and divisions of the army, and to prevent injustice by reports of straggling and misconduct through mistake as to their organizations, the chief quartermaster will

furnish without delay the following badges, to be worn by the officers
and enlisted men of all the regiments of the various corps mentioned.
They will be securely fastened upon the center of the cap. The inspecting officers will at all inspections see that these badges are worn
as designated.

First Corps—a sphere: red for First Division; white for Second;
blue for Third.

Second Corps—a trefoil: red for First Division; white for Second;
blue for Third.

Third Corps—a lozenge: red for First Division; white for Second;
blue for Third.

Fifth Corps—a Maltese cross: red for First Division; white for
Second; blue for Third.

Sixth Corps—a cross: red for First Division; white for Second;
blue for Third. (Light Division, green.)

Eleventh Corps—a crescent: red for First Division; white for
Second; blue for Third.

Twelfth Corps—a star: red for First Division; white for Second;
blue for Third.

The sizes and colors will be according to pattern.

By command of
MAJOR-GENERAL HOOKER
S. WILLIAMS, A.A.G.

Accompanying this order were paper patterns pasted on a
flyleaf, illustrating the size and color required. Diligent inquiry
and research in the departments at Washington fail to discover
any of the patterns referred to, or their dimensions; but there
were several veterans who preserved the first badge issued
to them in pursuance of this circular, from which it is inferred
that the patterns were of a size to please the eye rather than to
conform to any uniform scale of measurement. A trefoil which
I have measured is about an inch and seven-eighths each way.
It is a copy of an original. The stem is straight, turning neither
to the right nor left.

The arms of the Fifth Corps badge are often figured as concave, whereas those of a Maltese Cross are straight. This was believed to be a deviation from the original in the minds of many
veterans who wore them.

The Sixth Corps wore a St. Andrew's Cross till 1864, when
it changed to the Greek Cross.

That this circular of Hooker's was not intended to be a dead
letter was shown in an order issued from Falmouth, Va., May
12, 1863, in which he says: "The badges worn by the troops

when lost or torn off must be immediately replaced."

And then, after designating the only troops that are without badges, he adds: "Provost-marshals will arrest as stragglers all other troops found without badges, and return them to their commands under guard."

There was a badge worn by the artillery brigade of the Third Corps, which, so far as I know, had no counterpart in other corps. I think it was not adopted until after Gettysburg. It was the lozenge of the corps subdivided into four smaller lozenges, on the following basis: If a battery was attached to the first division, two of these smaller lozenges were red, one white, and one blue; if to the second, two were white, one red, and one blue; and if to the third, two were blue, one red, and one white. They were worn on the left side of the cap.

The original Fourth Corps, organized by McClellan, did not adopt a badge, but its successor of the same number wore an equilateral triangle prescribed by Major-General Thomas, April 26, 1864, in General Orders No. 62, Department of the Cumberland, in which he used much the same language as that used by Hooker in his circular, and designated divisions by the same colors.

The badge of the Seventh Corps was a crescent nearly encircling a star. It was not adopted until after the virtual close of the war, June 1, 1865. The following is a paragraph from the circular issued by Major-General J. J. Reynolds, Department of Arkansas, regarding it:

"This badge, cut two inches in diameter, from cloth of colors red, white and blue, for the 1st, 2d, and 3d Divisions respectively, may be worn by all enlisted men of the Corps."

This was an entirely different corps from the Seventh Corps, which served in Virginia, and which had no badge. The latter was discontinued Aug. 1, 1863, at the same time with the origiginal Fourth Corps.

The Eighth Corps wore a six-pointed star. I have not been able to ascertain the date of its adoption. There was no order issued.

The Ninth Corps was originally a part of the Army of the Potomac, but at the time Hooker issued his circular it was in another part of the Confederacy. Just before its return to the Army, General Burnside issued General Orders No. 6, April 10, 1864, announcing as the badge of his corps: "A shield with the figure nine in the center crossed with a foul anchor and

cannon, to be worn on the top of the cap or front of the hat."
This corps had a fourth division, whose badge was green. The
corps commander and his staff wore a badge "of red, white, and
blue, with gilt anchor, cannon, and green number."

December 23, 1864, Major-General John G. Parke, who
had succeeded to the command, issued General Orders No. 49,
of which the following is the first section:

"1. All officers and enlisted men in this command will be
required to wear the Corps Badge upon the cap or hat. For the
Divisions, the badges will be plain, made of cloth in the shape
of a shield—red for the first, white for the second, and blue for
the third. For the Artillery Brigade, the shield will be red, and
will be worn under the regulation cross cannon."

This order grew out of the difficulty experienced in obtaining the badge prescribed by General Burnside. The cannon,
anchor, etc., were made of gold bullion at Tiffany's, New York
City, and as it was scarcely practicable for the rank and file to
obtain such badges, they had virtually anticipated the order of
General Parke and were wearing the three plain colors after the
manner of the rest of Potomac's army. . . .

The Tenth Corps badge was the trace of a four-bastioned
fort. It was adopted by General Orders No. 18 issued by Major-General D. B. Birney, July 25, 1864.

The Eleventh and Twelfth Corps have already been referred
to, in General Hooker's circular. On the 18th of April, 1864,
these two corps were consolidated to form the Twentieth
Corps, and by General Orders No. 62 issued by Major-General
George H. Thomas, April 26, "a star, as heretofore worn by the
Twelfth Corps," was prescribed as the badge.

At this point it should be stated that many of the corps
combined the two badges in order not to lose their original
identity.

The Thirteenth Corps had no badge.

The badge of the Fourteenth Army Corps was an acorn.
Tradition has it that some time before the adoption of this
badge the members of this corps called themselves *Acorn Boys*,
because at one time in their history, probably when they were
hemmed in at Chattanooga by Bragg, rations were so scanty
that the men gladly gathered large quantities of acorns from an
oak grove, nearby which they were camped, and roasted and
ate them, repeating this operation while the scarcity of food
continued. Owing to this circumstance, when it became neces-

sary to select a badge, the acorn suggested itself as an exceedingly appropriate emblem for that purpose, and it was therefore adopted by General Orders No. 62, issued from Headquarters Department of the Cumberland, at Chattanooga, April 26, 1864.

The badge of the Fifteenth Corps derives its origin from the following incident: During the fall of 1863 the Eleventh and Twelfth Corps were taken from Meade's army, put under the command of General Joe Hooker and sent to aid in the relief of Chattanooga, where Thomas was closely besieged. They were undoubtedly better dressed than the soldiers of that department, and this fact, with the added circumstance of their wearing corps badges, which were a novelty to the Western armies at that time, led to some sharp tilts between the Eastern and Western soldiers. One day a veteran of Hooker's command met an Irishman of Logan's Corps at the spring where they went to fill their canteens. "What corps do you belong to?" said the Eastern veteran, proud in the possession of the distinguishing badge on his cap, which told his story for him. "What corps, is it?" said the gallant son of Erin, straightening his back; "the Fifteenth, to be sure." "Where is your badge?" "My badge, do ye say? There it is!" said Pat, clapping his hand on his cartridge box at his side; "forty rounds. Can you show me a betther?"

On the 14th of February, 1865, Major-General John A. Logan, the commander of this corps, issued General Orders No. 10, which prescribe that the badge shall be "A miniature cartridge box, one-eighth of an inch thick, fifteen-sixteenths of an inch wide, set transversely on a field of cloth or metal, one and five-eighths of an inch square. Above the cartridge box plate will be stamped or worked in a curve 'Forty Rounds.'" This corps had a fourth division, whose badge was yellow, and headquarters wore a badge including the four colors. Logan continues:

"It is expected that this badge will be worn constantly by every officer and soldier in the corps. If any corps in the Army has a right to take pride in its badge, surely that has which looks back through the long and glorious line of . . . [naming twenty-nine different battles], and scores of minor struggles; the corps which had its birth under Grant and Sherman in the darker days of our struggle, the corps which will keep on struggling until the death of the Rebellion."

The following correct description of the badge worn by the

Sixteenth Army Corps is given by the assistant-inspector general of that corps, Colonel J. J. Lyon: "The device is a circle with four Minie balls, the points towards the center, cut out of it." It was designed by Brevet Brigadier-General John Hough, the assistant adjutant-general of the corps, being selected out of many designs, submitted by Major-General A. J. Smith, the corps commander, and, in his honor, named the "A. J. Smith Cross." It is easily distinguished from the Maltese Cross in being bounded by curved instead of straight lines. No order for its adoption was issued.

The badge of the Seventeenth Corps, said to have been suggested by General M. F. Ford, and adopted in accordance with General Orders issued by his commander, Major-General Francis P. Blair, was an arrow. He says, "In its swiftness, in its surety of striking where wanted, and its destructive powers, when so intended, it is probably as emblematical of this corps as any design that could be adopted." The order was issued at Goldsboro, N. C., March 25, 1865. The order further provides that the arrow for divisions shall be two inches long, and for corps headquarters one and one-half inches long, and further requires the wagons and ambulances to be marked with the badge of their respective commands, the arrow being twelve inches long.

A circular issued from the headquarters of the Eighteenth Army Corps June 7, 1864, and General Orders No. 108, from the same source, dated August 25, 1864, furnish all the information on record regarding the badge of this body. While both are quite lengthy in description and prescription, neither states what the special design was to be. It was, however, a cross with equi-foliate arms. The circular prescribed that this cross should be worn by general officers, suspended by a tri-colored ribbon from the left breast. Division commanders were to have a triangle in the center of the badge, but brigade commanders were to have the number of their brigade instead; line officers were to suspend their badges by ribbons of the color of their division; cavalry and artillery officers also were to have distinctive badges. The whole system was quite complex, and somewhat expensive as well, as the badges were to be of metal and enamel in colors. Enlisted men were to wear the plain cross of cloth sewed to their left breast. This order was issued by General W. F. Smith.

General Orders 108, issued by General E. O. C. Ord, simplified the matter somewhat, requiring line officers and enlisted men both to wear the plain cross the color of their respective divisions, and enlisted men were required to wear theirs on the front of the hat or top of the cap.

By General Orders No. 11 issued by General Emory Nov. 17, 1864, the Nineteenth Corps adopted "a fan-leaved cross, with an octagonal center." The First Division was to wear red, the Second blue, and the Third white—the exception in the order of the colors which proved the rule. The badge of enlisted men was to be cloth, two inches square, and worn on the side of the hat or top of the cap, although they were allowed to supply themselves with metallic badges of the prescribed color, if so minded. The Twentieth Corps adopted a white star. The Twenty-First Corps never adopted a badge.

The Twenty-Second adopted (without orders) a badge quinquefarious in form, that is, opening into five parts, and having a circle in the center. This was the corps which served in the defence of Washington. Its membership was constantly changing.

The badge adopted by the Twenty-Third Corps (without General Orders) was a plain shield, differing somewhat in form from that of the Ninth Corps, with which it was for a time associated, and which led it to adopt a similar badge.

The following General Order tells the story of the next Corps' badge:

> Headquarters Twenty-Fourth Army Corps
> Before Richmond, Va., March 18, 1865
> [General Orders No. 32]
>
> By authority of the Major-General commanding the Army of the James the HEART is adopted as the badge of the Twenty-Fourth Army Corps.
> The symbol selected is one which testifies our affectionate regard for all our brave comrades—alike the living and the dead—who have braved the perils of the mighty conflict, and our devotion to the sacred cause—a cause which entitles us to the sympathy of every brave and true heart and the support of every strong and determined hand.
> The Major-General commanding the Corps does not doubt that soldiers who have given their strength and blood to the fame of their former badges, will unite in rendering the present one even more renowned than those under which they have heretofore marched to battle.
>
> By command of
> Major-General JOHN GIBBON
> A. HENRY EMBLER, A.A.A. General

This corps was largely made up of re-enlisted men, who had served nine months or three years elsewhere. Here is another General Order which speaks for itself:

Headquarters Twenty-Fifth Army Corps
Army of the James
In the Field, Va., Feb. 20, 1865
[Orders]

In view of the circumstances under which this Corps was raised and filled, the peculiar claims of its individual members upon the justice and fair dealing of the prejudiced, and the regularity of the troops which deserve those equal rights that have been hitherto denied the majority, the Commanding General has been induced to adopt the Square as the distinctive badge of the Twenty-Fifth Army Corps.

Wherever danger has been found and glory to be won, the heroes who have fought for immortality have been distinguished by some emblem to which every victory added a new luster. They looked upon their badge with pride, for to it they had given its fame. In the homes of smiling peace it recalled the days of courageous endurance and the hours of deadly strife—and it solaced the moment of death, for it was a symbol of a life of heroism and self-denial. The poets still sing of the Templar's Cross, the Crescent of the Turks, the Chalice of the hunted Christian, and the White Plume of Murat that crested the wave of valor sweeping resistlessly to victory.

Soldiers! to you is given a chance in this spring campaign of making this badge immortal. Let history record that on the banks of the James thirty thousand freemen not only gained their own liberty but shattered the prejudice of the world and gave to the land of their birth peace, union, and liberty,

GODFREY WEITZEL
Major-General Commanding

[Official]
W. L. GOODRICH
A.A.A. General

This corps was composed wholly of colored troops.

In the late, fall of 1864, Major-General W. S. Hancock resigned his command of the Second Corps to take charge of the First Veteran Corps,* then organizing. The badge adopted

---

* First established in April, 1863 as the Invalid Corps; name changed to Veterans Reserve Corps in March, 1864. It consisted of men who had recovered from wounds or sickness enough to do non-combat duty. [Ed.]

originated with Colonel C. H. Morgan, Hancock's chief-of-staff.

The center is a circle half the diameter of the whole design, surrounded by a wreath of laurel. Through the circle a wide red band passes vertically. From the wreath radiate rays in such a manner as to form a heptagon with concave sides. Seven hands spring from the wreath, each grasping a spear, whose heads point the several angles of the heptagon.

Sheridan's Cavalry Corps had a badge, but it was not generally worn. The device was "Gold crossed sabers on a blue field, surrounded by a glory in silver."

The design of Wilson's Cavalry Corps was a carbine from which was suspended by chains a red, swallow-tail guidon, bearing gilt crossed sabers.

The badge of the Engineer and Pontonnier Corps is thus described: "Two oars crossed over an anchor, the top of which is encircled by a scroll surmounted by a castle; the castle being the badge of the U.S. Corps of Engineers." As a fact, however, this fine body of men wore only the castle designed in brass.

The badge of the Signal Corps was two flags crossed on the staff of a flaming torch. This badge is sometimes represented with a red star in the center of one flag, but such was not the typical badge. This star was allowed on the headquarters flag of a very few signal officers, who were accorded this distinction for some meritorious service performed; but such a flag was rarely seen and should not be figured as part of the corps badge.

The Department of West Virginia, under the command of General Crook, adopted a spread eagle for a badge, Jan. 3, 1865.

The Pioneers of the Army [road clearers and axemen] wore a pair of crossed hatchets, the color of the division to which they belonged. Then, the Army of the Cumberland have a society badge. So likewise have the Army of the Potomac. There are also medals presented for distinguished gallantry. They are not numerous and are seldom to be seen—for this reason, if for no other, they are of precious value to the owner and are therefore carefully treasured.

In nearly every corps whose badge I have referred to, the plan was adopted of having the first three divisions take the national colors of red, white, and blue respectively. These corps emblems were not only worn by the men—I refer now to the Army of the Potomac—but they were also painted with stencil on . . . wagons and ambulances. And just here I may add that there was no army which became so devotedly attached to its badges as did the Army of the Potomac. There were reasons for this. They were the first to adopt them, being at least a year ahead of *all* other corps, and more than two years ahead of many. Then, by their use they were brought into sharper comparison in action and on the march, and, as General Weitzel says, "they looked upon their badge with pride, for to it they had given its fame."

13

Some Inventions and Devices
of the War

That "necessity is the mother of invention" nothing can more clearly and fully demonstrate than war. I will devote this chapter to presenting some facts which illustrate this maxim. . . .

A demand was at once made on both sides of Mason and Dixon's line for a new class of materials—the materials of war, for which there had been no demand of consequence for nearly fifty years. . . .

The few muskets remaining in the hands of the Government in 1861 were to equip the troops who left first for the seat of war. Then manufacturing began on an immense scale. The Government workshops could not produce a tithe of what were wanted, even though running night and day; and so private enterprise was called in to supplement the need. As one illustration, Grover & Baker of Roxbury turned their extensive sewing-machine workshop into a rifle manufactory, which employed several hundred hands, and this was only one of a large number in that section. Alger of South Boston poured the immense molten masses of his cupolas into the moulds of cannon, and his massive steam hammers pounded out and welded the ponderous shafts of gunboats and monitors. The descendants of Paul Revere diverted a part of their yellow metal [brass] from the mills which rolled it into sheathing for Government ships, to the founding of brass twelve-pounders or Napoleons, as they were called; and many a Rebel was laid low by shrapnel or canister hurled through the muzzle of guns on which was plainly stamped "Revere Copper Co., Canton, Mass." Plain smoothbore Springfield muskets soon became Springfield rifles, and directly the process of rifling was applied to cannon of various calibers. Then, muzzle-loading rifles became breech-loading; and from a breech-loader for a single cartridge the capacity was increased until some of the cavalry regiments that took the field in 1864 went equipped with Henry's sixteen-shooters, a breech-loading rifle which the Rebels said the Yanks loaded in the morning and fired all day.

Later I met at Chattanooga, Tenn., Captain Fort, of the old First Georgia Regulars, a Confederate regiment of distinguished service. In referring to these repeating rifles, he said that his first encounter with them was near Olustee, Fla. While he was skirmishing with a Massachusetts regiment (the Fortieth), he found them hard to move, as they seemed to load with marvellous speed, and never to have their fire drawn. Determined to see what sort of firearms were opposed to him, he ordered his men to concentrate their fire on a single skirmisher. They did so and laid him low and afterwards secured his repeating rifle—I think a Spencer's seven-shooter—which they carried along as a great curiosity for some time afterward.

In the Navy invention made equally rapid strides. When the war broke out, the available vessels were mainly a few ships-of-the-line, frigates, and screw-steamers; but these could be of little service in such a warfare as was evidently on hand, a warfare which must be carried on in rivers and bays, and coastwise generally, where such clumsy and deep-draft vessels could not be used. So sloops-of-war, gunboats, mortar-boats, double-enders, and ironclads came to the front, and the larger old-fashioned craft were used mainly as receiving ships. But with the increase in range and caliber of naval armament came a seeking by invention for something less vulnerable to their power, and after the encounter of the little Yankee Cheese Box, so called, and the Rebel Ram *Virginia*, the question of what should constitute the main reliance of the Navy was definitely settled, and monitors became the idols of the hour. . . .

I wish now to give it still further emphasis by citing some illustrations which the historian has neglected. Some of the inventions which I shall refer to were impractical and had only a brief existence. Of course your small inventor and would-be benefactor to his kind clearly foresaw that men who were about to cut loose from the amenities of civil life would be likely to spend money freely in providing themselves before their departure with everything portable that might have a tendency to ameliorate the condition of soldier life. With an eye single to this idea these inventors took the field.

One of the first products of their genius which I recall was a combination *knife-fork-and-spoon* arrangement, which was peddled through the state camping-grounds in great numbers and variety. Of course every man must have one. So much convenience in so small a compass must be taken advantage of. It was a sort of soldier's trinity, which they all thought that they understood and appreciated. But I doubt whether this invention, on the average, ever got beyond the first camp in active service.

I still have in my possession the remnants of a *water-filterer* in which I invested after enlistment. There was a metallic mouth-piece at one end of a small gutta-percha tube, which latter was about fifteen inches long. At the other end of the tube was a suction-chamber, an inch long by a half-inch in diameter, with the end perforated and containing a piece of bocking as a filter. Midway of the tubing was an air chamber. The tubing long since dried and crumbled away from the metal. It is possible that I used this instrument half a dozen times, though I do not recall a single instance, and on breaking camp just before the Gettysburg Campaign, I sent it, with some other effects, northward.

I remember another filterer, somewhat simpler. It consisted of the same kind of mouthpiece with rubber tubing attached to a small conical piece of pumice stone, through which the water was filtered. Neither of these was ever of any practical value.

I have spoken of the rapid improvements made in arms. This improvement extended to all classes of firearms alike. Revolvers were no exception, and *Colt's* revolver, which monopolized the field for some time, was soon crowded in the race by *Smith and Wesson, Remington,* and others. Thousands of them were sold monthly, and the newly fledged soldier who did not possess a revolver, either by his own purchase, or as a present from solicitous relatives, or admiring friends, or enthusiastic business associates, was something of a curiosity. Of course a present of this kind necessitated an outfit of special ammunition, and such was at once procured. But the personal armory of many heroes was not even then complete, and a dirk knife—a real "Arkansaw toothpick"—was no unusual sight to be seen hanging from the belt of some of the incipient but blood-thirsty warriors. The little town of Ashby in Massachusetts, at one of its earliest war meetings, voted "that each volunteer shall be provided with a revolver, a bowie-knife, and a Bible, and shall also receive ten dollars in money." The thought did not appear to find lodgement in the brain of the average soldier or his friends that by the time the Government had provided him with what arms, ammunition, and equipments it was thought necessary for him to have, he would then be loaded with about all he could bear without adding a personal armory and magazine. Nor did he realize that which afterwards in his experience must have come upon him with convincing force, that by the time he had done his duty faithfully and well with the arms which the Government had placed in his hands there would be little opportunity or need, even if his ambition still held out, to fall back on his personal arsenal for further supplies. Members of the later regiments got their eyes open to this fact either through correspondence with men at the front, or by having been associated with others who had seen service. But the troops of '61 and '62 took out hundreds of revolvers only to lose them, give them away, or throw them away; and as many regiments were forbidden by their colonels to wear them, a large number were sent back to the North. Revolvers were probably cheaper in Virginia in those years than in any other state in the Union.

There was another invention that must have been sufficiently popular to have paid the manufacturer a fair rate on his investment, and that was the steel-armor enterprise. There were a good many men who were anxious to be heroes, but they were particular. They preferred to be live heroes. They were willing to go to war and fight as never man fought before, if they could only be insured against bodily harm. They were not willing to assume all the risks which an enlistment involved without securing something in the shape of a drawback. Well, the iron tailors saw and appreciated the situation and sufferings of this class of men and came to the rescue with a vest of steel armor, worth, as I remember it, about a dozen dollars. Greaves I think, did not find so ready a market as the vests, which were comparatively common. These iron-clad warriors admitted that when panoplied for the fight their sensations were much as they might be if they were dressed up in an old-fashioned air-tight stove; still with all the discomforts of this casing, they felt a little safer with it on than off in battle, and reasoned that it was the right and duty of every man to adopt all honorable measures to assure his safety in the line of duty.

This seemed solid reasoning, surely; but, in spite of it all, a large
number of these vests never saw Rebéldom. Their owners were
subjected to such a storm of ridicule that they could not bear
up under it. It was a stale yet common joke to remind them
that in action these vests must be worn behind. Then, too,
the ownership of one of them was taken as evidence of faint-
heartedness. Of this the owner was often reminded; so that
when it came to the packing of the knapsack for departure,
the vest, taking as it did considerable space and adding no
small weight to his already too-heavy
burden, was in many cases left behind.
The officers, whose opportunity to take
baggage along was greater, clung to
them longest; but I think that they
were quite generally abandoned with
the first important reduction made in
the luggage.

A Havelock

One of the first supposed-to-be useful, if not ornamental stupidities, which
some of the earlier troops took to themselves by order, was the *Havelock*. True,
its invention antedated the time of
which I speak. It was a foreign conception and derived its name from an English general who distinguished himself
in the war in India, where they were
worn in 1857. It was a simple covering of white linen for the
cap, with a cape depending for the protection of the neck from
the sun. They may have been very essential to the comfort of
the troops in the Eastern climate, but while whole regiments
went South with them, if one of these articles survived active
service three months I have yet to hear of it.

Then there were fancy patent-leather haversacks, with two
or three compartments for the assortment of rations which
Uncle Sam was expected to furnish. But those who invested
in them were somewhat disgusted at a little later stage of their
service, when they were ordered to throw away all such "high-
toned" trappings and adopted the regulation pattern of painted
cloth. This was a bag about a foot square, with a broad strap
for the shoulder, into which soldiers soon learned to bundle
all their food and table furniture, which . . . after a day's hard
march were always found in such a delightful hodge-podge.

Now and then an invention was to be found which was a real convenience. I still have in my possession such a one, an article which, when not in use, is a compact roll eight and one-half inches long and two inches in diameter, and designed to hold pens, ink, and paper. Unrolled, it makes a little tablet of the length given and five and one-half inches wide, which was my writing-desk when no better was to be had.

A Zouave

The Turkish fez with pendent tassel was seen on the heads of some soldiers. Zouave regiments wore them. They did very well to lie around camp in, and in a degree marked their owner as a somewhat conspicuous man among his fellows, but they were not tolerated on line; few of them ever survived the first three months' campaigning.

And this recalls the large number of the soldiers of '62 who did not wear the forage cap furnished by the Government. They bought the "McClellan cap," so called, at the hatters' instead, which in most cases faded out in a month. This the Government caps did not do, with all their awkward appearance. They may have been coarse and unfashionable to the eye, but the colors would stand. Nearly every man embellished his cap with the number or letter of his company and regiment and the appropriate emblem. For infantry this emblem is a bugle, for artillery two crossed cannons, and for cavalry two crossed sabers.

One other item occurs to me; this was the great care exercised to have all equipments prominently marked with the regiment, company, and state to which the owner belonged. For example, on the back of the knapsack of every man in a regiment appeared in large lettering something like this: Co. B, 33d New York Regiment; or, if it was light artillery, this, 10th Mass. Battery. Nor did the advertising stop here, for the haversacks and canteens were often similarly labelled, and yet at the time it seemed necessary to somebody that it should be done. At any rate, nobody found any fault with it; and if it had been thought desirable that each article of apparel should be similarly placarded, there would have been a general acquiescence on the part of the untutored citizen soldiery, who were in the best of humor, and with Pope (Alexander not John) seemed to agree that "Whatever is, is right." But how many of these loudly marked equipments survived the strife? Perhaps not one. The knapsack may have been thrown aside in the first battle, and a simple roll composed of the woollen and rubber blanket substituted for it. The haversacks and canteens were soon lost, and new ones took their place; and they lasted just as long and were just as safe as if conspicuously marked. One of the comical sights of the service was to see Rebel prisoners brought in having strapped on their backs knapsacks bearing just such labelling as that which I have quoted. Of course, these were trophies which they had either taken from prisoners or had picked up on some battlefield or in the wake of the Union Army and appropriated to their own use.

Light-artillerymen went to the front decorated with brass scales on their shoulders, but, finding an utter absence of such ornaments on the persons of soldiers who had been in action, and feeling sensitive about being known as recruits, these decorations soon disappeared. Theoretically, they were worn to ward off the blows of a saber aimed by cavalrymen at the head; practically, it is doubtful whether they ever served such a purpose.

14

The Army Mule

It has often been said that the South could not have been worsted . . . had it not been for the steady re-enforcement brought to the Union side by the mule.* To just what extent his services hastened the desired end, it would be impossible to compute; but it is admitted by both parties to the war that they were invaluable.

It may not be generally known that Kentucky is the chief mule-producing state of the Union, with Missouri next, while St. Louis is perhaps the best mule market in the world; but the entire Southwest does something at mule raising. Mules vary more in size than horses. The largest and best come from Kentucky. The smaller ones are the result of a cross with the Mexican mustang. These were also extensively used. General Grant says, in his *Memoirs* (vol. 1. p. 69), that while Taylor's army was at Matamoras, contracts were made for mules between American traders and Mexican smugglers at from eight to eleven dollars each. But the main source of supply for the Western states, where they were very generally used, for the South, and for the Government during wartime was Kentucky. When the war broke out, efforts were made by Governor [Beriah] Magoffin of that state—or rather by the Legislature, for the Governor was in full sympathy with the Rebels—to have that commonwealth remain neutral. For this reason when the Government attempted to purchase mules there in 1861, they were refused; but in the course of a few weeks the neutrality nonsense was pretty thoroughly knocked out of the authorities, Kentucky took its stand on the side of the Union, and the United States Government began and continued its purchase of mules there in increasing numbers till the close of the war.

---

* MULE: The hybrid offspring of a horse and an ass, usually unable to breed. Some 450,000 mules served in the Union armies. [Ed.]

What were these mules used for? Well, when the war broke out, thousands of soldiers came pouring into Washington for its defence and afterwards went by thousands into other sections of Rebeldom. To supply these soldiers with the necessary rations, forage, and camp equipage, and keep them supplied, thousands of wagons were necessary. Some of the regiments took these wagons with them from their native state, but most did not. Some of the wagons were drawn by mules already owned by the Government, and more mules were purchased from time to time. The great advantage possessed by these animals over horses was not at that period fully appreciated, so that horses were also used in large numbers. But the magnitude of the Rebellion grew apace. Regiments of cavalry, each requiring 1200 horses, and light batteries 110, were now rapidly organizing, calling for an abundance of horseflesh. Then, disease, exposure, and hard usage consumed a great many more, so that these animals naturally grew scarcer as the demand increased. For certain kinds of work horses must be had, mules would not do. The horse was good for any kind of service as a beast of burden, up to the limits of his endurance. Not so his half-brother the mule. The latter was more particular as to the kind of service he performed. Like a great many bipeds that entered the Army, he preferred to do military duty in the safe rear. As a consequence, if he found himself under fire at the front, he was wont to make a stir in his neighborhood until he got out of such inhospitable surroundings.

This nervousness totally unfitted him for artillery or cavalry service; he must therefore be made available for draft in the trains, the ammunition and forage trains, the supply and bridge trains. So, as rapidly as it could conveniently be done, mules took the place of horses in all the trains, six mules replacing four horses.

Aside from this nervousness under fire, mules have a great advantage over horses in being better able to stand hard usage, bad feed, or no feed, and neglect generally. They can travel over rough ground unharmed where horses would be lamed or injured in some way They will eat brush and not be very hungry to do it, either. When forage was short, the drivers were wont to cut branches to throw before them for their refreshment. One m. d. (mule driver) tells of having his Army overcoat partly eaten by one of his team—actually chewed and swallowed. The operation made the driver blue, if the diet did not thus affect the mule.

In organizing a six-mule team, a large pair of heavy animals were selected for the pole, a smaller size for the swing, and a still smaller pair for leaders. There were advantages in this arrangement; in the first place, in going through a miry spot the small leaders soon place themselves, by their quick movements, on firm footing, where they can take hold and pull the pole-mules out of the wallow. Again, with a good heavy steady pair of wheel-mules, the driver can restrain the smaller ones that are more apt to be frisky and reckless at times, and assisted by the brake, hold back his loaded wagon in descending a hill. Then, there was more elasticity in such a team when well trained, and a good driver could handle them much more gracefully and dexterously than he could the same number of horses.

It was really wonderful to see some of the experts drive these teams. The driver rides the near pole-mule, holding in his left hand a single rein. This connects with the bits of the near lead-mule. By pulling this rein, of course the brutes would go to the left. To direct them to the right one or more short jerks of it were given, accompanied by a sort of gibberish which the mule drivers acquired in the business. The bits of the lead-mules being connected by an iron bar, whatever movement was made by the near one directed the movements of the off one. The pole-mules were controlled by short reins which hung over their necks. The driver carried in his right hand his *blacksnake*, that is, his black-leather whip, which was used with much effect on occasion.

When mules were brought to the Army they were enclosed in what was called a *corral*. To this place the driver in quest of a mule must repair to make and take his selection, having the proper authority to do so. I will illustrate how it was done. Here is a figure representing a corral, having on the inside a fence running from A to C. AD and BE are pairs of bars. The driver enters the yard, mounted, and, having selected the mule he wants, drives him toward BE. The bars at AD being up, and those at BE being down, the mule advances and the bars BE are put up behind him. He is now enclosed in the small space indicated by ABDE. The mule driver then mounts the fence, bridles the brute of his choice, lets down the bars at AD, and takes him out. Why does he bridle him from the fence? Well, because the mule is an uncertain animal.

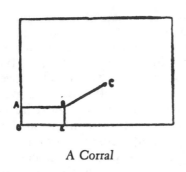

A Corral

In making his selection the driver did not always draw a prize. Sometimes his mule would be kind and tractable and sometimes not. Of course he would saddle him and start to ride him to camp; but the mule is not always docile under the saddle. He too often has a mind of his own. He may go along all right, or, if he is tricky, he may suddenly pause, bracing his forefeet and settling down on his hind ones, as if he had suddenly happened to think of the girl he left behind him and was debating whether or not to go back after her. It is when the mule strikes such an attitude as this, I suppose, that Josh Billings calls him "a stubborn fact." But the driver! Well, if at that moment he was off his guard, he would get off without previous preparation—as a man sometimes sits down on ice —and look at the mule. If, however, he was on the alert and well prepared, the mule in the end would generally come off second best. I have referred to the *blacksnake*. It was the badge of authority with which the mule driver enforced his orders.

It was the panacea for all the ills to which mule flesh was heir. It was a common sight to see a six-mule team, when left to itself, get into an entanglement, seeming inextricably mixed, unless it was unharnessed; but the appearance of the driver with his black wand would change the scene as if by magic. As the heel-cord of Achilles was his only vulnerable part, so the ears of the mule seemed to be the development through which his reasoning faculties could be the most quickly and surely reached, and one or two cracks of the whip on or near these little monuments, accompanied by the driver's very expressive ejaculation in the mule tongue, which I can only describe as a kind of cross between an unearthly screech and a groan, had the effect to disentangle them unaided and make them stand as if at a "present arms" to their master. When off duty in camp, they were usually hitched to the pole of their wagon, three on either side, and here, between meals, they were often as antic as kittens or puppies at play, leaping from one side of the pole to the other, lying down, tumbling over, and biting each other, until perhaps all six would be an apparently confused heap of mule. If the driver appeared at such a crisis with his black "ear-trumpet," one second was long enough to dissolve the pile into its original mule atoms and arrange them again on either side of the pole, looking as orderly and innocent as if on inspection.

An educated mule driver was, in his little sphere, as competent a disciplinarian as the colonel of a regiment. Nor did he always secure the prompt and exact obedience above described by applications of the *blacksnake* alone, or even when accompanied by the sternest objurgations delivered in the mule dialect. He was a terror to his subjects in yet another way: and old soldiers will sustain me in the assertion that the propulsive power of the mule driver was increased many-fold by the almost unlimited stock of profanity with which he greeted the sensitive ears of his muleship when the latter was stubborn. I have seen mules, but now most obdurate, jump into their collars the next moment with the utmost determination to do their whole duty when one of these Gatling guns of curses opened fire upon them. Some reader may prefer to adjudge as a reason for this good behavior the fear of the *blacksnake*, which was likely to be applied close upon the volley of oaths; but I prefer to assign as a motive the mule's interest in the advancement of good morals.

In all seriousness, however, dealing only with the fact, without attempting to prove or deny justification for it, it is undoubtedly true that the mule drivers, when duly aroused, could produce a deeper cerulean tint in the surrounding atmosphere than any other class of men in the service. The theory has been advanced that if all of these professional m. d.'s in the trains of the Army of the Potomac could have been put into the trenches around Petersburg and Richmond in the fall of 1864 and have been safely advanced to within ear-shot of the enemy, then, at a signal, set to swearing simultaneously at their level-worst, the Rebels would either have thrown down their arms and surrendered then and there, or have fled incontinently to the fastnesses of the Blue Ridge. There may have been devout mule drivers in Sherman's army, but I never saw one east. They may have been pious on taking up this important work. They were certainly impious before laying it down. Nevertheless, in those later days, when they were living better lives, any twinge of conscience they may have felt must have been relieved by the knowledge that General Grant had given them credit for being able to swear a mule team out of the mud when it could not be moved by any other process.

I have stated that the mule was uncertain; I mean as to his intentions. He cannot be trusted even when appearing honest and affectionate. His reputation as a kicker is worldwide. He was the Mugwump of the service. The mule that will not kick is a curiosity. A veteran relates how, after the battle of Antietam, he saw a colored mule driver approach his mules that were standing unhitched from the wagons, when, presto! one of them knocked him to the ground in a twinkling with one of those unexpected instantaneous kicks for which the mule is peerless. Slowly picking himself up, the Negro walked deliberately to his wagon, took out a long stake the size of his arm, returned with the same moderate pace to his muleship, dealt him a stunning blow on the head with the stake, which felled him to the ground. The stake was returned with the same deliberation. The mule lay quiet for a moment, then arose, shook his head, a truce was declared, and driver and mule were at peace and understood each other.

Here is another illustration of misplaced confidence. On the road to Harpers Ferry after the Antietam Campaign in 1862, the colored cook of the headquarters of the Sixtieth New York Regiment picked up a large and respectable looking mule, to whom, with a cook's usual foresight and ambition, he attached all the paraphernalia of the cook house together with his own personal belongings, and settled himself down proudly on his back among them. All went on serenely for a time, the mule apparently accepting the situation with composure until the Potomac was reached at Harpers Ferry. On arriving in the middle of the pontoon bridge upon which the Army was crossing, from some unexplained reason—perhaps because, on looking into the water, he saw himself as others saw him—the mule lifted up his voice in one of those soul-harrowing brays for which he is famous—or *infamous*—and lifting his hind legs aloft, in the next moment tossed his entire burden of cook and cook house into the river, where, weighted down with messkettles and other utensils of his craft, the cook must have drowned had not members of the regiment come to his rescue. Not at all daunted by this experience, the cookey harnessed the mule again as before, led him across the remaining portion of the bridge, where he remounted and settled himself among his household goods once more, where all was well till the Shenandoah was reached. Here, with another premonitory blast of his nasal trumpet, the mule once more dumped his load into the rapid rolling river, when the cook lost all confidence in mules as beasts of burden and abandoned him.

Josh Billings says somewhere that if he had a mule who would neither kick nor bite he would watch him dreadful "cluss" till he found out where his malice *did* lay. This same humorist must have had some experience with the mule, for he has said some very bright and pat things concerning him. Here are a few I recall:

"To break a mule—begin at his head."

"To find the solid contents of a mule's hind leg, feel of it clussly."

"The man who wont believe anything he kant see ain't so wise az a mule, for they will kick at a thing in the dark."

"The only thing which makes a mule so highly respectable is the great accuracy of his kicking."

"The mule is a sure-footed animal. I have known him to kick a man fifteen feet off ten times in a second."

These are a few samples, most all of which have reference to his great ability as a kicker. Unquestionably he had no equal in this field of amusement—to him. His legs were small, his feet were small, but his ambition in this direction was large.

He could kick with wonderful accuracy, as a matter of fact. Mule drivers tell me he could kick a fly off his ear, as he walked along in the team, with unerring accuracy. This being so, of course larger objects were never missed when they were within range. But the distance included within a mule's range had often to be decided by two or three expensive tests. One driver, whom I well knew, was knocked over with a mule's hind foot while standing directly in front of him. This shows something of their range.

I have remarked, in substance, that the mule was conquered only by laying hold of or striking his ears. It may be asked how he was shod if he was such a kicker. To do this, one of two methods was adopted; either to sling him up as oxen are slung, then strap his feet; or walk him into a noose, and cast him, by drawing it around his legs. Of course, he would struggle violently for a while, but when he gave in it was all over for that occasion, and he was as docile under the smith's hands as a kitten. Being surer-footed and more agile than a horse, of course he gets into fewer bad places or entanglements; but once in, and having made a desperate struggle for his relief, and failing, he seems utterly discouraged, and neither whip nor persuasion can move him. Then, as in the shoeing, the driver can handle him with the utmost disregard of heels; but when once on his feet again, stand aside! He has a short memory. He lives in the future, and his heels are in business, as usual, at the old stand.

I need not comment on the size of the mule's ears. Of course, everybody who has seen them knows them to be abnormal in size. But disproportionately large though they may be, there is one other organ in his possession which surpasses them; that is his voice. This is something simply tremendous. That place which the guinea-fowl occupies among the feathered bipeds of the barnyard in this respect, the mule holds facile princeps among the domestic quadrupeds. The poets who lived in the same time with Pericles said of the latter that "he lightened, thundered, and agitated all Greece," so powerful was his eloquence. So, likewise, when the mule raised his voice, all opposition was silent before him, for nothing short of rattling, crashing thunder, as it seemed, could successfully compete for precedence with him.

In addition to his great usefulness in the train, he was used a good deal under a pack-saddle. Each regiment usually had one that brought up the rear on the march, loaded with the implements of the cook house—sometimes with nothing to be seen but head and tail, so completely was he covered in. They were generally convoyed by a colored man. Sometimes these strong-minded creatures, in crossing a stream would decide to lie down, all encumbered as they were, right in the middle, and down they would settle in spite of the ludicrous opposition and pathetic protests of the convoy. Of course, it was no balm to his wound to have the passing column of soldiers keep up a running fire of banter. But there was no redress or relief to be had until his muleship got ready to move, which was generally after every ounce of his burden had been stripped off and placed on terra firma.

When the Army was lying in line of battle in such close proximity to the enemy that the ammunition wagons could not safely approach it, two boxes were taken and strapped on a mule, one on each side, "to keep his balance true," and thus the troops were supplied when needed.

At the terrible battle of Spotsylvania, May 12, 1864, a steady line of pack-mules loaded with ammunition filed up the open ravine opposite the captured salient for nearly twenty hours, in that way supplying our forces who were so hotly engaged there. Rations were furnished in the same manner under similar circumstances. But now and then a mule would lie down under his burden and refuse to budge.

Grant says (vol. i. p. 106): "I am not aware of ever having used a profane expletive in my life, but I would have the charity to excuse those who may have done so if they were in charge of a train of Mexican pack-mules. . . ."

I believe I have stated that the mule much preferred to do military duty in the safe rear; but if there was anything which the war proved with the utmost clearness to both Yanks and Rebs, it was that there was surely no safe rear. This being so, the vivacious mule did not always have a plain and peaceful pilgrimage as a member of the wagon train. I vividly recall the enjoyment of my company, during Lee's final retreat, whenever our guns were unlimbered, as they were again and again, to be trained on the columns of retreating wagon trains. The explosion of a shell or two over or among them would drive the long-ears wild and render them utterly unmanageable, and the driver's best and often his only recourse was to let them go if there was room ahead. But one demoralized, disorganized six-mule

team would sometimes so effectively block the way, when the
road was narrow and the pursuit close, as to cause the capture
of that part of the train behind it. . . .

From what I have stated, it will be seen that the mule would
be very unreliable in cavalry service, for in action he would be
so wild that if he did not dismount his rider he would carry
even the most valiant from the scene of conflict, or what was
just as likely, rush madly into the ranks of the enemy. The same
observations would suit equally well as objections to his service
with artillery. On the 5th of April, 1865, during the retreat of
Lee, we came upon a batch of wagons and a battery of steel
guns of the Armstrong pattern which Sheridan's troopers had
cut out of the enemy's retreating trains. The guns had apparently never been used since their arrival from England. The
harnesses were of russet leather and equally new; but the battery
was drawn by a sorry-looking lot of horses and mules, indiscriminately mingled. My explanation for finding the mules thus
tackled was that horses were scarce, and that it was not expected to use the guns at present, but simply to get them off
safely; but that if it became necessary to use them they could
do so with comparative safety as the guns were of long range.

I should have pronounced these particular mules safe anywhere, even under a hot fire, if extreme emaciation had been
a sure index of departed strength and nerve in this variety of
brute. But that is not mule at all. The next day, at Sailor's
Creek, my corps (Second), after a short, sharp contest, made
a capture of thirteen flags, three guns, 1,300 prisoners, and
over 200 army wagons with their mules. And such mules! the
skinniest, boniest animals that I ever saw retaining life. For a
full week they had been on the go, night and day, with rare
and brief halts for rest or food. Just before their capture they
would seem to have gone down a long hill into a valley, a literal
Valley of Humiliation as it proved, for there they were compelled to stay and surrender, either from inability to climb the
opposite hill and get away, or else because there was not opportunity for them to do so before our forces came upon them. And
yet, in spite of the worn and wasted state of those teams, it is
doubtful if their kicking capacity was materially reduced by it.

The question frequently raised among old soldiers is, What
became of all the Army mules? There are thousands of men
who would take a solemn oath that they never saw a dead
mule during the war. They can tell you of the carcasses of

horses which dotted the line of march, animals which had
fallen out from exhaustion or disease and left by the roadside
for the buzzards and crows. These they could recall by hundreds; but not the dimmest picture of a single dead mule, and
they would assure you, to the best of their knowledge and
belief, the Government did not lose one of these animals during
the war. I once conversed with an old soldier who remembered
having once seen, on the march, the four hoofs of a mule—
those and nothing more; and the conclusion that he arrived
at was that the mule in a fit of temper had kicked off his hoofs
and gone up. Another soldier, a mule driver, remembers seeing
a mule team which had run off the corduroy road into a mire of
quicksand. The wagon had settled down till its body rested in
the mire, but nothing of the team was visible save the ear tips
of the off-pole mule.

As a fact, however, the mules, though tough and hardy, died
of disease much as did the horses. Glanders took off a great
many, and black tongue, a disease peculiar to them, caused the
death of many more. But, with all their outs, they were of invaluable service to the armies and well deserve the good opinions which came to prevail regarding their many excellent
qualities as beasts of burden. Here is an incident of the war in
which the mule was the hero of the hour:

On the night of Oct. 28, 1863, when General Geary's Division of the Twelfth Corps repulsed the attacking forces of
Longstreet at Wauhatchie, Tennessee, about two hundred
mules, affrighted by the din of battle, rushed in the darkness
into the midst of Wade Hampton's Rebel troops, creating
something of a panic among them and causing a portion of
them to fall back, supposing that they were attacked by cavalry.
Someone in the Union Army, who knew the circumstances,
taking Tennyson's "Charge of the Light Brigade" as a basis,
composed and circulated the following description of the ludicrous event:

CHARGE OF THE MULE BRIGADE

Half a mile, half a mile,
Half a mile onward,
Right through the Georgia troops
Broke the two hundred.

"Forward the Mule Brigade!
Charge for the Rebs!" they neighed.
Straight for the Georgia troops
    Broke the two hundred.

"Forward the Mule Brigade!"
Was there a mule dismayed?
Not when the long ears felt
    All their ropes sundered.
Theirs not to make reply,
Theirs not to reason why,
Theirs but to make Rebs fly.
On! to the Georgia troops
    Broke the two hundred.

Mules to the right of them,
Mules to the left of them,
Mules behind them
    Pawed, neighed, and thundered.
Breaking their own confines,
Breaking through Longstreet's lines
Into the Georgia troops,
    Stormed the two hundred.

Wild all their eyes did glare,
Whisked all their tails in air
Scattering the chivalry there,
    While all the world wondered.
Not a mule back bestraddled,
Yet how they all skedaddled—
Fled every Georgian,
Unsabered, unsaddled,
    Scattered and sundered!
How they were routed there
    By the two hundred!

Mules to the right of them,
Mules to the left of them,
Mules behind them
    Pawed, neighed, and thundered;
Followed by hoof and head

Full many a hero fled,
Fain in the last ditch dead,
Back from an ass's jaw
All that was left of them—
    Left by the two hundred.

When can their glory fade?
Oh, the wild charge they made!
    All the world wondered.
Honor the charge they made!
Honor the Mule Brigade,
    Long-eared two hundred!

The following plaint in behalf of this veteran quadruped
will close this sketch:

THE ARMY MULE IN TIME OF PEACE

That men are ungrateful can plainly be seen
In the case of that mule standing out on the green.
His features are careworn, bowed down is his head,
His spirit is broken; his hopes have all fled.
He thinks of the time when the battle raged sore,
When he mingled his bray with the cannon's loud roar;
When Uncle Sam's soldiers watched for him to come,
Hauling stores of provisions and powder and rum;
When his coming was greeted with cheers and huzzas,
And the victory turned on the side of the stars.

These thoughts put new life into rickety bones—
He prances just once, then falls over and groans.
A vision comes over his poor mulish mind,
And he sees Uncle Sam, with his agents behind,
Granting pensions by thousands to all who apply,
From the private so low to the officer high;
To the rich and the poor, the wise man and fool,
But, alas! there is none for the poor army mule.

15

Hospitals and Ambulances

This chapter is an attempt . . . to give a more adequate idea of the Medical Department of the Army, what it was, how it grew up, and something of what it accomplished. . . .

At the time of the battle of Bull Run [July 21, 1861] there was no plan in operation by which the wounded in that battle were cared for. Before this engagement took place, while the troops were lying in and around Washington, general hospitals had been established to provide for the sick. For this purpose five or six hotels, seminaries, and infirmaries in Washington and Georgetown, and two or three in Alexandria, had been taken possession of, and these were all the hospital accommodations to be found at the end of the first three months. So general was the opinion that the war would be speedily ended no one thought of such a thing as building permanent structures for hospital purposes.

But this condition of affairs soon after changed. Preparations for war were made on a grander scale. The Army of the Potomac under the moulding hands of McClellan was assuming form, and the appointment by him, Aug. 12, 1861, of Surgeon Charles S. Tripler as medical director of that Army indicated a purpose of having a medical department set on foot and put in completeness for active service. . . .

Army Regulations were the written law to which it was attempted to have everything conform as far as possible. But when these regulations were drafted there was no expectation of such a war as finally came upon us, and to attempt to confine so large an army as then existed to them as a guide was as impossible and absurd as for the full-grown man to wear the suit of clothes he cast off at ten years.

So in certain directions Army Regulations had to be ignored. For example, they provided only for the establishment of regimental and general hospitals. A regimental hospital is

212

what its name indicates—the hospital of a particular regiment. But if such a hospital became full or received some patients whose ailments were not likely to submit readily to treatment, such cases were sent to a *General Hospital*, that is, one into which patients were taken regardless of the regiment to which they belonged. But in these early war times, in the absence of a system, any patient who was able could at his pleasure leave one general hospital and go to another for any reason which seemed sufficient to him, or he could desert the service entirely.

By general orders issued from the war department, May 25, 1861, Governors of states were directed to appoint a surgeon and assistant surgeon for each regiment. The men appointed were for the most part country physicians, many of them with little practice, who, on reaching the field, were in some respects as ignorant of their duties under the changed conditions as if they had not been educated to the practice of medicine; and the medical director of the Army found his hands more than full in attempting to get them to carry out his wishes. So, to simplify his labors and also to increase the efficiency of his department, brigade hospitals were organized about the beginning of 1862, and by general orders from the War Department brigade surgeons were appointed with the rank of major and assigned to the staffs of brigadier-generals. These brigade surgeons had supervision of the surgeons of their brigades and exercised this duty under the instructions of the medical director.

The regimental hospitals in the field were sometimes tents, and sometimes dwellings or barns near camp. It was partly to relieve these that brigade hospitals were established. The latter were located near their brigade or division.

The hospital tent I have already described at some length. I may add here that those in use for hospital purposes before the war were 24 feet long by 14 feet 6 inches wide, and 11 feet 6 inches high, but, owing to their great bulk and weight, and the difficulty of pitching them in windy weather, the size was reduced . . . to 14 feet by 14 feet 6 inches, and 11 feet high in the center, with the walls 4 feet 6 inches, and a "fly" 21 feet 6 inches by 14 feet. Each of these was designed to accommodate eight patients comfortably. Army Regulations assigned three such tents to a regiment, together with one Sibley and one Wedge or A tent.

The Sibley tent I have likewise quite fully described. I will only add here that, not having a "fly," it was very hot in warm weather. Then, on account of its center pole and the absence of walls, it was quite contracted and inconvenient. For these reasons it was little used for hospital purposes and not used at all after the early part of the war.

The hospital tents in the Army of the Potomac were heated for the most part, by what was called for some reason the *California Plan*. This consisted of a pit, dug just outside of the hospital door, two and a half feet deep, from which a trench passed through the tent, terminating outside the other end in a chimney built of barrels, or in such a manner as I have elsewhere described. This trench was covered throughout its entire extent with iron plates, which were issued by the Quartermaster's Department for that purpose. The radiation of the heat from the plates kept the tent very comfortable.

The honor of organizing the first field hospital in tents is said to belong to Dr. B. J. D. Irwin, U. S. A., of the Army of the Ohio. It occurred at the battle of Shiloh. While establishing a hospital near the camp of Prentiss' division of that Army, which had been captured the day before, the abandoned tents still standing suggested themselves to him as a convenient receptacle for his wounded. He at once appropriated the camp for this purpose and laid it out in systematic form. It was clearly shown by this and succeeding experiences during the war that the wounded treated under canvas did better and recovered more rapidly than those treated in permanent hospitals.

As fast as they could be procured, hospital tents were furnished, three to a regiment, in accordance with the provision of Army Regulations referred to. Each regiment provided its own nurses and cooks. In general hospitals one nurse was allowed to ten patients, and one cook to thirty.

The capacity of a regimental hospital tent, like a stagecoach, varied according to the demand for room. I have said they were designed to accommodate eight. An old Army surgeon says, "Only six can be comfortably accommodated in one of them, three on each side." But when the surgeons were crowded with the wounded, it was a common practice to set two long narrow boards edgewise through the center of the tent, about twenty inches apart. If boards were wanting, two good-sized *poles* were cut and used instead. Between these was the passage for the surgeons and nurses. Behind the boards or poles a filling of straw or fine boughs was made and covered with blankets. On these latter could be placed twenty patients, ten on either side; but they were crowded. When six single cots were put in one of these tents, three on each side, ample space was afforded to pass among them.

In the latter part of 1861, the Government, realizing its pressing needs, began to build general hospitals for the comfort and accommodation of its increasing thousands of sick and wounded, continuing to build as the needs increased to the very last year of the war, when they numbered 205.

Before the Civil War, the Government had never been supplied with carriages to convey the sick and wounded. Only two years before, a board appointed by the Secretary of War, had adopted for experiment a four-wheeled and a two-wheeled carriage. The four-wheeled vehicle was tried in an expedition sent into New Mexico and was favorably reported on; the two-wheeled was never tested but was judged to be the best adapted to badly wounded men (though the contrary proved to be the fact), and so the board reported in favor of adopting these carriages in the ratio of five two-wheeled to one four-wheeled.

A Two-Wheeled Ambulance

When Surgeon Tripler took charge, he found several of these two-wheeled carriages in Washington, but they were used chiefly as pleasure-carriages for officers or for some other private purpose. This was stopped, for a time at least, and an order was issued, leaving one to a regiment and requiring the rest to be turned over to the Quartermaster's Department. But the diversion of ambulances from their proper use, I will add in passing, continued to a greater or less extent till the end of the war. This very year McClellan issued an order for them not to be used except for the transportation of the sick and wounded unless by authority of the brigade commander, the medical director, or the quartermaster in charge, and the provost-marshal was ordered to arrest officers and confine non-commissioned officers and privates for violation of the order.

The most important steps taken towards organizing the Medical Department and placing it on that thorough basis which distinguished it in the later years of the war were the result of the foresight, energy, and skilful management of Dr. Jonathan Letterman, who was made medical director of the Army of the Potomac on the 19th of June, 1862. His labor was enormous: It was during the progress of the Peninsular Campaign. All was confusion; medical supplies were exhausted; thousands of sick and wounded men were dying for want of proper care and medicine. Yet this campaign, so disastrous in its results to our Army from a military point of view, was a valuable teacher in many respects, and one of its most pointed and practical lessons was the necessity shown of having the ambulances organized and under a competent head. It remained for Dr. Letterman to appreciate this need and effect an organization which remained practically unchanged till the close of the war. Here is the substance of the plan which he drew up and which General McClellan approved and published to the Army in orders, Aug. 2, 1862, and which General Meade reissued with some additions and slight changes a little more than a year later.

AMBULANCE CORPS

All the ambulances belonging to an army corps were to be placed under the control of the medical director of that corps, for now, in addition to a medical director of the Army, there was a subordinate medical director for each army corps. Such an ambulance corps was put into the hands of a captain as commandant. This corps was divided and sub-divided into division, brigade, and regimental trains corresponding to the divisions of the army corps to which it belonged, having a first lieutenant in charge of a division, a second lieutenant in charge of a brigade, and a sergeant in charge of a regimental detachment. Besides these, three privates, one of them being the driver, were to accompany each ambulance on the march and in battle. The duties of all these men, both officers and privates, were very carefully defined as well for camp as for the march and battle. Besides the ambulances, there accompanied each corps one medicine-wagon and one army wagon to a brigade, containing the requisite medicines, dressings, instruments, hospital stores, bedding, medical books, small furniture (like tumblers, basins, bed pans, spoons, vials, etc.).

In addition to the foregoing articles, which were carefully assorted both as to quantity and quality, each ambulance was required to carry in the box beneath the driver's seat, under lock and key, the following articles:

A Four-Wheeled Ambulance

Three bed-sacks, six 2-pound cans beef stock, one leather bucket, three camp kettles (assorted sizes), one lantern and candle, six tin plates, six tablespoons, six tin tumblers; and just before a battle ten pounds of hard bread were required to be put into the box.

There was another scheme, which was conceived and carried into execution by Dr. Letterman which deserves mention in this connection. This was the establishment of Field Hospitals "in order that the wounded might receive the most prompt and efficient attention during and after an engagement and that the necessary operations might be performed by the most skilful and responsible surgeons at the earliest moment." Under

Surgeon Tripler there had been rendezvous established in rear
of the Army to which all the wounded were taken for immediate attention before being sent to general hospitals. But
there was no recognized system and efficiency in regard to it.
Just before an engagement a field hospital for each division
was established. It was made by pitching a suitable number
of hospital tents. The location of such a hospital was left to
the medical director of the corps. Of course, it must be in the
rear of the division, out of all danger and in a place easily
reached by the ambulances. A division hospital of this description was under the charge of a surgeon, who was selected by
the surgeon-in-chief of the division. With him was an assistant
surgeon, similarly appointed, whose duty it was to pitch the
tents, provide straw, fuel, water, etc., and in general make
everything ready for the comfort of the wounded. For doing
this the hospital stewards and nurses of the division were placed
under his charge and special details made from the regiments
to assist. A kitchen or cook tent must be at once erected and
the cooks put in possession of the articles mentioned as carried in the ambulance boxes and hospital-wagons, so that a
sufficient amount of nourishing food could be prepared for immediate use.

Another assistant surgeon was detailed to keep a complete
record of patients, with name, rank, company, and regiment,
the nature of their wound, its treatment, etc. He was also
required to see to the proper interment of those who died, and

A Medicine Wagon

the placing of properly marked headboards at their graves.

Then, there were in each of these division hospitals three surgeons selected from the whole division "without regard to rank, but solely on account of their known prudence, judgment, and skill" whose duty it was to perform all important operations, or at least be responsible for their performance. Three other medical officers were detailed to assist these three. Nor was this all, for the remaining medical officers of the division, except one to a regiment, were also required to report at once to the hospital to act as dressers of wounds and assistants generally. In addition to these, a proper number of nurses and attendants were detailed to be on hand. The medical officers left with regiments were required to establish themselves during the fighting in the rear of their respective organizations at such a distance as not to unnecessarily expose themselves, where they could give such temporary aid to the wounded as they should stand in need of.

I have said that these hospitals were to be located out of all danger. That statment needs a little modifying. In case the tide of battle turned against our Army and it was compelled to retreat, what was before a safe place might at once be converted into a place of great danger. But a hospital could not be struck and its patients moved at a moment's or even a day's warning, as a rule, and so it was made the duty of the medical director of a corps to select a sufficient number of medical officers, who, in case a retreat was found necessary, should remain in charge of the wounded. When the Rebels captured such a hospital, it was their general practice to parole all the inmates—that is, require them to give their word of honor that they would not bear arms again until they had been properly exchanged as prisoners of war. Our Government established what were known as parole camps, where such prisoners were required to remain until duly exchanged.

I think it can now be readily understood . . . how the establishment of these field hospitals facilitated the care of the wounded and by their systematic workings saved hundreds of lives. With a skilful, energetic man as medical director of the Army, giving his orders to medical directors of corps, and these carefully superintending surgeons-in-chief of divisions, who in turn held the surgeons and assistant surgeons and officers of ambulance corps to a strict accountability for a careful performance of their duties, while the latter fortified themselves by judicious oversight of *their* subordinates, the result was to place this Department of the Army on a footing which endured with the most profitable of results to the service till the close of the war.

I vividly remember my first look into one of these field hospitals. It was, I think, on the 27th of November, 1863, during the Mine Run Campaign, so-called. General French, then commanding the Third Corps, was fighting the battle of Locust Grove, and General Warren with the Second Corps had also been engaged with the enemy and had driven him from the neighborhood of Robertson's Tavern, in the vicinity of which the terrific Battle of the Wilderness began the following May. Near this tavern the field hospital of Warren's Second Division had been located, and into this I peered while my battery stood in park not far away, awaiting orders. The surgeon had just completed an operation. It was the amputation of an arm about five inches below the shoulder, the stump being now carefully dressed and bandaged. As soon as the patient recovered from the effects of the ether, the attendants raised him to a sitting posture on the operating table. At that moment the thought of his wounded arm returned to him, and turning his eyes towards it, they met only the projecting stub. The awful reality dawned upon him for the first time. An arm had gone forever, and he dropped backwards on the table in a swoon. Many a poor fellow like him brought to the operator's table came to consciousness only to miss an arm or a leg which perhaps he had begged in his last conscious moments to have spared. But the medical officers first mentioned decided all such cases, and the patient had only to submit. At Peach Tree Creek, Col. Thomas Reynolds of the Western Army was shot in the leg, and while the surgeons were debating the propriety of amputating it, the colonel, who was of Irish birth, begged them to spare it as it was very valuable, being an *imported leg* —a piece of wit which saved the gallant officer his leg, although he became so much of a cripple that he was compelled to leave the service.

It has been charged that limbs and arms were often uselessly sacrificed by the operators; that they were specially fond of amputating, and just as likely to amputate for a flesh wound as for a fractured bone on the ground that they could do it more quickly than they could dress the wound; that it made a neater, job, thus gratifying professional pride: but how the victim might feel about it or be affected by it then or thereafter did not seem to enter their thoughts. It was undoubtedly true that many flesh wounds were so ugly the only safety for the patient lay in amputation. A fine fellow, both as a man and soldier, belonging to my company, lost his arm from a flesh wound— needlessly, as he and his friends always asserted and believed.

A corporal of the First Massachusetts Heavy Artillery suffered a compound fracture of the left knee joint from a piece of shell by which he was struck at the battle of Hatcher's Run, Oct. 27, 1864. In the course of time he reached the Lincoln Hospitals (well do I remember them as they stood on Capitol Hill where they were erected just before the bloody repulse at Fredericksburg), where a surgeon decided that his leg must come off, and after instructing the nurse to prepare him for the operating room, left the ward. But the corporal talked the matter over with a wounded cavalryman (this was a year when cavalrymen were wounded quite generally) and decided that his leg must not come off; so, obtaining the loaded revolver of his comrade, he put it under his pillow and awaited the reapperance of the surgeon. He returned not long after, accompanied by two men with a stretcher and approached the cot.

"What are you going to do?" asked the corporal.

"My boy, we will have to take your leg off," was the reply of the surgeon.

"Not if I know myself," rejoined the corporal with determination expressed in both looks and language.

For a moment the surgeon was taken aback by the soldier's resolute manner. But directly he turned to the men and said, "Come, boys, take him up carefully," whereupon the stretcher bearers advanced to obey the order. At the same instant the corporal drew the revolver from beneath his pillow, cocked it, and, in a voice which carried conviction, exclaimed, "*The man that puts a hand on me dies!*" At this the men stepped back, and the surgeon tried to reason with the corporal, assuring him that in no other way could his life be saved. But the corporal persisted in declaring that if he died it should be with both legs on.

At that "Sawbones" (as the men used to call them) lost his temper and sought out the surgeon in general charge, with whom he soon returned to the corporal. This head surgeon, first by threats and afterwards by persuasion, tried to secure the revolver, but failing to do so, turned away, exclaiming with an oath, "Let the d—— fool keep it and die!" but a moment after, on second thought, said to the first surgeon that, as they wanted a subject to try the water cure on, he thought the corporal would meet that want. After obtaining a promise from the surgeon that he would not himself take the leg off or allow any one else to, the corporal assented to the proposition. A can was then arranged over the wounded knee in such a manner as to drop water on the cloth which enwrapped it day and night, and a cure was finally effected.

This is the substance of the story as I received it from the lips of the corporal himself, who, let me say in passing, was reduced to the rank of private and mustered out of the service as such, for daring to keep two whole legs under him. His bravery in the hour of peril—to him—deserved better things from his country than that.

But to return to the field hospital again; on the ground lay one man, wounded in the knee, while another sat near, wounded in the finger. This latter was a suspicious wound. Men of doubtful courage had a way of shooting off the end of the trigger finger to get out of service. But they sometimes did it in such a bungling manner that they were found out. The powder blown into the wound was often the evidence which convicted them. These men must have been proud of such scars.

Three wounded Rebels also lay in the tent, waiting for surgical attention. Of course, they would not be put upon the tables until all of our own wounded were attended to; they did not expect it. In one part of the tent lay two or three of our men who were either lifeless or faint from loss of blood. Only a few rods away from the tent were some freshly made graves enclosing the forms of men whose wounds had proved fatal, either having died on their way to the hospital or soon after their arrival. Among these was the gallant Lieutenant-Colonel Theodore Hesser, who was shot in the head while bravely leading the Seventy-Second Pennsylvania Infantry in a charge. The graves were all plainly marked with small head boards. A drizzling rain added gloom to the scene; and my first call at a field hospital with its dismal surroundings was brief.

One regulation made for this department of the service was never enforced. It provided that no one but the proper medical officers or the officers, non-commissioned officers, and privates of the ambulance corps should conduct sick or wounded to the rear, either on the march or in battle, but as a matter of fact there were probably more wounded men helped off the field by soldiers *not* members of the ambulance corps than by members of that body. There were always plenty of men who hadn't the interests of the cause so nearly at heart but what they could be induced without much persuasion when bullets and shells were flying thick, to leave the front line and escort a suffering comrade to the rear. Very often such a sufferer found a larger body-guard than could well make his needs a pretext for their absence from the line. Then, too, many of these escorts were most unfortunate, and *lost their way*, so that they did not find their regiment again until after the battle was over. A large number of them would be included among the Shirks and Beats whom I have already described. But, in truth, it was not possible for the ambulance corps to do much more in a hot fight than keep their stretchers properly manned. Each ambulance was provided with two of these, and the severely wounded who could not help themselves must be placed on them and cared for first, so that there was often need for a helping hand to be given a comrade who was quite seriously wounded, yet could hobble along with a shoulder to lean on.

The designating mark of members of the ambulance corps was, for sergeants, a green band an inch and a quarter broad around the cap, and inverted chevrons of the same color on each arm above the elbow; for privates the same kind of band and a half chevron of the same material. By means of this designation they were easily recognized.

By orders of General Meade, issued in August, 1863, three ambulances were allowed to a regiment of infantry; two to a regiment of cavalry, and one to a battery of artillery, with which it was to remain permanently. Owing to this fact, an artillery company furnished its own stretcher-bearers when needed. I shall be pardoned the introduction of a personal incident, as it will illustrate in some measure the duties and trials of a stretcher bearer. It was at the battle of *Hatcher's Run* . . . or the *Boydton Plank Road*, as some called it. The guns had been ordered into position near Burgess' Tavern, leaving the caissons and ambulance nearly a half mile in the rear. Meanwhile, a flank attack of the enemy cut off our communications with the rear for a time, and we thought ourselves sure of an involuntary trip to Richmond; but the way was opened again by some of our advance charging to the rear, and by the destructive fire from our artillery. Soon orders came for the battery to return

to the rear. In common with the rest, the writer started to do
so when a sergeant asked him to remain and help take off one
of our lieutenants, who was lying in a barn near by, severely
wounded. So actively had we been engaged that this was my
first knowledge of the sad event. But, alas! what was to be
done? Our ambulance with its stretchers was to the rear. That
could not now avail us. We must resort to other means. Fortunately, they were at hand. An abandoned army blanket lay
near, and carefully placing the lieutenant on this with one man
at each corner, we started.

But the wounded officer was heavy, and it was . . . an awkward way of carrying him. Moreover, his wound was a serious
one—mortal as it soon proved—and every movement of ours
tortured him so that he begged of us to leave him there to die.
Just then we caught sight of a stretcher on which a wounded
Rebel was lying. Some Union stretcher bearers had been taking
him to the rear when the flank attack occurred, when they evidently abandoned him to look out for themselves. It was not
a time for sentiment; so, with the sergeant at one end of the
stretcher and the narrator at the other, our wounded enemy was
rolled off with as much care as time would allow. With the aid
of our other comrades we soon put the lieutenant in his place,
and raising the stretcher to our shoulders, started down the
road to the rear. We had gone but a few rods, however, before
the enemy's sharpshooters or outposts fired on us, driving us
to seek safety in the woods. But it was now dusk, and no easy
matter to take such a burden through woods, especially as it
rapidly grew darker. . . . After more than an hour's wandering
and plunging, our burden was delivered at the ambulance,
where another of our lieutenants, also mortally wounded, was
afterwards to join him. This fragment of personal experience
will well illustrate some of the many obstacles which stretcher
bearers had to contend with, and disclose the further truth that
in actual combat the chances for severely wounded men to be
taken from the field were few indeed, for at such a time
stretcher bearers . . . are scarce.

The men whose wounds were dressed in the field hospitals
were transported as rapidly as convenient to the general hospitals, where the best of care and attention could be given them.
Such hospitals were located in various places. Whenever it
was possible, transportation was by water in steamers specially
fitted up for such a purpose. . . .

Another invention for the transportation of the wounded from the field was the *Cacolet* or *Mule Litter*, which was borne either by a mule or a horse and arranged to carry, some one and some two, wounded men. But although it was at first supposed that they would be a great blessing for this purpose, yet being strapped tightly to the body of the animal, the men felt his every motion, thus making them an intensely uncomfortable carriage for a severely wounded soldier, so that they were used but very little.

16

Scattering Shots

Forty-two dollars was the sum allowed by the Government to clothe the private soldier for one year. The articles included in his outfit were a cap or hat (usually the former), blouse, over-coat, dress coat, trousers, shirts, drawers, socks, shoes, a woollen and a rubber blanket. This was the wardrobe of the *infantry.* It should be said, however, that many regiments never drew a dress coat after leaving the state, the blouse serving as the substitute for that garment. The *artillery* and *cavalry* had the same except that a jacket took the place of the dress coat, boots that of shoes, and their trousers had a re-enforce, that is, an extra thickness of cloth extending from the upper part of the seat down the inside of both legs for greater durability in the service required of these branches in the saddle.

This outfit was not sufficient to last the year through for various reasons, and so the quartermaster supplied duplicates of the garments when needed. But whatever was drawn from him beyond the amount allowed by the Government was charged to the individual and deducted from his pay at the end of the year. If, however, a man was so fortunate as not to overdraw his allowance, which rarely happened, he received the balance in cash.

The infantry made way with a large amount of clothing. Much of it was thrown away on the march. A soldier burdened with a musket, from forty to eighty rounds of ammunition, according to circumstances; a haversack stuffed plump as a pillow but not so soft, with three days rations; a canteen of water, a woollen and rubber blanket, and a half-shelter tent would be likely to take just what more he was obliged to. So, with the opening of the spring campaign away would go all extra clothing. A choice was made between the dress coat and blouse, for one of these must go. Then some men took

226

their overcoat and left their blanket. In brief, when a campaign was fairly under way the average infantryman's wardrobe was what he had on—only that and nothing more. At the first start from camp many would burden themselves with much more than the above, but after a few miles tramp the roadside would be sprinkled with the castaway articles. There seemed to be a difference between Eastern and Western troops in this respect, for reasons which I will not attempt now to analyze, for Grant says (*Memoirs*, vol. ii., pp. 190-191):

"I saw scattered along the road, from Culpeper to Germania Ford, wagonloads of new blankets and overcoats thrown away by the troops to lighten their knapsacks; an improvidence I had never witnessed before."

It was a way the Army of the Potomac had of getting into light marching order.

When the infantry were ordered in on a charge, they always left their knapsacks behind them, which they might or might not see again. And whenever they were surprised and compelled to fall back hastily, they were likely to throw aside everything that impeded their progress except musket and ammunition. Then, in the heat of battle, again there was a dispensing with all encumbrances that would impair their efficiency. For these and other reasons, the Governmental allowances would not have been at all adequate to cover the losses in clothing. Recognizing this fact, the Government supplied new articles gratis for everything lost in action, the quartermaster being required to make out a list of all such articles and certify they were so lost before new ones could be obtained.

But the men who did garrison duty were not exempt from long clothing bills more than were those who were active at the front. I have in mind the heavy artillerymen who garrisoned the forts around Washington. They were in receipt of visits at all hours in the day from the most distinguished of military and civil guests, and on this account were not only obliged to be efficient in drill but showy on parade. Hence their clothing had always to be of the best. No patched or untidy garments were tolerated. In the spring of 1864, twenty-four thousand of these men were despatched as re-enforcements to the Army of the Potomac, and a fine lot of men they were. They were soldiers, for the most part, who had enlisted early in the war, and having had so safe—or, as the boys used to say, "soft"—and easy a time of it in the forts, had re-enlisted only to be soon relieved of garrison duty and sent to the front as infantry. But while they were veterans in service in point of time, yet, so far as the real hardships of war were concerned, they were simply recruits. I shall never forget that muggy, muddy morning of the 18th of May, when, standing by the roadside near what was known as the "Brown House" at Spotsylvania, I saw this fine-looking lot of soldiers go by. Their uniforms and equipments all seemed new. Among the regiments was the First Maine Heavy Artillery.

"What regiment is this?" was inquired at the head of the column by bystanders.

"First Maine," was the reply.

After the columns had marched by a while, someone would again ask what regiment it was, only to find it still the First Maine. It numbered over two thousand strong, and, never having lost any men in battles and hard campaigning, its ranks were full. The strength of these regiments struck the Army of the Potomac with surprise. A single regiment larger than one of their own brigades!

These men had started from Washington with knapsacks that were immense in their proportions, and had clung to them manfully the first day or two out, but this morning in question, which was of the sultriest kind, was taxing them beyond endurance as they plunged along in the mire marching up to the front; and their course could have been followed by the well-stuffed knapsacks—or "bureaus," as some of the old vets called them—that sprinkled the roadside. It seemed rather sad to see a man step out of the ranks, unsling his knapsack, seat himself for a moment to overhaul its contents, transfer to his pocket some little keepsake, then, rising and casting one despairing look at it, hurry on after the column. Many would not even open their knapsacks, but, giving them a toss, would leave them to fate and sternly resume their march. It was the second in the list of sacrifices that active campaigning required of them. Their first was made in cutting loose from their comfortable quarters and accumulated conveniences in the forts which they had so recently left.

The knapsack, haversack, canteen, and shelter tent, like the arms, were Government property, for which the commanding officer of a company was responsible. At the end of a soldier's term of service they were to be turned in or properly accounted for.

ARMY CATTLE

An Army officer who was reputed to have been of high and hasty temper, who certainly seemed to have been capable of rash and inconsiderate remarks, was once overheard to say of soldiers that they were nothing but cattle and deserved to be treated only as such. In the short sketch here submitted on the subject of Army cattle, I do not include the variety above referred to, but rather the quadrupedal kind that furnished food for them. . . .

When there came an active demand for fresh and salt meat to feed the soldiers and sailors, at once the price advanced, and Northern farmers turned their attention more extensively to grazing. Of course, the great mass of the cattle were raised in the West, but yet even rugged New England contributed no inconsiderable quantity to swell the total. These were sent by hundreds and thousands by rail and shipboard to the various armies. On their arrival, they were put in a corral. Here they were subject, like all supplies, to the disposition of the Commissary General of the Army, who, through his subordinates, supplied them to the various organizations upon the presentation of a requisition signed by the commanding officer of a regiment or other body of troops, certifying to the number of rations of meat required.

When the army was investing Petersburg and Richmond, the cattle were in corral near City Point. On the 16th of September, 1864, the Rebels having learned through their scouts that this corral was but slightly guarded, and that by making a wide détour in the rear of our lines the chances were good for them to add a few rations of fresh beef to the bacon and corn-meal diet of the Rebel Army, a strong force of cavalry under Wade Hampton made the attempt, capturing 2500 beeves and 400 prisoners, and getting off with them before our cavalry could intervene. The beeves were a blessing to them, far more precious and valuable than as many Union prisoners would have been; for they already had more prisoners than they could or would feed. As for us, I do not remember that fresh meat was any the scarcer on account of this raid, for the North with its abundance was bountifully supplying the Government with whatever was needed, and the loss of a few hundred cattle could scarcely cause even a temporary inconvenience. Had the Army been on the march, away from its base of supplies, the loss might have been felt more severely.

Whenever the Army made a move its supply of fresh meat went along too. Who had charge of it? Men were detailed for the business from the various regiments, who acted both as butchers and drovers and were excused from all other duty. When a halt was made for the night, some of the steers would be slaughtered, and the meat furnished to the troops upon presentation of the proper requisitions by quartermasters. The butcher killed his victims with a rifle. The killing was not always done at night. It often took place in the morning or forenoon, and the men received their rations in time to cook for dinner.

The manner in which these cattle were taken along was rather interesting. One might very naturally suppose that they would be driven along the road just as they are driven in any neighborhood; but such was not exactly the case. The troops and trains must use the roads, and so the cattle must need travel elsewhere, which they did. Every herd had a steer that was used both as a pack animal and a leader. As a pack animal he bore the equipments and cooking utensils of the drovers. He was as docile as an old cow or horse, and could be led or called fully as readily. By day he was preceded in his lead by the herdsman in charge on horseback, while other herdsmen brought up the rear. It was necessary to keep the herd along with the troops for two reasons—safety and convenience; and, as they could not use the road, they skirted the fields and woods only a short remove from the highways and picked their way as best they could.

By night one of the herdsmen went ahead of the herd on foot, making a gentle hallooing sound which the sagacious steer on lead steadily followed and was in turn faithfully followed by the rest of the herd. The herdsman's course lay sometimes through the open but often through the woods, which made the hallooing sound necessary as a guide to keep the herd from straying. They kept nearer the road at night than in the day, partly for safety's sake, and partly to take advantage of the light from huge campfires which detachments of cavalry that preceded the Army kindled at intervals to light the way, making them nearer together in woods and swamps than elsewhere. Even then these drovers often had a thorny and difficult path to travel in picking their way through underbrush and brambles.

Such a herd got its living off the country in the summer, but not in the winter. It was a sad sight to see these animals, which followed the Army so patiently, sacrificed one after the other until but a half-dozen were left. When the number had been reduced to this extent, they seemed to realize the fate in store for them, and it often took the butcher some time before he could succeed in facing one long enough to shoot him. His aim was at the curl of the hair between the eyes, and they would avert their lowered heads whenever he raised his rifle, until at last his quick eye brought them to the ground.

From the manner in which I have spoken of these herds, it may be inferred that there was a common herd for the whole Army; but such was not the case. The same system prevailed here as elsewhere. For example, when the Army entered the Wilderness with three-days' rations of hard bread, and three-days' rations of meat in their haversacks, the fresh meat to accompany the other three-days' rations, which they had stowed in their knapsacks, was driven along in division herds. The remainder of the meat ration which they required to last them for the sixteen days during which it was expected the Army would be away from a base of supplies was driven as corps herds. In addition to these there was a general or Army herd to fall back upon when necessary to supply the corps herds, but this was always at the base of supplies. Probably from eight to ten thousand head of cattle accompanied the Army across the Rapidan when it entered upon the Wilderness Campaign.

THE ARMY HORSE

I have already stated that the horse* was the sole reliance of the artillery and cavalry, and have given the reasons why the mule was a failure in either branch. I have also stated that the mule replaced him for the most part in the wagon trains, six mules being substituted for four horses. I did not state that in the ambulance train the horses were retained because they were steadier. But I wish now to refer more particularly to their conduct in action and on duty generally.

First, I will come directly to the point by saying that the horse was a hero in action. That horses under fire behaved far better than men did under a similar exposure would naturally

---

* The Union Armies used about 650,000 horses.

be expected, for men knew what and whom to fear, whereas a horse, when hit by a bullet, if he could get loose, was fully as likely to run towards the enemy as from him. But not every horse would run or make a fuss when wounded. It depended partly upon the horse and partly upon the character and location of the wound. I have seen bullets buried in the neck or rump of steady-nerved horses without causing them to show more than a little temporary uneasiness. The best illustration of the fortitude of horseflesh that I ever witnessed occurred on the 25th of August, 1864, at Ream's Station on the Weldon Railroad. In this battle the fifty-seven or eight horses belonging to my company stood out in bold relief, a sightly target for the bullets of Rebel sharpshooters, who, from a woods and cornfield in our front, improved their opportunity to the full. Their object was to kill off our horses, and then by charging, take the guns, if possible.

It was painfully interesting to note the manner in which our brave limber-horses—those which drew the guns—succumbed to the bullets of the enemy. They stood harnessed in teams of six. A peculiar dull thud indicated that the bullet had penetrated some fleshy part of the animal, sounding much as a pebble does when thrown into the mud. The result of such wounds was to make the horse start for a moment or so, but finally he would settle down as if it was something to be endured without making a fuss, and thus he would remain until struck again. I remember having had my eye on one horse at the very moment when a bullet entered his neck, but the wound had no other effect upon him than to make him shake his head as if pestered by a fly. Some of the horses would go down when hit by the first bullet and after lying quiet awhile would struggle to their feet again only to receive additional wounds. Just before the close of this battle, while our gallant General Hancock was riding along endeavoring by his own personal fearlessness to rally his retreating troops, his horse received a bullet in the neck, from the effects of which he fell forward, dismounting the general, and appearing as if dead. Believing such to be the case, Hancock mounted another horse; but within five minutes the fallen brute arose, shook himself, was at once remounted by the general, and survived the war many years.

When a bullet struck the bone of a horse's leg in the lower part, it made a hollow snapping sound and took him off his feet. I saw one pole-horse shot thus, fracturing the bone. Down he went at once, but all encumbered as he was with harness and limber, he soon scrambled up and stood on three legs until a bullet hit him vitally. It seemed sad to see a single horse left standing, with his five companions all lying dead or dying around him, himself the object of a concentrated fire until the fatal shot finally laid him low. I saw one such brute struck by the seventh bullet before he fell for the last time. Several received as many as five bullets, and it was thought by some that they would average that number apiece. They were certainly very thoroughly riddled, and long before the serious fighting of the day occurred but two of the thirty-one nearest the enemy remained standing. These two had been struck, but not vitally, and survived some time longer. We took but four of our fifty-seven horses from that ill-starred fray.

But, aside from their wonderful heroism—for I can find no better name for it—they exhibited in many ways that sagacity for which the animal is famous. I have already referred to the readiness with which they responded to many of the bugle calls used on drill. In the cavalry service they knew their places as well as their riders did, and it was a frequent occurrence to see a horse, when his rider had been dismounted by some means, resume his place in line or column without him, seemingly not wishing to be left behind. This quality was often illustrated when a poor, crippled, or generally used-up beast, which had been turned out to die, would attempt to hobble along in his misery and join a column as it passed.

Captain W. S. Davis, a member of General Griffin's staff of the Fifth Corps, rode a horse which had the very singular but horse-sensible habit of sitting down on his haunches like a dog after his rider had dismounted. One morning he was missing, and nothing was seen of him for months; but one night after the corps had encamped, some of the men who knew the horse, in looking off towards the horizon, saw against the sky a silhouette of a horse sitting down. It was at once declared to be the missing brute, and Captain Davis, on being informed, recovered his eccentric but highly prized animal.

17

On the March

From the descriptions which I have already given of the various kinds of shelter used by the soldiers it will be readily understood that they got the most comfortably settled in their winter quarters, and that in a small way each hut became a miniature homestead, and for the time being possessed to a certain extent all the attractions of home. The bunk, the stools, and other furniture, the Army bric-à-brac, whether captured or of home production, which adorned the rough tenement within and without, all came to have a value by association in the soldier's thought, a value which was not fully computed till campaigning impended—that usually direful day, when marching orders came, and the boys folded their tents and marched away.

When the general commanding an army had decided upon a plan of campaign, and the proper time came to put it in operation, he at once issued his orders to his subordinate commanders to have their commands ready to take their place in column at a given hour on a given day. These orders came down through the various corps, division, brigade, regimental, or battery headquarters to the rank and file, whose instructions given them on line would be to the effect that at the stated hour they were to be ready to start with three-days' rations in their haversacks (this was the usual quantity), the infantry to have forty rounds of ammunition in their cartridge boxes. This latter quantity was very often exceeded. The Army of the Potomac went into the Wilderness having from eighty to a hundred rounds of ammunition to a man, stowed away in knapsacks, haversacks, or pockets, according to the space afforded, and six-days' rations similarly disposed of. When Hooker started on the Chancellorsville Campaign, *eleven-days' rations* were issued to the troops.

Sometimes marching orders came when least expected. I remember to have heard the long roll sounded one Saturday forenoon in the camp of the infantry that lay near us in the fall of '63; it was October 10. Our guns were unlimbered for action just outside of camp where we had been lying several days utterly unsuspicious of danger. It was quite a surprise to us; and such Lee intended it to be, he having set out to put himself between our army and Washington. We were not attacked, but started to the rear a few hours afterwards.

Before the opening of the spring campaign a reasonable notice was generally given. There was one orderly from each brigade headquarters who almost infallibly brought marching orders. The men knew the nature of the tidings when he cantered up to regimental headquarters with orders tucked under his belt. Very often they would good-naturedly rail at him as he rode into and out of camp, thus indicating their dislike of his errand; but the wise ones went directly to quarters and began to pack up.

When it was officially announced to the men on line at night that marching orders were received, and that at such an hour next morning tents would be struck . . . men . . . retired to their huts and took an account of stock in order to decide what to take and what to leave. As a soldier would lay out two articles on the bunk, of equally tender associations, one could seem to hear him murmur with [John] Gay:

> How happy could I be with either
> Were t'other dear charmer away

as he endeavored to choose between them, knowing too well that both could not be taken. The survival of the fittest was the question which received deeper and tenderer consideration here in one evening than Darwin has ever given it. . . . Then, there was the overcoat and the woollen blanket—which should be left? Perhaps he finally decided to try taking both along for a while. He will leave the dress coat and wear the blouse. He has two changes of flannels. He will throw away those he has on, don a clean set, and take a change with him. These flannels . . . from the Government stores were often as rough to the skin as coarse sandpaper, which they somewhat resembled in color.

From the head of his bunk he takes a collection of old letters which have accumulated during the winter. These he looks over one by one and commits to the flames with a sigh. Many of them are letters from home; some are from acquaintances. Possibly he read the *Waverly Magazine*, and may have carried on a correspondence with one or more of the many young women who advertised in it for a "soldier correspondent, who must not be over twenty," with all the virtues namable. There was no man in my company—from old Graylocks, of nearly sixty, down to the callow "chicken" of seventeen—but what felt qualified to fill such a bill, "just for the fun of it, you know." The young woman was generally "eighteen, of prepossessing appearance, good education, and would exchange photographs if desired."

An occasional letter from such a quarter would provoke a smile as the soldier glanced at its source and contents before committing it to. the yawn of his army fireplace. This rather unpleasant task completed, he continues his researches and work of destruction. He tucks his little collection of photographs, which perhaps he has encased in rubber or leather, into an inside pocket, and disposes other small keepsakes about his person. If he intends to take his effects in a knapsack, he will at the start have put by more to carry than if he simply takes his blankets (rubber and woollen) rolled and slung over his shoulder. Late in the war this latter was the most common plan, as the same weight could be borne with less fatigue in that manner than in a knapsack slung on the back.

I have assumed it to be evening or late afternoon when marching orders arrived, and have thus far related what the average soldier was wont to do immediately afterwards. There was a night ahead and the soldiers were wont to make a night of it. As a rule, there was little sleep to be had, the enforcement of the usual rules of camp being relaxed on such an occasion. Aside from the labor of personal packing and destroying, the rations were to be distributed, and each company had to fall into line, march to the cook house, and receive their three or more days' allowance of hardtack, pork, coffee, and sugar, all of which they must stow away as compactly as possible in the haversack or elsewhere. In the artillery, besides securing the rations, sacks of grain—usually oats—must be taken from the grainpile and strapped on to the ammunition chests; the axles must be greased, good spare horses selected to supply the vacancies in any teams where the horses were unfit for duty; the tents of regimental headquarters must be struck, likewise the cook tents, and these, with officers' baggage, must be put into the wagons which are to join the trains—in brief, everything must be prepared for the march of the morrow.

After this routine of preparation was completed, campfires were lighted, and about them would gather the happy-go-lucky boys of the rank and file, whose merry din would speedily stir the blood of the men who had hoped for a few hours' sleep before starting out on the morrow, to come out of their huts and join the jovial round; and soon they were as happy as the happiest, even if more reticent. As the fire died down, and the soldiers drew closer about it, some comrade would go to his hut, and with an armful of its furniture, stools, closets, and tables, reillumine and enliven the scene and drive back the circle of bystanders again. The conversation, which, with the going down of the fire, was likely to take on a somewhat sober aspect, would again assume a more cheerful strain. For a time conjectures on the plan of the coming campaign would be exchanged. Volumes of wisdom concerning what ought to be done changed hands at these campfires, mingled with much "I told you so" about the last battle. Alexanders simply swarmed, so numerous were those who could solve the Gordian knot of success at sight. . . .

When this slight matter of the proper thing for the Army to do was disposed of, someone would start a song, and then for an hour at least "John Brown's Body," "Marching Along," "Red, White, and Blue," "Rally 'round the Flag," and other popular and familiar songs would ring out on the clear evening air, following along in quick succession, and sung with great earnestness and enthusiasm as the chorus was increased by additions from neighboring campfires, until tired Nature began to assert herself, when one by one the company would withdraw, each going to his hut for two or three hours' rest, if possible, to partially prepare him for the toils of the morrow. Ah! is not that an all-wise provision of Providence which keeps the future a sealed book, placing it before us leaf by leaf only as the present? For some of these very men whose voices rang out so merrily at that campfire would lie cold and pale ere the week should close in the solemn stillness of death.

But morning dawned all too soon for those who gave up most of the night to hilarity, and all were summoned forth at the call of the bugle or the drum, and at a time agreed upon *The General* was sounded.

THE GENERAL

The above is the General of infantry. That of the artillery was less often used and entirely different.

At this signal, every tent in a regiment was struck. It was quite an interesting sight to see several acres of canvas disappear in a moment, where before it had been the prominent feature in the landscape. As a fact, I believe the General was little used in the latter part of the war. For about two years, when the troops were sheltered by the Sibley, Wedge, and Wall tents, it was necessary to have them struck at an early hour, in order that they might be packed away in the wagon train. But after the Shelter tent came into use, and each man was his own wagon, the General was seldom heard unless at the end of a long encampment; for when marching orders came, each man understood that he must be ready at the hour appointed even if his regiment waited another day before it left camp.

No more provoking incident of army life happened, I believe, than for a regiment to wait in camp long after the hour appointed to march. But such was the rule rather than the exception. Many a man's hearthstone was then desolate, for if the hour of departure was set for the morning, when morning came and the stockade was vacated, it often suffered demolition to increase the heat of the campfires, as previously noted. But as hour after hour wore on, and men still found themselves in camp with nothing to do . . . they began to wish that they had not been so hasty in breaking up housekeeping and tearing down their shanties, else they might resort to them and make their wait a little more endurable. Especially did they repent if rain came on as they lingered, or if night again overtook them there with their huts untenable, for it would have been the work of only a moment to re-cover them with the Shelter tents. Such waits and their consequences were severe tests to the patience of the men, and sometimes seemed to work more injury to their morale than the average Army chaplain could repair in days.

But there is an end to all things earthly. . . . The colors of corps headquarters borne at the heels of the corps commander and followed by his staff are at last seen moving into the road. The bugler of the division having the lead sounds the call *Attention.*

This call is the Attention of infantry at which the men, already in column, take their places, officers mount, and all await the next call, which is

FORWARD

At this signal the regiments take "right shoulder shift," and the march begins. Let the reader, in imagination, take post by the roadside as the column goes by. Take a look at corps headquarters. The commander is a major-general. His staff comprises an assistant adjutant-general, an assistant inspector-general, a topographical engineer, a commissary of musters, a commissary of subsistence, a judge-advocate, several aides-de-camp—and perhaps other officers of varying rank. Those mentioned usually ranked from colonel to captain. In the Union Army, major-generals might command either a division, a corps, or an army, but in the Confederate service each army of importance was commanded by a lieutenant-general. Take a look at the corps headquarters flag. Feb. 7, 1863, General Hooker decreed the flags of corps headquarters to be a blue swallow-tail field bearing a white Maltese cross, having in the center the number of the corps; but so far as I can learn, this decree was never enforced in a single instance. Mr. James Beale, in his exceedingly valuable and unique volume, *The*

Union Flags at Gettysburg, shows a nondescript cross on some of the headquarters' flags, which some quartermaster may have intended as a compliance with Hooker's order; but though true copies of originals they are monstrosities, which never could have had existence in a well-ordered brain, and which have no warrant in heraldry or general orders as far as can be ascertained. When the Army entered upon the Wilderness Campaign, each corps headquarters floated a blue swallow-tailed flag bearing its own particular emblem in white, in the center of which was the figure designating the corps in red.

Here comes the First Division. At the head rides its general commanding and staff. Behind him is the color-bearer carrying the division flag. If you are familiar with the corps badges, you will not need to ask what corps or division it is. The men's caps tell the story, but the flags are equally plain-spoken.

This flag is the first *division* color. It is *rectangular* in shape. The corps emblem is red in a, white field; the *second* has the emblem white in a blue field; the *third* has the emblem blue in a white field. The divisions had the lead of the corps of the march by turns, changing each day.

But here comes another headquarters. The color-bearer carries a *triangular* flag. That is a *brigade* flag. May 12, 1863, General Hooker issued an order prescribing division flags of the pattern I have described, and also designated what the brigade flags should be. They were to be, first of all, *triangular* in shape; the brigades of the first division should bear the corps symbol in *red* in the center of a *white* field, but, to distinguish them, the first brigade should have no other mark; the second should have a *blue* stripe next the staff, and the third a *blue* border four and one-half inches wide around the flag.

The brigades of the second division had the corps symbol in *white* in the center of a *blue* field, with a *red* stripe next the staff to designate the second brigade, and a *red* border the third.

The third division had its brigades similarly designated, with the symbol *blue*, the field *white*, and the stripes *red*.

Whenever there was a fourth brigade, it was designated by a triangular block of color in each corner of the flag.

The chief quartermaster of the corps and the chief of artillery each had his appropriate flag, but the arrangement of the colors in the flag of the chief quartermasters differed in different corps.

This scheme of Hooker's for distinguishing corps, division, and brigade headquarters remained unchanged till the end of the war.

The brigades took turns in having the lead—or, as military men say, the *right*—of the division, and regiments had the right of brigades by turns.

There goes Army Headquarters yonder—the commanding general, with his numerous staff—making for the head of the column. His flag is the simple Star-Spangled Banner. The Stars and Stripes were a common flag for Army Headquarters. It was General Meade's headquarters flag till Grant came to the Army of the Potomac, who also used it for the purpose. This made it necessary for Meade to change, which he did, finally adopting a lilac-colored, swallow-tailed flag, about the size of the corps headquarters flags, having in the field a wreath enclosing an eagle in gold.

You can easily count the regiments in column by their United States colors. A few of them, you will notice, have a battle flag, bearing the names of the engagements in which they have participated. Some regiments used the national colors for a battle flag, some the state colors. I think the volunteers did not adopt the idea early in the war. Originally battles were only inscribed on flags by authority of the Secretary of War, that is, in the regular Army. But the volunteers seemed to be a law unto themselves, and while many flags in existence today bear names of battles inscribed by order of the commanding general, there are some with inscriptions of battles which the troops were hardly in hearing of. The Rebel battle flag was a blue-spangled saltier in a red field; it originated with General Joe Johnston after First Bull Run.

You will have little difficulty in deciding where a regiment begins or ends. It begins with a field officer and ends with a mule. Originally it ended with several army wagons; but now that portion of regimental headquarters baggage which has not gone to the wagon train is to be found stowed about the mule, that is led along by a contraband. Yes, the head, ears, and feet which you see are the only visible externals of a mule. He is "clothed upon" with the various materials necessary to prepare a square meal for the colonel and other headquarters officers. His trappings would, seemingly, fit out a small family in household goods of a kind. There is a mess kettle, a fry pan, mess pans, tent poles, a fly (canvas), a valise, a knapsack and haver-

sack, a hamper on each side, a musket, and other matter which
goes to make the burden at least twice the size of the animal.
Four mules were regarded as having the carrying capacity of one
army wagon. At the end of the brigade you will see two or
three of these mules burdened with the belongings of brigade
headquarters.

The mule had company other than the Negro ofttimes. That
man who seems to be flour and grease from head to heels, who
needs no shelter nor rubber blanket because he is waterproof
already, inside and out, whose shabby, well-stuffed knapsack
furnishes the complement to the mule's lading, who shuffles
along with no style about him, is the cook, perhaps, for
the regiment, probably for headquarters, certainly not for
Delmonico. It is singular, but none the less true, that if a man
made a slovenly, indifferent soldier he was fully as likely to get a
berth in the cook house as to have any other fate befall him.
This remark applies to men who drifted into the business of
army caterer after trying other service, and not those who
entered at once upon it.

Here comes a light battery at the rear of the division. Possibly
it is to remain with this part of the corps for the campaign. Such
was sometimes the case, but later a battery was often used anywhere within the limits of a corps that it could be of advantage.
This battery has six brass Napoleons, 12-pounders. They are
very destructive at short range. It is followed by a battery of
steel guns. They are Parrots, three-inch rifles; best for long
range, but good anywhere—not so safe for close action, however, as the Napoleons.

Yonder you can see the Second Division moving across the
fields, made up like the one just passed. It will close in upon
the rear of this division farther up the road. What an interesting
spectacle it presents, the bright sunlight glinting from the
thousands of polished muskets, the moving masses of light and
dark blue inching along over the uneven ground, the various
flags streaming proudly in the air, marking off the separate
brigades and regiments. The column is moving at a moderate
pace. It takes some time for a corps to get under way. If we
wait long enough, the Third Division, made up like the others,
will pass by us, unless it has gone on a parallel road.

It is growing warmer. The column has now got straightened
out, and for the last hour has moved forward quite rapidly. The
road is evidently clear of all obstructions, but the heat and

speed begin to tell on the men. Look at the ground which that brigade has just vacated after its brief halt for rest. It is strewn with blankets, overcoats, dresscoats, pantaloons, shirts—in fact, a little of everything from the outfit of the common soldier. As the Second Corps advanced into the Wilderness on the morning of May 4, 1864, I saw an area of an acre or more almost literally covered with the articles above named, many of them probably extras, but some of them the sole garment of their kind left by the owners who felt compelled, from the increasing weight of their load, to lighten it to the extent of parting with the blankets which they would need that very night for shelter. This lightening of the load began before the columns had been on the road an hour. A soldier who had been through the mill would not wait for a general halt to occur before parting with a portion of his load if it oppressed him; but a recruit would hang to his until he bent over at an angle of 45°, with his eyes staring, his lower jaw hanging, and his face dripping with moisture. If you were to follow the column after the first two miles, you would find various articles scattered along at intervals by the roadside, where a soldier quietly stepped out of the ranks, sat down, unslung his knapsack or his blanket roll, took out what he had decided to throw away, again equipped himself, and thus relieved, hastened on to overtake the regiment. It did not take an army long to get into light marching order after it was once fairly on the road.

I have been dealing with the first day out of settled camp. On subsequent days, of course the same program would not be enacted. And, again, if a man clung to his efforts till noon, he was likely to do so for the day, as after noon the thought of shelter for the night nerved him to hold on. But men would drop out in the afternoon of the first day for another reason. They blistered or chafed their feet and sat down at the first stream to bathe them, after which, if the weather admitted, they could. be seen plodding along barefooted, their pantaloons rolled up a few inches, and their shoes dangling at the end of their musket barrel.

Then, this very crossing of a stream often furnished an interesting scene in the march of the column. A river broad and deep would be spanned by a pontoon bridge, but the common creeks of the South were crossed by fording. Once in a while (in warm weather) the men would take off most of their clothing and carry it with their equipment across on their heads. It was no uncommon experience for them to ford streams waist-deep even in cool weather. If the bottom was a treacherous one, and the current rapid, a line of cavalrymen was placed across the river just below the column to pick up such men as should lose their footing. Many were the mishaps of such a crossing, and unless the enemy was at hand, the first thing to be done after reaching shore was to strip and wring out such clothing as needed it. With those who had slipped and fallen this meant all they had on and what was in their knapsacks besides, but with most it included only trousers, drawers, and socks.

After the halt which allowed the soldiers time to perform this bit of laundry work had ended, and the column moved along, it was not an uncommon sight to see muskets used as clotheslines, from which depended socks, shoes, here and there a shirt, perhaps a towel or handkerchief. But if the weather was cool the wash did not hang out in this way. When it became necessary to cross a stream in the night, huge fires were built on its banks, with a picket at hand, whose duty it was to keep them burning until daylight, or until the army had crossed. A greater number of mishaps occurred in fording by night than by day even then. During Meade's retreat from Culpeper in the fall of 1863—it was the night of October 11— my company forded the Rappahannock after dark and went into camp a few rods away from the ford; and I remember what a jolly night the troops made of it when they came to this ford. At short intervals I was awakened from slumber by the laughter or cheers of the waders, as they made merry at the expense of some of their number, who came out after immersion using language which plainly indicated their disbelief in that kind of baptism. Here was the field for the tired, overloaded headquarters mule to display his obstinacy to a large and changing audience, by getting midway of the stream and refusing to budge. I can see the frenzied Ethiopian in charge, now, waist-deep in water, wild with despair at the situation, alternating reasoning with pulling and beating, while the brute lies down in the stream all encumbered with the baggage, the passing column jeering poor Sambo and making the adjacent woodland echo with loud guffaws at his helpless yet laughable condition.

That was a noisy night, and it has always been a matter of wonder to me that we remained undisturbed, with the enemy less than three miles up the river, as General Birney, with whom we then were, has left on record. There was no stopping to wring out. But "close up!" was the order after crossing, and the dull rattle made by the equipments, the striking of the coffee dipper on the canteen or buckles, as the column glided along in the darkness, or the whipping-up of belated mule teams, was heard until the gray of morning appeared.

The army on the march in a rain storm presented some aspects not seen in fair weather. As soon as it began to rain, or just before, each man would remove his rubber blanket from his roll or knapsack and put it over his shoulders, tying it in front. Some men used their shelter tent instead—a very poor substitute, however. But there was no fun in the marching business during the rain. It might settle the dust. It certainly settled about everything else. An order to go into camp while the rain was in progress was not much of an improvement, for the ground was wet, fence rails were wet, one's woollen blanket was likely also to be wet, hardtack in the haversack wet—in fact, nothing so abundant and out of place as water. I remember going into camp one night in particular, in Pleasant Valley, Md., on a side hill during a drenching rain, such as mountain regions know, and lying down under a hastily pitched shelter, with the water coursing freely along beneath me. I was fresh as a soldier then, and this experience, seeming so dreadful to me, made a strong impression. Such situations were too numerous afterwards to make note of even in memory.

Then, the horses! It made them ugly and vicious to stand in the pelting rain at the picket rope. I think they preferred being in harness on the road. But they were likely to get subdued the next day, when sloughs and mire were the rule. If two corps took the same road after a storm, the worse for the hindermost, for it found deep ruts and mud holes in abundance; and as it dragged forward it would come upon some piece of artillery or caisson in the mire to the hubs, doomed to stay, in spite of the shoutings and lashings of the drivers, the swearing of the officers, and the lifting and straining of mud-bedraggled cannoneers, until six more horses were added to extricate it. Anon the corps would arrive at a place utterly impassable, when down would go the fence by the roadside . . . and out would go the column into the field skirting the road, returning again beyond the mire. At another slough, a staff officer might be found posted to direct the artillery where to make a safe passage.

Such places by night were generally lighted by fires built for that purpose. I remember such a spot in particular—a reminiscence of the Mine Run Campaign; I think it was the night of Dec. 4, 1863. My battery was then attached to the Third Division of the Third Corps. By the edge of the slough in question sat General J. B. Carr, the division commander, with a portion of his command nearby, and, as a caisson went down in the mire, he called in his "Blue Diamonds" to lift it out, which they did right manfully. There was no turning into fields that night, for, while the roads were soft, the fields were softer, and worse traveling I believe the Army of the Potomac never saw, unless on the Mud March [after Fredericksburg].

When the army was expecting to run against the enemy in its advance, flankers were thrown out on either side of the column. These flankers were a single file of soldiers who marched along a few feet apart, parallel to the column, and perhaps ten or twelve rods distant from it in open country, but not more than half that distance when it was marching through woods. In the event of an attack, the flankers on that side became the skirmish line in action.

It was an interesting sight to see a column break up when the order came to halt, whether for rest or other reason. It would melt in a moment, dividing to the right and left, and scattering to the sides of the road, where the men would sit down or lie down, lying back on their knapsacks if they had them, or stretching out full length on the ground. If the latter was wet or muddy, cannoneers sat on their carriages and limber chests, while infantrymen would perhaps sit astride their muskets, if the halt was a short one. When the halt was expected to continue for some considerable time the troops of a corps or division ·were massed, that is, brought together in some large open tract of territory, then the muskets would be stacked, the equipments laid off, and each man rush for the "top rail" of the nearest fence, until not a rail remained. The coffee would soon begin to simmer, the pork to sputter in the flames, and when the march was resumed the men would start off refreshed with rest and rations.

But if the halt was for a few minutes only, and the marching had not been relieved by the regular rests usually allowed, the men stiffened up so much that with their equipments on, they could hardly arise without assistance and, goaded by their stiffened cords and tired muscles and swollen or chafed feet, made wry faces for the first few rods after the column started. In this manner they plodded on until ordered into camp for the night, or perhaps double-quicked into line of battle.

During that dismal night retreat of the Army of the Potomac from Chancellorsville, a little event occurred which showed what a choleric man General Meade was on occasion, and to what an exhausted bodily condition the rigors of a campaign often reduced men. While the general was sitting with General Warren at one of those campfires always found along the line of march after nightfall, a poor jaded, mud-bedraggled infantrymen came straggling and stumbling along the roadside, scarcely able in his wet and wearied condition to bear up under his burden of musket and equipments. As he staggered past the campfire, he struck by the merest accident against General Meade, who jumped immediately to his feet, drew his saber, and made a lunge at the innocent offender, which sent him staggering to the ground. There he lay motionless as if dead. At once Meade began to upbraid himself for his hasty temper and seemed filled with remorse for what he had done. Whereat General Warren made efforts to calm his fears by telling him it was probably not as serious as he supposed, and thereupon began to make investigation of the nature of the injury done the prostrate veteran. To General Meade's great gratification, it was found that while his saber had cut through the man's clothing, it had only grazed his side without drawing blood, but so completely worn out had the soldier become through the exactions of the recent campaign that matter dominated mind, and he lay in a double sense as if dust had returned to dust.

18

Army Wagon Trains

Before giving a history of the wagon trains which formed a part, and a necessary part, of every army, I will briefly refer to what was known as Grant's Military Railroad, which was really a railroad built for the Army and used solely by it. When the Army of the Potomac appeared before Petersburg, City Point on the James River was made Army Headquarters and the base of supplies, that is, the place to which supplies were brought from the North, and from which they were distributed to the various portions of the Army. The Lynchburg or Southside Railroad enters Petersburg from the west, and a short railroad known as the City Point Railroad connects it with City Point, ten miles eastward. The greater portion of this ten miles fell within the Union lines after our Army appeared before Petersburg, and as these lines were extended westward after the siege was determined upon, Grant conceived the plan of running a railroad inside our fortifications to save both time and mule flesh in distributing supplies along the line. It was soon done. About five miles of the City Point road were used, from which the new road extended to the southwest, perhaps ten miles, striking the Weldon Railroad, which had been wrested from the enemy. Down this the trains ran three miles; then a new branch of about two miles more to the west took them to the left of the Union lines.

Of course, there were stations along this road at which supplies were left for those troops nearby. These stations were named after different generals of the army. Meade and Patrick stations are two names which yet linger in my memory, near each of which my company was at some time located. The trains on this road were visible to the enemy for a time as they crossed an open plain in their trips, and brought upon themselves quite a lively shelling, resulting in no damage, I believe, but still making railroading so uncomfortable that a high embankment of earth was thrown up, which completely covered the engine and cars as they rolled along. . . . This railroad was what is known as a surface road, by which is meant that there were no cuts made, the track being laid on the natural surface of the ground. When a marsh was met with, instead of filling, the engineers built a trestling. The effect of such railroading to the eye was quite picturesque, as a train wound its serpentine course along the country, up hill and down dale, appearing much as if it had jumped the track and was going across lots to its destination.

But *the* trains of the Army were *wagon* trains. . . . The trains belong to what is known in French as the *materiel* of the Army, in distinction from the *personnel*, the men employed. In Roman history we frequently find the baggage trains of the army alluded to as the *impedimenta*. The *matériel*, then, or *impedimenta*, of our armies has very naturally been ignored by the historian; for the *personnel*, the actors, are of so much more consequence, they have absorbed the interest of both writers and readers. I say the persons are of much more consequence, but I must not be understood as belittling the importance of the trains. An army without its varied supplies, which the trains care for and provide, would soon be neither useful nor ornamental. In fact, an army is like a piece of machinery, each part of which is indispensable to every other part.

Army wagons . . . were heavy, lumbering affairs at best, built for hard service, all apparently after the same pattern, each one having its tool box in front, its feed trough behind, which in camp was placed lengthwise of the pole; its spare pole suspended at the side; its wooden bucket for water, and iron slush bucket for grease hanging from the hind axle; and its canvas cover, which when closely drawn in front and rear, as it always was on the march, made quite a satisfactory closed carriage. As a pleasure carriage, however, they were not considered a success. When the Third Corps was wintering at Brandy Station in 1863–4 the concert troupe, which my company boasted, was engaged to give a week of evening entertainments not far from Culpeper, in a large hexagonal stockade, which would seat six or seven hundred persons, and which had been erected for the purpose by one Lieutenant Lee. . . . To convey us thither over the intervening distance of four or five miles, as I now remember, we hired a mule driver with his Army wagon. Those twelve or fourteen rides after dark across the rough country and frozen ground around Brandy Station were so thoroughly jolted into my memory that I shall never forget them. The seven dollars apiece per night which we received for our services was but a trifling compensation for the battering and mellowing we endured *en route*, and no more than paid for wear and tear. No harder vehicle can be found to take a ride in than an Army wagon.

By some stroke of good luck, or perhaps good management, many of the regiments from New England took their transportation along with them. It consisted, in many cases, of twenty-five wagons, two for each company and five for regimental headquarters. These were drawn at first by four horses but afterwards by six mules. A light battery had three such wagons. They were designed to carry the baggage of the troops, and when a march was ordered they were filled with tents, stoves, kettles, pans, chairs, desks, trunks, valises, knapsacks, boards—in fact whatever conveniences had accumulated about the camps.

General Sherman, in his *Memoirs* (vol. i. p. 178), describes graphically the troops he saw about Washington in '61, as follows:

"Their uniforms were as various as the states and cities from which they came; their arms were also of every pattern and caliber; and they were so loaded down with overcoats, haversacks, knapsacks, tents, and baggage, that it took from twenty-five to fifty wagons to move the camp of a regiment from one place to another, and some of the camps had bakeries and cooking establishments that would have done credit to Delmonico."

General Sherman might have seen much the same situation near Washington even in '62 and '63. Every company in a regiment located in the defences of the capital city had one or more large cook stoves with other appointments to match, and when they moved only a few miles they took all their *lares* and *penates* with them. This could then be done without detriment to the service. It was only when they attempted to carry everything along in active campaigning that trouble ensued.

In October, 1861, McClellan issued an order which contained the following provisions:

1. No soldiers shall ride in loaded baggage wagons under any circumstances, nor in empty wagons unless by special instructions to that effect.

2. Knapsacks shall not be carried in the wagons except on the written recommendation of the surgeon, which shall be given in case of sickness.

3. Tent floors shall not be transported in public wagons, and hereafter no lumber shall be issued for tent floors except upon the recommendation of the medical director for hospital purposes.

This order was issued before the corps were organized, while the wagons were yet with their regiments, and while the men yet had their big knapsacks, which they were always ready to ride with or toss into a wagon when the regiment moved. This was the time of transporting tent floors, the luxurious fault-finding period before carpets, feather beds, and roast beef had entirely lost their charm; when each man was in his own way and belief fully the size of a major-general; when the medical director of the Army had time, unaided as yet by subordinates, to decide the question of tent floors *versus* no tent floors for individuals. Ah, the freshness and flavor of those early war days come back to me as I write—each day big with importance as our letters . . . faithfully record.

Not many months elapsed before it became apparent that the necessities of stern warfare would not permit and should not have so many of the equipments of civil life, when the Shelter tent, already described, took the place of the larger varieties; when campfires superseded stoves, and many other comfortable but unnecessary furnishings disappeared from the baggage. Not how *little* but how *much* could be dispensed with then became the question of the hour. The trains must be reduced in size, and they must be moved in a manner not to hamper the troops if possible; but the war was more than half-finished before they were brought into a satisfactory system of operation.

The greater number of the three-years' regiments that arrived in Washington in 1861 brought no transportation of any kind. After McClellan assumed command, a *depot of transportation* was established at Perryville on the Susquehanna; by this is meant a station where wagons and ambulances were kept and from which they were supplied.

From there Captain Sawtell . . . fitted out regiments as rapidly as he could, giving each *six* wagons instead of twenty-five, one of which was for medical supplies. Some regiments, however, by influence or favor at court, got more than that. A few wagons were supplied from the Quartermaster's Depot at Washington. A quartermaster is an officer whose duty it is to provide quarters, provisions, clothing, fuel, storage, and transportation for an army. The chief officer in the quartermaster's department is known as the Quartermaster-General. There was a chief quartermaster of the Army, and a chief quartermaster to each corps and division; then, there were brigade and regimental quartermasters, and finally the quartermaster-sergeants, all attending in their appropriate spheres to the special duties of this department.

During the march of the Army up the Peninsula in 1862, the fighting force advanced by brigades, each of which was followed by its long columns of transportation. But this plan was very unsatisfactory, for thereby the Army was extended along forest paths over an immense extent of country, and great delays and difficulties ensued in keeping the column closed up; for such was the nature of the roads that after the first few wagons had passed over them they were rendered impassable in places for those behind. At least a quarter of each regiment was occupied in escorting its wagons, piled up with ammunition, provisions, tents, etc.; and long after the head of the column had settled in bivouac could be heard the loud shouting of the teamsters to their jaded and mire-bedraggled brutes, the clatter of wagon and artillery wheels, the lowing of the driven herds, the rattling of sabers, canteens, and other equipment, as the men strode along in the darkness, anxious to reach the spot selected for their uncertain quantity of rest.

At times in this campaign it was necessary for the wagon trains to be massed and move together, but for some reason no order of march was issued, so that the most dire confusion ensued. A struggle for the lead would naturally set in, each division wanting it and fighting for it. Profanity, threats, and the flourishing of revolvers were sure to be prominent in the settling of the question, but the train which could run over the highest stumps and pull through the deepest mud holes was likely to come out ahead.

The verdancy which remained after the first fall of the Union Army at Bull Run was to be utterly overshadowed by the baptism of woe which was to follow in the Peninsular Campaign; and on arriving at Harrison's Landing on the James, McClellan issued the following order, which paved the way for better things:

Allowance of Transportation, Tents, and Baggage

HEADQUARTERS, ARMY OF THE POTOMAC

Camp near Harrison's Landing, Va., August 10, 1862

[General Orders, No. 153]

I. The following allowance of wagons is authorized:
For the Headquarters of an Army Corps .... Four
For the Headquarters of a Division or Brigade .... Three
For a Battery of Light Artillery or Squadron of Cavalry .... Three
For a full regiment of Infantry .... Six

This allowance will in no case be exceeded, but will be reduced to correspond as nearly as practicable with the number of officers and men actually present. All means of transportation in excess of the prescribed standard will be immediately turned in to the depot, with the exception of the authorized supply trains, which will be under the direction of the Chief Quartermasters of Corps. The Chief Quartermaster of this Army will direct the organization of the supply trains.

II. The Army must be prepared to bivouac when on marches away from the depots. The allowance of tents will therefore be immediately reduced to the following standard, and no other accommodations must be expected until a permanent depot is established:
For the Headquarters of an Army Corps, Division, or Brigade, one wall tent for the General Commanding, and one to every two officers of his staff.
To each full regiment, for the Colonel, Field and Staff officers, three wall tents.
For all other commissioned officers, one shelter tent each.
For every two non-commissioned officers, soldiers, officers' servants, and camp followers, as far as they can be supplied, one shelter tent.
One hospital tent will be allowed for office purposes at Corps Headquarters, and one wall tent at Division and Brigade Headquarters.
All tents in excess of this allowance will be immediately turned in to the depots.
Tents of other patterns required to be exchanged for shelter tents will be turned in as soon as the latter can be obtained from the Quartermaster's Department. Under no circumstances will they be allowed to be carried when the Army moves.

III. The allowance of officers' baggage will be limited to blankets, a small valise or carpet bag and a reasonable mess kit. All officers will at once reduce their baggage to this standard. The men will carry no baggage except blankets and shelter tents. The Chief Quartermaster will provide storage on the transports for the knapsacks of the men and for the officers' surplus baggage.

IV. Hospital tents must not be diverted from their legitimate use, except for offices, as authorized in paragraph II.

V. The wagons allowed to a regiment or battery must carry nothing but forage for the teams, cooking utensils for the men, hospital stores, small rations, and officers' baggage. One of the wagons allowed for a regiment will be used exclusively for hospital stores under the direction of the regimental surgeon. The wagon for regimental Headquarters will carry grain for the officers' horses. At least one and a half of the wagons allowed to a battery or squadron will carry grain.

VI. Hospital stores, ammunition, Quartermaster's Stores, and subsistence stores in bulk will be transported in special trains.

VII. Commanding officers will be held responsible that the reduction above ordered, especially of officers' baggage, is carried into effect at once, and Corps commanders are specially charged to see that this responsibility is enforced.

VIII. On all marches, Quartermasters will accompany and conduct their trains, under the orders of their commanding officers, so as never to obstruct the movement of troops.

IX. All Quartermasters and Commissaries of Subsistence will attend in person to the receipt and issue of supplies for their commands and will keep themselves constantly informed of the situation of the depots, roads, etc.

By command of Major-General McClellan:

S. WILLIAMS,
Assistant Adjutant General

Official:

Aide-de-Camp

This order quite distinctly shows some of the valuable lessons taught by that eventful campaign before Richmond, more especially the necessity of limiting the amount of camp equipage and the transportation to be used for that purpose. But it further outlines the beginnings of the *Supply Trains*, and to these I wish to direct special attention.

I have thus far only referred to the transportation provided for the *camp equipage*; but *subsistence* for man and beast must be taken along; *clothing*, to replace the wear and tear of service, must be provided; *ammunition* in quantity and variety must be at ready command; *intrenching tools* were indispensable in an active campaign—all of which was most forcibly demonstrated on the Peninsular. Some effort, I believe, was made to establish these trains before that campaign began, but everything was confusion when compared with the system which was inaugurated by Colonel Rufus Ingalls when he became Chief Quartermaster of the Army of the Potomac. Through his persevering zeal, trains for the above purposes were organized. All strife for the lead on the march vanished, for every movement was governed by orders from Army Headquarters under the direction of the chief quartermaster. He prescribed the roads to be traveled over, which corps trains should lead and which should bring up the rear—where more than one took the same roads. All of the corps trains were massed before a march, and the chief quartermaster of some corps was selected and put in charge of this consolidated train. The other corps quartermasters had charge of their respective trains, each in turn having his division and brigade quartermasters subject to his orders. "There never was a corps better organized than was the Quartermaster's Corps with the Army of the Potomac in 1864," says Grant in his *Memoirs*.

Let us see a little more clearly what a corps train included. I can do no better than to incorporate here the following order of General Meade:

HEADQUARTERS, ARMY OF THE POTOMAC
August 21, 1863

[General Orders, No. 83]

In order that the amount of transportation in this Army shall not in any instance exceed the maximum allowance prescribed in General Order No. 274 of August 7, 1863 from the War Department, and to further modify and reduce baggage and supply trains heretofore authorized, the following allowances are established and will be strictly conformed to, viz.:

1. The following is the maximum amount of transportation to be allowed to this Army in the field:

To the Headquarters of an Army Corps, 2 wagons or 8 pack mules.

To the Headquarters of a Division or Brigade, 1 wagon or 5 pack mules.

To every three company officers when detached or serving without wagons, 1 pack mule.

To every 12 company officers when detached, 1 wagon or 4 pack mules.

To every 2 staff officers not attached to any Headquarters, 1 pack mule.

To every 10 staff officers serving similarly, 1 wagon or 4 pack mules.

The above will include transportation for personal baggage, mess chests, cooking utensils, desks, papers, &c. The weight of officers' baggage in the field, specified in the Army Regulations, will be reduced so as to bring it within the foregoing schedule. All excess of transportation now with Army Corps, Divisions, Brigades, and Regiments, or Batteries over the allowances herein prescribed will be immediately turned in to the Quartermaster's Department to be used in the trains.

Commanding officers of Corps, Divisions, &c., will immediately cause inspections to be made, and will be held responsible for the strict execution of this order.

Commissary stores and forage will be transported by the trains. Where these are not convenient of access, and where troops act in detachments, the Quartermaster's Department will assign wagons or pack animals for that purpose; but the baggage of officers, or of troops, or camp equipage, will not be permitted to be carried in the wagons or on the pack animals so assigned. The assignment for transportation for ammunition, hospital stores, subsistence, and forage will be made in proportion to the amount ordered to be carried. The number of wagons is hereinafter prescribed.

The allowance of spring wagons and saddle horses for contingent wants, and of camp and garrison equipage, will remain as established by circular dated July 17, 1863.

2. For each full regiment of infantry and cavalry of 1000 men, for baggage, camp equipage, &c., 6 wagons.

For each regiment of infantry less than 700 men and more than 500 men, 5 wagons.

For each regiment of infantry less than 500 men and more than 300 men, 4 wagons.

For each regiment of infantry less than 300 men, 3 wagons.

3. For each battery of 4 and 6 guns—for personal baggage, mess chests, cooking utensils, desks, papers, &c., 1 and 2 wagons respectively.

For ammunition trains the number of wagons will be determined and assigned upon the following rules:

1st. Multiply each 12 pdr. gun by 122 and divide by 112.

2d. Multiply each rifle gun by 50 and divide by 140.

3d. For each 20 pdr. gun, 1½ wagons.

4th. For each siege gun, 2½ wagons.

5th. For the general supply train of reserve ammunition of 20 rounds to each gun in the Army to be kept habitually with Artillery Reserve, 54 wagons.

For each battery, to carry its proportion of subsistence, forage, &c., 2 wagons.

4. The supply train for forage, subsistence, quartermaster's stores, &c., to each 1000 men, cavalry and infantry, 7 wagons.

To every 1000 men, cavalry and infantry, for small arm ammunition, 5 wagons.

To each 1500 men, cavalry and infantry, for hospital supplies, 3 wagons.

To each Army Corps, except the Cavalry, for entrenching tools, &c., 6 wagons.

To each Corps Headquarters for the carrying of subsistence, forage and other stores not provided for herein, 3 wagons.

To each Division Headquarters for similar purpose as above, 2 wagons.

To each Brigade Headquarters for similar purpose as above, 1 wagon.

To each Brigade, cavalry and infantry, for commissary stores for sales to officers, 1 wagon.

To each Division, cavalry and infantry, for hauling forage for ambulance animals, portable forges, &c., 1 wagon.

To each Division, cavalry and infantry, for carrying armorer's tools, parts of muskets, extra arms and accoutrements, 1 wagon.

It is expected that each ambulance, and each wagon, whether in the baggage, supply or ammunition train, will carry the necessary forage for its own team.

By Command of Major-General Meade:

S. WILLIAMS
Assistant Adjutant General

Official:

Assistant Adjutant General

As the transportation was reduced in quantity, the capacity of what remained was put to a severer test. For example, when the Army of the Potomac went into the Wilderness in 1864, each wagon was required to carry five-days' forage for its animals (600 pounds), and if its other freight was rations it might be six barrels of salt pork and four barrels of coffee, or ten barrels of sugar. Forty boxes of hardtack was a load, not so much because of its weight as because a wagon would hold no more.

It even excluded the forage to carry such a number. In the

final campaign against Lee, Grant allowed for baggage and
camp equipage three wagons to a regiment of over seven hundred men, two wagons to a regiment of less than seven hundred
and more than three hundred, and one wagon to less than
three hundred. One wagon was allowed to a field battery. But,
notwithstanding the reductions ordered at different times,
extra wagons were often smuggled along. One captain, in
charge of a train, tells of keeping a wagon and six mules of his
own more than orders allowed, and whenever the inspecting
officer was announced as coming, the wagon, the charge of his
man Mike, was driven off under cover and not returned till
the inspection was completed. This enabled him to take along
quite a personal outfit for himself and friends. But his experience was not unique. There were many other "contraband"
mule teams smuggled along in the same way, and for the same
object.

In leaving Chattanooga to advance into Georgia, General
Sherman reduced his transportation to one baggage wagon and
one ambulance for a regiment, and a pack horse or mule for
the officers of each company. His supply trains were limited
in their loads to food, ammunition, and clothing; and wall
tents were forbidden to be taken along, barring one for each
headquarters, the gallant old veteran setting the example, by
taking only a tent fly, which was pitched over saplings or fence
rails.

The general has recorded in his Memoirs that his orders
were not strictly obeyed in this respect, Thomas being the
most noted exception, who could not give up his tent, and
"had a big wagon, which could be converted into an office, and
this we used to call 'Thomas's circus.' " In starting on his
march to the sea, Sherman issued Special Field Orders No.
120; paragraph 3 of this order reads as follows:

There will be no general train of supplies, but each corps will have
its ammunition train and provision train distributed habitually as
follows: Behind each regiment should follow one wagon and one
ambulance; behind each brigade should follow a due proportion of
ammunition wagons, provision wagons, and ambulances. In case of
danger each corps commander should change this order of march,
by having his advance and rear brigades unencumbered by wheels.
The separate columns will start habitually at 7 A.M., and make about
fifteen miles per day, unless otherwise fixed in orders.

I presume the allowance remained about the same for the Wilderness Campaign as that given in Orders No. 83. General Hancock says that he started into the Wilderness with 27,000 men. Now, using this fact in connection with the general order, a little rough reckoning will give an approximate idea of the size of the train of this corps. Without going into details, I may say that the total train of the Second Corps, not including the ambulances, could not have been far from 800 wagons, of which about 600 carried the various supplies, and the remainder the baggage—the camp equipage of the corps.

When the Army was in settled camp, the supply trains went into park by themselves, but the baggage wagons were retained with their corps, division, brigade, or regimental headquarters. When a march was ordered, however, these wagons waited only long enough to receive their freight of camp equipage, then away they went in charge of their respective quartermasters to join the corps supply train.

I have alluded to the strength of a single corps train. But the Second Corps comprised only about one-fifth of the Union Army in the Wilderness, from which a little arithmetic will enable one to get a tolerably definite idea of the *impedimenta* of this one army, even after a great reduction in the original amount had been made. There were probably over 4000 wagons following the Army of the Potomac into the Wilderness. An idea of the ground such a train would cover may be obtained by knowing that a six-mule team took up on the road, say forty feet, but of course they did not travel at close intervals. The nature of the country determined, in some degree, their distance apart. In going up or down hill a liberal allowance was made for balky or headstrong mules. Colonel Wilson, the Chief Commissary of the Army, in an interesting article to the *United Service Magazine* (1880), has stated that could the train which was requisite to accompany the Army on the Wilderness Campaign have been extended in a straight line it would have spanned the distance between Washington and Richmond, being about 130 miles. I presume this estimate includes the ambulance train also. On the basis of three to a regiment, there must have been as many as 150 to a corps. These, on ordinary marches, followed immediately in the rear of their respective divisions.

When General Sherman started for the sea, his army of

60,000 men was accompanied by about 2500 wagons and 600
ambulances. These were divided nearly equally between his
four corps, each corps commander managing his own train. In
this campaign the transportation had the roads, while the infantry plodded along by the roadside.

The supply trains, it will now be understood, were the
traveling depot or reservoir from which the Army replenished
its needs. When these wagons were emptied, they were at
once sent back to the base of supplies to be reloaded with
precisely the same kind of material as before; and empty
wagons had always to leave the road clear for loaded ones.
Unless under a pressure of circumstances, all issues except of
ammunition were made at night. By this plan the animals of
the supply consumed their forage at the base of supplies and
thus saved hauling it.

It was a welcome sight to the soldiers when rations drew
low or were exhausted, to see these wagons drive up to the
lines. They were not *impedimenta* to the Army then.

It has sometimes been thought that the wagon train was a
glorious refuge from the dangers and hard labors endured at
the front, but such was not the case. It was one of the most
wearing departments of the service. The officers in immediate
charge were especially burdened with responsibility. . . . They
were charged to have their trains at a given point at or before
a specified time. It *must* be there. There was no "if convenient"
or "if possible" attached to the order. The troops must have
their rations, or more important still, the ammunition must
be at hand in case of need. Sometimes they would accomplish
the task assigned without difficulty, but it was the exception.
Of course, they could not start until the Army had got out of
the way. Then, the roads already cut up somewhat by the
artillery were soon rendered next to impassable by the moving
trains. The quartermaster in charge of a train would be called
upon to extricate a wagon here that was blocking the way; to
supply the place of a worn-out horse or mule; to have a stalled
wagon unloaded and its contents distributed among other
wagons; to keep the train well closed up; to keep the right road
even by night, when of necessity much of their traveling was
done.

And if, with a series of such misfortunes befalling him,
the quartermaster reached his destination a few hours late, his

chances were very good for being roundly sworn at by his superior officers for his delinquency.

During the progress of the train . . . the quartermaster
would ease his nervous and troubled spirit by swearing at careless or unfortunate mule drivers, who, in turn would make the
air blue with profanity addressed to their mules, individually
or collectively, so that the anxiety to get through was felt by
all the moving forces in the train. A large number of these
drivers were civilians early in the war, but owing to the lack
of subordination which many of them showed, their places
were largely supplied later by enlisted men upon whom Uncle
Sam had his grip, and who could not resign or swear back
without penalty.

The place of the trains on an advance was in the rear of the
Army; on the retreat, in front as a rule. If they were passing
through a dangerous section of country, they were attended
by a guard, sometimes of infantry, sometimes cavalry. The
strength of the guard varied with the nature of the danger
expected. Sometimes a regiment, sometimes a brigade or division, was detailed from a corps for the duty. The nature of
Sherman's march was such that trains and troops went side by
side, as already referred to. The colored division of the Ninth
Corps served as train-guard for the transportation of the Army
of the Potomac from the Rapidan to the James in 1864.

When ammunition was wanted by a battery or a regiment
in the line of battle, a wagon was sent forward from the train
to supply it, the train remaining at a safe distance in the rear.
The nearness of the wagon's approach was governed somewhat
by the nature of the ground. If there was cover to screen it
from the enemy, like a hill or a piece of woods, it would come
pretty near, but if exposed, it would keep farther away. When
it was possible to do so, supplies both of subsistence and ammunition were brought up by night when the Army was in
line of battle, for, as I have said elsewhere, a mule team or a
mule train under fire was a diverting spectacle to every one
but the mule drivers.

One of the most striking reminiscences of the wagon train
I remember relates to a scene enacted in the fall of '63, in that
campaign of maneuvers between Meade and Lee. My own
corps (Third) had reached Centreville Heights before sun-
set. . . .

We had anticipated most of the trains. At that hour General

Warren was having a lively row with the enemy at Bristoe
Station, eight or nine miles away. As the twilight deepened,
the flash of his artillery and the smoke of the conflict were
distinctly visible on the horizon. The landscape . . . presented
one of the most animated spectacles I ever saw in the service.
Its most attractive feature was the numerous wagon trains,
whose long lines stretching away for miles over the open plain,
were hastening forward to a place of refuge, all converging
towards a common center—the high ground lying along the
hither side of Bull Run. The officers in charge of the trains,
made somewhat nervous by the sounds of conflict reaching
them from the rear, impatiently urged on the drivers, who in
turn, with lusty lungs uttered vigorous oaths at the mules,
punctuated by blows or cracks of the black snake that equalled
in volume the intonations of a rifle; and these jumped into
their harnesses and took the wagons along over stumps and
through gullies with as great alacrity as if the chief strain and
responsibility of the campaign centered in themselves. An additional feature of animation was presented by the columns
of infantry from the other corps, which alternated in the
landscape with the lines of wagons, winding along into camp
tired and footsore, but without apparent concern. I do not
now remember any other time in my experience when so large
a portion of the *matériel* and *personnel* of the Army could
have been covered by a single glance as I saw in the gathering
twilight of that October afternoon.

The system of designating the troops by corps badges was
extended to the transportation, and every wagon was marked
on the side of the canvas covering with the corps badge, perhaps eighteen inches in diameter, and of the appropriate color
to designate the division to which it belonged. In addition to
this, the number of its division, brigade, and the nature of its
contents, whether rations, forage, clothing, or ammunition—
and, if the latter, the kind, whether artillery or musket, and
the caliber—were plainly stencilled in quite large letters on the
cover.

All this and much more went to indicate as perfect organization in the trains as in the Army itself, and to these men who
were usually farthest from the fray, for whom few words of
appreciation have been uttered by distinguished writers on
the war, I gladly put on record my humble opinion that the
country is as much indebted as for the work of the soldiers in

line. They acted well their part; all honor to them for it.

A regular Army officer, who had a large experience in charge of trains, has suggested that a bugler for each brigade or division train would have been a valuable auxiliary for starting or halting the trains, or for regulating the camp duties as in artillery and cavalry. It seems strange that so commendable a proposition was not thought of at the time.

In 1863, while the Army was lying at Belle Plain after the memorable Mud March, large numbers of colored refugees came into camp. Every day saw some old cart or antiquated wagon, the relic of better days in the Old Dominion, unloading its freight of contrabands, who had thus made their entrance into the lines of Uncle Sam and Freedom. As a large number of these vehicles had accumulated near his headquarters, General Wadsworth, then commanding the first division of the First Corps, conceived the novel idea of forming a supply train of them, using as draft steers, to be selected from the corps cattle herd, and broken for that purpose. His plan . . . was to load the carts at the base of supplies with what rations they would safely carry, dispatch them to the troops wherever they might be, issue the rations, slaughter the oxen for fresh beef, and use the wagons for fuel to cook it. A very practical scheme, at first view, surely. A detail of mechanics was made to put the wagons in order, a requisition was drawn for yokes, and Captain Ford of a Wisconsin regiment, who had had experience in such work, was detailed to break in the steers to yoke and draft.

The captain spent all winter and the following spring in perfecting the Bull Train, as it was called. The first serious setback the plan received resulted from feeding the steers with unsoaked hard bread, causing several of them to swell up and die; but the general was not yet ready to give up the idea and so continued the organization. Chancellorsville battle came when all the trains remained in camp. But the day of trial was near. When the Army started on the Gettysburg Campaign, Captain Ford put his train in rear of the corps wagon train, and started with the inevitable result.

The mules and horses walked right away from the oxen, in spite of the goading and lashing and yelling of their drivers. By nightfall they were doomed to be two or three miles behind the main train—an easy prey for Mosby's guerilla band. At

last the labor of keeping it up and the anxiety for its safety
were so intense that before the Potomac was reached the animals were returned to the herd, the supplies were transferred
or issued, the wagons were burned, and the pet scheme of
General Wadsworth was abandoned as impracticable.

Quite nearly akin to this Bull Train was the train organized
by Grant after the battle of Port Gibson. His army was east of
the Mississippi, his ammunition train was west of it. Wagon
transportation for ammunition must be had. Provisions could
be taken from the country. He says: "I directed, therefore,
immediately on landing, that all the vehicles and draft animals,
whether horses, mules, or oxen, in the vicinity should be collected and loaded to their capacity with ammunition. Quite a
train was collected during the 30th, and a motley train it was.
In it could be found fine carriages, loaded nearly to the top
with boxes of cartridges that had been pitched in promiscu-
ously, drawn by mules with plow harness, straw collars, rope
lines, etc.; long-coupled wagons with racks for carrying cotton
bales, drawn by oxen, and everything that could be found in
the way of transportation on a plantation, either for use or
pleasure." [Vol. i., p. 488.]

Here is another incident which will well illustrate the trials
of a train quartermaster. At the opening of the campaign in
1864, Wilson's cavalry division joined the Army of the Potomac. Captain Ludington was chief quartermaster of its
supply train. It is a settled rule guiding the movement of trains
that the cavalry supplies shall take precedence in a move, as
the cavalry itself is wont to precede the rest of the army.
Through some oversight of the chief quartermaster of the
Army, General Ingalls, the captain had received no order of
march, and after waiting until the head of the infantry supply
trains appeared, well understanding that his place was ahead
of them on the march, he moved out of park into the road. At
once he encountered the chief quartermaster of the corps
train, and a hot and wordy contest ensued, in which vehement
language found ready expression. While this dispute for place
was at white heat, General Meade and his staff rode by, and
saw the altercation in progress without halting to inquire into
its cause. After he had passed some distance up the road,
Meade sent back an aid, with his compliments, to ascertain
what train that was struggling for the road, who was in charge

of it, and with what it was loaded. Captain Ludington informed him that it was Wilson's cavalry supply train loaded with forage and rations. These facts the aid reported faithfully to Meade, who sent him back again to inquire particularly if that really was Wilson's cavalry train. Upon receiving an affirmative answer, he again carried the same to General Meade, who immediately turned back in his tracks, and came furiously back to Ludington. Uttering a volley of oaths, he asked him what he meant by throwing trains into confusion. "You ought to have been out of here hours ago!" he continued. "I have a great mind to hang you to the nearest tree. You are not fit to be a quartermaster." In this manner General Meade rated the innocent captain for a few moments and then the general rode away.

When he had gone, General Ingalls dropped back from the staff a moment, with a laugh at the interview, and on learning the captain's case, told him to remain where he was until he received an order from him. Thereupon Ludington withdrew to a house that stood not far away from the road, and taking a seat on the veranda, entered into conversation with two young ladies who resided there. Soon after he had thus comfortably disposed himself, who should appear upon the highway but Sheridan, who was in command of all the cavalry with the army. On discovering the train at a standstill, he rode up and asked:

"What train is this?"

"The supply train of Wilson's Cavalry Division," was the reply of a teamster.

"Who's in charge of it?"

"Captain Ludington."

"Where is he?"

"There he sits yonder, talking to those ladies."

"Give him my compliments and tell him I want to see him," said Sheridan, much wrought up at the situation, apparently thinking that the train was being delayed that its quartermaster might spend further time in gentle dalliance with the young ladies.

As soon as the captain approached, the general charged forward impetuously, as if he would ride the captain down, and with one of those terrible oaths for which he was famous, demanded to know what he was there for, why he was not out at daylight, and on after his division. As Ludington attempted to explain, Sheridan cut him off by opening his battery of abuse again, threatening to have him shot for his incompetency and delay, and ordering him to take the road at once with his train. Having exhausted all the strong language in the vocabulary, he rode away, leaving the poor captain in a state of distress that can be only partially imagined. When he had finally got somewhat settled after this rough stirring-up, he took a review of the situation, and, having weighed the threatened hanging by General Meade, the request to await his orders from General Ingalls, the threatened shooting of General Sheridan, and the original order of General Wilson, which was to be on hand with the supplies at a certain specified time and place, Ludington decided to await orders from General Ingalls, and resumed the company of the ladies. At last the orders came, and the captain moved his train, spending the night on the road in the Wilderness, and when morning dawned had reached a creek over which it was necessary for him to throw a bridge before it could be crossed. So he set his teamsters at work to build a bridge. Hardly had they begun felling trees before up rode the chief quartermaster of the Sixth Corps train, anxious to cross.

An agreement was soon entered into, however, that they should build the bridge together; and the corps quartermaster set his pioneers to work with Ludington's men, and the bridge was soon finished. Recognizing the necessity for the cavalry train to take the lead, the corps quartermaster had assented that it should pass the bridge first when it was completed, and on the arrival of that moment the train was put in motion, but just then a prompt and determined chief quartermaster of a Sixth Corps division train, unaware of the understanding had between his superior, the corps quartermaster, and Captain Ludington, rode forward and insisted on crossing first. A struggle for precedence immediately set in. The contest waxed warm, and language more forcible than polite was waking the woodland echoes when who should appear on the scene again but General Meade. On seeing Ludington engaged as he saw him the day before, it aroused his wrath most unreasonably, and riding up to him, he shouted with an oath: "What! are you here again!" Then shaking his fist in his face, he continued: "I am sorry now that I did not hang you yesterday, as I threatened." The captain, exhausted and out of patience with the trials which he had encountered, replied that he sincerely wished he had and was sorry that he was not already dead. The arrival of the chief quartermaster of the Sixth Corps, at this time, ended the dispute for precedence, and Ludington went his way without further vexatious delays to overtake his cavalry division.

19

Army Road and Bridge Builders

If there was one class of men in this country who more than all others should have appreciated spacious, well-graded highways, or ready means of transit from one section to another, that class was the veterans of the Union Army; for those of them who hoofed it from two to four years in Rebeldom traveled more miles across country in that period than they did on regularly constituted thoroughfares. Now through the woods, now over the open, then crossing a swamp, or wading a river of varying depth, here tearing away a fence obstructing the march, there filling a ditch with rails to smooth the passage of the artillery—in fact, short cuts were so common and popular that the men endured the obstacles they often presented with the utmost good nature, knowing that every rod of travel thus saved meant fewer foot blisters and an earlier arrival in camp.

But there was a portion of the Army which could not often indulge in short cuts, which must find a way or make it, or have it made for them by others; and as some time and much skill and labor were necessary in laying out and completing such a way in an efficient manner, a body of men was enlisted for the exclusive purpose of doing this kind of work. Such a body was the *Engineer Corps*, often called the *Sappers and Miners* of the Army; but so little sapping and mining was done, and that little mainly by the fighting forces, I shall speak of this body of men as *Engineers*—the name which, I believe, they prefer.

In the Army of the Potomac this corps was composed of the Fifteenth and Fiftieth New York regiments of volunteers and a battalion of regulars comprising three companies. They started out with McClellan in the Peninsular Campaign, and from that time till the close of the war were identified with the movements of this army. These engineers went armed as

268

infantry for purposes of self-defence only, for fighting was not their legitimate business, nor was it expected of them. There were emergencies in the history of the Army when they were drawn up in line of battle. Such was the case with a part of them at least at Antietam, Gettysburg, and the Wilderness, but so far as I can learn, they were never actively engaged.

The engineers' special duties were to make roads passable for the Army by corduroying sloughs, building trestle bridges across small streams, laying pontoon bridges over rivers, and taking up the same, laying out and building fortifications, and slashing. Corduroying called at times for a large amount of labor, for Virginia mud was such a foe to rapid transit that miles upon miles of this sort of road had to be laid to keep ready communication between different portions of the Army.

Corduroying

Where the ground was miry, two stringers were laid longitudinally of the road, and on these the corduroy of logs, averaging, perhaps, four inches in diameter, was laid, and a cover of brush was sometimes spread upon it to prevent mules from thrusting their legs through. Where the surface was simply muddy, no stringers were used. It should be said here that by far the greater portion of this variety of work fell to fatigue details from the infantry, as did much more of the labor which came within the scope of the engineers' duties; for the latter could not have accomplished one-fifth of the tasks devolved upon them in time. In fact, if I except the laying and taking-up of pontoon bridges, and the laying-out and superintending of the building of forts, there were none of the engineers' duties which were not performed by the fighting force to a large extent. I state this not in detraction of the engineers, who always did well, but in justice to the infantry, who so often supplemented the many and trying duties of their own department with the accomplishments of the engineer corps. The quartermaster of the Army had a large number of wagons loaded with intrenching tools with which to supply the troops when their services were required as engineers.

The building of trestle bridges called for much labor from the engineers with the Army of the Potomac, for Virginia is gridironed with small streams. These, bear in mind, the troops could ford easily, but the heavily loaded trains must have bridges to cross on, or each ford would soon have been choked with mired teams. Sometimes the bridges built by the natives were still standing, but they had originally been put up for local travel only, not to endure the tramp and rack of moving armies and their thousands of tons of *impedimenta;* wherefore the engineers would take them in hand and strengthen them to the point of present efficiency.

When a line of works was laid out through woods, much *slashing,* or felling of trees, was necessary in its front. This was especially necessary in front of forts and batteries. Much of this labor was done by the engineers. The trees were felled with their tops toward the enemy, leaving stumps about three feet high. The territory covered by these fallen trees was called *the Slashes,* hence *Slashing.* No large body of the enemy could safely attempt a passage through such an obstacle. It was a strong defence for a weak line of works.

The *Gabions,* being hollow cylinders of wicker-work without bottom, filled with earth, and placed on the earthworks; the *Fascines,* being bundles of small sticks bound at both ends and intermediate points, to aid in raising batteries, filling ditches, etc.; *Chevaux-de-frise,* a piece of timber traversed with wooden spikes, used especially as a defence against cavalry; the *Abatis,* a row of the large branches of trees, sharpened and laid close together, points outward, with the butts pinned to the ground; the *Fraise,* a defence of pointed sticks, fastened into the ground at such an incline as to bring the points breast-high—all these were fashioned by the Engineer Corps in vast numbers when the Army was besieging Petersburg in 1864.

But the crowning work of this corps, as it always seemed to me, the department of their labor for which, I believe, they

A Large Gabion

will be the longest remembered, was that of ponton-bridge laying. The word *ponton*, or pontoon, is borrowed from both the Spanish and French languages, which, in turn, derive it from the parent Latin, *pons*, meaning a bridge, but it has now come to mean a *boat*, and the men who build such bridges are called by the French *pontonniers*. In fact, the system of pontoon bridges in use during the Rebellion was copied, I believe, almost exactly from the French model.

The first pontoon bridge which I recall in history was built by Xerxes, nearly 2400 years ago, across the Hellespont. It was over 4000 feet long. A violent storm broke it up, whereupon the Persian got square by throwing two pairs of shackles into the sea and ordering his men to give it three hundred strokes of a whip, while he addressed it in imperious language. Then he ordered all those persons who had been charged with the construction of the bridge to be beheaded. Immediately

Chevaux-de-Frise

afterwards he had two other bridges built, "one for the army to pass over, and the other for the baggage and beasts of burden. He appointed workmen more able and expert than the former, who went about it in this manner. They placed 360 vessels across, some of them having three banks of oars and others fifty oars apiece, with their sides turned towards the Euxine (Black) Sea; and on the side that faced the Aegean Sea they put 314. They then cast large anchors into the water on both sides, in order to fix and secure all these vessels against the violence of the winds and the current of the water. On the east side they left three passages or vacant spaces between the vessels that there might be room for small boats to go and come easily, when there was occasion, to and from the Euxine Sea. After this, upon the land of both sides, they drove large piles into the earth, with huge rings fastened to them, to which were tied six vast cables, which went over each of the two bridges: two of which cables were made of hemp, and four of a sort of reeds called BIBLOS, which were made use of in those times for the making of cordage. Those that were made of hemp must have been of an extraordinary strength and thickness since every cubit in length weighed a talent (42 pounds). The cables, laid over the whole extent of the vessels lengthwise, reached from one side to the other of the sea. When this part of the work was finished, quite over the vessels from side to side, and over the cables just described, they laid the trunks of trees cut for that purpose, and planks again over them, fastened and joined together to serve as a kind of floor or solid bottom; all which they covered over the earth, and added rails or battlements on each side that the horses and cattle might not be frightened at seeing the sea in their passage."

Fascines

Compare this bridge of Xerxes with that hereinafter described, and note the points of similarity.

One of the earliest pontoons used in the Rebellion was made of India-rubber. It was a sort of sack, shaped not unlike a torpedo, which had to be inflated before use. When thus inflated, two of these sacks were placed side by side, and on this buoyant foundation the bridge was laid. Their extreme lightness was a great advantage in transportation, but for some reason they were not used by the engineers of the Army of the Potomac. They were used in the western army, however, somewhat. General F. P. Blair's division used them in the Vicksburg campaign of 1863.

Abatis

Another pontoon which was adopted for bridge service may be described as a skeleton boat frame, over which was stretched a cotton-canvas cover. This was a great improvement over the tin or copper-covered boat frames, which had been thoroughly tested and condemned. It was the variety used by Sherman's Army almost exclusively. In starting for Savannah, he distributed his pontoon trains among his four corps, giving to each about 900 feet of bridge material. These pontoons were suitably hinged to form a wagon body, in which was carried the canvas cover, anchor, chains, and a due proportion of other bridge materials. This kind of bridge was used by the volunteer engineers of the Army of the Potomac. I recall two such bridges.

One spanned the Rapidan at Ely's Ford, and was crossed by the Second Corps the night of May 3, 1864, when it entered upon the Wilderness Campaign. The other was laid across the Po River, by the Fiftieth New York Engineers, seven days afterwards, and over this Hancock's Veterans crossed— those, at least, who survived the battle of that eventful Tuesday —before nightfall.

But all of the long bridges, notably those crossing the Chickahominy, the James, the Appomattox, which now come to my mind, were supported by wooden boats of the French pattern. These were thirty-one feet long, two feet six inches deep, five feet four inches wide at the top, and four feet at the bottom. They tapered so little at the bows and sterns as to be nearly rectangular, and when afloat the gunwales were about horizontal, having little of the curve of a skiff.

The floor timbers of the bridge, known as *Balks*, were twenty-five and one-half feet long, and four and one-half inches square on the end. Five continuous lines of these were laid on the boats two feet ten inches apart.

The flooring of the bridge, called *chesses*, consisted of boards having a uniform length of fourteen feet, a width of twelve inches, and a thickness of one and a half inches.

To secure the chesses in place, *side rails* of about the same dimensions as the balks were laid upon them over the outer balks, to which the rails were fastened by cords known as *rack lashings*.

The distance between the centers of two boats in position is called a *bay*. The distance between the boats is thirteen feet ten inches. The distance between the side rails is eleven feet, this being the width of the roadway.

An *abutment* had to be constructed at either end of a bridge, which was generally done by settling a heavy timber horizontally in the ground, level with the top of the bridge, confining it there by stakes. A proper approach was then made to this,

The Fraise

sometimes by grading, sometimes by corduroying, sometimes by cutting away the bank.

The boats, with all other bridge equipage, were carried upon wagons, which together were known as the Pontoon Train. Each wagon was drawn by six mules. A single boat with its anchor and cable formed the entire load for one team. The balks were loaded on wagons by themselves, as were also the chesses, and the side rails on others. This system facilitated the work of the pontonniers. In camp, the Pontoon Train was located near Army Headquarters. On the march it would naturally be in rear of the Army, unless its services were soon to be made use of. If, when the column had halted, we saw this train and its bodyguard, the engineers, passing to the front, we at once concluded that there was one wide river to cross, and we might as well settle down for a while, cook some coffee, and take a nap.

In order to get a better idea of pontoon-bridge laying, let us follow such a train to the river and note the various steps in the operation. If the enemy is not holding the opposite bank, the wagons are driven as near as practicable to the brink of the water, unloaded, and driven out of the way. To avoid confusion and expedite the work, the corps is divided up into the abutment, boat, balk, lashing, chess, and side-rail parties Each man, therefore, knows just what he has to do. The abutment party takes the initiative, by laying the abutment, and preparing the approaches as already described. Sometimes, when the shore was quite marshy, trestle work or a crib of logs was necessary in completing this duty, but, as the Army rarely approached a river except over a recognized thoroughfare, such work was the exception.

While this party has been vigorously prosecuting its special labors, the *boat party*, six in number, have got a pontoon afloat, manned it, and ridden to a point a proper distance above the line of the proposed bridge, dropped anchor, and paying out cable, drop down alongside the abutment, and go ashore. The *balk party* are on hand with five balks, two men to each, and having placed these so that one end projects six inches beyond the outer gunwale of the boat, they make way for the *lashing party*, who lash them in place at proper intervals as indicated on the gunwales. The boat is then pushed into the stream the length of the balks, the hither ends of which are at once made fast to the abutment.

The *chess party* now step to the front and cover the balks with flooring to within one foot of the pontoon. Meanwhile the boat party has launched another pontoon, dropped anchor in the proper place, and brought it alongside the first; the balk party, also ready with another bay of balks, lay them for the lashing party to make fast; the boat being then pushed off broadside-to as before, and the free end of the balks lashed so as to project six inches over the *shore* gunwale of the first boat. By this plan it may be seen that each balk and bay of balks completely spans two pontoons. This gives the bridge a firm foundation. The chess party continue their operations, as before, to within a foot of the second boat. And now, when the third bay of the bridge is begun, the *side-rail* party appears, placing their rails on the chesses over the outside balks, to which they firmly lash them, the chesses being so constructed that the lashings pass between them for this purpose.

The foregoing operations are repeated bay after bay till the bridge reaches the farther shore, when the building of another abutment and its approaches completes the main part of the work. It then remains to scatter the roadway of the bridge with a light covering of hay, or straw, or sand, to protect it from wear, and, perhaps, some straightening here and tightening there may be necessary, but the work is now done, and all of the *personnel* and *matériel* may cross with perfect safety. No rapid movements are allowed, however, and man and beast must pass over at a walk. A guard of the engineers is posted at the abutment, ordering "Route step!" "Route step!" as the troops strike the bridge, and sentries at intervals repeat the caution further along. By keeping the cadence in crossing, the troops would subject the bridge to a much greater strain, and settle it deeper in the water. It was shown over and over again that nothing so tried the bridge as a column of infantry. The idea that the artillery and the trains must have given it the severest test was not the case.

In taking up a bridge, the order adopted was the reverse of that followed in laying it, beginning with the end next to the enemy, and carrying the chess and balks back to the other shore by hand. The work was sometimes accelerated by weighing all anchors, and detaching the bridge from the further abutment, allow it to swing bodily around to the hither shore to be dismantled. One instance is remembered when this maneuver was executed with exceeding despatch. It was after the Army had recrossed the Rappahannock, following the battle of Chancellorsville. So nervous were the engineers lest the enemy should come upon them at their labors they did not even wait to pull up anchors, but cut every cable and cast loose, glad enough to see their flotilla on the retreat after the Army, and more delighted still not to be attacked by the enemy during the operation,—so says one of their number. . . .

When the Army of the Potomac retreated from before Richmond in 1862 it crossed the lower Chickahominy on a bridge of boats and rafts 1980 feet long. This was constructed by three separate working parties, employed at the same time, one engaged at each end and one in the center. It was the longest bridge built in the war of which I have any knowledge, save one, and that the bridge built across the James, below Wilcox's Landing in 1864. This latter was a remarkable achievement in pontoon engineering. It was over 2000 feet long, and the channel boats were firmly anchored in thirteen fathoms of water. The engineers began it during the forenoon of June 14, and completed the task at midnight. It was built under the direction of General Benham for the passage of the wagon trains and a part of the troops, while the rest crossed in steamers and ferryboats.

But pontoon bridges were not always laid without opposition or interference from the enemy. Perhaps they made the most stubborn contest to prevent the laying of the bridges across the Rappahannock before Fredericksburg in December, 1862.

The pontonniers had partially laid one bridge before daylight, but when dawn appeared, the enemy's sharpshooters, who had been posted in buildings on the opposite bank, opened so destructive a fire upon them that they were compelled to desist, and two subsequent attempts to continue the work, though desperately made, were likewise brought to naught by the deadly fire of Mississippi rifles. At last three regiments, the Seventh Michigan, and the Nineteenth and Twentieth Massachusetts, volunteered to cross the river and drive the enemy out of cover, which they did most gallantly, though not without considerable loss. They crossed the river in pontoon boats, charged up the steep bank opposite, drove out or captured the Rebels holding the buildings, and in a short time the first pontoon bridge was completed. Others were laid nearby soon after. I think the engineers lost more men here—I mean now in actual combat—than in all their previous and subsequent service combined.

Pontoon bridges were a source of great satisfaction to the soldiers. They were perfect marvels of stability and steadiness. No swaying motion was visible. To one passing across with a column of troops or wagons no motion was discernible. They seemed as safe and secure as mother earth, and the Army walked them with the same serene confidence as if they were. I remember one night while my company was crossing the

Appomattox on the bridge laid at Point of Rocks that . . . a cannoneer, who stood about six feet and a quarter in boots, being well-nigh asleep from the fatigue of the all-night march . . . walked off the bridge. Fortunately for him, he stepped— not into four or five fathoms of water, but—onto a pontoon. As can readily be imagined, an unexpected step down of two feet and a half was quite an eye-opener to him, but, barring a little lameness, he suffered no harm.

The engineers, as a whole, led an enjoyable life in the service. Their labors were quite fatiguing while they lasted, but they were a privileged class when compared with the infantry. Yet they did well all that was required of them, and there was no finer body of men in the service.

The winter quarters of the engineers were, perhaps, the most unique of any in the Army. In erecting them they gave their mechanical skill full play. Some of their officers' quarters were marvels of rustic design. The houses of one regiment in the winter of '63–4 were fashioned out of the straight cedar, which, being undressed, gave the settlement a quaint but at- tractive and comfortable appearance.

Their streets were corduroyed, and they even boasted side- walks of similar construction. Poplar Grove Church, erected by the Fiftieth New York Engineers a few miles below Peters- burg in 1864 [was] a monument to their skill in rustic design.

20

Talking Flags and Torches

The corps, division, and brigade flags told a story of their own in a manner already described. But there were other flags whose sole business it was to talk to one another, and the stories they told were immediately written down for the benefit of the soldiers or sailors. These flags were *Signal flags*, and the men who used them and made them talk were known in the service as the *Signal Corps*. . . .

The system of signals used in both armies during the Rebellion originated with one man—Albert J. Myer, who was born in Newburg, N. Y. He entered the Army as assistant surgeon in 1854, and while on duty in New Mexico and vicinity, the desirability of some better method of rapid communication than that of a messenger impressed itself upon him. This conviction, strengthened by his previous lines of thought in the same direction, he finally wrought out in a system of motion telegraphy.

Recognizing to some extent the value of his system, Congress created the position of Chief Signal Officer of the Army, and Surgeon Myer was appointed by President Buchanan to fill it. Up to some time in 1863 Myer was not the *Chief* Signal Officer alone, but the *only* signal officer commissioned as such, all others then in the corps—and there were a quite a number —being simply *acting* signal officers on detached service from various regiments.

One of the officers in the regular Army, whom Surgeon Myer had instructed in signalling while in New Mexico, went over to the enemy when the war broke out and organized a corps for them. [General E. P. Alexander, C. S. A.]

From this small beginning of one man grew up the Signal Corps. As soon as the value of the idea had fairly penetrated the brains of those whose appreciation was needed to make it of practical value, details of men were made from the various regiments around Washington and placed in camps of instruction to learn the use of the Signal Kit, so called. The chief article in this kit was a series of seven flags, varying from two feet to six feet square. Three of these flags, one six feet, one four feet, and one two feet square, were white, and each had a block of red in the center one-third the dimensions of the flag; that is, a flag six feet square had a center two feet square; two flags were black with white centers, and two were red with white centers. When the flags were in use, they were tied to a staff whose length varied with the size of the flag to be used. If the distance to signal was great, or obstructions intervened, a long staff and a large flag were necessary; but the four-foot flag was the one in most common use.

It will be readily inferred that the language of these flags was to be addressed to the eye and not the ear. To make that language plain, then, they must be distinctly seen by the persons whom they addressed. This will explain why they were of different colors. In making signals, the color of flag to be used depended upon the color of background against which it was to appear. For example, a white flag, even with its red center, could not be easily seen against the sky as a background. In such a situation a black flag was necessary. With green or dark-colored backgrounds the white flag was used, and in fact this was the flag of the signal service, having been used, in all probability, nine times out of every ten that signals were made.

Before the deaf and dumb could be taught to talk, certain motions were agreed upon to represent particular ideas, letters, and figures. In like manner, a key, or code was constructed which interpreted the motions of the signal flag—for it talked by motions—and in accord with which the motions were made. Let me illustrate these motions by the accompanying cuts.

Plate 1 represents a member of the Signal Corps in position, holding the flag directly above his head, the staff vertical, and grasped by both hands. This is the position from which all the motions were made.

Plate 2 represents the flagman making the numeral "2" or the letter "i." This was done by waving the flag to the right and instantly returning it to a vertical position. To make "1" the flag was waved to the left, and instantly returned as before. See plate 3. This the code translated as the letter "t"

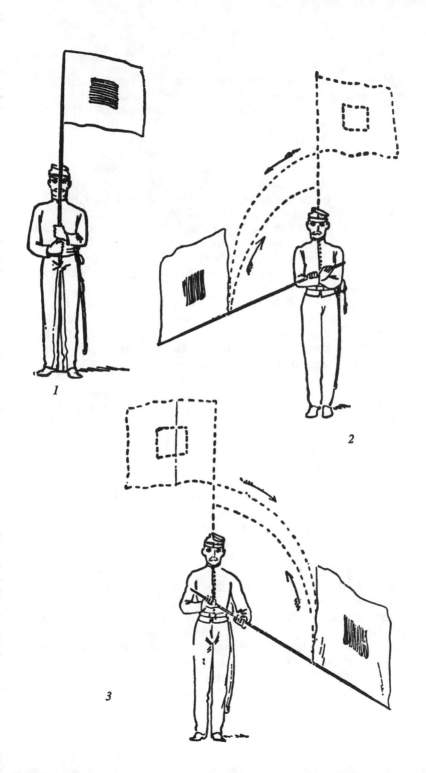

1

2

3

and the word "the." "5" was made by waving the flag directly to the front, and returning at once to the vertical.

The signal code most commonly used included but two symbols, which made it simple to use. With these, not only could all the letters of the alphabet and the numerals be communicated, but an endless variety of syllables, words, phrases, and statements besides. As a matter of fact, however, it contained several thousand combinations of numerals with the significance of each combination attached to it. Let me illustrate still further by using the symbols "2" and "1."

Let us suppose the flagman to make the signal for "1" and follow it immediately with the motion for "2." This would naturally be read as 12, which the code showed to mean O. Similarly, two consecutive waves to the right, or 22, represented the letter N. Three waves to the right and one to the left, or 2221, stood for the syllable *tion*. So by repeating the symbols and changing the combinations we might have, for example, 2122, meaning *the enemy are advancing*; or 1122, *the cavalry have halted*; or 12211, *three guns in position*; or 1112, *two miles to the left*—all of which would appear in the code.

Let us join a signal party for the sake of observing the method of communicating a message. Such a party, if complete, was composed of three persons, viz., the signal officer (commissioned) in charge, with a telescope and field glass; the flagman, with his kit, and an orderly to take charge of the horses if the station was only temporary. The point selected from which to signal must be a commanding position, whether a mountain, a hill, a treetop, or a housetop. The station having been attained, the flagman takes position, and the officer sweeps the horizon and intermediate territory with his telescope to discover another signal station, where a second officer and flagman are posted.

Having discovered such a station, the officer directs his man to call that station. This he does by signalling the number of the station (for each station had a number), repeating the same until his signal is seen and answered. It was the custom at stations to keep a man on the lookout with the telescope for signals constantly. Having got the attention of the opposite station, the officer sends his message. The flagman was not supposed to know the import of the message which he waved out with his flag. The officer called the numerals, and the flagman responded with the required motions almost automatically, when well practised.

At the end of each word motion "5" was made once; at the end of a sentence "55"; and of a message "555." There were a few words and syllables which were conveyed 'by a single motion of the flag; but as a rule the words had to be spelled out letter by letter, at least by beginners. Skilled signalists, however, used many abbreviations and rarely found it necessary to spell out a word in full.

So much for the manner of *sending* a message. Now let us join the party at the station where the message is being *received*. There we simply find the officer sitting at his telescope reading the message being sent to him. Should he fail to understand any word, his own flagman signals an interruption and asks a repetition of the message from the last word understood. Such occurrences were not frequent, however.

The services of the Signal Corps were just as needful and valuable by night as in daylight; but, as the flags could not then talk understandingly, *Talking Torches* were substituted for them. As a "point of reference" was needful, by which to interpret the torch signals made, the flagman lighted a "foot torch," at which he stood firmly while he signalled with the "flying torch." This latter was attached to a staff of the same length as the flagstaff, in fact, usually the flagstaff itself. These torches were of copper filled with turpentine. At the end of a message the flying torch was extinguished.

The rapidity with which messages were sent by experienced operators was something wonderful to the uneducated looker-on. An ordinary message of a few lines can be sent in ten minutes, and the rate of speed is much increased where officers have worked long together and understand each other's methods and abbreviations.

Signal messages have been sent twenty-eight miles; but that is exceptional. The conditions of the atmosphere and the location of stations were seldom favorable to such long-distance signalling. Ordinarily, messages were not sent more than six or seven miles, but there were exceptions. Here is a noted one:

In the latter part of September, 1864, the Rebel Army under Hood set out to destroy the railroad communications of Sherman, who was then at Atlanta. The latter soon learned that

Allatoona was the objective point of the enemy. As it was only held by a small brigade, whereas the enemy was seen advancing upon it in much superior numbers, Sherman signalled a dispatch from Vining's Station to Kenesaw, and from Kenesaw to Allatoona, whence it was again signalled to Rome. It requested General Corse, who was at the latter place, to hurry back to the assistance of Allatoona. Meanwhile, Sherman was propelling the main body of his army in the same direction. On reaching Kenesaw, "the signal officer reported," says Sherman, in his *Memoirs*, "that since daylight he had failed to obtain any answer to his call for Allatoona; but while I was with him he caught a faint glimpse of the telltale flag through an embrasure, and after much time he made out these letters

'C' 'R' 'S' 'E' 'H' 'E' 'R'

and translated the message 'Corse is here.' It was a source of great relief, for it gave me the first assurance that General Corse had received his orders, and that the place was adequately garrisoned."

General Corse has informed me that the distance between the two signal stations was about sixteen miles in an air line. Several other messages passed later between these stations, among them this one, which has been often referred to:

ALLATOONA, Georgia, Oct. 6, 1864—2 P.M.

Captain L. M. DAYTON, Aide-de-Camp:
I am short a cheekbone and an ear, but am able to whip all hell yet. My losses are heavy. A force moving from Stilesboro to Kingston gives me some anxiety. Tell me where Sherman is.

JOHN M. CORSE, Brigadier-General

The occasions which called the Signal Corps into activity were various, but they were most frequently employed in reporting the movements of troops, sometimes of the Union, sometimes of the enemy. . . . If nature did not always provide a suitable place for lookout, art came to the rescue, and signal towers of considerable height were built for this class of workers, who, like the cavalry, were the eyes of the Army. . . . I remember several of these towers which stood before Petersburg in 1864. They were of especial use there in observing the movements of troops within the enemy's lines, as they stood, I should judge, from one hundred to one hundred and fifty feet high. Although these towers were erected somewhat to the rear of the Union main lines and were a very open trestling, they were yet a conspicuous target for the enemy's long-range guns and mortar shells.

Sometimes the nerve of the flagman was put to a very severe test, as he stood on the summit of one of these frail structures waving his flag, his situation too like that of Mahomet's coffin, while the Whitworth bolts whistled sociably by him, saying, "Where is he? Where is he?" or, by another interpretation, "Which one? Which one?" Had one of these bolts hit a cornerpost of the lookout, the chances for the flagman and his lieutenant to reach the earth by a new route would have been favorable, although the engineers who built them claimed that with three posts cut away the tower would still stand. But, as a matter of fact, I believe no shot ever seriously injured one of the towers, though tons of iron must have been hurled at them. The roof of the Avery House, before Petersburg, was used for a signal station, and the shells of the enemy's guns often tore through below, much to the alarm of the signal men above.

Signalling was carried on during an engagement between different parts of the Army. By calling for needed re-enforcements, or giving news of their approach, or requesting ammunition, or reporting movements of the enemy, or noting the effects of shelling—in these and a hundred kindred ways the corps made their services invaluable to the troops. Sometimes signal officers on shore communicated with others on shipboard, and, in one instance, Lieutenant Brown told me that through the information he imparted to a gunboat off Suffolk, in 1863, regarding the effects of the shot which were thrown from it, General Longstreet had since written him that the fire was so accurate he was compelled to withdraw his troops. The signals were made from the tower of the Masonic Hall in Suffolk, whence they were taken up by another signal party on the river bluff, and thence communicated to the gunboat.

Not long after, General Sherman alluded to a correspondent of the New York Herald whom he had threatened to hang, declaring that had he done so his "death would have saved ten thousand lives." The relation of this anecdote brings out another interesting phase of signal-corps operations. It seems

that one of our signal officers had succeeded in reading the
signal code of the enemy, and had communicated the same
to his fellow officers. With this code in their possession, the
corps was enabled to furnish valuable information directly from
Rebel headquarters, by reading the Rebel signals, continuing
to do so during the Chattanooga and much of the Atlanta
campaign, when the enemy's signal flags were often plainly
visible. Suddenly this source of information was completely
cut off by the ambition of the correspondent to publish all
the news, and the natural result was the enemy changed the
code. This took place just before Sherman's attack on Kenesaw
Mountain (June, 1864), and it is to the hundreds slaughtered
there that he probably refers. General Thomas was ordered
to arrest the reporter, and have him hanged as a spy; but old
"Pap" Thomas' kind heart banished him to the north of the
Ohio for the remainder of the war instead.

When Sherman's headquarters were at Big Shanty, there
was a signal station located in his rear, on the roof of an old
gin house, and this signal officer, having the key to the enemy's signals, reported to Sherman that he had translated this
signal from Pine Mountain to Marietta: "Send an ambulance
for General Polk's body"—which was the first tidings received
by our Army that the fighting bishop had been slain. He was
hit by a shell from a volley of artillery fired by order of General Sherman.

To the men in the other arms of the service who saw this
mysterious and almost continuous waving of flags, it seemed
as if every motion was fraught with momentous import.
"What could it all be about?" they would ask one another.
A signal station was located in '61–2, on the top of what was
known as the Town Hall (since burned) in Poolesville, Md.,
within a few rods of my company's camp, and to the best of
my recollection, not an hour of daylight passed without more
or less flag waving from that point. This particular squad of
men did not seem at all fraternal, but kept aloof, as if (so
we thought) they feared they might in an unguarded moment
impart some of the important secret information which had
been received by them from the station at Sugar Loaf Mountain or Seneca. Since the war I have learned that their apparently excited and energetic performances were, for the most
part, only practice between stations for the purpose of acquir-
ing familiarity with the code and facility in using it.

It may be thought that the duties of the Signal Corps were always performed in positions where their personal safety was never imperilled. But such was far from the fact. At the battle of Atlanta, July 22, 1864, a signal officer had climbed a tall pine tree for the purpose of directing the fire of a section of Union artillery which was stationed at its foot, the country being so wooded and broken that the artillerists could not certainly see the position of the enemy. The officer had nailed a succession of cleats up the trunk, and was on the platform which he had made in the top of the tree, acting as signal officer, when the Rebels made a charge, capturing the two guns, and shot the officer dead at his post.

From the important nature of the duties which they performed, the enemy could not look upon them with very tender regard, and this fact they made apparent on every opportunity. Here is an incident which, I think, has never been published:

When General Nelson's division arrived at Shiloh, Lieutenant Joseph Hinson, commanding the Signal Corps attached to it, crossed the Tennessee and reported to General Buell, after which he established a station on that side of the river, from which messages were sent having reference to the disposition of Nelson's troops. The crowd of stragglers (presumably from Grant's army) was so great as to continually obstruct his view, and in consequence he pressed into service a guard from among the stragglers themselves to keep his view clear, and placed his associate, Lieutenant Hart, in charge. Presently General Grant himself came riding up the bank, and, as luck would have it, came into Lieutenant Hinson's line of vision. Catching sight of a cavalry boot, without stopping to see who was in it, in his impatience, Lieutenant Hart sang out: "Git out of the way there! Ain't you got no sense?" Whereupon Grant very quietly apologized for his carelessness, and rode over to the side of General Buell. When the lieutenant found he had been addressing or "dressing" a major-general, his confusion can be imagined.

After arriving before Fort McAllister, General Sherman sent General Hazen down the right bank of the Ogeechee to take the fort by assault, and himself rode down the left bank to a rice plantation where General Howard had established a signal station to overlook the river and watch for vessels. The station was built on the top of a rice mill. From this point the fort was visible, three miles away. In due time a commotion in the fort indicated the approach of Hazen's troops, and the signal officer discovered a signal flag about three miles above the fort, which he found was Hazen's, the latter inquiring if Sherman was there. He was answered affirmatively and informed that Sherman expected the fort to be carried before night. Finally Hazen signalled that he was ready and was told to go ahead. Meanwhile, a small United States steamer had been descried coming up the river, and, noticing the party at the rice mill, this dialogue between signal flags ensued:

"Who are you?"

"General Sherman."

"Is Fort McAllister taken?"

"Not yet; but it will be in a minute."

And in a few minutes it was taken, and the fact signalled to the naval officers' on the boat, who were not in sight of the fort.

During the battle of Gettysburg, or at least while Sickles was contending at the Peach Orchard against odds, the signal men had their flags flying from Little Round Top; but when the day was lost, and Hood with his Texans pressed towards that important point, the signal officers folded their flags, and prepared to visit other and less dangerous scenes. At that moment, however, General Warren of the Fifth Corps appeared, and ordered them to keep their signals waving as if a host were. immediately behind them, which they did.

General E. P. Alexander, the officer referred to as having organized the Rebel Signal Corps, in an article in the Century Magazine for January, 1887, describing Pickett's charge, says that he was "particularly cautioned in moving the artillery, to keep it out of sight of the signal station upon Round Top." In a footnote referring to this caution he says:

"This suggests the remark that I have never understood why the enemy abandoned the use of military balloons early in 1863, after having used them extensively up to that time. Even if the observer never saw anything, they would have been worth all they cost for the annoyance and delays they caused us in trying to keep our movements out of their sight. That wretched little signal station upon Round Top that day caused one of our divisions to lose over two hours, and probably delayed our assault nearly that long. During that time a Federal corps arrived near Round Top and became an important factor in the action which followed."

In a note addressed to the historian of the Signal Corps Association, to whom General Alexander has furnished a sketch of the organization of the Rebel Signal Corps, he says:

"You are more than welcome to the compliment I paid the signal station on Round Top in my article in the January Century. I have forgiven all my enemies now; and though you fellows there were about the last that I did forgive, I took you in several years ago and concluded to let by-gones be by-gones."

Soldier Life

in the Confederate Army

from

DETAILED MINUTIAE OF SOLDIER
LIFE IN THE ARMY OF NORTHERN
VIRGINIA
by Carlton McCarthy

1

The Outfit Modified

With the men who composed the Army of Northern Virginia will die the memory of those little things which made the Confederate soldier peculiarly what he was.

The historian who essays to write the grand movements will hardly stop to tell how the hungry private fried his bacon, baked his biscuit, and smoked his pipe; how he was changed from time to time by the necessities of the service, until the gentleman, the student, the merchant, the mechanic, and the farmer were merged into a perfect, all-enduring, never-tiring, and invincible soldier. To preserve these little details, familiar to all soldiers, and by them not thought worthy of mention to others because of their familiarity, but ever dear to them and always the substance of their war talks, is the object of this book.

The volunteer of 1861 made extensive preparations for the field. Boots, he thought, were an absolute necessity, and the heavier the soles and longer the tops the better. His pants were stuffed inside the tops of his boots, of course. A double-breasted coat, heavily wadded, with two rows of big brass buttons and a long skirt was considered comfortable. A small stiff cap with a narrow brim took the place of the comfortable felt, or the shining and towering tile worn in civil life.

Then over all was a huge overcoat, long and heavy, with a cape reaching nearly to the waist. On his back he strapped a knapsack containing a full stock of underwear, soap, towels, comb, brush, looking glass, tooth brush, paper and envelopes, pens, ink, pencils, blacking, photographs, smoking and chewing tobacco, pipes, twine string, and cotton strips for wounds and other emergencies, needles and thread, buttons, knife, fork, and spoon, and many other things as each man's idea of what he was to encounter varied. On the outside of the knapsack, solidly folded, were two great blankets and a rubber or oilcloth.

This knapsack, etc., weighed from fifteen to twenty-five pounds, sometimes even more. All seemed to think it was impossible to have on too many or too heavy clothes, or to have too many conveniences, and each had an idea that to be a good soldier he must be provided against every possible emergency.

In addition to the knapsack, each man had a haversack, more or less costly, some of cloth and some of fine morocco, and stored with provisions always as though he expected any moment to receive orders to march across the Great Desert and supply his own wants on the way. A canteen was considered indispensable, and at the outset it was thought prudent to keep it full of water. Many, expecting terrific hand-to-hand encounters, carried revolvers, and even bowie knives. Merino shirts (and flannel) were thought to be the right thing, but experience demonstrated the contrary. Gloves were also thought to be very necessary and good things to have in winter time, the favorite style being buck gauntlets with long cuffs.

In addition to each man's private luggage, each mess, generally composed of from five to ten men, drawn together by similar tastes and associations, had *its* outfit, consisting of a large camp chest containing skillet, frying pan, coffee boiler, bucket for lard, coffee box, salt box, sugar box, meal box, flour box, knives, forks, spoons, plates, cups, etc., etc. These chests were so large that eight or ten of them filled up an army wagon, and were so heavy that two strong men had all they could do to get one of them into the wagon. In addition to the chest each mess owned an axe, water bucket, and bread tray. Then the tents of each company, and little sheet-iron stoves, and stove pipe, and the trunks and valises of the company officers, made an immense pile of stuff, so that each company had a small wagon train of its own.

All thought money to be absolutely necessary, and for a while rations were disdained and the mess supplied with the best that could be bought with the mess fund. Quite a large number had a "boy" along to do the cooking and washing. Think of it! a Confederate soldier with a body servant all his own, to bring him a drink of water, black his boots, dust his clothes, cook his corn bread and bacon, and put wood on his fire. Never was there fonder admiration than these darkies displayed for their masters. Their chief delight and glory was to praise the courage and good looks of Mahse Tom and prophesy great things about his future. Many a ringing laugh and shout of fun originated in the queer remarks, shining countenance, and glistening teeth of this now forever departed character.

It is amusing to think of the follies of the early part of the war, as illustrated by the outfits of the volunteers. They were so heavily clad, and so burdened with all manner of things, that a march was torture, and the wagon trains were so immense in proportion to the number of troops that it would have been impossible to guard them in an enemy's country. Subordinate officers thought themselves entitled to transportation for trunks, mattresses, and folding bedsteads, and the privates were as ridiculous in their demands.

Thus much by way of introduction. The change came rapidly, and stayed not until the transformation was complete. Nor was this change attributed alone to the orders of the general officers. The men soon learned the inconvenience and danger of so much luggage, and as they became more experienced they vied with each other in reducing themselves to light-marching trim.

Experience soon demonstrated that boots were not agreeable on a long march. They were heavy and irksome, and when the heels were worn a little one-sided, the wearer would find his ankle twisted nearly out of joint by every unevenness of the road. When thoroughly wet, it was a laborious undertaking to get them off, and worse to get them on in time to answer the morning roll call. And so, good, strong brogues or brogans with broad bottoms and big, flat heels succeeded the boots and were found much more comfortable and agreeable, easier put on and off and altogether the more sensible.

A short-waisted and single-breasted jacket usurped the place of the long-tailed coat and became universal. The enemy noticed this peculiarity, and called the Confederates gray jackets, which name was immediately transferred to those lively creatures which were the constant admirers and inseparable companions of the Boys in Gray and in Blue.

Caps were destined to hold out longer than some other uncomfortable things, but they finally yielded to the demands of comfort and common sense, and a good soft felt hat was worn instead. A man who has never been a soldier does not know, nor indeed can know, the amount of comfort there is in a good soft hat in camp, and how utterly useless is a "soldier hat" as they are generally made. Why the Prussians, with all their experience, wore their heavy, unyielding helmets, and the French their little caps, was a mystery to a Confederate who had enjoyed the comfort of an old slouch.

Overcoats an inexperienced man would think an absolute necessity for men exposed to the rigors of a northern Virginia winter, but they grew scarcer and scarcer; they were found to be a great inconvenience. The men came to the conclusion that the trouble of carrying them on hot days outweighed the comfort of having them when the cold day arrived. Besides they found that life in the open air hardened them to such an extent that changes in the temperatures were not felt to any degree. Some clung to their overcoats to the last, but the majority got tired lugging them around, and either discarded them altogether or trusted to capturing one about the time it would be needed. Nearly every overcoat in the army in the later years was one of Uncle Sam's captured from his boys.

The knapsack vanished early in the struggle. It was inconvenient to change the underwear too often, and the disposition not to change grew, as the knapsack was found to gall the back and shoulders and weary the man before half the march was accomplished. The better way was to dress out and out, and wear that outfit until the enemy's knapsack or the folks at home supplied a change. Certainly it did not pay to carry around clean clothes while waiting for the time to use them.

Very little washing was done, as a matter of course. Clothes once given up were parted with forever. There were good reasons for this: cold water would not cleanse them or destroy the vermin, and hot water was not always to be had. One blanket to each man was found to be as much as could be carried and amply sufficient for the severest weather. This was carried generally by rolling it lengthwise, with the rubber cloth outside, tying the ends of the roll together and throwing the loop thus made over the left shoulder with the ends fastened together hanging under the right arm.

The haversack held its own to the last and was found practical and useful. It very seldom, however, contained rations but was used to carry all the articles generally carried in the knapsack; of course the stock was small. Somehow or other, many men managed to do without the haversack, and carried absolutely nothing but what they wore and had in their pockets.

The infantry threw away their heavy cap boxes and cartridge boxes, and carried their caps and cartridges in their pockets. Canteens were very useful at times, but they were as a general thing discarded. They were not much used to carry water but were found useful when the men were driven to the necessity of foraging, for conveying buttermilk, cider, sorghum, etc., to camp. A good strong tin cup was found better than a canteen, as it was easier to fill at a well or spring and was serviceable as a boiler for making coffee when the column halted for the night.

A Haversack and Dipper

Revolvers were found to be about as useless and heavy lumber as a private soldier could carry, and early in the war were sent home to be used by the women and children in protecting themselves from insult and violence at the hands of the ruffians who prowled about the country shirking duty.

Strong cotton was adopted in place of flannel and merino for two reasons: first, because easier to wash; and second, because the vermin did not propagate so rapidly in cotton as in wool. Common white cotton shirts and drawers proved the best that could be used by the private soldier.

Gloves to any but a mounted man were found useless, worse than useless. With the gloves on, it was impossible to handle an axe, buckle harness, load a musket, or handle a rammer at the piece. Wearing them was found to be simply a habit, and so, on the principle that the less luggage the less labor, they were discarded.

The camp chest soon vanished. The brigadiers and major-generals, even, found them too troublesome, and soon they were left entirely to the quartermasters and commissaries. One skillet and a couple of frying pans, a bag for flour or meal, another bag for salt, sugar, and coffee, divided by a knot tied between, served the purpose as well. The skillet passed from mess to mess. Each mess generally owned a frying pan, but often one served a company. The oilcloth was found to be as good as the wooden tray for making up the dough. The water bucket held its own to the last!

Tents were rarely seen. All the poetry about the "tented field" died. Two men slept together, each having a blanket and an oilcloth; one oilcloth went next to the ground. The two laid on this, covered themselves with two blankets, protected from the rain with the second oilcloth on top, and slept very comfortably through rain, snow or hail, as it might be.

Very little money was seen in camp. The men did not expect, did not care for, or often get any pay, and they were not willing to deprive the old folks at home of their supply, so they learned to do without any money.

When the rations got short and were getting shorter, it became necessary to dismiss the darkey servants. Some, however, became company servants, instead, of private institutions, and held out faithfully to the end, cooking the rations away in the rear and at the risk of life, carrying them to the line of battle to their "young mahsters."

Reduced to the minimum, the private soldier consisted of one man, one hat, one jacket, one shirt, one pair of pants, one pair of drawers, one pair of shoes, and one pair of socks. His baggage was one blanket, one rubber blanket, and one haversack. The haversack generally contained smoking tobacco and a pipe, and a small piece of soap, with temporary additions of apples, persimmons, blackberries, and such other commodities as he could pick up on the march.

The company property consisted of two or three skillets and frying pans, which were sometimes carried in the wagon, but oftener in the hands of the soldiers. The infantrymen generally preferred to stick the handle of the frying pan in the barrel of a musket and so carry it.

The wagon trains were devoted entirely to the transportation of ammunition and commissary and quartermaster's stores which had not been issued. Rations which had become company property, and the baggage of the men when they had any, were carried by the men themselves. If, as was sometimes the case, three–days' rations were issued at one time and the troops ordered to cook them, and be prepared to march, they did cook them *and eat them if possible*, so as to avoid the labor of carrying them. It was not such an undertaking either, to eat three-day's rations in one, as frequently none had been issued for more than a day, and when issued were cut down one half.

The infantry found out that bayonets were not of much use, and did not hesitate to throw them, with the scabbard, away.

The artillerymen, who started out with heavy sabers hanging to their belts, stuck them up in the mud as they marched, and left them for the ordnance officers to pick up and turn over to the cavalry.

The cavalrymen found sabers very tiresome when hung to the belt, and adopted the plan of fastening them to the saddle on the left side, with the hilt in front and in reach of the hand. Finally sabers got very scarce even among the cavalrymen, who relied more and more on their short rifles.

No soldiers ever marched with less to encumber them, and none marched faster or held out longer.

The courage and devotion of the men rose equal to every hardship and privation, and the very intensity of their sufferings became a source of merriment. Instead of growling and deserting, they laughed at their own bare feet, ragged clothes, and pinched faces; and weak, hungry, cold, wet, worried with vermin and itch, dirty, with no hope of reward or rest, marched cheerfully to meet the well-fed and warmly clad hosts of the enemy.

2

Romantic Ideas Dissipated

To offer a man promotion in the early part of the war was equivalent to an insult. The higher the social position, the greater the wealth, the more patriotic it would be to serve in the humble position of a private; and many men of education and ability in the various professions, refusing promotion, served under the command of men greatly their inferiors, mentally, morally, and as soldiers. It soon became apparent that the country wanted knowledge and ability as well as muscle and endurance, and those who had capacity to serve in higher positions were promoted. Still it remained true that inferior men commanded their superiors in every respect, save one—rank; and leaving out the one difference of rank, the officers and men were about on a par.

It took years to teach the educated privates in the Army that it was their duty to give unquestioning obedience to officers because they were such, who were awhile ago their playmates and associates in business. It frequently happened that the private, feeling hurt by the stern authority of the officer, would ask him to one side, challenge him to personal combat, and thrash him well. After awhile these privates learned all about extra duty, half rations, and courts martial.

It was only to conquer this independent resistance of discipline that punishment or force was necessary. The privates were as willing and anxious to fight and serve as the officers and needed no pushing up to their duty. It is amusing to recall the disgust with which the men would hear of their assignment to the rear as reserves. They regarded the order as a deliberate insult, planned by some officer who had a grudge against their regiment or battery, who had adopted this plan to prevent their presence in battle and thus humiliate them. How soon did they learn the sweetness of a day's repose in the rear!

300

Another romantic notion which for awhile possessed the boys was that soldiers should not try to be comfortable but glory in getting wet, being cold, hungry, and tired. So they refused shelter in houses or barns, and "like true soldiers" paddled about in the mud and rain, thinking thereby to serve their country better. The real troubles had not come, and they were in a hurry to suffer some. They had not long thus impatiently to wait, nor could they latterly complain of the want of a chance to do or die. Volunteering for perilous or very onerous duty was popular at the outset, but as duties of this kind thickened it began to be thought time enough when the orders were peremptory, or the orderly read the detail.

Another fancy idea was that the principal occupation of a soldier should be actual conflict with the enemy. They didn't dream of such a thing as camping for six months at a time without firing a gun, or marching and countermarching to mislead the enemy, or driving wagons and ambulances, building bridges, currying horses, and the thousand commonplace duties of the soldier.

On the other hand, great importance was attached to some duties which soon became mere drudgery. Sometimes the whole detail for guard—first, second, and third relief—would make it a point of honor to sit up the entire night and watch and listen as though the enemy might pounce upon them at any moment and hurry them off to prison. Of course they soon learned how sweet it was after two hours' walking of the beat to turn in for four hours! which seemed to the sleepy man an eternity in anticipation but only a brief time in retrospect, when the corporal gave him a chunk, and remarked: "Time to go on guard."

Everybody remembers how we used to talk about one Confederate whipping a dozen Yankees. Literally true sometimes, but generally speaking two to one made hard work for the boys. They didn't know at the beginning anything about the advantage the enemy had in being able to present man for man in front and then send as many more to worry the flanks and rear. They learned something about this very soon and had to contend against it on almost every field they won.

Wounds were in great demand after the first wounded hero made his appearance. His wound was the envy of thousands of unfortunates who had not so much as a scratch to boast, and who felt small and of little consequence before the man with a bloody bandage. Many became despondent and groaned as they thought that perchance after all they were doomed to go home safe and sound, and hear for all time the praises of the fellow who had lost his arm by a cannon shot, or had his face ripped by a saber, or his head smashed with a fragment of shell. After a while the wound was regarded as a practical benefit. It secured a furlough of indefinite length, good eating, the attention and admiration of the fair, and, if permanently disabling, a discharge. Wisdom born of experience soon taught all hands better sense, and the fences and trees and ditches and rocks became valuable and eagerly sought after when the music of minie and the roar of the Napoleon twelve-pounders was heard. Death on the field, glorious first and last, was dared for duty's sake, but the good soldier learned to guard his life and yield it only at the call of duty.

Only the wisest men, those who had seen war before, imagined that the war would last more than a few months. The young volunteers thought one good battle would settle the whole matter; and, indeed, after First Manassas many thought they might as well go home! The whole North was frightened, and no more armies would dare assail the soil of Old Virginia. Colonels and brigadiers with flesh wounds not worthy of notice rushed to Richmond to report victory and the end of the war! They had seen sights in the way of wounded and killed, plunder, etc., and according to their views, no sane people would try again to conquer the heroes of that remarkable day.

The newspaper men delighted in telling the soldiers that the Yankees were a diminutive race, of feeble constitution, timid as hares, with no enthusiasm, and that they would perish in short order under the glow of our Southern sun. Anyone who had seen a regiment from Ohio or Maine knew how true these statements were. And besides, the newspapers did not mention the English, Irish, German, French, Italian, Spanish, Swiss, Portuguese, and Negroes who were to swell the numbers of the enemy, and as our army grew less make his larger. True, there was not much fight in all this rubbish, but they answered well enough for drivers of wagons and ambulances, guarding stores and lines of communication, and doing all sorts of duty, while the good material was doing the fighting. Sherman's army, marching through Richmond after the surrender of Lee and Johnston, seemed to be composed of a race of giants, well-fed and well-clad.

Many feared the war would end before they would have a fair chance to make a record, and that when the cruel war was over they would have to sit by, dumb, and hear the more fortunate ones, who had smelt the battle, tell to admiring home circles the story of the bloody field. Most of these got in in time to satisfy their longings, and got out to learn that the man who did not go, but kept out and made money, was more admired and courted than the poor fellow with one leg or arm less than is allowed.

It was fortunate for those who skulked that the war ended as it did, for had the South been successful, the soldiers would have been favored with every mark of distinction and honor, and they, despised and rejected, as they deserved to be. While the war lasted it was the delight of some of the stoutly built fellows to go home for a few days, and kick and cuff and tongue-lash the able-bodied bombproofs. How coolly and submissively they took it all! How big they were later!

The rubbish accumulated by the hope of recognition burdened the soldiers nearly to the end. England was to abolish the blockade and send us immense supplies of fine arms, large and small. France was thinking about landing an imperial force in Mexico and marching thence to the relief of the South. But the Confederate yell never had an echo in the "Marseillaise," or "God Save the Queen;" and Old Dixie was destined to sing her own song, without the help even of "Maryland, My Maryland." The war with England, which was to give Uncle Sam trouble and the South an ally, never came.

Those immense balloons which somebody was always inventing, and which were to sail over the enemy's camps dropping whole cargoes of explosives never tugged at their anchors or sailed majestically away.

As discipline improved and the men began to feel that they were no longer simply volunteers, but enlisted volunteers, the romantic devotion which they had felt was succeeded by a feeling of constraint and necessity, and while the Army was in reality very much improved and strengthened by the change, the soldiers imagined the contrary to be the case. And if discipline had been pushed to too great an extent, the army would have been deprived of the very essence of its life and power.

When the officers began to assert superiority by withdrawing from the messes and organizing officers' messes, the bond of brotherhood was weakened; and who will say that the dignity which was thus maintained was compensation for the loss of personal devotion as between comrades?

At the outset, the fact that men were in the same company put them somewhat on the same level and produced an almost perfect bond of sympathy; but as time wore on, the various peculiarities and weaknesses of the men showed themselves, and each company, as a community, separated into distinct circles, as indifferent to each other, save in the common cause, as though they had never met as friends.

The pride of the volunteers was sorely tried by the incoming of conscripts—the most despised class in the Army—and their devotion to company and regiment was visibly lessened. They could not bear the thought of having these men for comrades, and felt the flag insulted when claimed by one of them as his flag. It was a great source of annoyance to the true men, but was a necessity. Conscripts crowded together in companies, regiments, and brigades would have been useless, but scattered here and there among the good men, were utilized. And so, gradually, the pleasure that men had in being associated with others whom they respected as equals was taken away, and the social aspect of army life seriously marred.

The next serious blow to romance was the abolishment of elections, and the appointment of officers. Instead of the privilege and pleasure of picking out some good-hearted, brave comrade and making him captain, the lieutenant was promoted without the consent of the men, or, what was harder to bear, some officer hitherto unknown was sent to take command. This was no doubt better for the service, but it had a serious effect on the minds of volunteer patriot soldiers, and looked to them too much like arbitrary power exercised over men who were fighting that very principle. They frequently had to acknowledge, however, that the officers were all they could ask, and in many instances became devotedly attached to them.

As the companies were decimated by disease, wounds, desertions, and death, it became necessary to consolidate them, and the social pleasures received another blow. Men from the same neighborhoods and villages, who had been schoolmates together, were no longer in companies, but mingled indiscriminately with all sorts of men from anywhere and everywhere.

Those who have not served in the Army as privates can

form no idea of the extent to which such changes as those just mentioned affect the spirits and general worth of a soldier. Men who, when surrounded by their old companions, were brave and daring soldiers, full of spirit and hope, when thrust among strangers for whom they cared not, and who cared not for them, became dull and listless, lost their courage, and were slowly but surely demoralized. They did, it is true, in many cases, stand up to the last, but they did it on dry principle, having none of that enthusiasm and delight in duty which once characterized them.

The Confederate soldier was peculiar in that he was ever ready to fight, but never ready to submit to the routine duty and discipline of the camp or the march. The soldiers were determined to be soldiers after their own notions, and do their duty, for the love of it, as they thought best. The officers saw the necessity for doing otherwise, and so the conflict was commenced and maintained to the end.

It is doubtful whether the Southern soldier would have submitted to any hardships which were purely the result of discipline; on the other hand, no amount of hardship, clearly of necessity, could cool his ardor. And in spite of all this antagonism between the officers and men, the presence of conscripts, the consolidation of commands, and many other discouraging facts, the privates in the ranks so conducted themselves that the historians of the North were forced to call them the finest body of infantry ever assembled.

But to know the men, we must see them divested of all their false notions of soldier life, and enduring the incomparable hardships which marked the latter half of the war.

3

On the March

It is a common mistake of those who write on subjects familiar to themselves to omit the details, which to one not so conversant with the matters discussed are necessary to a clear appreciation of the meaning of the writer. This mistake is fatal when the writer lives and writes in one age and his readers live in another. And so a soldier, writing for the information of the citizen, should forget his own familiarity with the everyday scenes of soldier life and strive to record even those things which seem to him too common to mention.

Who does not know all about the marching of soldiers? Those who have never marched with them and some who have. The varied experience of thousands would not tell the whole story of the march. Every man must be heard before the story is told, and even then the part of those who fell by the way is wanting.

Orders to move! Where? when? what for?—are the eager questions of the men as they begin their preparations to march. Generally nobody can answer, and the journey is commenced in utter ignorance of where it is to end. But shrewd guesses are made, and scraps of information will be picked up on the way. The main thought must be to get ready to move. The orderly sergeant is shouting "Fall in!" and there is no time to lose. The probability is that before you get your blanket rolled up, find your frying pan, haversack, axe, etc., and fall in, the roll call will be over, and some extra duty provided.

No wonder there is bustle in the camp. Rapid decisions are to be made between the various conveniences which have accumulated, for some must be left. One fellow picks up the skillet, holds it awhile, mentally determining how much it weighs, and what will be the weight of it after carrying it five miles, and reluctantly, with a half-ashamed, shy look, drops it and takes his place in ranks. Another having added to his store of blankets too freely, now has to decide which of the two or three he will leave. The old water bucket looks large and heavy, but one stout-hearted, strong-armed man has taken it affectionately to his care.

This is the time to say farewell to the bread tray, farewell to the little piles of clean straw laid between two logs, where it was so easy to sleep; farewell to those piles of wood, cut

Breaking Camp

with so much labor; farewell to the girls in the neighborhood; farewell to the spring, farewell to "our tree' and "our fire," good-by to the fellows who are not going, and a general good-by to the very hills and valleys. Soldiers commonly threw away the most valuable articles they possessed. Blankets, overcoats, shoes, bread and meat—all gave way to the necessities of the march; and what one man threw away would frequently be the very article that another wanted and would immediately pick up; so there was not much lost after all.

The first hour or so of the march was generally quite orderly, the men preserving their places in ranks and marching in solid column; but soon some lively fellow whistles an air, somebody else starts a song, the whole column breaks out with roars of laughter; route step takes the place of order, and the jolly singing, laughing, talking, and joking that follows no one could describe.

Now let any young officer who sports a new hat, coat, saddle, or anything odd, or fine, dare to pass along, and how nicely he is attended to. The expressions of good-natured fun, or contempt, which one regiment of infantry was capable of uttering in a day for the benefit of such passers-by, would fill a volume. As one thing or another in the dress of the subject of their remarks attracted attention, they would shout, "Come out of that hat!—you can't hide in thar!" "Come out of that coat, come out—there's a man in it!" "Come out of them boots!"

The infantry seemed to know exactly what to say to torment cavalry and artillery, and generally said it. If any one on the roadside was simple enough to recognize and address by name a man in the ranks, the whole column would kindly respond, and add all sorts of pleasant remarks, such as, "Halloa, John, here's your brother!" "Bill! oh Bill! here's your ma!" "Glad to see you! How's your grandma?" "How d'ye do!" "Come out of that 'biled shirt'!"

Troops on the march were generally so cheerful and gay that an outsider, looking on them as they marched, would hardly imagine how they suffered. In summer time, the dust combined with the heat, caused great suffering. The nostrils of the men, filled with dust, became dry and feverish, and even the throat did not escape. The grit was felt between the teeth, and the eyes were rendered almost useless. There was dust in eyes, mouth, ears, and hair. The shoes were full of sand, and the dust, penetrating the clothes, and getting in at the neck, wrists, and ankles, mixed with perspiration, produced an irritant almost as active as cantharides. The heat was at times terrific, but the men became greatly accustomed to it and endured it with wonderful ease. Their heavy woolen clothes were a great annoyance; tough linen or cotton clothes would have been a great relief; indeed, there are many objections to woolen clothing for soldiers, even in winter. The sun produced great changes in the appearance of the men: their skins, tanned to a dark brown or red, their hands black almost, and long uncut beard and hair, burned to a strange color, made them barely recognizable to the home folks.

If the dust and the heat were not on hand to annoy, their very able substitutes were; mud, cold, rain, snow, hail and wind took their places. Rain was the greatest discomfort a soldier could have; it was more uncomfortable than the severest cold with clear weather. Wet clothes, shoes, and blankets; wet meat and bread; wet feet and wet ground; wet wood to burn, or rather not to burn; wet arms and ammunition; wet ground to sleep on, mud to wade through, swollen creeks to ford, muddy springs, and a thousand other discomforts attended the rain. There was no comfort on a rainy day or night except in "bed" —that is, under your blanket and oilcloth. Cold winds, blowing the rain in the faces of the men, increased the discomfort, Mud was often so deep as to submerge the horses and mules, and at times it was necessary for one man or more to extricate another from the mud holes in the road. Night marching was attended with additional discomforts and dangers, such as falling off bridges, stumbling into ditches, tearing the face and injuring the eyes against the bushes and projecting limbs of trees, and getting separated from your own company and hopelessly lost in the multitude. Of course, a man lost had no sympathy. If he dared to ask a question, every man in hearing would answer, each differently, and then the whole multitude would roar with laughter at the lost man and ask him "if his mother knew he was out?"

Very few men had comfortable or fitting shoes, and fewer had socks, and as a consequence the suffering from bruised and inflamed feet was terrible. It was a common practice on long marches for the men to take off their shoes and carry them in their hands or swung over the shoulder. Bloody footprints in the snow were not unknown to the soldiers of the Army of Northern Virginia!

When large bodies of troops were moving on the same road, the alternate "halt" and "forward" was very harassing. Every obstacle produced a halt, and caused the men at once to sit and lie down on the roadside where shade or grass tempted them; about the time they got fixed they would hear the word "forward!" and then have to move at increased speed to close up the gap in the column. Sitting down for a few minutes on a long march is pleasant, but it does not always pay; when the march is resumed the limbs are stiff and sore, and the man rather worsted by the halt.

About noon on a hot day, some fellow with the water instinct would determine in his own mind that a well was not far ahead, and start off in a trot to reach it before the column. Of course another and another followed, till a stream of men were hurrying to the well, which was soon completely surrounded by a thirsty mob, yelling and pushing and pulling to get to the bucket as the windlass brought it again and again to the surface. But their impatience and haste would soon overturn the windlass, and spatter the water all around the well till the whole crowd were wading in mud, the rope would break, and the bucket fall to the bottom. But there was a substitute for rope and bucket. The men would hasten away and get long, slim poles, and on them tie by the straps a number of canteens, which they lowered into the well and filled; and unless, as was frequently the case, the whole lot slipped off and fell to the

The Rush to a Well

bottom, drew them to the top and distributed them to their owners, who at once threw their heads back, inserted the nozzles in their mouths, and drank the last drop, hastening at once to rejoin the marching column, leaving behind them a dismantled and dry well. It was in vain that the officers tried to stop the stream of men making for the water, and equally vain to attempt to move the crowd while a drop remained accessible. Many, who were thoughtful, carried full canteens to comrades in the column, who had not been able to get to the well; and no one who has not had experience of it knows the thrill of gratification and delight which those fellows felt when the cool stream gurgled from the battered canteen down their parched throats.

In very hot weather, when the necessities of the service permitted there was a halt about noon of an hour or so to rest the men and give them a chance to cool off and get the sand and gravel out of their shoes. This time was spent by some in absolute repose; but the lively boys told many a yarn, cracked many a joke, and sung many a song between "Halt" and "Column forward!" Some took the opportunity, if water was near, to bathe their feet, hands, and face; nothing could be more enjoyable.

The passage of a cider cart (a barrel on wheels) was a rare and exciting occurrence. The rapidity with which a barrel of sweet cider was consumed would astonish any one who saw it for the first time, and generally the owner had cause to wonder at the small return in cash. Sometimes a desperately enterprising darkey would approach the column with a cartload of pies, "so-called." It would be impossible to describe accurately the taste or appearance of those pies. They were generally similar in appearance, size, and thickness to a pale specimen of Old Virginia buckwheat cakes, and had a taste which resembled a combination of rancid lard and crab apples.

It was generally supposed that they contained dried apples, and the sellers were careful to state that they had "sugar in 'em" and were "mighty nice." It was rarely that any sugar was found, but they filled up a hungry man wonderfully.

Men of sense, and there were many such in the ranks, were necessarily desirous of knowing where or how far they were to march, and suffered greatly from a feeling of helpless ignorance of where they were and whither bound—whether to battle or camp. Frequently, when anticipating the quiet and rest of an ideal camp, they were thrown, weary and exhausted, into the face of a waiting enemy, and at times, after anticipating a sharp fight, having formed line of battle and braced themselves for the coming danger, suffered all the apprehension and got themselves in good fighting trim, they were marched off in the driest and prosiest sort of style and ordered into camp, where, in all probability, they had to wait for the wagon, and for the bread and meat therein, until the proverb "Patient waiting is no loss" lost all force and beauty.

Occasionally, when the column extended for a mile or more, and the road was one dense moving mass of men, a cheer would be heard away ahead—increasing in volume as it approached, until there was one universal shout. Then some favorite general officer, dashing by, followed by his staff, would explain the cause. At other times, the same cheering and enthusiasm would result from the passage down the column of some obscure and despised officer, who knew it was all a joke and looked mean and sheepish accordingly. But no man could produce more prolonged or hearty cheers than the old hare which jumped the fence and invited the column to a chase; and often it was said, when the rolling shout arose: "There goes old General Lee or a Molly Cotton Tail!"

The men would help each other when in real distress, but their delight was to torment anyone who was unfortunate in a ridiculous way. If, for instance, a piece of artillery was fast in the mud, the infantry and cavalry passing around the obstruction would rack their brains for words and phrases applicable to the situation, and most calculated to worry the cannoneers, who, waist deep in the mud, were tugging at the wheels.

Brass bands, at first quite numerous and good, became very rare and their music very poor in the latter years of the war. It was a fine thing to see the fellows trying to keep the

music going as they waded through the mud. But poor as the music was, it helped the foot-sore and weary to make another mile, and encouraged a cheer and a brisker step from the lagging and tired column.

As the men tired, there was less and less talking, until the whole mass became quiet and serious. Each man was occupied with his own thoughts. For miles nothing could be heard but the steady tramp of the men, the rattling and jingling of canteens and accoutrements, and the occasional "Close up, men, —close up!" of the officers.

The most refreshing incidents of the march occurred when the column entered some clean and cosy village where the people loved the troops. Matron and maid vied with each other in their efforts to express their devotion to the defenders of their cause. Remembering with tearful eyes the absent soldier brother or husband, they yet smiled through their tears, and with hearts and voices welcomed the coming of the road-stained troops. Their scanty larders poured out the last morsel, and their bravest words were spoken as the column moved by. But who will tell the bitterness of the lot of the man who thus passed by his own sweet home, or the anguish of the mother as she renewed her farewell to her darling boy? Then it was that men and women learned to long for the country where partings are no more.

As evening came on, questioning of the officers was in order, and for an hour it would be, "Captain, when are we going into camp?" "I say, Lieutenant, are we going to —— or to ——?" "Seen anything of our wagon?" "How long are we to stay here?" "Where's the spring?" Sometimes these questions were meant simply to tease, but generally they betrayed anxiety of some sort, and a close observer would easily detect the seriousness of the man who asked after "our wagon," because he spoke feelingly, as one who wanted his supper and was in doubt as to whether or not he would get it. People who live on country roads rarely know how far it is from anywhere to anywhere else. This is a distinguishing peculiarity of that class of people. If they do know, then they are a malicious crew. "Just over the hill there," "Just beyond those woods," " 'Bout a mile," "Round the bend," and other such encouraging replies mean anything from a mile to a day's march!

An accomplished straggler could assume more misery, look more horribly emaciated, tell more dismal stories of distress, eat more and march further (to the rear), than any ten ordinary men. Most stragglers were real sufferers, but many of were ingenious liars, energetic foragers, plunder hunters, and gormandizers. Thousands who kept their place in ranks to the very end were equally as tired, as sick, as hungry, and as hopeless as these scamps, but too proud to tell it or use it as a means of escape from hardship. But many a poor fellow dropped in the road and breathed his last in the corner of a fence with no one to hear his last fond mention of his loved ones. And many whose ambition it was to share every danger and discomfort with their comrades, overcome by the heat, or worn out with disease, were compelled to leave the ranks, and while friend and brother marched to battle, drag their weak and staggering frames to the rear, perhaps to die pitiably alone in some hospital.

After all, the march had more pleasure than pain. Chosen friends walked and talked and smoked together; the hills and valleys made themselves a panorama for the feasting of the soldiers' eyes; a turnip patch here and an onion patch there invited him to occasional refreshment; and it was sweet to think that camp was near at hand, and rest, and the journey almost ended.

4

Cooking and Eating

Rations in the Army of Northern Virginia were alternately superabundant and altogether wanting. The quality, quantity, and frequency of them depended upon the amount of stores in the hands of the commissaries, the relative position of the troops and the wagon trains, and the many accidents and mishaps of the campaign. During the latter years and months of the war, so uncertain was the issue as to time, quantity, and composition, that the men became in large measure independent of this seeming absolute necessity, and by some mysterious means, known only to purely patriotic soldiers, learned to fight without pay and to find subsistence in the field, the stream, or the forest, and a shelter on the bleak mountain side.

Sometimes there was an abundant issue of bread and no meat; then meat in any quantity, and no flour or meal; sugar in abundance and no coffee to be had for love or money; and then coffee in plenty without a grain of sugar; for months nothing but flour for bread and then nothing but meal (till all hands longed for a biscuit); or fresh meat until it was nauseating and then salt pork without intermission.

To be one day without anything to eat was common. Two days' fasting, marching and fighting was not uncommon, and there were times when no rations were issued for three or four days. On one march, from Petersburg to Appomattox, no rations were issued to Cutshaw's battalion of artillery for one entire week, and the men subsisted on the corn intended for the battery horses, raw bacon captured from the enemy, and the water of springs, creeks, and rivers.

A soldier in the Army of Northern Virginia was fortunate when he had his flour, meat, sugar, and coffee all at the same time and in proper quantity. Having these, the most skillful axeman of the mess hewed down a fine hickory or oak and cut it into lengths. All hands helped to tote it to the fire. When wood was convenient, the fire was large, the red coals abundant, and the meal soon prepared.

The man most gifted in the use of the skillet was the one most highly appreciated about the fire, and as tyrannical as a Turk; but when he raised the lid of the oven and exposed the brown-crusted tops of the biscuits, animosity subsided. The frying pan full of grease then became the center of attraction. As the hollow-cheeked boy sopped his biscuit, his poor, pinched countenance wrinkled into a smile, and his sunken eyes glistened with delight. And the coffee, too—how delicious the aroma of it, and how readily each man disposed of a quart! The strong men gathered round, chuckling at their good luck, and cooing like a child with a big piece of cake. Ah, this was a sight which but few of those who live and die are permitted to see!

And now the last biscuit is gone, the last drop of coffee, and the frying pan is wiped clean. The tobacco bag is pulled wide open, pipes are scraped, knocked out, and filled, the red coal is applied, and the blue smoke rises in wreaths and curls from the mouths of the no longer hungry but happy and contented soldiers. Songs rise on the still night air, the merry laugh resounds, the woods are bright with the rising flame of the fire, story after story is told, song after song is sung, and at midnight the soldiers steal away one by one to their blankets on the ground, and sleep till reveillé. Such was a meal when the mess was fortunate.

How different when the wagons have not been heard from for forty-eight hours. Now the question is, how to do the largest amount of good to the largest number with the smallest amount of material? The most experienced men discuss the situation and decide that somebody must go foraging. Though the stock on hand is small, no one seems anxious to leave the small certainty and go in search of the large uncertainty of supper from some farmer's well-filled table; but at last several comrades start out, and as they disappear the preparations for immediate consumption commence. The meat is too little to cook alone, and the flour will scarcely make six biscuits. The result is that "slosh" or "coosh" must do. So the bacon is fried out till the pan is half full of boiling grease. The flour is mixed with water until it flows like milk, poured into the grease and rapidly stirred till the whole is a dirty brown mixture. It is now ready to be served. Perhaps some dainty fellow prefers the more imposing slapjack. If so, the flour is mixed with less water, the grease reduced, and the paste poured in till it covers the bottom of the pan, and, when brown on the underside, is by a nimble twist of the pan, turned and browned again. If there is any sugar in camp it makes a delicious addition.

About the time the last scrap of slapjack and the last spoonful of "slosh" are disposed of, the unhappy foragers return. They take in the situation at a glance, realize with painful distinctness that they have sacrificed the homely slosh for the vain expectancy of apple butter, shortcake, and milk, and, with woeful countenance and mournful voice, narrate their adventure and disappointment thus: "Well, boys we have done the best we could. We have walked about nine miles over the mountain, and haven't found a mouthful to eat. Sorry, but it's a fact. Give us our biscuits." Of course there are none, and, as it is not contrary to army etiquette to do so, the whole mess professes to be very sorry. Sometimes, however, the foragers returned well laden with good things, and as good comrades should, shared the fruits of their toilsome hunt with their comrades.

Foragers thought it not indelicate to linger about the house of the unsuspecting farmer till the lamp revealed the family at supper, and then modestly approach and knock at the door. As the good-hearted man knew that his guests were posted about the meal in progress in the next room, the invitation to supper was given, and, shall I say it, accepted with an unbecoming lack of reluctance.

The following illustrates the ingenuity of the average forager. There was great scarcity of meat, and no prospect of a supply from the wagons. Two experienced foragers were sent out, and as a farmer about ten miles from the camp was killing hogs, guided by soldier instinct, they went directly to his house and found the meat nicely cut up, the various pieces of each hog making a separate pile on the floor of an outhouse. The proposition to buy met with a surprisingly ready response on the part of the farmer. He offered one entire pile of meat, being one whole hog, for such a small sum that the foragers instantly closed the bargain, and as promptly opened their eyes to the danger which menaced them. They gave the old gentleman a ten-dollar bill and requested change. Pleased with their honest method he hastened away to his house to obtain it. The two honest foragers hastily examined the particular pile of pork which the simple-hearted farmer designated as theirs, found it very rank and totally unfit for food, transferred half of it to another pile, from which they took half and added to theirs, and awaited the return of the farmer. On giving them their change, he assured them that they had a bargain. They agreed that they had, tossed good and bad together in a bag, said good-by, and departed as rapidly as artillerymen on foot can. The result of the trip was a pot-pie of large dimensions; and some six or eight men gorged with fat pork declared that they had never cared for and would not again wish to eat pork—especially pork pies.

A large proportion of the eating of the Army was done in the houses and at the tables of the people, not by the use of force, but by the wish and invitation of the people. It was at times necessary that whole towns should help to sustain the army of defense, and when this was the case, it was done voluntarily and cheerfully. The soldiers—all who conducted themselves properly—were received as honored guests and given the best in the house. There was a wonderful absence of stealing or plundering, and even when the people suffered from depredation they attributed the cause to terrible necessity rather than to wanton disregard of the rights of property. And when armed guards were placed over the smoke-houses and barns, it was not so much because the commanding general doubted the honesty as that he knew the necessities of his troops. But even pinching hunger was not held to be an excuse for marauding expeditions.

The inability of the government to furnish supplies forced the men to depend largely upon their own energy and ingenuity to obtain them. The officers, knowing this, relaxed discipline to an extent which would seem, to a European officer, for instance, ruinous. It was no uncommon sight to see a brigade or division, which was but a moment before marching in solid column along the road, scattered over an immense field searching for luscious blackberries. And it was wonderful to see how promptly and cheerfully all returned to the ranks when the field was gleaned. In the fall of the year a persimmon tree on the roadside would halt a column and detain it till the last persimmon disappeared.

The sutler's wagon, loaded with luxuries, which was so common in the Federal Army, was unknown in the Army of Northern Virginia for two reasons: the men had no money to buy sutlers' stores, and the country no men to spare for sutlers. The nearest approach to the sutler's wagon was the cider cart of some old darkey, or a basket of pies and cakes displayed on the roadside for sale.

The Confederate soldier relied greatly upon the abundant supplies of eatables which the enemy was kind enough to bring him, and he cheerfully risked his life for the accomplishment of the twofold purpose of whipping the enemy and getting what he called a square meal. After a battle there was general feasting on the Confederate side. Good things, scarcely ever seen at other times, filled the haversacks and the stomachs of the Boys in Gray. Imagine the feelings of men half famished when they rush into a camp at one side, while the enemy flees from the other, and find the coffee on the fire, sugar at hand ready to be dropped into the coffee, bread in the oven, crackers by the box, fine beef ready cooked, desiccated vegetables by the bushel, canned peaches, lobsters, tomatoes, milk, barrels of ground and roasted coffee, soda, salt, and in short everything a hungry soldier craves. Then add the liquors, wines, cigars, and tobacco found in the tents of the officers and the wagons of the sutlers, and, remembering the condition of the victorious party, hungry, thirsty, and weary; say if it did not require wonderful devotion to duty, and great self-denial to push on, trampling under foot the plunder of the camp, and pursue the enemy till the sun went down.

When it was allowable to halt, what a glorious time it was! Men, who a moment before would have been delighted with a pone of corn bread and a piece of fat meal, discuss the comparative merits of peaches and milk and fresh tomatoes, lobster and roast beef, and, forgetting the briar-root pipe, faithful companion of the vicissitudes of the soldier's life, snuff the aroma of imported Havanas.

In sharp contrast with the mess-cooking at the big fire was the serious and diligent work of the man separated from his comrades, out of reach of the woods, but bent on cooking and eating. He has found a coal of fire, and having placed over it in an ingenious manner the few leaves and twigs near his post, he fans the little pile with his hat. It soon blazes. Fearing the utter consumption of his fuel, he hastens to balance on the little fire his tin cup of water. When it boils, from some secure place in his clothes he takes a little coffee and drops it in the cup, and almost instantly the cup is removed and set aside;

then a slice of fat meat is laid on the coals, and when brown and crisp, completes the meal—for the crackers or biscuits are ready. No one but a soldier would have undertaken to cook with such a fire, as frequently it was no bigger than a quart cup.

Crackers, or hardtack as they were called, are notoriously poor eating, but in the hands of the Confederate soldier were made to do good duty. When on the march and pressed for time, a piece of solid fat pork and a dry cracker was passable or luscious, as the time was long or short since the last meal.

A Hardtack—Full Size

When there was leisure to do it, hardtack was soaked well and then fried in bacon grease. Prepared thus, it was a dish which no Confederate had the weakness or the strength to refuse.

Sorghum, in the absence of the better molasses of peace times, was greatly prized and eagerly sought after. A "Union" man living near the Confederate lines was one day busy boiling his crop. Naturally enough, some of our boys smelt out the place and determined to have some of the sweet fluid. They had found a yearling dead in the field hard by, and in thinking over the matter determined to sell the Union man if possible. So they cut from the dead animal a choice piece of beef, carried it to the old fellow and offered to trade. He accepted the offer, and the whole party walked off with canteens full.

Artillerymen, having tender consciences and no muskets, seldom if ever shot stray pigs; but they did sometimes, as an act of friendship, wholly disinterested, point out to the infantry a pig which seemed to need shooting, and by way of dividing the danger and responsibility of the act, accept privately a choice part of the deceased.

On one occasion, when a civilian was dining with the mess, there was a fine pig for dinner. This circumstance caused the civilian to remark on the good fare. The forager replied that pig was an uncommon dish, this one having been kicked by one of the battery horses while stealing corn, and instantly killed. The civilian seemed to doubt the statement after his teeth had come down hard on a pistol bullet, and continued to doubt, though assured that it was the head of a horseshoe nail.

The most melancholy eating a soldier was ever forced to do, was, when pinched with hunger, cold, wet, and dejected, he wandered over the deserted field of battle and satisfied his craving with the contents of the haversacks of the dead. If there is anything which will overcome the natural abhorrence which a man feels for the enemy, the loathing of the bloated dead, and the awe engendered by the presence of death, solitude, and silence, it is hunger. Impelled by its clamoring, men of high principle and tenderest humanity become for the time void of sensibility, and condescend to acts which, though justified by their extremity, seem afterwards, even to the doers, too shameless to mention.

When rations became so very small that it was absolutely necessary to supplement them, and the camp was permanently established, those men who had the physical ability worked for the neighborhood farmers at cutting cord-word, harvesting the crops, killing hogs, or any other farm work. A stout man would cut a cord of wood a day and receive fifty cents in money or its equivalent in something eatable. Hogs were slaughtered for the "fifth quarter." When the corn became large enough to eat, the roasting ears, thrown in the ashes with the shucks on, and nicely roasted, made a grateful meal. Turnip and onion patches also furnished delightful and much-needed food, good raw or cooked.

Occasionally, when a mess was hard pushed for eatables, it became necessary to resort to some ingenious method of disgusting a part of the mess, that the others might eat their fill. The "pepper treatment" was a common method practiced with the soup, which once failed. A shrewd fellow, who loved things "hot," decided to have plenty of soup, and to accomplish his purpose, as he passed and repassed the boiling pot, dropped in a pod of red pepper. But, alas! for him, there was another man like minded who adopted the same plan, and the result was that all the mess waited in vain for that pot of soup to cool.

The individual coffee boiler of one man in the Army of Northern Virginia was always kept at the boiling point. The owner of it was an enigma to his comrades. They could not understand his strange fondness for red-hot coffee. After the war's end he explained that he found the heat of the coffee prevented its use by others, and adopted the plan of placing his cup on the fire after every sip. This same character never troubled himself to carry a canteen, though a great water drinker. When he found a good canteen he would kindly give it to a comrade, reserving the privilege of an occasional drink when in need. He soon had an interest in thirty or forty canteens and their contents and could always get a drink of water if it was to be found on any of them. He pursued the same plan with blankets and always had plenty in that line. His entire outfit was the clothes on his back and a haversack accurately shaped to hold one half-pone of corn bread.

Roasting-ear time was a trying time for the hungry private. Having been fed during the whole of the winter on salt meat and coarse bread, his system craved the fresh, luscious juice of the corn, and at times his honesty gave way under the pressure. How could he resist? He didn't—he took some roasting ears! Sometimes the farmer grumbled, sometimes he quarreled, and sometimes he complained to the officers of the depredations of the men. The officers apologized, ate what corn they had on hand, and sent their boy for some more. One old farmer conceived the happy plan of inviting some privates to his house, stating his grievances, and securing their coöperation in the effort to protect his corn. He told them that of course *they* were not the *gentlemen* who took his corn! Oh no! of course *they* would not do such a thing; but wouldn't they please speak to the others and ask them please not to take his corn? Of course; certainly! oh, yes! they would remonstrate with their comrades. How they burned, though, as they thought of the past and contemplated the near future. As they returned to camp through the field they filled their haversacks with the silky ears and were met on the other side of the field by the kind farmer and a file of men who were only too eager to secure the plucked corn in the line of duty.

A faithful officer, worn out with the long, weary march, sick, hungry, and dejected, leaned his back against a tree and and groaned to think of his inability to join in the chase of an old hare, which, he knew, from the wild yells in the wood, his men were pursuing. But the uproar approached him— nearer, nearer, and nearer, until he saw the hare bounding towards him with a regiment at her heels. She spied an opening made by the folds of the officer's cloak and jumped in, and he embraced his first meal for forty-eight hours.

An artilleryman, camped for a day where no water was to be found easily, awakened during the night by thirst, went stumbling about in search of water; and to his great delight found a large bucketful. He drank his fill, and in the morning found that what he drank had washed a bullock's head and was crimson with its blood.

Some stragglers came up one night and found the camp silent. All hands asleep. Being hungry they sought and to their great delight found a large pot of soup. It had a peculiar taste, but they worried it down, and in the morning bragged of their good fortune. The soup had defied the stomachs of the whole battery, being strongly impregnated with the peculiar flavor of defunct cockroaches.

Shortly before the evacuation of Petersburg, a country boy went hunting. He killed and brought to camp a muskrat. It was skinned, cleaned, buried a day or two, disinterred, cooked, and eaten with great relish. It was splendid.

During the Seven Days' Battles around Richmond, a studious private observed the rats as they entered and emerged from a corn crib. He killed one, cooked it privately, and invited a friend to join him in eating a fine squirrel. The comrade consented, ate heartily, and when told what he had eaten, forthwith disgorged. But he confessed that up to the time when he was enlightened he had greatly enjoyed the meal.

It was at this time, when rats were a delicacy, that the troops around Richmond agreed to divide their rations with the poor of the city, and they were actually hauled in and distributed. Comment here would be like complimenting the sun on its brilliancy.

Orators dwell on the genius and skill of the general officers; historians tell of the movements of divisions and army corps, and the student of the art of war studies the geography and topography of the country and the returns of the various crops: they all seek to find and to tell the secret of success or failure. The Confederate soldier knows the elements of his success—courage, endurance, and devotion. He knows also by whom he was defeated—sickness, starvation, death. He fought not men only, but food, raiment, pay, glory, fame, and fanaticism. He endured privation, toil, and contempt. He won, and despite the cold indifference of all and the hearty hatred of some, he will have for all time, in all places where generosity is, a fame untarnished.

5

Comforts, Conveniences, and Consolations

Have you ever been a soldier? No? Then you do not know what comforts are! Conveniences you never had; animal consolations, never! You have not enjoyed the great exceptional luxuries which once in a century, perhaps, bless a limited number of men. How sad that you have allowed your opportunity to pass unimproved!

But you *have* been a soldier! Ah, then let us together recall with pleasure the past! once more be hungry, and eat; once more tired, and rest; once more thirsty, and drink; once more cold and wet, let us sit by the roaring fire and feel comfort creep over us. So!—isn't it very pleasant? Now let us recount, repossess rather, the treasures which once were ours, not forgetting that values have shrunk, and that the times have changed, and that men also are changed; some happily, some woefully. Possibly we, also, are somewhat modified.

Eating, you will remember, was more than a convenience; it was a comfort which rose almost to the height of a consolation. Probably the most universally desired comfort of the Confederate soldier was something to eat. But this, like all greatly desired blessings, was shy, and when obtained was, to the average seeker, not replete with satisfaction.

But he did eat, at times, with great energy, great endurance, great capacity, and great satisfaction; the luscious slapjack, sweetened perhaps with sorghum, the yellow and odoriferous soda-biscuit, ash-cake, or, it might chance to be, the faithful hardtack (which our friends the enemy called "crackers") serving in rotation as bread.

The faithful hog was everywhere represented. His cheering presence was manifested most agreeably by the sweet odors flung to the breeze from the frying pan,—that never-failing and

325

always reliable utensil. The solid slices of meat, lean and fat, the limpid gravy, the brown pan of slosh inviting you to sop it, and the rare, delicate shortness of the biscuit, made the homely animal to be in high esteem.

Beef, glorious beef! How seldom were you seen, and how welcome was your presence. In the generous pot you parted with your mysterious strength and sweetness. Impaled upon the cruel ramrod you suffered slow torture over the fire. Sliced, chopped, and pounded; boiled, stewed, fried, or broiled, always a trusty friend and sweet comforter.

Happy the fire where the "stray" pig found a lover, and unhappy the pig! Innocence and youth were no protection to him, and his cries of distress availed him not as against the cruel purpose of the rude soldiery.

What is that faint aroma which steals about on the night air? Is it a celestial breeze? No! it is the mist of the coffee boiler. Do you not hear the tumult of the tumbling water? Poor man! you have eaten, and now other joys press upon you. Drink! drink more! Near the bottom it is sweeter. Providence hath now joined together for you the bitter and the sweet—there is sugar in that cup!

Some poor fellows, after eating, could only sleep. They were incapable of the noble satisfaction of a good smoke. But there were some good men and true, thoughtful men, quietly disposed men, gentle and kind, who next to a good square meal prized a smoke. Possibly, here begins consolation. Who can find words to tell the story of the soldier's affection for his faithful briar-root pipe! As the cloudy incense of the weed rises in circling wreaths about his head, as he hears the murmuring of the fire, and watches the glowing and fading of the embers, and feels the comfort of the hour pervading his mortal frame, what bliss!

But yonder sits a man who scorns the pipe—and why? He is a chewer of the weed. To him, the sweetness of it seems not to be drawn out by the fiery test, but rather by the persuasion of moisture and pressure. But he, too, is under the spell. There are pictures in the fire for him, also, and he watches them come and go. Now draw near. Are not those cheerful voices? Do you not hear the contented tones of men sitting in a cosy home? What glowing hopes here leap out in rapid words! No bitterness of hate, no revenge, no cruel purpose; but simply the firm resolve to march in the front of their country's defenders. Would you hear a song? You shall—for even now they sing:

> *Aha! a song for the trumpet's tongue!*
> *For the bugle to sing before us,*
> *When our gleaming guns, like clarions,*
> *Shall thunder in battle chorus!*

Would you hear a soldier's prayer? Well, there kneels one, behind that tree, but he talks with God: you may not hear him —nor I!

But now, there they go, one by one; no, two by two. Down goes an old rubber blanket, and then a good, thick, woolen one, probably with a big "U.S." in the center of it. Down go two men. They are hidden under another of the U.S. blankets. They are resting their heads on their old battered haversacks. They love each other to the death, those men, and sleep there, like little children, locked in close embrace. They are asleep now —no, not quite; they are thinking of home, and it may be, of heaven. But now, surely they are asleep! No, they are not quite asleep, they are falling off to sleep. Happy soldiers, they are asleep.

At early dawn the bugle sounds the réveillé. Shout answers to shout, the roll is called and the day begins. What new joys will it bring?

Let us stay and see.

The sun gladdens the landscape; the fresh air, dashing and whirling over the fields and through the pines is almost intoxicating. Here are noble chestnut oaks, ready for the axe and the fire; and there, at the foot of the hill, a mossy spring. The oven sits enthroned on glowing coals, crowned with fire; the coffee boils, the meat fries, the soldier—smiles and waits.

But waiting is so very trying that some, seizing towels, soap, and comb from their haversacks, step briskly down the hill and plunge their heads into the cool water of the brook. Then their cheeks glow with rich color, and chatting merrily, they seek again the fire, carrying the old bucket brimming full of water for the mess. All hands welcome the bucket, and breakfast begins. Now see the value of a good tin plate. What a treasure that tin cup is, and that old fork! Who would have a more comfortable seat than that log affords!

But here comes the mail—papers, letters, packages. Here comes news from home, sweet, tender, tearful, hopeful, sad, distressing news; joyful news of victory and sad news of defeat; pictures of happy homes, or sad wailing over homes destroyed! But the mail has arrived and we cannot change the burden it has brought. We can only pity the man who goes empty away from the little group assembled about the mail bag, and rejoice with him who strolls away with a letter near his heart. Suppose he finds therein the picture of a curly head. Just four years old! Suppose the last word in it is "Mother." Or suppose it concludes with a signature having that peculiarly helpless, but courageous and hopeful air, imparted by the hand of a girl whose heart goes with the letter! Once more, happy soldier!

The artilleryman tarrying for a day only in a camp had only time to eat and do his work. Roll call, drill, watering the horses, greasing caissons and gun carriages; cleaning, repairing, and greasing harness; cleaning the chests of the limbers and caissons; storing and arranging ammunition; and many little duties, filled the day. In the midst of a campaign, comfortable arrangements for staying were hardly completed by the time the bugle sounded the assembly and orders to move were given. But however short the stay might be, the departure always partook of the nature of a move from home. More especially was this true in the case of the sick man, whose weary body was finding needed rest in the camp; and peculiarly true of the man who had fed at the table of a hospitable neighbor, and for a day, perhaps, enjoyed the society of the fair daughters of the house.

Orders to move were frequently heralded by the presence of the courier, a man who rarely knew a word of the orders he had brought; who was always besieged with innumerable questions, always tried to appear to know more than his position allowed him to disclose, and who never ceased to be an object of interest to every camp he entered. Many a gallant fellow rode the country over; many a one led in the thickest of the fight and died bravely, known only as "my courier."

When the leaves began to fall and the wind to rush in furious frolics through the woods, the soldier's heart yearned for comfort. Chilling rains, cutting sleet, drifting snow, muddy roads, all the miseries of approaching winter, pressed him to ask and repeat the question, "When will we go into winter quarters?"

After all, the time did come. But first the place was known. The time was always doubtful. Leisurely and steady movement towards the place might be called the first comfort of winter quarters; and as each day's march brought the column nearer the appointed camp, the anticipated pleasures assumed almost the sweetness of present enjoyment.

But at last comes the welcome "Left into park!" and the fence goes down, the first piece wheels through the gap, the battery is parked, the horses are turned over to the horse sergeant, the old guns are snugly stowed under the tarpaulins, and the winter has commenced. The woods soon resound with the ring of the axe; trees rush down, crashing and snapping to the ground; fires start here and there till the woods are illuminated, and the brightest, happiest, busiest night of all the year falls upon the camp. Now around each fire gathers the little group who are, for a while, to make it the center of operations. Hasty plans for comfort and convenience are eagerly discussed till late into the night, and await only the dawn of another day for execution.

Roll call over and breakfast eaten, the work of the day commences with the preparation of comfortable sleeping places, varying according to the material on hand. A favorite arrangement for two men consisted of a bed of clean straw between the halves of a large oak log, covered, in the event of rain, with a rubber blanket. The more ambitious builders made straw pens, several logs high, and pitched over these a fly tent, adding sometimes a chimney. In this structure, by the aid of a bountiful supply of dry, clean straw, and their blankets, the occupants bade defiance to cold, rain, and snow.

Other men, gifted with that strange facility for comfort without work which characterizes some people, found resting-places ready made. They managed to steal away night after night and sleep in the sweet security of a haystack, a barn, a stable, a porch, or, if fortune favored them, in some farmer's feather bed.

Others still, but more especially the infantry and cavalry, built shelters open to the south, covered them with pine-tags and brush, built a huge fire in front, and made themselves at home for a season.

But all these things were mere makeshifts, temporary stopping places, occupying about the same relation to winter quarters as the boardinghouse does to a happy and comfortable home. During the occupancy of these, and while the work of building was progressing, the Confederate soldier wrote many letters home. He saw an opportunity for enjoyment ahead, and tried to improve it. His letters were somewhat after the following order:

CAMP NEAR WILLIAMS' MILL
December 2, 1864

DEAR FATHER, You will no doubt be glad to hear that we are at last in winter quarters! We are quite comfortably fixed, though we arrived here only two days ago. We are working constantly on our log cabins and hope to be in them next week. We are near the —— railroad, and anything you may desire to send us may be shipped to —— depot. If you can possibly spare the money to buy them, please send at once four pounds ten-penny nails; one pair wrought hinges (for door); one good axe; two pairs shoes (one for me and one for J.); four pairs socks (two for me and two for J.); five pounds Killickinick smoking tobacco; one pound bi-carb. soda. Please send also two or three old church music books, and any good books you are willing to part with forever. Underclothing of any sort, shirts, drawers, socks—cotton or woollen—would be very, very acceptable, as it is much less trouble to put on the clean and throw away the soiled clothes than to wash them. Some coffee, roasted and ground, with sugar to match, and *anything good to eat* would do to fill up. Do not imagine, however, that we are suffering or unhappy. Our only concern is for all at home; and if compliance with the above requests would cost you the slightest self-denial at home, we would rather withdraw them.

Why don't——and——go into the Army? They are old enough, hearty enough, able to provide themselves with every comfort, and ought to be here.

Many furloughs will be granted during the winter, and we may get home, some of us, before another month is past.

Love to mother, dear mother; and to sister, and tell them

we are happy and contented. Write as soon as you can, and believe me, Your affectionate son,

P. S. Don't forget the tobacco.   W.

And now another night comes to the soldier, inviting him to nestle in clean straw, under dry blankets, and sleep. Tomorrow he will lay the foundation of a village destined to live till the grass grows again. Tomorrow he will be architect, builder, and proprietor of a cosy cabin in the woods. Let him sleep.

A pine wood of heavy original growth furnishes the ground and the timber. Each company is to have two rows of houses with a street between, and each street is to end on the main road to the railroad depot. The width of the street is decided; it is staked off; each mess selects its site, and work begins.

The old pines fall rapidly under the energetic strokes of the axes which glide into the hearts of the trees with a malicious and cruel willingness; the logs are cut into lengths, notched and fitted one upon another, and the structure begins to rise. The builders stagger about here and there under the weight of the huge logs, occasionally falling and rolling in the snow. They shout and whistle and sing, as merry as children at play.

At last the topmost log is rolled into place and the artistic work commences—the riving of slabs. Short logs of oak are to be split into huge shingles for the roof, and tough and tedious work it is. But it is done; the roof is covered in, and the house is far enough advanced for occupancy.

Now the bunks which are simply broad shelves one above another, wide enough to accommodate two men spoon fashion, are built. Merry parties sally forth to seek the straw stack of the genial farmer of the period, and returning heavily laden with sweet clean straw, bestow it in the bunks. Here they rest for a night. Next day the chimney, built like the house, of notched sticks or small logs, rises rapidly till it reaches the apex of the roof and is crowned with a nail keg or flour barrel.

Next, a pit is dug deep enough to reach the clay; water is poured in and the clay well mixed, and the whole mess takes in hand the daubing of the chinks. Every crack and crevice of house and chimney receives attention at the hands of the builders, and when the sun goes down the house is proof against the most searching winter wind. The most skillful man contrives a door and swings it on its hinges; another makes a shelf for the old water bucket; a short bench or two appear like magicians' work before the fire, and the family is settled for the winter.

It would be a vain man indeed who thought himself able to describe the happy days and cozy nights of that camp. First among the luxuries of settled life was the opportunity to part forever with a suit of underwear which had been on constant duty for possibly three months, and put on the sweet clean clothes from home. They looked so pure, the very smell of them was sweet. Then there was the ever-present thought of a dry, warm, undisturbed sleep the night through.

Remember, now, there is a pile of splendid oak ready cut for the fire within easy reach of the door—several cords of it—all ours. It will keep a fire night and day for a month.

The wagons, which have been over the mountains and far away have come into camp loaded with the best flour in abundance; droves of cattle are bellowing in the road, and our commissary, as he hurries from camp to camp with the glad tidings, is the embodiment of happiness. All this means plenty to eat.

This is a good time to make and carve beautiful pipes of hard wood with horn mouthpieces, very comfortable chairs, bread trays, haversacks, and a thousand other conveniences.

At night the visiting commences, and soon in many huts are little social groups close around the fire. The various incidents of the campaign pass in review, and pealing laughter rings out upon the crisp winter air. Then a soft, sweet melody floats out of that cabin door as the favorite singer yields to the entreaty of his little circle of friends; or a swelling chorus of manly voices, in a grand and solemn anthem, stirs every heart.

Now think of an old Confederate veteran, who passed through Fredericksburg, Chancellorsville, and the Wilderness, sitting in front of a cheerful fire in a snug log cabin, reading, say, *The Spectator!* Think of another by his side reading a letter from his sweetheart; and another still, a warm and yearning letter from his mother. Think of two others in the corner playing old sledge, or, it may be, chess. Hear another, off guard, snoring in his bunk. Ah! what an amount of condensed contentment that little hut contains.

And now the stables are finished. The whole battalion did the work, and the poor old shivering and groaning horses are under cover. And the guardhouse, another joint production, opens wide its door every day to receive the unhappy men whose time for detail has at last arrived. The chapel is also ready, having been duly dedicated to the worship of God.

Men thus comfortably fixed, with light guard duty and little else to do, found time, of course, to do a little foraging in the country around. By this means often during the winter the camp enjoyed great abundance and variety of food. Apples and apple butter, fresh pork, dried fruit, milk, eggs, risen bread, and even cakes and preserves. Occasionally a whole mess would be filled with the liveliest expectations by the information that Bob or Joe was expecting a box from home. The wagon comes into camp escorted by the expectant Bob and several of his intimate friends; the box is dropped from the wagon to the ground; off goes the top and in go busy hands and eyes. Here are clothes, shoes, and hats; here is coffee, sugar, soda, salt, bread, fresh butter, roast beef, and turkey; here is a bottle! marked "to be used in case of sickness or wounds." What shall be done with this treasure? One man cannot eat the eatables or smoke the tobacco. Call in the willing comrades. They come; they see; they devour!

And now the ever-true and devoted citizens of the much and often besieged city of Richmond conclude to send a New Year's dinner to their defenders in the army. That portion destined for the camp above described arrived in due time in the shape of one good turkey. Each of the three companies composing the battalion appointed a man to "draw straws" for the turkey; the successful company appointed a man from each detachment to draw again; then the detachment messes took a draw, and the fortunate mess devoured the turkey. But the soldiers, remembering that in times past they had felt constrained to divide their rations with the poor of that city, did not fail in gratitude, or question the liberality of those who had remembered with self-denying affection the soldiers in the field.

Not the least among the comforts of life in winter quarters, was the pleasure of sitting under the ministrations of an amateur barber and hearing the snip of his scissors as the long growth of hair fell to the ground. The luxury of a shave; the possession of comb, brush, small mirror, towels and soap; boots blacked every day; white collars, and occasionally a starched bosom, called, in the expressive language of the day, a "biled shirt," completed the restoration of the man to decency. Now, also, the soldier with painful care threaded his needle with huge thread, and with a sort of lefthanded awkwardness sewed on the long-absent button, or, with even greater trepidation, attempted a patch. At such a time the soldier pondered on the

peculiar fact that war separates men from women. A man cannot thread a needle with ease; certainly not with grace.

In winter quarters every man had his chum or bunkmate,
with whom he slept, walked, talked, and divided hardship or
comfort as they came along; and the affectionate regard of each
for the other was often beautiful to see. Many such attachments
led to heroic self-denials and death, one for the other.

It was a rare occurrence, but occasionally the father or
mother or brother or sister of some man paid him a visit. The
males were almost sure to be very old or very young. In either
case they were received with great hospitality, given the best
place to sleep, the best the camp afforded in the way of eatables,
and treated with the greatest courtesy and kindness by the
whole command. But the lady visitors! the girls! Who could
describe the effect of their appearance in camp! They produced
conflict in the soldier's breast. They looked so clean, they were
so gentle, they were so different from all around them, they
were so attractive, they were so agreeable, and sweet, and fresh,
and happy, that the poor fellows would have liked above all
things to have gotten very near to them and have heard their
kind words—possibly shake hands; but no, some were barefooted, some almost bareheaded; some were still expecting
clean clothes from home; some were sick and disheartened;
some were on guard; some in the guardhouse, and others too
modest; and so, to many, the innocent visitor became a sort of
pleasant agony; as it were, a bitter sweet. Nothing ever so
promptly convinced a Confederate soldier that he was dilap-
idated and not altogether as neat as he might be, as sudden
precipitation into the presence of a neatly dressed, refined, and
modest woman. Fortunately for the men, the women loved
the very rags they wore, if they were gray; and when the war
ended they welcomed with open arms the man and his rags.

Preaching in camp was to many a great pleasure and greatly
profitable. At times intense religious interest pervaded the
whole army, and thousands of men gladly heard the tidings of
salvation. Many afterwards died triumphant, and many others
became witnesses of the great change wrought in them by the
preaching of the faithful and able men who, as chaplains, shared
the dangers, hardships, and pleasures of the campaign.

To all the foregoing comforts and conveniences must be
added the consolation afforded by the anticipation and daily
expectation of a furlough; which meant, of course, a blissful re-

union with the dear ones at home—perhaps an interview or two with that historic maid who is left behind by the soldier of all times; plenty to eat; general admiration of friends and relatives; invitations to dine, to spend a week; and last, but not least, an opportunity to express contempt for every able-bodied bomb-proof found sneaking about home. Food, shelter, and rest, the great concerns, being thus all provided for, the soldier enjoyed intensely his freedom from care and responsibility, living as near as a man may the innocent life of a child. He played marbles, spun his top, played at football, bandy, and was happy. He had time now comfortably to review the toils, dangers, and hardships of the past campaign, and with allowable pride to dwell on the cheerfulness and courage with which he had endured them all; and to feel the supporting effect of the unanimity of feeling and pervasive sympathy which linked together the rank and file of the Army.

He realized he was resisting manfully the coercive force of other men, and was resolved to die rather than yield his liberty. He felt that he was beyond doubt in the line of duty, and expected no relief from toil by any other means than the accomplishment of his purpose and the end of the war. To strengthen his resolve he had ever present with him the unchanging love of the people for whom he fought; the respect and confidence of his officers; unshaken faith in the valor of his comrades and the justice of his cause. And, finally, he had an opportunity to brace himself for another, and, if need be, for still another struggle, with the ever increasing multitude of invaders, hoping that each would usher in the peace so eagerly coveted and the liberty for which already a great price had been paid. Was he not badly disappointed?

6

Fun and Fury on the Field

A battlefield, when only a few thousands of men are engaged, is a more extensive area than most persons would suppose. When large bodies of men—twenty to fifty thousand on each side—are engaged, a mounted man at liberty to gallop from place to place could scarcely travel the field over during the continuance of the battle; and a private soldier in the smallest affair sees very little of the field. What occurs in his own regiment, or probably in his own company, is about all and is sometimes more than he actually sees or knows. Thus it is that while the field is extensive, it is to each individual limited to the narrow space of which he is cognizant.

The dense woods of Virginia, often choked with heavy undergrowth, added greatly to the difficulty of observing the movements of large bodies of troops extended in line of battle. The commanders were compelled to rely almost entirely upon the information gained from their staff officers and the couriers of those in immediate command on the lines.

The beasts of burden which travel the Great Desert scent the oasis and the well miles away, and cheered by the prospect of rest and refreshment, press on with renewed vigor; and in the book of Job it is said of the horse, "He saith among the trumpets, Ha! ha! and he smelleth the battle afar off, the thunder of the captains, and the shoutings." So a soldier, weary and worn, recognizing the signs of approaching battle, did quicken his lagging steps and cry out for joy at the prospect.

The column, hitherto moving forward with the steadiness of a mighty river, hesitates, halts, steps back, then forward, hesitates again, halts. The colonels talk to the brigadier, the brigadiers talk to the major-general, some officers hurry forward and others hurry to the rear. Infantry stands to one side of the road while cavalry trots by to the front. Now some old wagons marked "Ord. Dept." go creaking and rumbling by. One or

336

two light ambulances with a gay and careless air seem to trip
along with the ease of a dancing girl. They and the surgeons
seem cheerful. Some, not many, ask "What is the matter?"
Most of the men there know exactly: they are on the edge of
battle.

Presently a very quiet, almost sleepy looking man on horseback says, "Forward, 19th!" and away goes the leading regiment. A little way ahead the regiment jumps a fence, and—
pop! bang! whiz! thud! is all that can be heard until the rebel
yell reverberates through the woods. Battle? No! skirmishers
advancing.

Step into the woods now and watch these skirmishers. See
how cheerfully they go in. How rapidly they load, fire, and reload. They stand six and twelve feet apart, calling to each
other, laughing, shouting and cheering, but advancing. There:
one fellow has dropped his musket like something red hot.
His finger is shot away. His friends congratulate him, and he
walks sadly away to the rear. Another staggers and falls with a
ball through his neck, mortally wounded. Two comrades raise
him to his feet and try to lead him away, but one of them receives a ball in his thigh which crushes the bone, and he falls
groaning to the ground. The other advises his poor dying friend
to lie down, helps him to do so, and runs to join his advancing
comrades. When he overtakes them he finds every man securely
posted behind a tree, loading, firing, and conducting himself
generally with great deliberation and prudence. They have at
last driven the enemy's skirmishers in upon the line of battle
and are waiting. A score of men have fallen here, some killed
outright, some slightly, some sorely, and some mortally
wounded.

The elements now add to the horrors of the hour. Dense
clouds hovering near the tree tops add deeper shadows to the
woods. Thunder, deep and ominous, rolls in prolonged peals
across the sky, and lurid lightning darts among the trees and
glistens on the gun barrels. But still they stand.

Now a battery has been hurried into position, the heavy
trails have fallen to the ground, and at the command "Commence firing!" the cannoneers have stepped in briskly and
loaded. The first gun blazes at the muzzle and away goes a
shell. The poor fellows back in the woods rejoice as it crashes
through the trees over their heads and cheer when it explodes
over the enemy's line. Now, what a chorus! Thunder, gun after

gun, shell after shell, musketry, pelting rain, shouts, groans, cheers, and commands!

But help is coming. At the edge of the woods, where the skirmishers entered, the brigade is in line. Somebody has ordered, "Load!"

The ramrods glisten and rattle down the barrels of a thousand muskets. "F-o-o-o-o-r-r-r-r-w-a-a-a-r-r-r-d!" is the next command, and the brigade disappears in the woods, the canteens rattling, the bushes crackling, and the officers never ceasing to say, "Close up, men; close up! guide c-e-n-t-e-r-r-r-r!"

The men on that skirmish line have at last found it advisable to lie down at full length on the ground, though it is so wet, and place their heads against the trees in front. They cannot advance and they cannot retire without in either case exposing themselves to almost certain death. They are waiting for the line of battle to come to their relief.

At last, before they see, they hear the line advancing through the pines. The snapping of the twigs, the neighing of horses, and hoarse commands, inspire a husky cheer, and when the line of the old brigade breaks through the trees in full view, they fairly yell! Every man jumps to his feet, the brigade presses firmly forward, and soon the roll of musketry tells all who are waiting to hear that serious work is progressing away down in the woods. All honor to the devoted infantry. The hour of glory has arrived for couriers, aides-de-camp, and staff officers generally. They dash about from place to place like spirits of unrest. Brigade after brigade and division after division is hurried into line and pressed forward into action. Battalions of artillery open fire from the crests of many hills, and the battle is begun.

Ammunition trains climb impassable places, cross ditches without bridges, and manage somehow to place themselves in reach of the troops. Ambulances, which an hour before went gayly forward, now slowly and solemnly return loaded. Shells and musket balls which must have lost their way, go flitting about here and there, wounding and killing men who deem themselves far away from danger. The Negro cooks turn pale as these unexpected visitors enter the camps at the rear, and the rear is extended at once.

But our place now is at the front, on the field. We are to watch the details of a small part of the great expanse. As we approach, a ludicrous scene presents itself. A strong-armed artilleryman is energetically thrashing a dejected looking individual with a hickory bush and urging him to the front. He has managed to keep out of many a fight, but now he *must* go in. The captain has detailed a man to *whip* him in, and the man is doing it. With every blow the poor fellow yells and begs to be spared, but his determined guardian will not cease. They press on, the one screaming and the other lashing, till they reach the battery in position and firing on the retiring enemy.

The Rear Guard of the Regiment

A battery of the enemy is replying, and shells are bursting overhead, or plowing huge furrows in the ground. Musket balls are rapping on the rims of the wheels and sinking with a deep thud into the bodies of the poor horses. Smoke obscures the scene, but the cannoneers in faint outline can be seen cheerfully serving the guns.

As the opposing battery ceases firing, and having limbered up, scampers away, and the last of the enemy's infantry slowly sinks into the woods out of sight and out of reach, a wild cheer breaks from the cannoneers, who toss their caps in the air and shout, shake hands and shout again while the curtain of smoke is raised by the breeze and borne away.

The cavalry is gone. With jingle and clatter they have

passed through the lines and down the hill and are already demanding surrender from many a belated man. There will be no rest for that retreating column. Stuart, with a twinkle in his eye, his lips puckered as if to whistle a merry lay, is on their flanks, in their rear, and in their front. The enemy will send their cavalry after him, of course, but he will stay with them, nevertheless.

Add now the stream of wounded men slowly making their way to the rear; the groups of dejected prisoners plodding along under guard, and you have about as much of a battle as one private soldier ever sees.

But after the battle, man will tell to man what each has seen and felt, until every man will feel that he has seen the whole. Hear, then, the stories of battle.

An artilleryman—he must have been a driver—says: when the firing had ceased, an old battery horse, his lower jaw carried away by a shot, with blood streaming from his wound, staggered up to him, gazed beseechingly at him, and, groaning piteously, laid his bloody jaws on his shoulder and so made his appeal for sympathy. He was beyond help.

The pathetic nature of this story reminds a comrade that a new man in the battery, desiring to save the labor incident to running up the gun after the rebound, determined to hold on to the handspike, press the trail into the ground, and hold her fast. He did try, but the rebound proceeded as usual, and the labor-saving man was shocked at the failure of his effort. Nothing daunted, the same individual soon after applied his lips to the vent of the gun, which was choked, and endeavored to clear it by an energetic blast from his lungs. The vent was not cleared but the lips of the recruit were nicely browned, and the detachment greatly amused.

At another gun it has happened that [gunner] No. 1 and No. 3 have had a difficulty. No. 3 having failed to serve the vent, there was a premature explosion, and No. 1, being about to withdraw the rammer, fell heavily to the ground, apparently dead. No. 3, seeing what a calamity he had caused, hung over the dead man and begged him to speak and exonerate him from blame. After No. 3 had exhausted all his eloquence and was a joke intended to warn him that if he ever failed again the premature explosion was a fact, but the death of No. 1 to serve that vent, he would have his head broken by a blow pathos, No. 1 suddenly rose to his feet and informed him that from a rammer head. This joke having been completed in all its details, the firing was continued.

Another man tells how Eggleston had his arm torn away by a solid shot, and as he walked away, held up the bleeding, quivering stump, exclaiming, "Never mind, boys; I'll come back soon and try 'em with this other one." Alas! poor fellow, he had fought his last fight.

Poor Tom, he who was always, as he said, "willing to give 'em half a leg, or so," was struck about the waist by a shot which almost cut him in two. He fell heavily to the ground, and though in awful agony, managed to say: "Tell mother I died doing my duty."

While the fight lasted, several of the best and bravest received wounds apparently mortal, and were laid aside covered by an old army blanket. They refused to die, however, and remained for years to tell their own stories of the war and of their marvelous recovery.

At the battle of the Wilderness, May, 1864, a man from North Carolina precipitated a severe fight by asking a very simple and reasonable question. The line of battle had been pressed forward and was in close proximity to the enemy. The thick and tangled undergrowth prevented a sight of the enemy, but every man felt he was near. Everything was hushed and still. No one dared to speak above a whisper. It was evening and growing dark. As the men lay on the ground, keenly sensible to every sound, and anxiously waiting, they heard the firm tread of a man walking along the line. As he walked they heard also the jingle-jangle of a pile of canteens hung around his neck. He advanced with deliberate mien to within a few yards of the line and opened a terrific fight by quietly saying, "Can any you fellows tell a man whar he can git some water?" Instantly the thicket was illumined by the flash of a thousand muskets, the men leaped to their feet, the officers shouted, and the battle was begun. Neither side would yield, and there they fought till many died.

Soon, however, the reserve brigade began to make its way through the thicket. The first man to appear was the brigadier, thirty yards ahead of his brigade, his sword between his teeth, and parting the bushes with both hands as he spurred his horse through the tangled growth. Eager for the fight, his eyes glaring and his countenance lit up with fury, his first word was "Forward!" and forward went the line.

On the march from Petersburg to Appomattox, after a sharp engagement, some men of Cutshaw's artillery battalion, acting as infantry, made a stand for a while on a piece of high ground. They noticed, hanging around in a lonely, distracted way, a tall, lean, shaggy fellow holding, or rather leaning on, a long staff, around which hung a faded battle flag. Thinking him out of his place and skulking, they suggested to him that it would be well for him to join his regiment. He replied that his regiment had all run away, and he was merely waiting a chance to be useful. Just then the enemy's advancing skirmishers poured a hot fire into the group, and the artillerymen began to discuss the propriety of leaving. The colorbearer, remembering their insinuations, saw an opportunity for retaliation. Standing, as he was, in the midst of a shower of musket balls, he seemed almost ready to fall asleep. But suddenly his face was illumined with a singularly pleased and childish smile. Quietly walking up close to the group, he said, "Any you boys want to charge?" The boys answered, "Yes." "Well," said the imperturbable, "I'm the man to carry this here old flag for you. Just follow me." So saying he led the squad full into the face of the advancing enemy and never once seemed to think of stopping until he was urged to retire with the squad. He came back smiling from head to foot, and suffered no more insinuations.

At Gettysburg, when the artillery fire was at its height, a brawny fellow who seemed happy at the prospect for a hot time, broke out singing:—

Backward, roll backward, O Time in thy flight:
Make me a child again, just for this fight!

Another fellow near him replied, "Yes, and a gal child at that."

At Fredericksburg a good soldier . . . was desperately wounded and lay on the field all night. In the morning a surgeon approached him and inquired the nature of his wound. Finding a wound which is always considered fatal, he advised the man to remain quietly where he was and die. The man insisted on being removed to a hospital, saying in the most emphatic manner that though every man ever wounded as he was (his bowels were punctured by the ball) had died, he was determined not to die. The surgeon, struck by the man's courage and nerve, consented to remove him, advising him, how-

ever, not to cherish the hope of recovery. After a hard struggle
he did recover, and is forever a fine example of the power of
a determined will.

At the Wilderness, when the fight was raging in the tangled
woods, and a man could scarcely trust himself to move in
any direction for fear of going astray or running into the hands
of the enemy, a mere boy was wounded. Rushing out of the
woods, his eyes staring and his face pale with fright, he shouted,
"Where's the rear? Mister! I say, Mister! where's the rear?"
Of course he was laughed at. The very grim fact that there
was no rear, in the sense of safety, made the question irresistibly
ludicrous. The conduct of this boy was not exceptional. It
was no uncommon thing to see the best men badly demoralized
and eager to go to the rear because of a wound scarcely worthy
of the name. On the other hand, it sometimes happened that
men seriously wounded could not be convinced of their danger
and remained on the field.

The day General Stuart fell, mortally wounded, there was a
severe fight in the woods not far from the old Brook Church,
a few miles from Richmond; the enemy was making a determined stand in order to gain time to repair a bridge which they
were compelled to use, and the Confederate infantry skirmishers were pushing them hard. The fighting was stubborn
and the casualties on the Confederate side very numerous. In
the midst of the fight a voice was heard shouting, "Where's
my boy? I'm looking for my boy!" Soon the owner of the voice
appeared, tall, slim, aged, with silver gray hair, dressed in a
full suit of broadcloth. A tall silk hat and a clerical collar and
cravat completed his attire. His voice, familiar to the people of
Virginia, was deep and powerful. As he continued to shout,
the men replied, "Go back, old gentleman; you'll get hurt
here. Go back; go back!" "No, no;" said he, "I can go anywhere my boy has to go, and the Lord is here. I want to see my
boy, and I will see him!" Then the order, "Forward!" was
given, and the men made once more for the enemy. The old
gentleman, his beaver in one hand, a big stick in the other, his
long hair flying, shouting, "Come on, boys!" disappeared in the
depths of the woods, well in front. He was a Methodist minister, an old member of the Virginia Conference, but his carriage that day was soldierly and grand. One thought—that
his boy was there—made the old man feel that he might brave
the danger, too. No man who saw him then could ever forget

the parson who led the charge at Brook Church.

At the battle of Spottsylvania Court House, a gun in position somewhat in advance of the line was so much exposed to the enemy's fire that it was abandoned. Later in the day the battery being ordered to move, the captain directed the sergeant to take his detachment and bring in the gun. The sergeant and his gunner, with a number of men, went out to bring in the gun by hand. Two men lifted the trail and the sergeant ordered, "All together!" The gun moved, but moved *in a circle*. The fire was hot, and *all hands were on the same side*—the side farthest from the enemy! After some persuasion the corporal and the sergeant managed to induce a man or two to get on the other side with them, and they were moving along very comfortably when a shrapnel whacked the sergeant on his breast, breaking his ribs and tearing away the muscle of one arm. He fell into the arms of the corporal. Seeing that their only hope of escaping from this fire was work, the cannoneers bent to the wheels, and the gun rolled slowly to shelter.

It was at Spottsylvania Court House that the Federal infantry rushed over the works and, engaging in a hand-to-hand fight, drove out the Confederate infantry. On one part of the line the artillerymen stood to their posts, and when the Federal troops passing the works had massed themselves inside, fired to the right and left, up and down the lines, cutting roadways through the compact masses of men, and holding their positions until the Confederate infantry reformed, drove out the enemy and re-occupied the line. Several batteries were completely overrun, and the cannoneers sought and found safety *in front of the works*, whence the enemy had made their charge.

At another point on the lines, where there was no infantry support, the enemy charged repeatedly and·made every effort to carry the works, but were handsomely repulsed by *artillery alone*. An examination of the ground in front of the works after the fight, disclosed the fact that all the dead and wounded were victims of artillery fire. The dead were literally torn to pieces, and the wounded dreadfully mangled. Scarcely a man was hurt on the Confederate side.

At Fort Harrison, a few miles below Richmond, in 1864, a ludicrous scene resulted from the firing of a salute with shotted guns. Federal artillery occupied the fort, and the lines immediately in front of it were held by the Department Battalion, composed of the clerks in the various government offices in Richmond, who had been ordered out to meet an emergency. Just before sundown the detail for picket duty was formed and about to march out to the picket line, the clerks presenting quite a soldierly appearance. Suddenly bang! went a gun in the fort, and a shell came tearing over. Bang! again, and bang! bang! and more shells exploding. Pow! pow! what consternation! In an instant the beautiful line melted away as by magic. Every man took to shelter, and the place was desolate. The firing was rapid, regular, and apparently aimed to strike the Confederate lines, but ceased as suddenly as it had begun. General Custis Lee, whose tent was near by, observing the panic, stepped quietly up to the parapet of the works, folded his arms, and walked back and forth without uttering a word or looking to the right or to the left. His cool behavior, coupled with the silence of the guns, soon reassured the trembling clerks, and one by one they dropped into line again. General Butler had heard some news that pleased him, and ordered a salute with shotted guns. That was all.

Two boys who had volunteered for service with the militia in the same neighborhood were detailed for picket duty. It was the custom to put three men on each post—two militia boys and one veteran. The boys and an old soldier of Johnston's division were marched to their post, where they found, ready dug, a pit about five feet deep and three feet wide. It was quite dark, and the boys, realizing fully their exposed position, at once occupied the pit. The old soldier saw he had an opportunity to have a good time, knowing that those boys would keep wide awake. Giving them a short lecture about the importance of great watchfulness, he warned them to be ready to leave there very rapidly at any moment, and above all to keep very quiet. His words were wasted, as the boys would not have closed their eyes or uttered a word for the world. These little details arranged, the cunning old soldier prepared to make himself comfortable. First he gathered a few small twigs and made a very small fire. On the fire he put a battered old tin cup. Into this he poured some coffee from his canteen. From some mysterious place in his clothes he drew forth sugar and dropped it into the cup. Next, from an old worn haversack, he took a chunk of raw bacon and a pone of corn bread. Then, drawing a large pocket knife, in a dexterous manner he sliced and ate his bread and meat, occasionally sipping his coffee.

His evening meal leisurely completed, he filled his pipe, smoked, and stirred up the imaginations of the boys by telling how dangerous a duty they were performing; told them how easy it would be for the Yankees to creep up and shoot them or capture and carry them off. Having finished his smoke, he knocked out the ashes and dropped the pipe in his pocket. Then he actually unrolled his blanket and oilcloth. It made the perspiration start on the brows of the boys to see the man's folly. Then taking off his shoes, he laid down on one edge, took hold of the blanket and oilcloth, rolled himself over to the other side, and with a kind "good night" to the boys, began to snore. The poor boys stood like statues in the pit till broad day. In the morning the old soldier thanked them for not disturbing him and quietly proceeded to prepare his breakfast.

After the fight at Fisher's Hill in 1864, Early's army, in full retreat and greatly demoralized, was strung out along the valley pike. The Federal cavalry was darting around picking up prisoners, shooting drivers, and making themselves generally disagreeable. It happened that an artilleryman who was separated from his gun was making pretty good time on foot, getting to the rear, and had the appearance of a demoralized infantryman who had thrown away his musket. So one of these lively cavalrymen trotted up, and, waving his saber, told the artilleryman to surrender! But he didn't stop. He merely glanced over his shoulder, and kept on. Then the cavalryman became indignant and shouted, "Halt, d——n you; halt!" And still he would not. "Halt," said the cavalryman, "halt, you d——n s— of a ——; halt!" Then the artilleryman halted, and remarking that he didn't allow any man to speak to him that way, seized a huge stick, turned on the cavalryman, knocked him out of his saddle, and proceeded on his journey to the rear.

This artilleryman fought with a musket at Sailor's Creek. He found himself surrounded by the enemy, who demanded surrender. He refused; said they must take him; and laid about him with the butt of his musket till he had damaged some of the party considerably. He was, however, overpowered and made a prisoner.

Experienced men, in battle, always availed themselves of any shelter within reach. A tree, a fence, a mound of earth, a ditch, anything. Sometimes their efforts to find shelter were very amusing and even silly. Men lying on the ground have been seen to put an old canteen before their heads as a shelter from musket balls; and during a heavy fire of artillery, seemed to feel safer under a tent. Only recruits and fools neglected the smallest shelter.

The more experienced troops knew better when to give up than green ones, and never fought well after they were satisfied that they could not accomplish their purpose. Consequently it often happened that the best troops failed where the raw ones did well. The old Confederate soldier would decide some questions for himself. To the last he maintained the right of private judgment, especially on the field of battle.

7

The Road to Appomattox

Sunday, April 2, 1865, found Cutshaw's battalion of artillery occupying the earthworks at Fort Clifton on the Appomattox, about two miles below Petersburg, Virginia. The command was composed of the Second Company Richmond Howitzers, Captain Lorraine F. Jones, Garber's battery, Fry's battery, and remnants of five other batteries (saved from the battle of Spottsylvania Court House, May 12, 1864), and had present for duty nearly five hundred men, with a total muster roll, including the men in prison, of one thousand and eighty.

The place—the old Clifton House—was well fortified and had the additional protection of the river along the entire front of perhaps a mile. The works extended from the Appomattox on the right to Swift Creek on the left. There were some guns of heavy caliber mounted and ready for action, and in addition to these some fieldpieces disposed along the line at suitable points. The enemy had formidable works opposite but had not used their guns to disturb the quiet routine of the camp. The river bank was picketed by details from the artillery, armed as infantry but without the usual equipments. The guard duty was so heavy that half the men were always on guard.

The huts built by the troops who had formerly occupied the place were located with a view to protection from the enemy's fire, under the hills on the sides of the ravines or gullies which divided them and were underground to the eaves of the roof. Consequently, the soil being sandy, there was a constant filtering of sand through the cracks, and in spite of the greatest care, the grit found its way into the flour and meal, stuck to the greasy frying pan, and even filled the hair of the men as they slept in their bunks.

At this time rations were reduced to the minimum of quantity and quality, being generally worm-eaten peas, sour or

348

rancid mess-pork, and unbolted corn meal, relieved occasionally with a small supply of luscious canned beef imported from England, good flour (half rations), a little coffee and sugar, and—once—apple brandy for all hands. Ragged, barefooted, and even bareheaded men were so common that they did not excite notice or comment and did not expect or seem to feel the want of sympathy. And yet there was scarcely a complaint or murmur of dissatisfaction and not the slightest indication of fear or doubt. The spirit of the men was as good as ever, and the possibility of immediate disaster had not cast its shadow there.

Several incidents occurred during the stay of the battalion at Fort Clifton which will serve to illustrate everyday life on the lines. It occurred to a man picketing the river bank that it would be amusing to take careful aim at the man on the other side doing the same duty for the enemy, fire, laugh to see the fellow jump and dodge, and then try again. He fired, laughed, dropped his musket to reload, and while smiling with satisfaction, heard the thud of a bullet and felt an agonizing pain in his arm. His musket fell to the ground, and he walked back to camp with his arm swinging heavily at his side. The surgeon soon relieved him of it altogether. The poor fellow learned a lesson. The Yank had beat him at his own game.

The guardhouse was a two-story framed building, about twelve feet square, having two rooms, one above the other. The detail for guard duty was required to stay in the guardhouse; those who wished to sleep going upstairs, while others just relieved or about to go on duty clustered around the fire in the lower room. One night, when the upper floor was covered with sleeping men, an improvised infantryman who had been relieved from duty walked in, and preparatory to taking his stand at the fire, threw his musket carelessly in the corner. A loud report and angry exclamations immediately followed. The sergeant of the guard, noticing the direction of the ball, hurried upstairs, and to the disgust of the sleepy fellows, ordered all hands to turn out. Grumbling, growling, stretching, and rubbing their eyes, the men got up. Some one inquired, "Where's Pryor?" His chum, who had been sleeping by his side, replied, "there he is, asleep; shake him." His blanket was drawn aside, and with a shake he was commanded to get up. But there was no motion, no reply. The ball had passed through his heart, and he had passed without a groan or a sigh from deep sleep to death. The man who was killed and the man who was sleeping by his side under the same blanket were members of the Second Company Richmond Howitzers. The careless man who made the trouble was also an artilleryman, from one of the other batteries.

Shortly after this accident, after a quiet day, the men retired to their huts, and the whole camp was still as a country churchyard. The pickets on the river's edge could hear those on the opposite side asking the corporal of the guard the hour and complaining that they had not been promptly relieved. Suddenly a terrific bombardment commenced, and the earth fairly trembled. The men, suddenly awakened, heard the roar of the guns, the rush of the shots, and the explosion of the shells. To a man only half awake, the shells seemed to pass very near and in every direction. In a moment all were rushing out of their houses, and soon the hillsides and bluffs were covered with an excited crowd, gazing awestruck on the sight. The firing was away to the right, and there was not the slightest danger. Having realized this fact, the interest was intense. The shells from the opposite lines met and passed in mid-air—their burning fuses forming an arch of fire, which paled occasionally as a shell burst, illuminating the heavens with its blaze. The uproar, even at such a distance, was terrible. The officers, fearing that fire would be opened along the whole line, ordered the cannoneers to their posts; men were sent down into the magazine with lanterns to arrange the ammunition for the heavy guns; the lids of the limbers of the fieldpieces were thrown up; the cannoneers were counted off at their posts; the brush which had been piled before the embrasures was torn away; and, with implements in hand, all stood at attention till the last shot was fired. The heavens were dark again, and silence reigned. Soon all hands were as sound asleep as though nothing had occurred.

The next morning an artilleryman came walking leisurely towards the camp, and being recognized as belonging to a battery which was in position on that part of the line where the firing of the last night occurred, was plied with questions as to the loss on our side, who was hurt, etc., etc. Smiling at the anxious faces and eager questions, he replied: "When? Last night? Nobody!" It was astounding, but nevertheless true.

On another occasion some scattering shots were heard up the river, and after a while a body came floating down the stream. It was hauled on shore and buried in the sand a little above highwater mark. It was a poor Confederate who had attempted to desert to the enemy, but was shot while swimming for the opposite bank of the river. His grave was the center of the beat of one of the picket posts on the river bank, and there were few men so indifferent to the presence of the dead as not to prefer some other post.

And so, while there had been no fighting, there were always incidents to remind the soldier that danger lurked around, and that he could not long avoid his share. The camp was not as joyous as it had been, and all felt that the time was near which would try the courage of the stoutest. The struggles of the troops on the right with overwhelming numbers and reports of adversities, caused a general expectation that the troops lying so idly at the Clifton House would be ordered to the point of danger. They had not long to wait.

Sunday came and went as many a Sunday had. There was nothing unusual apparent, unless, perhaps, the dull and listless attitudes of the men, and the monotonous calls of those on guard were more oppressive than usual. The sun went down, the hills and valleys and the river were veiled in darkness. Here and there twinkling lights were visible. On the other side of the river could be heard a low rumbling which experienced men said was the movement of artillery and ammunition trains bound to the enemy's left to press the already broken right of the Confederate line.

Some had actually gone to sleep for the night. Others were huddled around the fires in the little huts, and a few sat out on the hillside discussing the probabilities of the near future. A most peaceful scene; a most peaceful spot. Hymns were sung and prayers were made, though no preacher was there. Memory reverted fondly to the past, to home and friends. The spirit of the soldier soared away to other scenes, and left him to sit blankly down, gaze at the stars, and feel unspeakable longings for undefined joys, and weep, for very tenderness of heart, at his own sad loneliness.

At ten P.M. some man mounted on horseback rode up to one of the huts, and said the battalion had orders to move. It was so dark that his face was scarcely visible. In a few minutes orders were received to destroy what could be destroyed without noise or fire. This was promptly done. Then the companies were formed, the roll was called, and the battalion marched slowly and solemnly away. No one doubted that the command would march at once to the assistance of the troops at or near Five Forks. It was thought that before morning every man would have his musket and his supply of ammunition, and the crack of day would see the battalion rushing into battle in regular infantry style, whooping and yelling like demons. But they got no arms that night. The march was steady till broad day of Monday the 3d of April. Of course the men felt mortified at having to leave the guns, but there was no help for it, as the battery horses which had been sent away to winter had not returned. It was evident that the battalion had bid farewell to artillery, and commenced a new career as infantry.

As the night wore on the men learned that the command was not going to any point on the lines. That being determined, no one could guess its destination. Later in the night, probably as day approached, the sky in the direction of Richmond was lit with the red glare of distant conflagration, and at short intervals there were deep, growling explosions of magazines. The roads were filled with other troops, all hurrying in the same direction. There was no sign of panic or fear, but the very wheels seemed turning with unusual energy. The men wore the look of determination, haste, and eagerness. One could feel the energy which surrounded him and animated the men and things which moved so steadily on, on, on! There was no laughing, singing, or talking. Nothing but the steady tread of the column and the surly rumbling of the trains.

As morning dawned the battalion struck the main road leading from Richmond. Refugees told the story of the evacuation, and informed the boys from the city that it was in the hands of the enemy and burning, and the chances were that not one house would be left standing. Here it became clearly understood that the whole army was in full retreat. From this point the men began to say, as they marched, that it was easier to march away than it would be to get back, but that they expected and hoped to fight their way back if they had to contest every inch. Some even regretted the celerity of the march, for, they said, "the farther we march the more difficult it will be to win our way back." Little did they know of the immense pressure at the rear, and the earnest push of the enemy on the flank as he strove to reach and overlap the advance of his hitherto defiant but now retreating foe.

A detail had been left at Fort Clifton with orders to spike

the guns, blow up the magazine, destroy everything which could be of value to the enemy, and rejoin the command. The order was obeyed, and every man of the detail resumed his place in the ranks.

From this point to Appomattox the march was almost continuous, day and night, and it is with the greatest difficulty that a private in the ranks can recall with accuracy the dates and places on the march. Night was day—day was night. There was no stated time to sleep, eat, or rest, and the events of morning became strangely intermingled with the events of evening. Breakfast, dinner, and supper were merged into "something to eat," whenever and wherever it could be had. The incidents of the march, however, lose none of their significance on this account, and so far as possible they will be given in the order in which they occurred, and the day and hour fixed as accurately as they can be by those who witnessed and participated in its dangers and hardships.

Monday the 3d the column was pushed along without ceremony at a rapid pace until night, when a halt was ordered and the battalion laid down in a piece of pine woods to rest. There was some desultory eating in this camp, but so little of it that there was no lasting effect. At early dawn of Tuesday the 4th the men struggled to their feet, and with empty stomachs and brave hearts resumed their places in the ranks and struggled on with the column as it marched steadily in the direction of Moore's Church in Amelia County, where it arrived in the night. The men laid down under the shelter of a fine grove, and friend divided with friend the little supplies of raw bacon and bread picked up on the day's march. They were scarcely stretched on the ground ready for a good nap when the orderly of the Howitzers commenced bawling, "Detail for guard! detail for guard! Fall in here; fall in!" then followed the names of the detail. Four men answered to their names, but declared they could not keep awake if placed on guard. Their remonstrance was in vain. They were marched off to picket a road leading to camp, and when they were relieved, said they had slept soundly on their posts. No one blamed them.

While it was yet night all hands were roused from profound sleep; the battalion was formed, and away they went, stumbling, bumping against each other, and sleeping as they walked. Whenever the column halted for a moment, as it did frequently during the night, the men dropped heavily to the ground and were instantly asleep. Then the officers would commence: "Forward! column forward!" Those first on their feet went stumbling on over their prostrate comrades, who would in turn be awakened, and again the column was in motion, and nothing heard but the monotonous tread of the weary feet, the ringing and rattling of the trappings of the horses, and the never-ending cry of "Close up, men; close up!"

Through the long, weary night there was no rest. The alternate halting and hurrying was terribly trying, and taxed the endurance of the most determined men to the very utmost; and yet on the morning of Wednesday the 5th, when the battalion reached the neighborhood of Scott's Shops, every man was in place and ready for duty. From this point, after some ineffectual efforts to get breakfast, the column pushed on in the direction of Amelia Court House, at which point Colonel Cutshaw was ordered to report to General James A. Walker, and the battalion was thereafter a part of Walker's division. The 5th was spent at or near the Court House—how, it is difficult to remember; but the day was marked by several incidents worthy of record.

About 225 muskets (not enough to arm all the men), cartridges, and caps were issued to the battalion—simply the muskets and ammunition. Not a cartridge-box, cap box, belt, or any other convenience ornamented the persons of these newborn infantrymen. They stored their ammunition in their pockets along with their corn, salt, pipes, and tobacco.

When application was made for rations, it was found that the last morsel belonging to the division had been issued to the command, and the battalion was again thrown on its own resources, to wit: corn on the cob intended for the horses. Two ears were issued to each man. It was parched in the coals, mixed with salt, stored in the pockets, and eaten on the road. Chewing the corn was hard work. It made the jaws ache and the gums and teeth so sore as to cause almost unendurable pain.

After the muskets were issued, a line of battle was formed with Cutshaw on the right. For what purpose the line was formed the men could not tell. A short distance from the right of the line there was a grove which concealed an ammunition train which had been sent from Richmond to meet the army. The ammunition had been piled up ready for destruction. An occasional musket ball passed over near enough and often enough to produce a realizing sense of the proximity of the enemy and solemnize the occasion. Towards evening the muskets were stacked, artillery style of course, the men were lying around, chatting and eating raw bacon, and there was general quiet, when suddenly the earth shook with a tremendous explosion and an immense column of smoke rushed up into the air to a great height. For a moment there was the greatest consternation. Whole regiments broke and fled in wild confusion. Cutshaw's men stood up, seized their muskets, and stood at attention till it was known that the ammunition had been purposely fired and no enemy was threatening the line. Then what laughter and hilarity prevailed for a while among these famishing men!

Order having been restored, the march was resumed, and moving by way of Amelia Springs, the column arrived near Deatonsville about ten o'clock on the morning of Thursday the 6th. The march, though not a long one, was exceedingly tiresome, as the main roads being crowded, the column moved by plantation roads, which were in wretched condition and crowded with troops and trains. That the night was spent in the most trying manner may best be learned from the fact that when morning dawned the column was only six or seven miles from the starting point of the evening before.

This delay was fatal. The whole army—trains and all—left Amelia Court House in advance of Walker's division, which was left to cover the retreat, Cutshaw's battalion being the last to leave the Court House, thus bringing up the rear of the Army, and being in constant view of the enemy's hovering cavalry. The movement of the division was regulated to suit the movements of the wagon trains, which should have been destroyed on the spot, and the column allowed to make its best time, as, owing to the delay they occasioned, the Army lost the time it had gained on the enemy in the start and was overtaken the next day.

At Deatonsville another effort to cook was made, but before the simplest articles of food could be prepared, the order to march was given, and the battalion took the road once more.

A short while after passing Deatonsville the column was formed in line of battle—Cutshaw's battalion near the road and in an old field with woods in front and rear. The officers, anticipating an immediate attack, ordered the men to do what they could for their protection. They immediately scattered along the fence on the roadside, and taking down the rails stalked back to their position in line, laid the rails on the ground, and returned for another load. This they continued to do until the whole fence was removed. Behind this slim defense they silently awaited the advance of the enemy.

Soon it was decided that this was not the place to make a stand. The first detachment of the Second Company of Richmond Howitzers, and twenty men each from Garber and Fry, under the command of Lieutenant Henry Jones, were left behind the fence-rail work with orders to resist and retard the advance of the enemy while the column continued its march.

This little band was composed of true spirits—the best material in the battalion. Right well did they do their duty. Left alone to face the advance of the immense host eagerly pursuing the worn remnant of the invincible army, they waited until the enemy's skirmishers appeared in the field, when, with perfect deliberation, they commenced their fire. Though greatly outnumbered and flanked right and left, they stubbornly held on till the line of battle following the skirmishers broke from the woods, and, advancing, rapidly poured into them a murderous volley. And yet, so unused were they to running, they moved not till the infantry skirmishers had retired, and the word of command was heard. Then stubbornly contesting the ground, they fought their way back through the woods. The gallant Lieutenant Jones fell mortally wounded, having held control of his little band to the moment he fell. His friend Kemp refused to leave him, and they were captured together but were immediately separated by the enemy. Pearson was pierced through by a musket ball as he was hurrying through the woods and fell heavily to the ground. Binford was severely wounded but managed to escape. Hamilton was killed outright.

The battalion had left this point but a short time, marching in column of fours with the division, and had reached the brow of a gently sloping hill, perfectly open for perhaps a mile with a broad valley on the left and beyond it a range of hills partly wooded. In an open space on this range the enemy placed a battery in position, and in anticipation of doing great slaughter from a safe distance, opened a rapid fire on the exposed and helpless column. The shells came hurtling over the valley, exploding in front, rear, and overhead, and tearing up the ground in every direction. Ah! how it grieved those artillerymen to stand, musket in hand, and receive that shower of insolence. How they longed for the old friends they had left at Fort Clifton. They knew how those rascals on the other side of the valley were enjoying the sport. They could hear, in imagination, the shouts of the cannoneers as they saw their shells bursting so prettily and rammed home another shot.

There was some impediment ahead, and there the column stood, a fair mark for these rascals. There was no help near, and all that could be done was to stand firm and wait orders; but help was coming.

A cloud of dust was approaching from the rear of the column. All eyes were strained to see what it might mean. Presently the artillerymen recognized a well-known sound. A battery was coming in full gallop, the drivers lashing their horses and yelling like madmen. The guns bounded along as though they would outrun the horses, and with rush, roar, and rattle they approached the front of the battalion. Some fellow in the Second Company Howitzers sung out, "Old Henry Carter! Hurrah! for the Third Company! Give it to 'em, boys!" It was, indeed, the Third Company of Howitzers, long separated from the Second, with their gallant captain at their head!

Not a moment was lost. The guns were in battery, and the smoke of the first shot was curling about the heads of the men in the column in marvelously quick time. Friends and comrades in the column called to the men at the guns, and they, as they stepped in and out, responded with cheerful, ringing voices, "Hello, Bill!" "How are you, Joe?" Bang! "Pretty"— Bang!—"well, I thank you." Bang! "Oh! we're giving it to 'em now." Bang!

As the battalion moved on, the gallant boys of the Third Company finished their work. The disappointed enemy limbered up, slipped into the woods and departed. Cheered by this fortunate meeting with old comrades, with the pleasant odor of the smoke lingering around them, these hitherto bereft and mournful artillerymen pushed on, laughing at the discomfiture of the enemy, and feeling that though deprived of their guns by the misfortunes of war, there was still left at least one battery worthy to represent the artillery of the Army.

As the column marched slowly along, some sharp-eyed man discovered three of the enemy's skirmishers in a field away on the left. More for amusement than anything else, it was proposed to fire at them. A group of men gathered on the roadside, a volley was fired, and, to the amazement of the marksmen, for the distance was great, one of the skirmishers fell. One of his comrades started on a run to his assistance, and he, too, was stopped. The third man then scampered away as fast as his legs could carry him. The battalion applauded the good shots and marched on.

At Sailor's Creek the detachment which had been left at Deatonsville behind the fence rails to watch and retard the approach of the enemy, having slowly retired before their advance, rejoined the command. Indeed, their resistance and retreat was the beginning of and ended in the battle of Sailor's Creek.

The line of battle was formed on Locket's Hill, which sloped gently down from the line to the creek about one hundred and fifty or two hundred yards in rear of and running nearly parallel with the line of battle. A road divided the battalion near the center. The Howitzers were on the left of this road and in the woods; Garber's men were on the right of the Howitzers, on the opposite side of the road, in a field; Fry's men on the extreme left. To cross the road dividing the line was a hazardous experiment, as the enemy, thinking it an important avenue, swept it with musketry.

It was amusing to see the men hauling out of their pockets a mixture of corn, salt, caps, and cartridges, and, selecting the material needed, loading. They were getting ready to stand. They did not expect to run and did not until ordered to do so.

The enemy's skirmishers advanced confidently and in rather free and easy style, but suddenly met a volley which drove them to cover. Again they advanced in better order, and again the improvised infantry forced them back. Then came their line of battle with overwhelming numbers; but the battalion stubbornly resisted their advance. The men, not accustomed to the orderly manner of infantry, dodged about from tree to tree, and with the deliberation of huntsmen picked off here and there a man. When a shot told, the marksman hurrahed, all to himself. There was an evident desire to press forward and drive the advancing foe. Several of the men were so enthusiastic that they had pushed ahead of the line, and several yards in advance they could be seen loading and firing as deliberately as though practicing at a mark.

Colonel Cutshaw received a wound which so shattered his leg that he had to be lifted from his horse into an ambulance. He was near being captured, but by hurrying away the ambulance at a gallop, he escaped to a house a short distance in the rear, where he fell into the hands of the enemy. The same night he suffered amputation of a leg. Captain Garber was struck, and called for the ambulance corps, but on examination found the ball in his pocket. It had lodged against the rowel of a spur which he found the day before and dropped into his pocket.

At last the enemy appeared in strong force on both flanks, while he pushed hard in front. It was useless to attempt a further stand. The voice of Captain Jones of the Howitzers rang out loud and clear, "Boys, take care of yourselves!" Saying this, he planted himself against a pine, and as his men rushed by him, emptied every chamber of his revolver at the enemy, and then reluctantly made his way in company with several privates down the hill to the creek.

At the foot of the hill a group of perhaps a dozen men gathered around Lieutenant McRae. He was indignant. He proposed another stand, and his comrades agreed. They stood in the road, facing the gentle slope of the hill from which they had been ordered to retire. The enemy's skirmishers were already on the brow of the hill, dodging about among the trees and shouting to those behind to hurry up. Their favorite expressions were, "Come along, boys; here are the damned Rebel wagons!" "Damn 'em, shoot 'em down!"

In a few moments their line of battle in beautiful order

stepped out of the woods with colors flying, and for a moment
halted. In front of the center of that portion of the line which
was visible—probably a full regimental front—marched the
colors, and color guard. McRae saw his opportunity. He ordered his squad to rise and fire on the colors. His order was
promptly obeyed. The color bearer pitched forward and fell,
with his colors, heavily to the ground. The guard of two men
on either side shared the same fate, or else feigned it. Immediately the line of battle broke into disorder, and came swarm-
ing down the hill, firing, yelling, and cursing as they came. An
officer, mounted, rode his horse close to the fence on the
roadside, and with the most superb insolence mocked McRae
and his squad, already, as he thought, hopelessly intermingled
with the enemy. McRae, in his rage, swore back at him, and
in the hearing of the man, called on a man near him to shoot
"that—— ——," calling him a fearfully hard name. But the
private's gun was not in working order, and the fellow escaped
for the time. Before he reached the woods, whither he was
going to hurry up the "boys," a Howitzer let fly at him, and at
the shock of the bullet's stroke he threw his arms up in the air,
and his horse bore him into the woods a corpse.

A little to the left, where the road crossed the creek, the
crack of pistols and the bang of muskets was continuous. The
enemy had surrounded the wagons and were mercilessly shooting down the unarmed and helpless drivers, some of whom,
however, managed to cut the traces, mount, and ride away.

In order to escape from the right of the line, it was necessary to follow the road, which was along the foot of the hill,
some distance to the left. The enemy seeing this were pushing
their men rapidly at a right oblique to gain the road and cut
off retreat. Consequently those who attempted escape in that
direction had to run the gauntlet of a constant fusilade from a
mass of troops near enough to select individuals, curse them,
and command them to throw down their arms or be shot.

Most of McRae's squad, in spite of the difficulties surrounding them, gained the creek, plunged in, and began a race for
life up the long, open hillside of plowed ground, fired upon
at every step by the swarm of men behind, and before they
reached the top, by a battery in close proximity, which poured
down a shower of canister.

The race to the top of the long hill was exceedingly trying
to men already exhausted by continual marching, hunger,

thirst, and loss of sleep. They ran, panting for breath, like chased animals, fairly staggering as they went.

On the top of this long hill there was a skirmish line of cavalry posted with orders to stop all men with arms in their hands, and form a new line; but the view down the hill to the creek and beyond revealed such a host of the enemy, and the men retiring before them were so few, that the order was disregarded and the fleeing band allowed to pass through.

The men's faces were black with powder. They had bitten cartridges until there was a deep black circle around their mouths. The burnt powder from the ramrods had blackened their hands, and in their efforts to remove the perspiration from their faces they had completed the coloring from the roots of the hair to the chin. Here was no place for rest, however, as the enemy's battery behind the creek on the opposite hills, having gotten the range, was pouring in a lively fire. Soon after passing the brow of the hill darkness came on. Groups of men from the battalion halted on the roadside, near a framed building of some sort, and commenced shouting, "Fall in, Howitzers!" "This way, Garber's men!" "Fry's battery!" "Fall in!" "Cutshaw's battalion, fall in here!" thus of their own accord trying to recover the organization from its disorder. Quite a number of the battalion got together, and in spite of hunger, thirst, defeat, and dreadful weariness, pushed on to the High Bridge. So anxious were the men to escape capture and the insinuation of desertion, that when threatened with shooting by the rear guard if they did not move on they scarcely turned to see who spoke: but the simple announcement, "The Yankees are coming!" gave them a little new strength, and again they struggled painfully along, dropping in the road sound asleep, however, at the slightest halt of the column.

At the bridge there was quite a halt, and in the darkness the men commenced calling to each other by name—the rascally infantry around, still ready for fun, answering for every name. Brother called brother, comrade called comrade, friend called friend; and there were many happy reunions there that night. Some alas! of the best and bravest did not answer the cry of anxious friends.

Before the dawn of day the column was again in motion. What strange sensations the men had as they marched slowly across the High Bridge. They knew its great height, but the night was so dark that they could not see the abyss on either side. Arrived on the other side, the worn-out soldiers fell to the ground and slept, more dead than alive. Some had slept as they marched across the bridge, and declared that they had no distinct recollection of when they left it or how long they were upon it.

Early on the morning of the 7th the march was resumed and continued through Farmville, across the bridge and to Cumberland Heights, overlooking the town. Here, on the bare hillside, a line of battle was formed, for what purpose the men did not know—the Howitzers occupying a central place in the line, and standing with their feet in the midst of a number of the graves of soldiers who had perished in the hospitals in the town.

While standing thus in line a detail was sent into the town to hunt up some rations. They found a tierce of bacon surrounded by a ravenous crowd, fighting and quarreling. The man on duty guarding the bacon was quickly overpowered, and the bacon was distributed to the crowd. The detail secured a piece and marched back triumphantly to their waiting comrades.

After considerable delay the line broke into column and marched away in the direction of Curdsville. It was on this march that Cutshaw's battalion showed itself proof against the demoralization which was appearing, and received, almost from the lips of the Commander-in-Chief, a compliment of which any regiment in the Army might be proud.

All along the line of march the enemy's cavalry followed close on the flanks of the column, and whenever an opportunity offered swooped down upon the trains. Whenever this occurred the battalion, with the division, was faced towards the advancing cavalry and marched in line to meet them, generally repulsing them with ease. In one of these attacks the cavalry approached so near the column that a dash was made at them, and the infantry returned to the road with General Gregg, of the enemy's cavalry, a prisoner. He was splendidly equipped and greatly admired by the ragged crowd around him. He was, or pretended to be, greatly surprised at his capture. When the column had reached a point two or three miles beyond Farmville, it was found that the enemy was driving in the force which was protecting the marching column and trains. The troops hurrying back were panic-stricken; all efforts to rally them were vain, and the enemy was almost upon the column. General

Gordon ordered General Walker to form his division and drive the enemy back from the road. The division advanced gallantly, and conspicuous in the charge was Cutshaw's battalion. When the line was formed, the battalion occupied rising ground on the right. The line was visible for a considerable distance. In rear of the battalion there was a group of unarmed men under command of Sergeant Ellett of the Howitzers. In the distribution of muskets at Amelia Court House the supply fell short of the demand, and this squad had made the trip so far unarmed. Some, too, had been compelled to ground their arms at Sailor's Creek. A few yards to the left and rear of the battalion, in the road, was General Lee, surrounded by a number of officers gazing eagerly about him. An occasional musket ball whistled over, but there was no enemy in sight. In the midst of this quiet a general officer, at the left and rear of the battalion, fell from his horse, severely wounded. A messenger was sent from the group in the road to ask the extent of his injury. After a short while the enemy appeared, and the stampeded troops came rushing by. Cutshaw's battalion stood firmly and quietly, as if on parade, awaiting orders. General officers galloped about, begging the fleeing men to halt, but in vain. Several of the fugitives, as they passed the battalion, were collared by the disarmed squad, relieved of their muskets and ammunition, and with a kick allowed to proceed to the rear. There was now between the group in the road and the enemy only the battalion of improvised infantry. There they stood, on the crest of the hill, in sharp relief. Not a man moved from his place. Did they know the Great Commander was watching them? Some one said, "Forward!" The cry passed from lip to lip, and with cheers the battalion moved rapidly to meet the enemy, while the field was full of the stampeded troops making to the rear. A courier came out with orders to stop the advance, but they heeded him not. Again he came, but on they went. Following the line was the unarmed squad, unable to do more than swell the volume of the wild shouts of their comrades. Following them, also, was the commissary department, consisting of two men with a piece of bacon swung on a pole between them, yelling and hurrahing. As the line advanced, the bluejackets sprang up and ran through the broomstraw like hares, followed by a shower of balls. Finally an officer—some say General Gordon, and others an aide of Longstreet's—rode out to the front of the battalion, ordered a halt, and in the name of General Lee thanked the men for their gallant conduct and complimented them in handsome style. His words were greeted with loud cheers, and the battalion marched back to the road carrying several prisoners and having retaken two pieces of artillery which had been abandoned to the enemy. After the enemy was driven back out of reach of our trains and column of march, and the troops were in line of battle, General Lee in person rode up in rear of the division, and addressing himself directly to the men in ranks (a thing very unusual with him) used language to this effect: "That is right, men; that is all I want you to do. Just keep those people back awhile. I do not wish you to expose yourselves to unnecessary danger."

Mahone's division then coming up took the place of Walker's, and the march was resumed. The battalion passed on, the men cutting slices from their piece of bacon and eagerly devouring them. As night came on the signs of disaster increased.

At several places whole trains were standing in the road abandoned; artillery, chopped down and burning, blocked the way, and wagonloads of ammunition were dumped out in the road and trampled under foot. There were abundant signs of disaster. So many muskets were dropped on the road that Cutshaw's unarmed squad armed itself with abandoned muskets, ammunition, and equipments.

There was a halt during the night in a piece of stunted woods. The land was low and sobby. In the road passing through the woods were several batteries, chopped down and deserted. There was a little flour on hand, which had been picked up on the road. An oilcloth was spread, the flour placed on it, water was found, and the dough mixed. Then some clean partition boards were knocked out of a limber chest, the dough was spread on them and held near the fire till partially cooked. Then with what delight it was devoured!

At daybreak, Saturday, the march was resumed, and continued almost without interruption during the whole day; the men, those whose gums and teeth were not already too sore, crunching parched corn and raw bacon as they trudged along. Saturday night the battalion rested near Appomattox Court House in a pine woods. Sunday morning, April 9th, after a short march, the column entered the village of Appomattox Court House by what seemed to be the main road. Several dead men dressed in the uniform of United States regular artillery were lying on the roadside, their faces turned up to the blaze of the sun. One had a ghastly wound in the breast, which must have been made by grape or canister.

On through the village without halting marched the column. Whitworth shots went hurtling through the air every few minutes, indicating very clearly that the enemy was ahead of the column and awaiting its arrival. On the outskirts of the village the line of battle was formed. Indeed, there seemed to be two lines, one slightly in advance of the other. Wagons passed along the line and dropped boxes of cartridges. The men were ordered to knock them open and supply themselves with forty rounds each. They filled their breeches' pockets to the brim. The general officers galloped up and down the line, apparently hurrying everything as much as possible. The shots from a battery in advance were continually passing over the line, going in the direction of the village but without harm to any one. The more experienced men predicted a severe struggle. It was supposed that this was to be an attack with the whole army in mass for the purpose of breaking through the enemy's line and making one more effort to move on.

Finally the order "Forward!" ran along the line, and as it advanced, the chiefs of detachments, gunners, and commissioned officers marched in rear, keeping up a continual cry of "Close up, men; close up!" "Go ahead, now; don't lag!" "Keep up!" Thus marching, the line entered a body of woods, proceeding some distance, changed direction to the left, and, emerging from the woods, halted in a large open field beyond which was another body of woods which concealed further view in front.

After some delay, a detail for skirmish duty was ordered. Captain Jones detailed four men, Fry and Garber the same number. Lieutenant McRae was placed in command. The infantry detailed skirmishers for their front. All arrangements completed, the men deployed and entered the woods. They had advanced but a short distance, when they encountered a strong line of picket posts. Firing and cheering they rushed on the surprised men, who scampered away, leaving all their little conveniences behind them and retreating for about a mile. From this point large bodies of the enemy were visible, crowding the hilltops like a blue or black cloud. It was not many minutes before a strong line of dismounted cavalry, followed by mounted men, deployed from this mass to cover the retreat of their fleeing brethren and restore the picket line. They came down the hills and across the fields, firing as they came. On looking around to see what were the chances for making a stand, Lieutenant McRae found that the infantry skirmishers had been withdrawn. The officer who had commanded them could be seen galloping away in the distance. The little squad, knowing they were alone, kept up a brisk fire on the advancing enemy till he was close up in front, and well to the rear of both flanks. On the left, not more than two hundred yards, a column of cavalry, marching by twos, had crossed the line and were still marching, as unconcernedly as possible, to the rear of Mc-Rae. Seeing this, McRae ordered his squad to retire, saying at the same time, "But don't let them see you running, boys!"

So they retired, slowly, stubbornly, and returning shot for shot with the enemy, who came on at a trot, cheering valiantly as they pursued four men and a lieutenant. The men dragged the butts of their old muskets behind them, loading as they walked. All loaded, they turned, halted, fired, received a shower of balls in return and then again moved doggedly to the rear. A little lieutenant of infantry, who had been on the skirmish line, joined the squad. He was armed with a revolver, and had his sword by his side. Stopping behind the corner of a corncrib he swore he would not go any farther to the rear. The squad moved on and left him standing there, pistol in hand, waiting for the enemy, who were now jumping the fences and coming across the field, running at the top of their speed. What became of this singular man no one knows. He was, as he said, determined to make a stand. A little farther on, the squad found a single piece of artillery manned by a lieutenant and two or three men. They were selecting individuals in the enemy's skirmish line and firing at them with solid shot! Lieutenant McRae laughed at the ridiculous sight, remonstrated with the officer, and offered his squad to serve the gun if there was any canister in the limber chest. The offer was refused, and again the squad moved on. Passing a cowshed about this time, the squad halted to look with horror upon several dead and wounded Confederates who lay there upon the manure pile. They had suffered wounds and death upon this the last day of their country's struggle. Their wounds had received no attention, and those living were famished and burning with fever.

Lieutenant McRae, noticing a number of wagons and guns parked in a field near by, surprised at what he considered great carelessness in the immediate presence of the enemy, approached an officer on horseback and said, in his usual impressive manner, "I say there, what does this mean?" The man took his hand and quietly said, "We have surrendered." "I don't believe it, sir!" replied McRae, strutting around as mad as a hornet. "You mustn't talk so, sir! you will demoralize my men!" He was soon convinced, however, by seeing Yankee cavalrymen walking their horses around as composedly as though the Army of Northern Virginia had never existed. To say that McRae was surprised, disgusted, indignant, and incredulous, is a mild way of expressing his state of mind as he turned to his squad and said, "Well, boys it must be so, but it's very strange behavior. Let's move on and see about it." As though dreaming, the squad and the disgusted officer moved on.

Learning that the Army had gone into camp, the skirmishers went on in the direction of the village and found the battalion in the woods near the main road. Fires were burning, and those who had been fortunate enough to find anything eatable were cooking. Federal troops were riding up and down the road and loafing about the camps trying to be familiar. They seemed to think that "How are you, Johnny?" spoken in condescending style was sufficient introduction.

During the day a line of men came single file over the hill near the camp, each bearing on his shoulder a box of hardtack or crackers. Behind these came a beef, driven by soldiers. The crackers and beef were a present from the Federal troops near, who, knowing the famishing condition of the surrounded army, had contributed their day's rations for its relief. All honor to them. It was a soldierly act which was thoroughly appreciated.

The beef was immediately shot and butchered, and before the animal heat had left the meat, it was impaled in little strips on sticks, bayonets, swords, and pocketknives and roasting over the fires.

Though numbers of the enemy visited the camps and plied the men with all sorts of questions, seeming very curious and inquisitive, not an unkind word was said that day. When the skirmishers under McRae entered the camp of the battalion, their enthusiastic descriptions of driving the enemy and being driven in turn failed to produce any effect. Many of the men were sobbing and crying like children recovering from convulsions of grief after a severe whipping. They were sorely grieved, mortified, and humiliated. Of course they had not the slightest conception of the numbers of the enemy who surrounded them. Other men fairly raved with indignation and declared their desire to escape or die in the attempt; but not a man was heard to blame General Lee. On the contrary, all expressed the greatest sympathy for him and declared their willingness to submit at once or fight to the last man, as he ordered. At no period of the war was he held in higher veneration or regarded with more sincere affection than on that sad and tearful day.

In the afternoon the little remnant of the Army was massed in a field. General Gordon spoke to them most eloquently and bade them farewell. General Walker addressed his division, to which Cutshaw's battalion was attached, bidding them farewell. In the course of his remarks he denounced fiercely the men who had thrown down their arms on the march and called upon the true men before him to go home and tell their wives, mothers, sisters, and sweethearts how shamefully these cowards had behaved.

General Henry A. Wise also spoke, sitting on his horse and bending forward over the pommel of his saddle. Referring to the surrender, he said, "I would rather have embraced the tabernacle of death."

There were many heaving bosoms and tear-stained faces during the speaking. A tall, manly fellow, with his colors pressed to his side, stood near General Gordon, convulsed with grief.

The speaking over, the assembly dispersed, and once more the campfires burned brightly. Night brought long-needed rest. The heroes of many hard-fought battles, the conquerors of human nature's cravings, the brave old army, fell asleep—securely guarded by the encircling hosts of the enemy. Who will write the history of that march? Who will be able to tell the story? Alas! how many heroes fell!

The paroles, which were distributed on Tuesday the 11th were printed on paper about the size of an ordinary bank check with blank spaces for the date, name of the prisoner, company and regiment, and signature of the commandant of the company or regiment. They were signed by the Confederate officers themselves and were as much respected by all picket officers, patrols, etc., of the Federal Army as though they bore the signature of U. S. Grant. The following is a copy of one of these paroles, made from the original:

APPOMATTOX COURT HOUSE, VIRGINIA,
April 10, 1865

The bearer, Private — —, of Second Company Howitzers, Cutshaw's Battalion, a paroled prisoner of the Army of Northern Virginia, has permission to go to his home and there remain undisturbed.

L. F. JONES,
Captain Commanding Second Company Howitzers

The guidon, or colorbearer, of the Howitzers had concealed the battle flag of the company about his person, and before the final separation cut it into pieces of about four by six inches, giving each man present a piece. Many of these scraps of faded silk will be handed down to future generations. Captain Fry, who commanded after Colonel Cutshaw was wounded, assembled the battalion, thanked the men for their faithfulness, bade them farewell, and read the following:

HEADQUARTERS ARMY, NORTHERN VIRGINIA,
APPOMATTOX COURT HOUSE, April 10, 1865

GENERAL ORDER No. 9

After four years of arduous service, marked by unsurpassed courage and fortitude, the Army of Northern Virginia has been compelled to yield to overwhelming numbers and resources.

I need not tell the brave survivors of so many hard-fought battles, who have remained steadfast to the last, that I have consented to this result from no distrust of them; but feeling that valor and devotion could accomplish nothing that would compensate for the loss that must have attended a continuance of the contest, I determined to avoid the useless sacrifice of those whose past services have endeared them to their countrymen.

By the terms of agreement, officers and men can return to their homes and remain until exchanged. You will take with you the satisfaction that proceeds from the consciousness of duty faithfully performed, and I earnestly pray that a merciful God will extend to you his blessing and protection.

With an unceasing admiration of your constancy and devotion to your country, and a grateful remembrance of your kind and generous consideration for myself, I bid you all an affectionate farewell.

R. E. LEE

This grand farewell from the man who had in the past personified the glory of his army and now bore its grief in his own

great heart, was the signal for tearful partings. Comrades wept
as they gazed upon each other and with choking voices said
farewell! And so—they parted. Little groups of two or three
or four, without food, without money, but with "the satisfaction that proceeds from the consciousness of duty faithfully
performed," were soon plodding their way homeward.

8

Campfires of the Boys in Gray

The soldier may forget the long, weary march, with its dust, heat, and thirst, and he may forget the horrors and blood of the battlefield or he may recall them sadly, as he thinks of the loved dead; but the cheerful, happy scenes of the campfire he will never forget. How willingly he closes his eyes once more to dream of those happy, careless days and nights! Around the fire crystallize the memories of the soldier's life. It was his home, his place of rest, where he met with good companionship. Who kindled the fire? Nobody had matches, there was no fire in sight, and yet scarcely was the camp determined when the bright blaze of the campfire was seen. He was a shadowy fellow who kindled the fire. Nobody knows who he was; but no matter how wet the leaves, how sobby the twigs, no matter if there was no fire in a mile of the camp, that fellow could start one. Some men might get down on hands and knees and blow it and fan it, rear and charge, and fume and fret, and yet "she wouldn't burn." But this fellow would come, kick it all around, scatter it, rake it together again, shake it up a little, and oh, how it burned! The little flames would bite the twigs and snap at the branches, embrace the logs and leap and dance and laugh at the touch of the master's hand, and soon lay at his feet a bed of glowing coals.

As soon as the fire is kindled all hands want water. Who can find it? Where is it? Never mind; we have a man who knows where to go. He says, "Where's our bucket?" and then we hear the rattle of the old tin cup as it drops to the bottom of it, and away he goes, nobody knows where. But he knows, and he doesn't stop to think, but without the slightest hesitation or doubt strikes out in the darkness. From the campfire as a center, draw 500 radii, and start an ordinary man on any of them, and let him walk a mile on each, and he will miss the water. But that fellow in the mess with the water instinct never failed. He would

371

go as straight for the spring, or well, or creek, or river, as though he had lived in that immediate neighborhood all his life and never got water anywhere else. What a valuable man he was! A modest fellow who never knew his own greatness. But others remember and honor him. May he never want for any good thing!

Having a roaring fire and a bucket of good water, we settle down. A man cannot be comfortable "anywhere;" so each man and his chum picks out a tree, and that particular tree becomes the homestead of the two. They hang their canteens on it, lay their haversacks and spread their blankets at the foot of it, and sit down and lean their weary backs against it, and feel that they are at home. How gloomy the woods are beyond the glow of our fire! How cosy and comfortable we are who stand around it and inhale the aroma of the coffee boiler and skillet!

The man squatting by the fire is a person of importance. He doesn't talk, not he; his whole mind is concentrated on that skillet. He is our cook,—volunteer, natural and talented cook. Not in a vulgar sense. He doesn't mix, but simply bakes, the biscuit. Every faculty, all the energy, of the man is employed in that great work. Don't suggest anything to him if you value his friendship. Don't attempt to put on or take off from the top of that skillet one single coal, and don't be in a hurry for the biscuit. You need not say you like yours half done, etc. Simply wait. When he thinks they are ready, and not before, you get them. He may raise the lid cautiously now and then and look in, but don't you look in. Don't say you think they are done, because it's useless. Ah! his face relaxes; he raises the lid, turns it upside down to throw off the coals, and says, *All right, boys!* And now, with the air of wealthy philanthropist, he distributes the solid and weighty product of his skill to, as it were, the humble dependents around him.

The "General" of the mess, having satisfied the cravings of the inner man, now proceeds to enlighten the ordinary members of it as to when, how, and why, and where, the campaign will open and what will be the result. He arranges for every possible and impossible contingency, and brings the war to a favorable and early termination. The greatest mistake General Lee ever made was that he failed to consult this man. Who can tell what might have been if he had?

Now, to the consternation of all hands, our old friend "the Bore," familiarly known as "the old Auger," opens his mouth to tell us of a little incident illustrative of his personal prowess, and by way of preface commences at Eden and goes laboriously through the Patriarchal Age, on through the Mosaic dispensation, to the Christian era, takes in Grecian and Roman history by the way, then Spain and Germany and England and colonial times, and the early history of our grand republic, the causes of and necessity for our war, and a complete history up to date, and then slowly unfolds the little matter. We always loved to hear this man, and prided ourselves on being the only mess in the Army having such treasure all our own.

The "Auger," having been detailed for guard duty, walks off; his voice grows fainter and fainter in the distance, and we call forth our poet. One eye is bandaged with a dirty cotton rag. He is bare-headed, and his hair resembles a dismantled straw stack. His elbows and knees are out, and his pants, from the knee down, have a brown-toasted tinge imparted by the genial heat of many a fire. His toes protrude themselves prominently from his shoes. You would say, "What a dirty, ignorant fellow." But listen to his rich, well-modulated voice. How perfect his memory! What graceful gestures! How his single eye glows! See the color on his cheek! See the strained and still attention of the little group around him as he steps into the light of the fire! Hear him!

> I am dying, Egypt, dying!
>   Ebbs the crimson life-tide fast,
> And the dark Plutonian shadows
>   Gather on the evening blast.
> Let thine arms, O Queen, support me,
>   Hush thy sobs and bow thine ear;
> Listen to the great heart secrets—
>   Thou, and thou alone, must hear.
>
>   .   .   .   .
>
> I am dying, Egypt, dying!
>   Hark! the insulting foeman's cry.
> They are coming! quick! my falchion!!
>   Let me front them ere I die.
> Ah! no more amid the battle
>   Shall my heart exulting swell—
> Isis and Osiris guard thee—
>   Cleopatra! Rome! Farewell!

"Good!" "Bully!" "Go ahead, Jack!" "Give us some more, old fellow!" And he generally did, much to everybody's satisfaction. We all loved Jack, the Poet of our mess. . . .

The Singing man generally put in towards the last and sung us to bed. He was generally a diminutive man with a sweet voice and a sweetheart at home. His songs had in them rosy lips, blue eyes, golden hair, pearly teeth, and all that sort of thing. Of course he would sing some good rollicking songs, in order to give all a chance. And so, with hearty chorus, "Three times Around Went She," "Virginia, Virginia, the Land of the Free," 'No Surrender," "Lula, Lula, Lula Is Gone," "John Brown's Body" with many variations, "Dixie," "The Bonny Blue Flag," 'Farewell to the Star-Spangled Banner," "Hail Columbia" with immense variations, and "Maryland, My Maryland" till about the third year of the war, when we began to think Maryland had "breathed and burned" long enough, and ought to "come." What part of her did come was first-class.

How the woods did ring with song! There were patriotic songs, romantic and love songs, sarcastic, comic, and war songs, pirates' glees, plantation melodies, lullabies, good old hymn tunes, anthems, Sunday-school songs, and everything but vulgar and obscene songs; these were scarcely ever heard, and were nowhere in the Army well received or encouraged.

The recruit—our latest acquisition—was so interesting. His nice clean clothes, new hat, new shoes, trimming on his shirt front, letters and cross-guns on his hat, new knife for all the fellows to borrow, nice comb for general use, nice little glass to shave by, good smoking tobacco, money in his pocket to lend out, oh, what a great convenience he was! How many things he had that a fellow could borrow, and how willing he was to go on guard and get wet, and give away his rations, and bring water and cut wood, and ride horses to water! And he was so clean and sweet, and his cheeks so rosy, all the fellows wanted to bunk with him under his nice new blanket, and impart to him some of their numerous and energetic "tormentors."

And then it was so interesting to hear him talk. He knew so much about war, arms, tents, knapsacks, ammunition, marching, fighting, camping, cooking, shooting, and everything a soldier is and does. It is remarkable how much a recruit and how little an old soldier knows about such things. After a while the recruit forgets all and is as ignorant as any veteran. How good the fellows were to a really gentlemanly boy! How they loved him!

The *Scribe* was a wonderful fellow and very useful. He could write a two-hours' pass, sign the captain's name better than the captain himself, and endorse it "respectfully forwarded approved," sign the colonel's name after "respectfully forwarded approved," and then on up to the commanding officer. And do it so well! Nobody wanted anything better. The boys had great veneration for the scribe and used him constantly.

The *Mischievous* man was very useful. He made fun. He knew how to volunteer to shave a fellow with a big beard and moustache. He wouldn't lend his razor, but he'd shave him very well. He shaves one cheek, one half the chin, one side of the upper lip, puts his razor in his pocket, walks off, and leaves his customer the most one-sided chap in the Army. He knew how to do something like this every day. What a treasure to a mess!

The *Forager* was a good fellow. He always divided with the mess. If there was buttermilk anywhere inside of ten miles he found it. Apples he could smell from afar off. If anybody was killing pork in the county he got the spare ribs. If a man had a cider cart on the road he saw him first and bought him out. No hound had a keener scent, no eagle a sharper eye. How indefatigable he was! Distance, rivers, mountains, pickets, patrols, roll calls—nothing could stop or hinder him. He never bragged about his exploits; simply brought in the spoils, laid them down, and said, "Pitch in." Not a word of the weary miles he had traveled, how he begged or how much he paid—simply "Pitch in."

The *Commissary* man—he happened to be in our mess—never had any sugar over, any salt, any soda, any coffee—oh, no! But beg him, plead with him, bear with him when he says, "Go way, boy! Am I the commissary-general? Have I got all the sugar in Confederacy? Don't you know rations are short now?" Then see him relax. "Come here, my son; untie that bag there, and look in that old jacket and you will find another bag —a little bag—and look in there, and you will find some sugar. Now go round and tell everybody in camp, won't you? Tell 'em all to come and get some sugar. Oh! I know you won't. Oh yes, of course!"

As a general rule every mess had a "Bully" and an "Argument man." Time would fail me to tell of the "lazy man," the "brave man," the "worthless man," the "ingenious man," the "helpless man," the "sensitive man," and the "gentleman," but they are as familiar to the members of the mess as the "honest man," who would not eat stolen pig, but would take a little of the gravy.

Every soldier remembers—indeed, was personally acquainted with—the *Universal* man. How he denied vehemently his own identity, and talked about poison oak, and heat, and itch, and all those things, and strove in the presence of those who knew how it was themselves to prove his absolute freedom from anything like "universality!" Poor fellow! sulphur internally and externally would not do. Alas! his only hope was to acknowledge his unhappy state and stand in the presence of his peers, confessed.

The Boys in Blue generally preferred to camp in the open fields. The Confeds took to the woods, and so the Confederate camp was not as orderly or as systematically arranged, but the more picturesque of the two. The blazing fire lit up the forms and faces and trees around it with a ruddy glow, but only deepened the gloom of the surrounding woods; so that the soldier pitied the poor fellows away off on guard in the darkness, and hugging himself, felt how good it was to be with the fellows around the fire. How companionable was the blaze and the glow of the coals! They warmed the heart as well as the foot. The imagination seemed to feed on the glowing coals and surrounding gloom, and when the soldier gazed on the fire, peace, liberty, home, strolls in the woods and streets with friends, the church, the school, playmates, and sweethearts all passed before him and even the dead came to mind. Sadly, yet pleasantly, he thought of the loved and lost; the future loomed up, and the possibility of death and prison and the grief at home would stir his heart, and the tears would fall trickling to the ground. Then was the time to fondle the little gifts from home; simple things —the little pin-cushion, the needle-case, with thread and buttons, the embroidered tobacco bag, and the knitted gloves. Then the time to gaze on photographs, and to read and re-read the letter telling of the struggles at home, and the coming box of good things—butter and bread, toasted and ground coffee, sugar cakes and pies, and other comfortable things, prepared by self-denial for the soldier, brother, and son. Then the time to call on God to spare, protect, and bless the dear, defenseless, helpless ones at home. Then the time for high resolves; to read to himself his duty; to reenlist for the war. Then his heart grew to his comrades, his general, and his country; and as the trees, swept by the wintry winds, moaned around him, the soldier slept and dreamed, and dreamed of home, sweet home.

Those whose knowledge of war and its effects on the character of the soldier was gleaned from the history of the wars of Europe and of ancient times, greatly dreaded the demoralization which they supposed would result from the Confederate war for independence, and their solicitude was directed mainly towards the young men of Virginia and the South who were to compose the armies of the Confederate States. It was feared by many that the bivouac, the campfires, and the march would accustom the ears of their bright and innocent boys to obscenity oaths, and blasphemy, and forever destroy that purity of mind and soul which was their priceless possession when they bid farewell to home and mother. Some feared the destruction of the battlefield; the wiser feared hardship and disease; and others, more than all, the destruction of morals and everything good and pure in character. That the fears of the last named were realized in some cases cannot be denied; but that the general result was demoralization can be denied, and the contrary demonstrated.

Let us consider the effect of camp life upon a pure and noble boy; and to make the picture complete, let us go to his home and witness the parting. The boy is clothed as a soldier. His pockets and his haversack are stored with little conveniences made by the loving hands of mother, sister, and sweetheart, and the sad yet proud hour has arrived. Sisters, smiling through their tears, filled with commingled pride and sorrow, kiss and embrace their great hero. The mother, with calm heroism suppressing her tender maternal grief, impresses upon his lips a fervent, never-to-be-forgotten kiss, presses him to her heart, and resigns him to God, his country, and his honor. The father, last to part, presses his hand, gazes with ineffable love into his bright eyes, and, fearing to trust his feelings for a more lengthy farewell, says, "Good-by, my boy; God bless you; be a man!"

Let those scoff who will; but let them know that such a parting is itself a new and wonderful power, a soul-enlarging, purifying, and elevating power, worth the danger, toil, and suffering of the soldier. The sisters' tears, the father's words, the mother's kiss, planted in the memory of that boy, will surely bring forth fruit beautiful as a mother's love.

As he journeys to the camp, how dear do all at home become! Oh, what holy tears he sheds! His heart, how tender! Then, as he nears the line and sees for the first time the realities of war, the passing sick and weary, and the wounded and bloody dead, his soldier spirit is born; he smiles, his chest expands, his eyes brighten, his heart swells with pride. He hurries on, and soon stands in the magic circle around the glowing fire, the admired and loved pet of a dozen true hearts. Is he happy? Aye! Never before has he felt such glorious, swelling, panting joy. He's a soldier now! He is put on guard. No longer the object of care and solicitude he stands in the solitude of the night, himself a guardian of those who sleep. Courage is his now. He feels he is trusted as a man and is ready at once nobly to perish in the defense of his comrades.

He marches. Dare he murmur or complain? No; the eyes of all are upon him, and endurance grows silently, till pain and weariness are familiar and cheerfully borne. At home he would be pitied and petted; but now he must endure or have the contempt of the strong spirits around him.

He is hungry—so are others; and he must not only bear the privation, but he must divide his pitiful meal, when he gets it, with his comrades; and so generosity strikes down selfishness. In a thousand ways he is tried, and that by sharp critics. His smallest faults are necessarily apparent, for in the varying conditions of the soldier every quality is put to the test. If he shows the least cowardice he is undone. His courage must never fail. He must be manly and independent, or.he will be told he's a baby, ridiculed, teased, and despised. When war assumes her serious dress, he sees the helplessness of women and children, he hears their piteous appeals, and chivalry burns him till he does his utmost of sacrifice and effort to protect and comfort and cheer them.

It is a mistake to suppose that the older men in the army encourage vulgarity and obscenity in the young recruit; for even those who themselves indulged in these would frown on the first show of them in a boy and without hesitation put him down mercilessly. No parent could watch a boy as closely as his mess-mates did and could, because they saw him at all hours of the day and night, dependent on himself alone, and were merciless critics who demanded more of their protégé than they were willing to submit to themselves.

The young soldier's piety had to perish ignominiously, or

else assume a boldness and strength which nothing else could so well impart as the temptations, sneers, and dangers of the Army. Religion had to be bold, practical, and courageous, or die.

In the Army the young man learned to value men for what they were and not on account of education, wealth, or station; and so his attachments, when formed, were sincere and durable, and he learned what constitutes a man and a desirable and reliable friend. The stern demands upon the boy, and the unrelenting criticisms of the mess, soon bring to mind the gentle forbearance, kind remonstrance, and loving counsels of parents and homefolks; and while he thinks, he weeps, and loves, and reverences, and yearns after the things against which he once strove, and under which he chafed and complained. Home, father, mother, sister—oh, how far away; oh, how dear! Himself, how contemptible ever to have felt cold and indifferent to such love! Then, how vividly he recalls the warm pressure of his mother's lips on the forehead of her boy! How he loves his mother! See him as he fills his pipe from the silk-embroidered bag. There is his name embroidered carefully, beautifully, by his sister's hand. Does he forget her? Does he not now love her more sincerely and truly and tenderly than ever? Could he love her quite as much had he never parted; never longed to see her and could not; never been uncertain if she was safe; never felt she might be homeless, helpless, insulted, a refugee from home? Can he ever now look on a little girl and not treat her kindly, gently, and lovingly, remembering his sister? A boy having ordinary natural goodness, and the home supports described, and the constant watching of men, ready to criticise, could but improve. The least exhibition of selfishness, cowardice, vulgarity, dishonesty, or meanness of any kind, brought down the dislike of every man upon him, and persistence in any one disreputable practice, or habitual laziness and worthlessness, resulted in complete ostracism, loneliness, and misery; while, on the other hand, he might by good behavior and genuine generosity and courage secure unbounded love and sincere respect from all.

Visits home, after prolonged absence and danger, open to the young soldier new treasures—new, because, though possessed always, never before felt and realized. The affection once seen only in everyday attention, when he reaches home, breaks out in unrestrained vehemence. The warm embrace of the hitherto dignified father, the ecstatic pleasure beaming in the

mother's eye, the proud welcome of the sister, and the wild enthusiasm even of the old black mammy, crowd on him the
knowledge of their love and make him braver, and stronger,
and nobler. He's a hero from that hour! Death for these, how
easy!

The dangers of the battlefield, and the demands upon his
energy, strength, and courage, not only strengthen the old, but
almost create new, faculties of mind and heart. The death, sudden and terrible, of those dear to him, the imperative necessity
of standing to his duty while the wounded cry and groan, and
while his heart yearns after them to help them, the terrible
thirst, hunger, heat, and weariness—all these teach a boy self-
denial, attachment to duty, the value of peace and safety; and
instead of hardening him, as some suppose they do, make him
pity and love even the enemy of his country, who bleeds and
dies for his country.

The acquirement of subordination is a useful one, and that
the soldier perforce has; and that not in an abject, cringing way,
but as realizing the necessity of it, and seeing the result of it
in the good order and consequent effectiveness and success of
the Army as a whole, but more particularly of his own company
and detachment. And if the soldier rises to office, the responsibility of command, attention to detail and minutiae, the
critical eyes of his subordinates and the demands of his superiors, all withdraw him from the enticements of vice, and
mold him into a solid, substantial character, both capable and
willing to meet and overcome difficulties.

The effect of outdoor life on the physical constitution is undoubtedly good, and as the physical improves, the mental is
improved; and as the mind is enlightened, the spirit is enno-
bled. Who can calculate the benefit derived from the contem-
plation of the beautiful in nature, as the soldier sees? Mountains and valleys, dreary wastes and verdant fields, rivers, se-
questered homes, quiet, sleepy villages as they lay in the morning light, doomed to the flames at evening; scenes which alternately stir and calm his mind, and store it with a panorama
whose pictures he may pass before him year after year with
quiet pleasure. War is horrible, but still it is in a sense a privilege to have lived in time of war. The emotions are never so
stirred as then. Imagination takes her highest flights, poetry
blazes, song stirs the soul, and every noble attribute is brought
into full play.

It does seem that the production of one Lee and one Jackson is worth much blood and treasure, and the building of a noble character all the toil and sacrifice of war. The campfires of the Army of Northern Virginia were not places of revelry and debauchery. They often exhibited scenes of love and humanity, and the purest sentiments and gentlest feelings of man were there admired and loved, while vice and debauch, in any from highest to lowest, were condemned and punished more severely than they are among those who stay at home and shirk the dangers and toils of the solidier's life. Indeed, the demoralizing effects of that war were far more visible at home among the skulks and bomb-proofs and suddenly diseased, than in the army. And the demoralized men were not among those who served in the army. The defaulters, the renegades, the bummers and cheats, were those who enjoyed fat places and salaries and easy comfort; while the solid, respected, and reliable men of the community were men who did their duty as soldiers, and having learned to suffer in war, then preferred to labor and suffer and earn, rather than steal, in peace.

And, strange to say, it was not those who suffered most and lost most, fought and bled, saw friend after friend fall, wept the dead and buried their hopes—who became bitter and dissatisfied, quarrelsome and fretful, growling and complaining; no, they were the peaceful, submissive, law-abiding, order-loving, of the country, ready to join hands with all good men in every good work, and prove themselves as brave and good in peace as they were stubborn and unconquerable in war.

Many a weak, puny boy was returned to his parents a robust, healthy, manly man. Many a timid, helpless boy went home a brave, independent man. Many a wild, reckless boy went home sobered, serious, and trustworthy. And many whose career at home was wicked and blasphemous went home changed in heart, with principles fixed, to comfort and sustain the old age of those who gave them to their country, not expecting to receive them again. Men learned that life was passable and enjoyable without a roof or even a tent to shelter from the storm; that cheerfulness was compatible with cold and hunger; and that a man without money, food, or shelter need not feel utterly hopeless, but might, by employing his wits, find something to eat where he never found it before; and feel that, like a terrapin, he might make himself at home wherever he might be. Men did actually become as independent of the imaginary ne-

cessities as the wild beasts. And can a man learn all this and not
know better than another how to economize what he has, and
how to appreciate the numberless superfluities of life? Is he
not made, by the knowledge he has of how little he really
needs, more independent and less liable to dishonest exertions
to procure a competency?

Strange as it may seem, religion flourished in the Army. So
great was the work of the chaplains that whole volumes have
been written to describe the religious history of the four years
of war. Officers who were ungodly men found themselves re-
strained alike by the grandeur of the piety of the great chiefs,
and the earnestness of the humble privates around them. Thousands embraced the Gospel, and died triumphing over death.
Instead of the degradation so dreaded, was the strange enno-
bling and purifying which made men despise all the things for
which they ordinarily strive, and glory in the sternest hardships,
the most bitter self-denials, cruel suffering, and death. Love
for home, kindred, and friends, intensified, was denied the
gratification of its yearnings, and made the motive for more
complete surrender to the stern demands of duty. Discipline,
the cold master of our enemies, never caught up with the gallant devotion of our Christian soldiers, and the science of war
quailed before the majesty of an army singing hymns.

Hypocrisy went home to dwell with the able-bodied skulkers,
being too closely watched in the Army, and too thoroughly
known to thrive. And so the campfire often lighted the pages
of the best Book, while the soldier read the orders of the Captain of his salvation. And often did the songs of Zion ring out
loud and clear on the cold night air, while the muskets rattled
and the guns boomed in the distance, each intensifying the
significance of the other, testing the sincerity of the Christian
while trying the courage of the soldier. Stripped of all sensual
allurements, and offering only self-denial, patience, and endurance, the Gospel took hold of the deepest and purest motives
of the soldiers, won them thoroughly, and made the Army as
famous for its forbearance, temperance, respect for women and
children, sobriety, honesty, and morality as it was for endurance and invincible courage.

Never was there an army where feeble old age received such
sympathy, consideration, and protection. Women, deprived of
their natural protectors, fled from the advancing hosts of the
enemy, and found safe retreat and chivalrous protection and

shelter in the lines of the Army of Northern Virginia. Children played in the camps, delighted to nestle in the arms of the roughly-clad but tender-hearted soldiers. Such was the behavior of the troops on the campaign in Pennsylvania, that the citizens of Gettysburg have expressed wonder and surprise at their perfect immunity from insult, violence, or even intrusion, when their city was occupied by and in complete possession of the Boys in Gray.

Index

Index

387

Seasoned troops, 347
"Secesh," 174
Seneca, 286
Sentences, military, 97
Sergeants, duties of, 67, 81, 110,
116, 132, 147
Servants, soldiers', 294, 298
Seven Days' Battles, 324
Sharp practices, 322
Shelter, taking, 346, 347
Shelter (or Dog) tent, 28, 29, 29
ill., 238, 239
Shelters, Army, 22-32, 234, 331
Sheridan, General P. H., 92, 266,
267
Sheridan's Cavalry Corps, 190
Sheridan's troopers, 208
Sherman, General W. T., 171,
186, 259, 283, 285-88
Sherman's Army, 302, 304
Sherman's "Bummers," 170
Sherman's Memoirs, 171, 250,
284
"Sherman's Special Field Orders
120," 170
Shiloh, 287, 288
Shortages, food, see under Food
Sibley, Henry, 23
Sibley (or Bell) tent, 22 ill., 23,
24, 26, 35, 36, 36 ill., 58, 213,
214, 238
Sick, care of, see Medical care
Sick Call, 119, 119 ill., 120, 121
Signal code, 280, 281 ill., 282
Signal Corps,
Confederate, 288, 289
Union, 190, 279, 283-89
Signal Kit, 280
Signal towers, 284, 285, 288, 289
Signalling (see also Signal code),
with flags, 282-89
with torches, 283
Silver shortage, 36, 63
Singing, camp, 316
"Skillygalee," 76
Skirmishing tactics, 337-40
Slapjacks, 316

Slashes (fortifications), 270
Sleeping arrangements, 25 ill.,
28, 29, 36, 58, 298, 327, 329
Sleeping on duty, punishment
for, 106
"Slosh," 316, 317
Slush lamps, 48
Smith, Major-General A. J., 187
Smith, General Kirby, 109
Smith, General W. F., 187
Smith and Wesson revolver, 194
"Smith Cross, A. J.," 187
Smoking, 326
Soldiers, character of, see under
Character
Soldiers, personalities of, 58-70,
372-75
Soldier's Aid Society, 53, 54
Soldiers' dependents, care of, 16,
17
Soldiers' views, Confederate, 300-
14, 324, 335
Songs, Army, 41-43, 77-78, 90,
91, 116, 117, 119, 135, 153,
237, 316, 326, 342, 374
Sorghum, 321
Soup, Army, 86
Souvenirs, Army, 37-39
"Spare Men," 118
"Spooning Together," 25 ill., 26
Spotsylvania, 207, 228
Spottsylvania Court House, 344,
348
Stable Call, 116 ill., 117, 130
Stables, Army, 332
308-10, 328
Steak, cooking of, 86
Stealing, 318
Stevensburg, 112, 126
Stevenson, Major J. T., 16
Stilesboro, 284
Stockades, Army, 31
Stockading, 26, 30
Stragglers, 313, 314
Strategy, amateur, 372
Strawberry ration, 92
Streams, fording of, 243, 244